U.S.S. (BB-56) Washington

TURNER PUBLISHING COMPANY

Turner Publishing Company
412 Broadway • P.O. Box 3101
Paducah Kentucky 42002-3101
Phone: (502) 443-0121

Turner Publishing Company Staff:
Production Coordinator: John Mark Jackson
Designer: Heather R. Warren

Copyright © 1998
Turner Publishing Company
All Rights Reserved.

This book or any part thereof may not be reproduced without the written consent of Turner Publishing Company.

ISBN 978-1-63026-963-0

Library of Congress Catalog
Card Number: 97-60753

Limited Edition

This publication was produced using available materials. The publisher regrets it cannot assume liability for errors or omissions.

TABLE OF CONTENTS

Executive Director's Message 6

Publisher's Message 7

U.S.S. Washington History 10

Commanding Officers 26

Special Stories 30

Biographies 72

Active Members 115

Associates Roster 117

Non-Active Shipmates 119

Honorary Life Members 120

Widow-Relative Roster 121

Deceased Roster 123

Index 126

EXECUTIVE DIRECTOR'S MESSAGE

**U.S.S. WASHINGTON (BB56)
REUNION GROUP INC. BOX 13047
COLUMBUS, OHIO 43213-0047
1-614-237-6775
JOHN A. BROWN, EXECUTIVE DIRECTOR**

★ ★ ★ ★ ★ ★ ★ ★ ★ ★ ★ ★ ★ ★ ★

Brief History of Battleship, U.S.S. Washington, BB56

The eighth Washington, BB56, was laid down on June 14, 1938 - Philadelphia Navy Yard. Launched on June 1, 1940. Sponsored by Miss Virginia Marshall, Commissioned May 15, 1941 Captain Howard H.J. Benson in Command.

Served early 1942 for four months with British Home Fleet as Flagship Task Force 39, escorted convoys to Murmansk and Archangel Russia. Sailed for Pacific Aug. 23, 1942 and served there for 34 months. Arriving Puget Sound Navy Yard, June 23, 1945. During service in Pacific, at Guadalcanal she fought and won a classic ship to ship duel with the Japanese Battleship Kirishima, becoming the first U.S. Battleship to fight an enemy battleship and the only one to singly destroy one.

She patrolled the enemy waters for 5 weeks alone, being the only U.S. Battleship in the Pacific. Set a record steaming 31,494 miles for 79 consecutive days, fueled destroyers 59 times, was fueled 16 times itself.

She had damaged three enemy cruisers, a destroyer, and sank a battleship, destroyer, oil tanker, and several transports. She shot down twelve enemy planes and bombarded ten enemy islands. Steamed 289,609 miles during World War Two, and repelled 53 air attacks. Fired 3535 rounds of 16 inch shells and 28,062 rounds of 5 inch projectiles, over 350,000 rounds of 20 millimeter machine gun bullets. She earned 15 Battle Stars and was never hit or lost a man to the enemy. She was struck from the Navy list June 1, 1960.

She sank more combat tonnage than any U.S. Battleship in World War II.

North Atlantic Duty
Convoy Escort Murmansk and Archangel Russia

Service in the Pacific
NOVEMBER 1942 - MAY 1945
Battles, Air strikes,
and Bombardments*

15 November 1942
Washington's sinking of Kirishima and Ayanami

19 November - 5 December 1943
Operation GALVANIC

8 December 1943
Bombardment of Nauru

31 December 1943 - 5 January 1944
Kavieng raids

29 January - 2 February 1944
Operation FLINTLOCK - bombardment of Kwajalein and collision with Indiana

12 June - 7 July 1944
Operation FORAGER - bombardment of Saipan and Battle of the Philippine Sea

25 July 1944
Air strikes on Palau Islands

10 - 21 October 1944
Air strikes on Okinawa, Taiwan, Luzon, and Visayan Islands

24 - 27 October 1944
Battles for Leyte Gulf

18 December 1944
Third Fleet's encounter with typhoon

3 - 9 January 1945
Air strikes on Taiwan and Okinawa

10 - 22 January 1945
Air strikes on Indochina, Canton, Hong Kong, and Taiwan

16 - 18 February 1945
Air strikes on Tokyo

19 - 22 February 1945
Bombardment of Iwo Jima

18 - 22 March 1945
Air strikes on Kyushu

24 March 1945
Bombardment of Okinawa

29 March 1945
Air strikes on Kyushu

1 April - 28 May 1945
Support of Okinawa operations

John A. Brown Family.

The reunion group is proud to present this book to USS *Washington* (BB-56) former shipmates, widows, associate unit members and friends of ship and group.

Our many thanks to the Turner Publishing Company for being interested in our naval history.

We are so fortunate to be served by this very much dedicated reunion committee: Elmer Cox, Ray and LaVerne Krueger, Bob and Kitty Sutherland, Jim and Mary Ann Loewe, Howard Wright and John and Gladys Brown. Our many thanks to the volunteers that have been assisting us.

Howard Wright now serves as the first associate unit president and Mike Jackson as the secretary-treasurer, assuring excellent representation in preserving the proud name and history of the ship. This letterhead spells out a brief history that is unmatched in naval history.

Gladys and I are in the 50th year in serving the organization and still much enthused. God Bless.

John A. and Gladys Brown
Executive Director
Ship Fitter 2/c R.Div.

PUBLISHER'S MESSAGE

Dave Turner, President.

As the son of a World War II U.S. Navy veteran, I understand and appreciate the significant role American military ships and their crews have played in defending freedom around the globe. Turner Publishing Company is proud to present the documented history of one such ship, the USS *Washington*.

From its commissioning in 1941 to its decommissioning in 1960, the USS *Washington* proved to be one of the U.S. Navy's most formidable battleships. The eighth *Washington*, BB-56, saw duty in both the North Atlantic, serving with the British Home Fleet as Flagship Task Force 39, and the Pacific, becoming the first U. S. Battleship to fight an enemy battleship and the only one to singly destroy one. The *Washington* sank more combat tonnage than any U. S. Battleship in World War II, earning 15 Battle Stars without sustaining a hit or losing a man to the enemy. This history book is a tribute the *Washington* and its crew rightfully deserve.

Our sincere thanks goes out to John A. Brown, Executive Director of the USS *Washington* Reunion Group Inc., for the countless hours he spent compiling and organizing materials for this history book. We also want to thank Charles D. Melson for composing the history text.

Finally, we would like to thank the veterans of the USS *Washington* for their heroic service to our country and for contributing photographs and stories for use in the book. Without them this book would not be possible.

It our hope that this history book raises awareness and helps to bring about the recognition the USS *Washington* and its crew deserve for their meritorious service.

Dave Turner, President
Turner Publishing Company

USS WASHINGTON HISTORY

BATTLE LOG OF THE USS *WASHINGTON* (BB-56) IN WWII, 1941-45

"Tell me, O muse, of that ingenious hero who traveled far and wide... Many cities did he visit, and many were the customs he was acquainted; moreover he suffered much by sea while trying to save his own life and bring his men safely home..."
Homer, The Odyssey, I (1).

Introduction: Piping Aboard

This account follows the wartime cruise of the USS *Washington* "from Pearl Harbor to Tokyo Bay," December 1941 through August 1945. The intention is to provide an outline of where the ship and its crew went and what they did within the larger context of the war. The story follows the "battle stars" earned by the ship and crew in both the Atlantic and Pacific theaters of operations in the course of the conflict that took them around the world and back again.

Battleships continue to fascinate, as even a recent Discovery Channel Documentary celebrated the exploits of the huge floating fighters that could fire 2,700 pound projectiles up to 25 miles from their 16-inch guns. The story of these fastest and most powerful warships can be traced from their search-and-destroy mission in WWI, to the race for bigger and better battleships in WWII, to the modernized versions deployed in Korea, Vietnam and the Persian Gulf.

No attempt was made to duplicate numerous and more complete published accounts. In this story the *Washington* itself is the main character as the embodiment of the many individuals that made up its officers, petty officers, sailors and Marines. The need for this approach will be evident to those who served and provides an introduction to their experience for their extended families and friends.

The Ship and Crew

The North Carolina Class battleships provided America with its first "fast battleships," capable of competing with nearly all of the post WWI capital ships constructed by foreign navies.

The design of the USS *Washington* and *North Carolina* proved to be distinctive, incorporating innovations in hull shape and propulsion as well as in layout. The most notable and unique element of the ships was their hulls design. Traditional battleships tended to follow one of two hull forms. Ships were either built with a broad, but relatively short hull, or with a long narrow hull. The former design allowed for tight turning radii and compact armor arrangements, however the broad beam associated with such hulls did not permit speeds greater than 20 knots. The long, narrow hulls permitted speeds in excess of 20 knots to be reached, but such ships proved to have inferior maneuverability and their armor tended to be distributed over a greater area than the armor of a shorter ship of similar tonnage. The *North Carolina* Class's design provided an optimum balance between speed, maneuverability, and armor protection. The maximum beam of the hull was not placed directly amidships, but at about three quarters aft. In turn, the machinery spaces were concentrated in the region of maximum beam, permitting a compact ship, in terms of length, while allowing for high speed. Another distinctly American requirement was met; *Washington* was sufficiently compact enough to pass through the Panama Canal, which played a critical role in the naval strategies of the time.

The innovative hull design was coupled with another technology developed by the US Navy, the propeller skeg. Previous battleship's propellers were mounted outside of the hull with drive shafts connecting the screw to the propulsion units. Drive shafts became particularly vulnerable to torpedo damage when they were required to turn outboard propellers, such as were found on battleships requiring multiple screws. The *Washington* sought too change this.

The skeg was a narrow vertical extension of the hull that extended from aft of the third turret to nearly the stern. The two inboard propellers and shafts were mounted on the skeg. The skegs would improve the durability of the ship by protecting two of the four drive shafts and, theoretically, the skegs would improve the performance of the ship.

Skegs were added to the *Washington* primarily for hydrodynamic reasons. This reasoning limited the use of skegs to the two innermost propellers. The channel formed by the two skegs was thought to provide a means of directing the flow of water under the ship, thereby reducing drag and in turn increasing the ship's

Courtesy of William Paul Weidert.

Courtesy of William Paul Weidert

maximum speed. While the *Washington* could make 32 knots at full steam, the role of the skegs in this accomplishment was dubious.

The more obvious and important advance found in the *Washington* was the layout of the main battery. No previous battleship had ever mounted nine 16-inch "rifles," some of the most powerful weapons ever put to sea. Just as notable was the use of triple turrets. Each turret and barbette assembly weighted nearly 3,000 tons, a figure unmatched in previous American battleships. Thus, Herculean effort was required to construct and install *Washington's* main armament.

The massive main battery reflected the superiority of the *Washington* over practically every other class of battleship. The 16-inch rifles could accurately fire a one tone shell nearly 20 miles. More importantly, "SG" surface search radar was used to obtain fire control information, limiting the need for visual references to a target. The combination of an accurate main battery and the most advanced radar of the time proved decisive in *Washington's* engagements off Savo Island in November 1942.

The main battery was supported by a secondary battery of 20 5/38" guns mounted in 10 twin turrets. The mounts were distributed on both sides of the superstructure. The *Washington* secondary battery provided firepower for use against both surface vessels and aircraft, as such they were the American battleships to be built with dual-purpose 5-inch guns.

Fire control for the secondary battery was provided, at first, by optical range finders and directors. Following their initial deployments, *Washington* had radar units installed to direct the 5-inch mounts. Later, radar would be used to detonate proximity fuses in the 5-inch rounds. This development made the 5/38" the superlative naval anti-aircraft weapon of WWII.

The skill with which the 5/38"s were handled contributed just as much or more to their success as a weapon. Emory J. Jernigan, a member of the *Washington's* crew recalled "we had quite a battle going on between the sailors and the marines on the 5-inch mounts as to which group was the best shot. We started real slow and built up to 22 rounds per minute. Such a combination of an excellent weapon and an able crew proved to be capable of repelling even the most determined air attacks. Even the Japanese kamikaze aircraft were unable to penetrate the intense barrages created by the 5/38.

A battery of light anti-aircraft weapons provided close range defense. Initially this consisted of 18 Browning 0.5" machine guns mounted on the deck, and 16 1.1" automatic cannons, mounted in four quadruple mounts on the superstructure. The machine guns proved to be deficient in range and stopping power, so 20 mm Oerklion automatic cannons supplanted and then replaced them. The 1.1" cannons did not prove to be effective, either. They were prone to jamming and did not provide adequate fire power. However inefficient the 1.1" cannons were, *Washington's* remained in place until 1943.

The Oerklion 40 mm automatic cannon replaced the 1.1" mounts. The 40 mm guns initially were arranged in six quadruple mounts, but, following a trend common to all American warships in WWII, more mounts were added. A total of 15 mounts were added during the course of the war.

The 20 mm Oerklion cannons provided further anti-aircraft protection. Dispersed over the deck and superstructure the 20 mm guns became the most numerous light weapon on the North Carolina class vessels. Many of the mounts were simply placed in any available space. Some mounts, particularly those on the bow, remained awash in all but the calmest seas. Other mounts gave no protection from the blast effects of the secondary 5/38" battery that provided heavy anti-aircraft fire.

Protecting the armament, crew, and machinery of the *Washington* was a veritable aegis of steel. The ship's armor scheme concentrated on placing armor only where it provided the most benefit: turrets, magazines, engineering spaces, command and control centers. A belt of hardened steel, 16 inches deep, ran along both sides of the hull, at the water line. Atop the belts lay an armored deck, five inches thick.

The stoutest armor protected the turrets and barbettes containing the 16-inch guns. Attaining a maximum thickness of 16 inches, the armor defending the main battery could not be penetrated by any foreign naval weapon, save for the 18-inch rifles of the ill-fated Japanese Yamato Class. Junior officer Douglas Fairbanks Jr. described the *Washington's* massive turrets as "great 12-inch steel homes for ... 16-inch guns." While *Washington* never received any damage that tested the main armor, few would doubt that the great steel shield protecting the battleships survive even the greatest of ordeals.

The last pre-war American battleships, the North Carolina Class embodied decades of battleship experience and refinement. The soundness of the design of the *Washington* was reflected in the balance of speed, firepower, and protection, as well as in the exemplary performance that the ships achieved when manned by their able crews.

Ship's design meant nothing without a crew organized to make things work. Ivan Musicant, the *Washington's* popular wartime chronicler, broke the 2,500-man complement down by tasks for the general reader: ordnance and fire control, ship control, communications and electronics, propulsion, ground tackle, aircraft and boats, damage control, pumps-tanks-voids, and personnel. Machinist Jernigan described it somewhat differently: "Each ship is like a city, large or small...Everything that was done in the home happened right on board the ship. The bakers baked, the cooks cooked, and the engineers ran the ship's propulsion division; the gunners had their guns and learned to use them."

WASHINGTON GOES TO WAR

Construction of the USS *Washington* began on June 14, 1938, at the Philadelphia Navy Yard and she was launched on June 1, 1940, after fighting in Europe had begun. The early 1940s saw Nazi Germany with its Axis partner, Italy, spreading war through Western Europe's cities and villages.

The *Washington* was commissioned amidst this background of conflict on May 15, 1941, the eighth US Navy ship of that name. The ship was sponsored by a direct descendant of Chief Justice John Marshall, Miss Virginia Marshall. Commissioned a year and a half ahead of schedule, on that date Captain Howard H.J. Benson became the ship's first "skipper." This was a prize assignment, as no battleships had been built since WWI, and the hand-picked crew was "all Old Navy and proud to be aboard."

In the Far East, Japan had already occupied China and was expanding to include Allied territory throughout the Pacific. The December 7, 1941, attack on Pearl Harbor found the ship and crew on a shakedown cruise. Both the USS *Washington* and its' sister ship the USS *North Carolina* left Norfolk, Virginia, for

The USS Washington. (Courtesy of Captain Wm. B. Fargo.)

Left to Right: Captain J.D. Hittle, USMC, Lt. JG. Douglas Fairbanks, Jr. BB56, Ensign C.R. Knowlton, USNR. (Courtesy of CDR. C.R. Knowlton.)

Commissioning Ceremony. May 15, 1941.

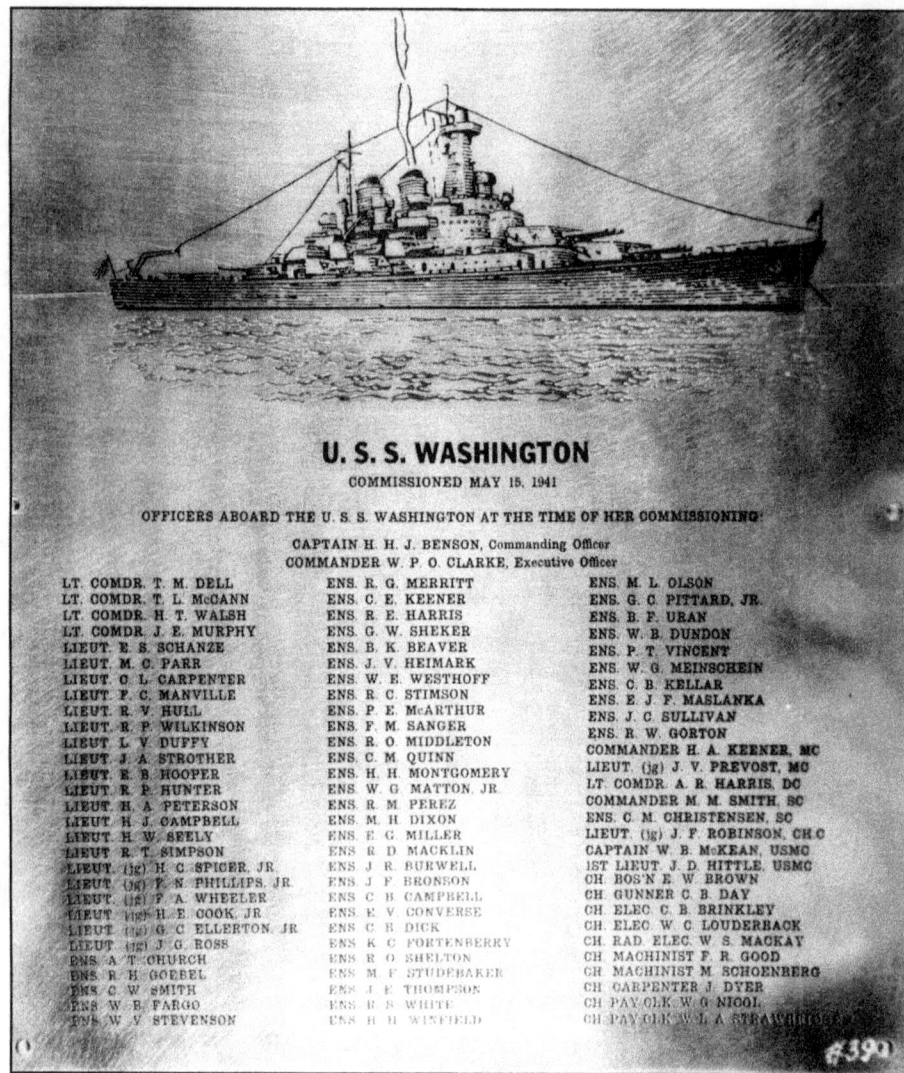

Courtesy of Walter R. Krause.

battle and gunnery trials in the Gulf of Mexico. In addition to the spectacle of the nine 16-inch rifles that fired a heavier projectile than previously designed, the *Washington's* gunnery officer, Lieutenant Commander Harvey T. Walsh, also proceeded to ensure the ship had the best trained anti-aircraft gunners in the fleet - in recognition of where the main threat of enemy attack might come from. This was the beginning its reputation as "the ship that liked to shoot."

Atlantic Theater

By year's end the Axis powers, Germany, Italy and Japan, were at war with the United States. Roosevelt and Churchill conceived a strategy of defeating Germany first, then Japan. The Battle of the Atlantic was already underway and a deadly war of attrition was waged for the oceanic lines of communications between stalking Axis submarines and Allied convoys and escorts. After the United States entered the war, U-boats prowled the East Coast in months dubbed the "Happy Time," where because of lack of convoys and seaboard blackouts, they sank thousands of tons of Allied merchant shipping - 500,000 in the first four months of 1942 alone.

Undersea "Wolf Packs" had almost crippled Great Britain's war making abilities, by sinking three million tons of Allied merchant shipping before anti-submarine techniques, especially increased air cover, began to have an effect. British "Ultra" communications intercepts and decryption helped reduce merchant losses by using radio intelligence to reroute convoys. Also, the more than a million tons a month of new Allied ship construction vastly exceeded the tonnage sunk at a time when German submarine launchings barely replaced losses.

The *Washington* entered the war assigned as flagship for Battleship Division 6 and Task Force 39 with Rear Admiral John W. Wilcox on board. On March 26, 1942, the *Washington* set out from Casco Bay, Maine and headed northeast for Iceland, the Orkneys, and into the menace of war and German submarines on the notorious Murmansk runs to keep Russia in the war by providing urgently needed war material and food. Setting sail with the carrier USS *Wasp* and cruisers, *Wichita* and *Tuscaloosa*, the first day out Admiral Wilcox went overboard in moderately heavy seas. Despite "man overboard" drills and searches, the admiral's body was not recovered and the task force proceeded on its mission.

Russian Convoy Operations

The *Washington* was not designated the flagship of Rear Admiral Robert C. "Ike" Giffen's Task Force 99 and tasked to support the British Home Fleet. The force's mission was to "engage in reconnaissance for the protection of the vital convoys running lend-lease supplies to Murmansk in the Soviet Union."

The Russian north run had lend-lease convoys from Great Britain heading to Murmansk and Archangel routed west of Iceland and north towards Spitzbergen during the summer. Winter ice caused convoys to be driven south and east of Iceland, where German units based in Norway would punish them with sea and air attacks. For the next four months, through July 1942, the *Washington* ranged the North Atlantic, from Iceland to the northern tip of Norway, to Scapa Flow, and to Spitzbergen. It was on the Spitzbergen trip that the *Washington* went to within 800 miles of the North Pole, farther north than any other battleship had ever been know to go - the crew becoming members of the Royal Order of Blue Noses.

The North Atlantic is stormy by nature and no exception was made for the *Washington*. But cold weather and rough seas did not lessen the danger of the German submarines, and a constant watch was kept for this undersea enemy that threatened to sever the highly important lifeline of the early war. In the back of the mind of every officer and man was the name of the Tirpitz, the German battleship that was the most deadly threat of all to the shipping routes from America.

One memorable incident was the May 1, 1942, ramming of the HMS *Punjabi* by the *King George V*. As the two halves of the Tribal Class destroyer went down, the *Washington* passed over the stern just when the depth charges went off, lifting the hull and damaging some electronic fire control systems. Some 187 British survivors were picked from the icy ocean, one of whom recalled at the 1973 *Washington* reunion "it was cold in the water!"

Long days of tenseness and alertness were relieved at intervals when the *Washington* dropped anchor in Iceland or Scapa Flow in rotation. There was little relaxation for the crew in either of these places, but just to rest for a few days was enough, and there were interesting visits to the old city of Kirkwall in Scotland and the unique town of Reykjavik in Iceland. Lieutenant (jg) Douglas Fairbanks Jr. left a description of his arrival for duty on the *Washington*. "The first gray, misty sight of all those ships of two mighty navies lying there in that huge landlocked sea shelter of Scapa Flow, in far northern Scotland, was breathtaking. In a setting of drama in both world wars rode about every type of warship and naval auxiliary."

While in Scapa Flow on June 7, 1942, his Majesty King George VI inspected the crew and signed the ship's log 12-14 entry "Moored as before." Also aboard at this time was Commander, Naval Forces Europe, Admiral Harold R. Stark who broke out his flag while establishing a temporary administrative headquarters.

After several more convoy missions the

Washington headed back to the States with a "screen" of four destroyers. The crew gave a "mighty cheer" as the New York City skyline came into view the morning of July 21, 1942. This was followed by a stay at the Brooklyn Navy Yard for refit. However, the stay there was not long; there was urgent need of a fast battleship in the Pacific. Of note was that none of the crew wished to rotate shore duty with some 180 applicants who wanted to come aboard! Captain Benson was relieved by Captain Glenn B. Davis on July 25, 1942. In August Davis took the *Washington* through the Panama Canal and headed her west with an escort of three destroyers, "steaming into three years of the greatest sea and air battles in history."

Pacific Theater

The Pacific Theater absorbed one third of the earth's surface with only 1/145 of its total land mass. These vast distances called for new strategy, tactics, equipment and weapons of war. It involved not just Japan and the United States, but Great Britain, Australia, New Zealand, France, Holland, Canada, China and the Soviet Union. It also caught up the people of the Pacific Islands upon whose waters and homelands the battles were fought. A wild run had gained Japan an empire of over 20 million square miles of Asia and the Pacific, an area five times greater than that taken by Germany at its heights of conquest.

While the *Washington* had been fighting the Battle of the Atlantic, events in the Pacific had moved on at a pace from the Japanese attack in December 1941. Six months after Pearl Harbor, the Philippines had fallen to Japan and Australia was being cut off by Japanese naval and air forces. In May 1942 the Battle of the Coral Sea was fought, the first naval battle in history in which all the fighting was by carrier-based aircraft and the opposing ships never saw each other. This was a tactical victory and a strategic defeat for Japan. It was followed by the Battle of Midway in June, the American victory that dealt Japan its first major naval defeat. The battle swung back and forth, until three Japanese carriers were hit in a single five minute attack, and a fourth was taken out later in the day, altering the course of the Pacific Campaign. It confirmed the power of the aircraft carrier as an offensive weapon in the Pacific War, command of the sea now rode on command of the air.

The Japanese continued to expand in the Aleutian Islands to the north and at New Guinea to the south. In August 1942, the US Marines land on Guadalcanal in the Solomon Islands in the first American offense of the war. The landing forged the joint tactics that would win the Pacific War; landing Marine or army assault troops, supported by ground attack aircraft and naval gunfire, on island stepping stones to Japan. Naval construction crews, Seabees, would follow ashore with the assault and build docks, roads, and airfields to support the next rung up the ladder.

Japanese efforts to recapture Guadalcanal failed, but with serious air and naval fighting, beginning with the First Battle of Savo Island on August 8-9 that sunk four Allied cruisers. On August 24, in the Battle of the Eastern Solomons, a Japanese carrier is sunk by aircraft from the USS *Enterprise* and *Saratoga*. It was into this arena that the *Washington* joined the Pacific combat.

On September 3, 1942, the *Washington* celebrated "crossing the line" by hoisting the "Jolly Roger" and welcoming King Neptune and his royal entourage aboard. Unlike the visit of the King of England, this saw the trials marking the transition from "polliwog" to "shellback"

King George at Scapa Flow in June or April of 1942.

Captain HHJ Benson. (Courtesy of Captain Wm. B. Fargo.)

Rear Admiral Robert C. "Ike" Giffen assumed Wilcox duties, commander Task Force 39.

Captain Glen Davis. (Courtesy of Captain Wm B. Fargo.)

The King of England visits the USS Washington in 1942.

for most of the crew. This time-honored ceremony was to be repeated four times, once each year, before the *Washington* finished its WWII career in the Pacific, making an immeasurable contribution to unit spirit. The *Washington* arrived at Tonga Tabu, Friendly Islands on September 14 with several hundred lowly polliwogs "properly and thoroughly" initiated and emerged as "tried and true" shellbacks. The stay at Tonga was short and all hands left with regret, for, of all the islands in the Pacific, the people of Tonga were the friendliest and the island itself closest to a tourist's idea of a South Sea island.

Soon after arrival, Rear Admiral William A. (Ching Chong China) Lee Jr. came on board as Commander Task Group 12.2 and Battleship Division 6. Lee was himself a fanatic about efficient gunnery that went along well with the ship's priorities. Walsh continued his emphasis on gunnery, aided by his assistant Lieutenant Edwin B. Hooper and air defense officer Lieutenant Harry W. Seeley. On September 15, the *Washington* sailed to join Task Force 17 formed around the aircraft carrier USS *Hornet*.

CAPTURE AND DEFENSE OF GUADALCANAL

From October 1942 to May 1943, operating from Noumea, New Caldonia and Espiritu Santo, New Hebrides the *Washington* supported the capture and occupation of the Solomon Islands. For the first five weeks, the *Washington* was the only fast battleship in the South Pacific and the US Navy was down to a single aircraft carrier, the *Enterprise*, with the loss of the *Wasp* in September and the *Hornet* in October 1942. It covered the approaches to the Solomon Islands and the tenuous hold on Guadalcanal. Cruisers, destroyers, an even cargo ships bore the brunt of forward action, but the *Washington* was there, backing the line, a potential major threat to Japanese surface and air counter moves.

By November, the massive Japanese air and surface attempts to wrest Allied control of the island were at their peak. The Allies held daylight air superiority while the Japanese had dominance at night while moving up and down "The Slot." This meant Allied surface units moved in the day and the Japanese in the hours of darkness, "subjecting Henderson Field on Guadalcanal to heavy bombardments with disturbing regularity." It was during this period the *Washington* then flagship for Rear Admiral Lee and Task Force 64, played the leading role in the 3rd Battle of Savo which was fought and won in infamous "Iron Bottom Sound."

The night of November 12-13 a Japanese bombardment group was driven back from Guadalcanal by a naval force commanded by Rear Admiral Daniel J. Callaghan and planes from Henderson Field. The damage to Callaghan's ships left Allied forces ashore exposed to further Japanese attacks. On November 13 Admiral Lee learned that three groups of Japanese ships, one consisting of 24 transports with escorts, were streaming towards Guadalcanal. An enemy force sighted that morn-

Adm. Lee greeting officers aboard the USS Washington

H. Division mates crossing the equator for the first time. Hazing was the order of the day!

ing was reported to consist of two battleships, a light cruiser, and 11 destroyers. This included a reinforcement group commanded by Rear Admiral Raizo Tanaka, with a support group under Vice Admiral Gunichi Mikawa and a separate bombardment group under Vice Admiral Nobutake Kondo.

At dusk on November 13, Lee took the *Washington*, *South Dakota*, and four destroyers towards Guadalcanal to intercept the Japanese convoy and covering force. Late the afternoon of November 14, Task Force 64 spent much of the day trying to avoid Japanese air reconnaissance some 50 miles southwest of Guadalcanal. Meanwhile, aircraft from Espiritu Santo and the USS *Enterprise* attacked the Japanese transports headed for Guadalcanal with troops of the 38th Division and supplies.

The engagement on the night of November 14, 1942, marked a turning point against the Japanese forces in the Southwest Pacific. Naval historian Theodore Roscoe's chronology and plot is followed by this account, other variations exist and can be found elsewhere (Portions of the actual November 14-15, 1942, deck log of the USS *Washington* are included as an appendix).

GUADALCANAL, THIRD BATTLE OF SAVO

The evening of November 14, the *Washington* was en route to intercept the suspected Japanese bombardment group approaching Guadalcanal. While the *Washington* acted as flagship, the battleship *South Dakota* provided support and four destroyers supplied an escort. Lee identified his task force to baffled American patrol boats, aircraft, and shore defenses over the radio with his fabled "This is Ching Chong China Lee... Get the hell out of the way; I am coming through!"

Traveling at high speed, the ships approached Savo Island. The *Walke* lead the vanguard of destroyers, with the *Benham*, the *Preston*, and the *Gwin* following in column. About 4,000 yards behind the destroyers cruised the *Washington* and the *South Dakota*. The two battleships provided the force with a set of search radar each and this technology was appreciated by the *Washington's* senior commander, "Ching" Lee. The *Washington's* cruise book recounts: ...the small group, steaming in column with the destroyers ahead rounded Savo in hopes of intercepting a large Japanese force of battleship, cruisers, destroyers, and transports. Contact with the Japanese forces was made just as hopes were growing dim.

The column of ships approached Savo Island from the north, then began to proceed southwest towards Guadalcanal. The *Washington's* radar made contact with an unidentified ship around 2300. It appeared as if the Japanese fleet had been discovered. Approximately 17 minutes later the *Washington* opened fire on the distant target; the 16-inch shells sped towards their targets, but no damage could be seen on the enemy vessels. The four American destroyers salvoed their guns with apparent scant results.

By the ship's account: ...suddenly, the command "Load!" came over the battle-circuit. In the turrets, eager hands smoothly worked hoists and rammers, loaded ammunition, and closed the heavy breach plugs. Still no sight of the enemy, but the "radar" said they were there. "Commence Firing!" Nine huge armor-piercing shells roared into the darkness. The *Washington* shuddering with the shock of that first salvo, felt at last the fulfillment of her purpose, the reward for her long preparation for action.

The Japanese warships that had been fired on were the light cruiser *Sendai* and four destroyers. The *Washington's* fire forced the *Sendai* and two destroyers to retreat while the remaining destroyers advanced towards the American ships. The bulk of the Japanese force, approaching the *Washington* from the north and northwest, still had not been engaged.

The American column of ships entered the channel between Savo Island and Cape Esperance by about 2300. The four destroyers still led the two battleships, and the *Washington* occupied the same position ahead of the *South Dakota*. Shortly thereafter, the four destroyers came under intense fire from the *Nagara* and four Japanese destroyers, in addition to the two destroyers that had accompanied the *Sendai*.

The USS *Preston* sank first. Raked by accurate gunfire from the *Nagara*, at close range, the destroyer began listing as soon as the first Japanese salvo struck home. A series of 5-inch rounds were directed at the *Nagara*, but insignificant damage was done. The *Preston* suffered mortal damage. Depth charges on the fantail began to explode and propulsion was soon lost. Little more than five minutes had passed between the arrival of the first Japanese salvos and the order to abandon ship. The *Preston* heeled over in the water and sank.

The other American destroyers, the *Walke*, *Benham* and *Gwin*, suffered similar fates. Surprised by the same attack that had sunk the *Preston*, they all suffered extensive damage. The *Walke* and *Benham* both received shells and torpedoes from the *Nagara* and its escorts. These two American destroyers managed to return fire, but to no avail; they sank shortly after the *Preston*. The *Gwin* took shell hits in its engineering spaces, but further damage was fortunately avoided and the *Gwin* successfully escaped the chaotic battle.

The *Washington* and *South Dakota* remained as the only two battle worthy American vessels. During the destruction of the American destroyers *Washington* managed to engage both the 16-inch and 5-inch batteries; *South Dakota* followed with similar action. The battleships damaged several of the Japanese cruisers and destroyers, although none sank.

The battleships entered the narrows between Savo Island and Cape Esperance to find it choked with the remains of the four American destroyers. In the water, hundreds of men struggled to find life rafts or to swim to shore. *Washington* and *South Dakota* dropped their life rafts to the beleaguered sailors as they passed. Unfortunately, at this moment the *South Dakota* lost power and use of all radar. The two battleships parted; *Washington* headed left to flank the Japanese fleet and *South Dakota* headed right.

Without the benefit of radar *South Dakota* could not detect the approach of *Sendai* and several Japanese destroyers which had been traveling a parallel course. *South Dakota's* turn to starboard had only brought it closer to the Japanese guns. The *Sendai* and its escort opened up with all of their batteries at 2400, striking *South Dakota* shortly after it regained power. Even thought near a dozen Japanese torpedoes were avoided, gunfire jammed *South Dakota's* #3 turret and riddled its superstructure. Salvo after salvo struck

South Dakota causing little if any flotation damage, but destroying more vulnerable components, like radar antenna and fire control equipment. While *South Dakota's* 5-inch batteries struck at the Japanese ships, the rest of the ship's damage put it out of action for the night. Soon, *Washington* was the only American ship left in fighting condition.

During the melee near Savo Island, the Japanese battle ship, *Kirishima*, sped towards the now burning *South Dakota*. Unknown to the Japanese, *Washington* occupied a station off of their right flank. Moonset had occurred and save for the few burning ships near Savo Island, all was dark. *Washington's* radar proved invaluable in spotting the approaching battleship through the darkness. Admiral Lee knew that the *Kirishima* was approaching and he maintained course to the starboard side.

At 2400, *Washington* opened fire on *Kirishima* with all batteries. The 16-inch batteries obtained a hit on the first and second salvo, while the 5-inch batteries delivered numerous blows. *Kirishima* did not return fire on *Washington* which was cloaked in darkness. The aged Japanese battleship was gutted in a matter of minutes. The Japanese destroyers accompanying *Kirishima* fired a spread of torpedoes at *Washington*; but none found their target.

Washington launched 75 16-inch shells at *Kirishima*, a majority of which found their mark. After seven minutes of firing *Washington* silenced its batteries. A blazing hulk, the *Kirishima* sank rapidly after being scuttled by its escort, signaling the defeat of the Japanese naval forces at Guadalcanal. *Washington* swung starboard to search out any remaining enemy vessels, but none were to be found. Only a few ill-aimed torpedoes were directed at *Washington* and the Japanese fleet was in retreat. Having accomplished his mission, Admiral Lee headed southward.

The official after-action report later recorded: This ship was fired on only sporadically. She was not illuminated. No hits were sustained and the nearest miss was the splash, apparently of a major-caliber shell about 200 yards on the port quarter. Observers who witnessed other ships of our force under concentrated fire reported the Japanese gunnery to be accurate. Enemy ships close to Savo fired automatic weapons accurately at our destroyers. The Japanese ships were, apparently, not equipped with radar. Their searchlights provided excellent illumination of *South Dakota*, but attracted our fire and provided a point of aim.

Famed naval historian, Samuel Eliot Morrison, remarked in *Two Ocean War*, "This night battleship action was vastly better fought by the US Navy... *Washington,* conned by Captain Glen Davis and directed by Admiral Lee with a skill and imperturbability worthy of her eponym saved the day for the United States." The *Washington* undoubtedly saved *South Dakota* from destruction and, moreover, halted further attempts by the Japanese fleet to bombard Henderson field.

The Naval Historical Center's account of fast battleship experience during the war wrote: In this decisive action *Washington* and *South Dakota* engaged a Japanese force formed around the battleship *Kirishima*. *South Dakota* suffered extensive topside damage, but *Washington's* accurate fire mortally injured *Kirishima*. Set aflame and wracked by explosions, *Kirishima* was scuttled by her crew. The last major Japanese naval thrust at Guadalcanal had been turned back, and *Washington* had done what she had been designed to do - sink one of her own kind in gunnery action. *Washington* was the only American fast battleship to defeat another capital ship. Surprisingly, *Washington* remained unscathed throughout the intense combat and its victory must be credited to the crew. It was apparent to all that took part in the action that a decisive victory had been secured. Shipfitter John Brown closed with "...spent 28 hours at General Quarters stations...sank first Japanese battleship."

The ship's history concluded: During the course of the fast but bitter action that followed, the *Washington,* as her part in the action, sank outright the enemy battleship *Kirishima* as well as assisting in the damage of several enemy cruisers and destroyers. Had the *Washington's* career terminated at this point, she would, even then, have more than justified her existence. She was, however, undamaged, had not lost a man, and was destined to sail on to less spectacular though no less important aggressive actions.

CONSOLIDATION OF THE SOUTHERN SOLOMON'S

The Allies continued on the offensive against Japan with a strategy that established a string of land bases and overlapping zones of air control in the Solomon's. General Douglas MacArthur and Admiral William F. Halsey correlated their South Pacific drives, while Admiral Chester W. Nimitz planned to island hop through the Central Pacific, beginning with the Gilbert Islands. These islands served as the means to recapture the Philippines, while the main Japanese base at Rabaul was left to wither on the vine.

Barr Collin #259, "And then there was one." Big E and support ships at Noumea Harbor, New Calidonia, November 1942.

For the next six months the *Washington* seemed to have little to do. The enemy had been dealt a serious blow, and our forces were gathering but were not strong enough for the vigorous removal of the Japanese from their other Solomon Island bases. From February through April 1943, the *Washington* continued to serve as Admiral Lee's flagship and provided protection to convoy and carrier groups, primarily with Task Force 11 and the *Saratoga* and Task Force 16 with the *Enterprise*.

During this stretch, a recreation beach was established near the anchorage of Noumea and aptly named Shangri-La. The crew spent many cheerful hours there swimming and playing ball. Captain Davis was relieved by Captain James E. (Silent Jim) Maher on April 27, 1943, and the month of May found the *Washington* off to Pearl Harbor for a short overhaul and a taste of civilization again. On the way they were joined by Task Force 16.

As Task Force 60, maneuvers were conducted from Pearl Harbor, Hawaii. While at Pearl Harbor the antiaircraft machine gun battery was improved and enlarged. Overhaul was completed and on July 27, 1943, and the ship headed south again as Task Group 56.14 to take part in the beginning of the Central Pacific push that was to end ultimately in Tokyo Bay. The *Washington* operated in support of fast carrier forces out of Efate, New Hebrides. This began the ship's extended service in the Pacific that witnessed participation in numerous battles, bombardments, and air strikes.

Gilbert Islands Operations

Admiral Nimitz advanced through the vast Central Pacific because the Navy's battle wagon fleets had been replaced with faster, more heavily armed ships and Essex and Independence class aircraft carriers. From November to December 1943, the *Washington* in the Fiji Island area, became a unit in a fast carrier task force for the first time as part of Task Group 53.2 with four battleships and six destroyers. They rendezvoused with the carriers *Enterprise*, *Essex* and *Independence* as well as other screening units under Rear Admiral Lee, now Commander Battleships, Pacific.

Following joint maneuvers, the formation split up and the *Washington* and escorts returned to the Fiji Island area on November 7, 1943. A few days later the first of the great Central Pacific island campaigns was launched against the Gilberts "by what was then the mightiest naval force in history." On November 15 the battleship groups joined with the carrier group of Rear Admiral Charles A. (Baldy) Pownall on the *Yorktown*.

As Task Force 50, the combined force proceeded to join the air and naval pounding of the Gilbert and Marshall Islands to "soften" them up for amphibious assault by Navy, Army and Marine forces. On November 19 aircraft attacked Mili, Jaluit, and Makin for the first time through November 20 when landings began.

On November 25, regrouping occurred which found the *Washington* with Task Group 50.4 under Rear Admiral Frederick C. (Ted) Sherman. This powerful fast carrier group was built around the *Bunker Hill* and *Monterey*, screened by the *Washington, South Dakota, Alabama* and eight destroyers. The group provided surface, submarine, and air protection north of Makin Island. The Naval Historical Center recorded "Enemy planes attacked the group on the 27th and 28th but were driven off without inflicting any damage..."

During this campaign several air attacks were successfully repelled, and the operation was finished with the *Washington* blasting Nauru Island to impotency, as part of Task Group 50.8 with Rear Admiral Lee on board. This was in concert with the *North Carolina, Massachusetts, Indiana, South Dakota* and *Alabama*. Two fleet aircraft carriers, *Bunker Hill* and *Monterey*, and 11 destroyers completed the force that steamed north and south of Ocean Island.

The carrier's launched their planes at daybreak December 8, as the aircraft strike groups formed, the battleships approached in column and fired 135 rounds 16-inch fire at Japanese installations on the island. The secondary batteries and spotter aircraft also contributed to the devastation ashore. Air strikes finished the attack and the task group sailed for Efate for further reorganization as Task Force 57 became Task Force 37.

Bismarck Archipelago Operations

The year ended with gunnery and maneuver practice in preparation for the next round of fighting. In early January 1944, the *Washington* took part in a strike on Kavieng in the Bismarck Archipelago, at the time beyond the range of land-based fighters and unescorted bombers. This was with the *North Carolina* and a screen of four destroyers under Rear Admiral Lee. They returned to the New Hebrides afterwards.

Marshall Islands Operations

The *Washington* joined with Task Group 37.2 consisting the carriers *Bunker Hill, Monterey* and four destroyers en route to the Ellice Islands. From there they linked up with the famed Task Force 58 under the overall command of Vice Admiral Marc A. (Pete) Mitscher. In late January and February 1944, as Task Group 58.1, The *Washington* served as a screen for the carriers as they launched their strikes against Kwajalein and Taroa. With the *Massachusetts, Indiana,* and four destroyers they shelled Kwajalein on January 30. Even more air strikes followed the next day.

Captain Jim Maher

On February 1 the *Washington* and *Indiana* collided while maneuvering and collapsed some 60 feet of the *Washington's* bow. Both ships pulled into the Majuro Atoll lagoon, after immediate repairs, on February 11, and the *Washington* went on the Pearl Harbor Navy Yard for a temporary bow. Following this, the ship turned east and headed for the States for its first visit home in 19 months. The ship's history recorded "Great was the jubilation of her officers and crew as she passed through the Straights of Juan de Fuca into Puget Sound.

Experienced men were sent to new ships and replacement drafts took their place, causing a certain amount of turmoil until these new shipmates became a part of the "family." There was another change of command when Captain Thomas R. (Old Tom) Cooley relieved Maher on April 23, 1944. Six short weeks of leave, liberty, hard work at the Bremerton Navy Yard, and again the *Washington* headed west to continue her record of participation in the Pacific campaigns. On the outgoing leg of the voyage, some extra 500 servicemen were transported to Hawaii.

Marianas Operations

On May 30, 1944, the *Washington* rejoined Task Force 58 at Majuro and as Vice Admiral Lee's flagship supported the invasion of the Marianas Islands. On June 7 she joined the fast carriers again. This time the targets were Saipan, Tinian, Guam, Rota and Pagan. It was becoming routine now; air attacks, naval bombardments and more air attacks with both the 3rd and 5th Fleets.

Advancing Japanese naval task forces were met on June 12 and damaged by Task Force 58 flyers. On June 13 Admiral Lee's battleship-destroyer task group conducted naval gunfire bombardment of Saipan and Tinian in support of the amphibious landings. Relieved the next day, on June 15, Task Force 58 conducted air strikes on Iwo, Chichi and Haha Jima. Intensive air and naval gunfire support continued to cover the hard fought Saipan landing. On this same day, the Japanese Combined Fleet under Admiral Jisaburo Ozawa attempted further counter strikes. In this action Japanese naval air made a desperate attempt to cripple permanently the American Pacific Fleet. A sea and air battle was fought from June 19-21, the first battle of the Philippine Sea, during which the famed "Marianas Turkey Shoot" took place. The Japanese attempt ended in total defeat when almost 300 enemy aircraft were destroyed. The result of this battle was the "complete destruction of the major portion of the air arm of the Imperial Japanese navy."

The *Washington* found itself deployed as part of the protective screen around the vital fleet carriers. The screen of seven US Navy battleships, four cruisers and 14 destroyers served to protect the "flattops" from effective counter action. Nearly all of the enemy planes were destroyed by our aircraft, but those few that filtered through the deadly carrier air groups met similar destruction in the anti-aircraft fire of the surface ships. History recorded "The tremendous firepower of the screen...together with the aggressive combat air patrols flown, the American carriers proved too much for even the aggressive Japanese."

This was not without cost to the Americans, what Japanese aircraft that did get through scored its on the *South Dakota, Wasp, Bunker Hill, Minneapolis* and *Indiana*. Some 29 American aircraft were also lost of the more than 300 carrier aircraft involved.

Breaking off from this engagement, the *Washington* refueled east of the Marianas. After this, the *Washington* and Task Group 58-4 returned to protecting the Saipan landing and other strikes in the Marianas through the end of July, concentrating by then on the landing at Guam.

Leyte Operation

Beginning on July 25 and for the next four months, operations found the *Washington* engaged in "softening up" action preliminary to the eventual invasion of the Philippines and included the capture of Peleliu and Anguar.

After refueling and replenishment at Eniwetok Atoll, Admiral Lee's Task Group 58.7 headed for first the Admiralty and then Palau Islands. The *Washington's* heavy guns shelled Peleliu and Angaur through the end of August.

With the American return to the Philippines, the Japanese defenders virtually sacrificed their entire force of over 500,000 and a weapon of desperation appeared, suicide pilots who flew their bomb laden aircraft into ships. The naval fighting, the largest of the war, cost Japan four carriers and its fleet air arm.

Newsman Fred Tucker wrote about one incident of many, with an account of an air attack at this point in the war. For the machine gunner at general quarters, completely exposed on deck, a "few moments were always utilized preparing himself for flash burns by tucking his trouser legs into his socks, rolling down sleeves, buttoning collar and debating whether or not to fasten helmet straps." At least the later model did not fly off the older "tin kellys" had at the start of the war. Word would be passed: "Now set Condition Zebra, secure all watertight compartments, close all watertight doors..." And the wait would begin broken only by the training of a gun mount or sights. "We have a bogey bearing 045, range 15,000 yards, closing... "came over the speaker, followed by "stations" and the sharp click of 20 mm guns being cocked. A lone aircraft approached from the starboard-quarter headed straight for the ship. The sound of aircraft machine guns, the buzzing of misses and ricochets, were met with the "sudden thunder" of 40 mm and 20 mm opening up and sending out streams of

Captain Ross Cooley. (Courtesy of Wm. B. Fargo.)

Captain Roscoe F. Good.

tracers converging on the kamikaze. "From behind all sorts of cover, men peered out in time to see the approaching plane, now within 50 yards, lose one of its wings!"

In October, there followed further support of air and surface strikes on the Philippines, Okinawa, Formosa, and a battle off Cape Engano. Captain Roscoe F. Good relieved Cooley on November 16. On the same day Captain Cooley made rear admiral and was designated Commander Battleship Division 6 with his flag aboard the *Washington* (after the war, Rear Admiral Cooley returned as Commander Battleship Division 4).

LUZON OPERATION

From November 5, 1944, through January 1945, there rapidly ensued more air strikes and more raids, this time closer to the enemy's strongest points; Okinawa, Formosa and Luzon were again hit, as were Cam Ranh Bay, Saigon, Hong Kong, Canton, Nansei Shoto, and the heart of Japan itself - Tokyo. The "kamikaze craze" seemed to wane as better pilots were lost and aircraft were destroyed on the ground.

On the *Washington*, a crew member wrote about the end of the year typhoon that struck viciously, a reminder that at sea the enemy was not the only threat: "Salt water was blowing horizontally at bridge level. There seemed to be no separation between sea and sky." Deck gear, aircraft, and several destroyers did not survive the 100 mile per hour gusts and high seas.

IWO JIMA OPERATION

An island nation, Japan depended upon secure sea lanes for food and raw material and to resupply and reinforce its armed forces. By 1945 half its merchant fleet had been destroyed, mostly by American submarines. At war's end, 95% percent of Japan's merchant tonnage would be destroyed. With its lifeline cut at sea, the proximity of American air bases brought an increase in strategic bombing attacks by land based aircraft. The various Allied cross Pacific drives were closing in as integrated operations took on suicidal defense.

The next step on the road to Tokyo Bay was bloody Iwo Jima from February through March 1945. Hardly more than a small volcanic rock, Iwo was the scene of the fiercest battles of the Pacific. Just prior to this a catapult and aircraft were lost in a fueling accident with the *Hailey*, that left that ship's anchor on board 75 miles west of Chichi Jima.

On February 19, the *Washington* took part in the initial bombardment of the island and then lay for five days "within a stone's throw of the beaches, tossing shells with pinpoint accuracy in close support of our advancing troops." The Naval Historical Center credits the main and secondary batteries as having "destroyed gun positions, troop concentrations, and other ground installations."

One Marine sergeant wounded with the assault force on Iwo sent a letter to his brother serving on the *Washington* which perhaps is one of the finest tributes ever paid the ship. The letter simply expressed the gratitude of the Marines for fire support in their time of need ashore. He wrote. "We couldn't ask for greater support than what you gave us. I wish you would tell every man on your ship from the captain on down, that the boys from my outfit thank you for helping us complete the hardest task in our history."

As Iwo was subdued, from February 23 through March 16, the carrier task forces, of which the *Washington* was part, again raided Tokyo as well as other parts of Japan and Nansei Shoto. Following these raids, the ship was detached and made a quick run to Manus in the Admiralty Islands for dry dock repairs. While there, a reunion was held with the British crews of the HMS *Argonaut, Black Prince, Indefatigable, Indomitable, Victorious* and *King George V.* Just like old times at Scapa Flow!

OKINAWA GUNTO OPERATION

In the Pacific War's final months, the United States planned large scale amphibious operations that involved both the Army and Navy. In March 1945, the ship joined Task Force 58 in support of the capture of Okinawa. By now, the island invasion had taken on a set pattern. The *Washington* took part in this with two surface bombardments of Okinawa on March 24 and April 19 that began the amphibious landings and later supported operations ashore. During the second bombardment the main battery alone fired 45,000 pounds of high explosives at the bitterly resisting enemy.

Japan hoped that suicidal resistance, as conducted at Okinawa, would inflict unacceptable costs on these forces and delay defeat. On the *Washington*, a crew member recalled March 19, 1995: "I was topside when off our port-quarter the *Franklin* was wrecked by Japanese bombs in a surprise attack. Seven hundred twenty-four were killed and the ship was deemed the most badly damaged capital ship that survived during the war." On May 11 he related the same happened to the *Bunker Hill*.

During the Okinawa Campaign the *Washington* remained at sea for 88 consecutive days, setting a record for battleships; steamed 31,494 miles, fueled destroyers 59 times, and was itself fueled 16 times. She received all her supplies and ammunition while underway and also transferred patients in stretchers to a hospital ship steaming alongside. Several other strikes were made on Kyushu during this period. There were also 33 air raids by the notorious Japanese Special Attack Corps, with kamikaze suicide-crash attacks on our ships as well as typhoon weather conditions. These suicide attacks added to the American dread about the costs of invading Japan. In the spring and summer of 1945, American B-29 Superfortresses fire bombed towns and cities in anticipation of the next Allied move. At the end of this, the *Washington* sailed for the Philippines and anchored at San Pedro Bay, Leyte on June 1, 1945.

The *Washington* emerged with a tired but unscathed crew, after the short stop in Leyte, a change of command followed, and on June 5, 1945, Captain Francis X. McInerney took over through war's end. Next, the ship was on her way to the continental United States for a complete overhaul, terminating three year's participation in the Pacific War. Little was it realized that this was the end of four years of practically continuous combat duty.

Stops were made at Guam and Pearl Harbor, reaching Puget Sound Navy Yard on June 23. This is where the *Washington* would be on V-J Day, August 14, 1945. At 1605, at commercial radio broadcast announced that "hostilities between the Allies and Japanese were suspended." A week earlier, a single B-29 had dropped an atomic bomb on Hiroshima, killing tens of thousands. This was followed by a second bomb on Nagasaki and Japan's unconditional surrender without a costly invasion. Work on the ship and at the Navy yard "ceased except for maintenance" until the next day. Victory in the Pacific was to bring the *Washington's* wartime saga to an end and changed forever America's place in the world.

Conclusion: Piping Aside

It would have been more fitting for the *Washington* to have been able to finish her wartime career in Tokyo Bay; however, such a reward was not in store for the ship. After a major overhaul at Puget Sound Navy Yard during July and August 1945, then an intensive 10 day underway training period off San Clemente Island, the *Washington* passed through the Panama Canal for the second time on her way to Philadelphia, arriving on October 17, 1945, just prior to Navy Day in October.

After being visited by over 100,000 grateful citizens, the *Washington* became a part of the Navy's "magic carpet," carrying returning veterans home from Europe. This began on November 21 after a dockyard stop for additional berthing. The crew was stripped to just 84 officers and 835 men who set sail in the Atlantic again on November 15. She was the only fast battleship to participate in this "operation," in which she made two trips between South Hampton, England and New York City. The second trip was memorable for the United States Army passengers and many of the crew. It was on this trip that the *Washington* weathered eight terrific storms in as many consecutive days.

Looking back on active wartime service, the *Washington* earned 15 Battle Stars. Its wartime deeds accounted for a battleship, three damaged cruisers, one destroyer, twelve aircraft, and strikes on ten enemy-held islands. With its place in history ensured, the *Washington* was decommissioned on June 19, 1947, at Bayonne, New Jersey. After staying in the Atlantic Reserve Fleet through the 1950s, the *Washington* was dropped from the Navy list and sold for scrap on May 24, 1961.

Distinguished journalist and historian, Fletcher Pratt, wrote a fitting epitaph after the war: She was too good. Other ships were raked by Japanese gunfire, got hit by torpedoes and kamikazes, and performed heroic acts of bravery in the face of death; they got the newspaper publicity. Nothing like that ever happened to the battleship *Washington*. In four years of the fiercest sea-fighting the world had seen, she was never touched, and the only casualty aboard her occurred when a descending shell fragment hit a Forty mm gunner in the butt. Yet she played a decisive role in one of the biggest naval battles of the war, and her guns sent more Japanese to drink saltwater than those of any other ship in our Navy.

Captain F.X. McInerney, U.S.N.

DECK LOG BOOK
U.S.S. Washington
Saturday, November 14-Sunday, November 15, 1942

Zone Description - 12

18 to 20: Steaming as before. 1905 darkened ship. 1915 sounded general quarters. 1925 main and secondary batteries manned. 1927 material condition Zed set. 1950 ceased zigzagging, resumed base course. 1957 changed course to 128 true 105 psc. average steam 587.5; average RPM 157.0.

R.P. Hunter, Lieutenant Commander, USN

20 to 24: Steaming as before. 2008 changed speed to 18 knots (118 RPM). 2015 set material condition Yoke, condition Z Mike. 2040 commenced zig zagging. 2040 changed speed to 21 knots (139 RPM). 2050 passed through heavy rain squall. 2240 radio voice contact with escort on bearing 068 true, distant 10 miles. 2242 ceased zig zagging, resumed base curse. 2250 passed through heavy rain squall. 2330 escorts ordered to form anti-submarine screen. Squally weather. Average steam 592; average RPM 134.8.

R.P. Hunter, Lieutenant Commander, USN

00 to 04: Steaming on course 270 true at 17 knots on boiler 1, 2, 3, 4, 5, 6, 7, 8 in company with *Walke, Benham, Gwin, Preston* and *South Dakota* - with Rear Admiral W.A. Lee Jr., USN, Commander Task Force 64, SOPA in *Washington*, proceeded in vicinity of Savo Island, Solomon Islands group, hunting Japanese vessels. 0016 commenced firing with main and secondary batteries on unknown enemy ship, increased speed to 23 knots... 0018 changed course to 3 (—) true. Steaming on same course at various speeds engaging unknown enemy ships. 0038 while steering 280 true, passed Savo Island abeam to starboard, distant 3.2 miles. 0107 ...proceeded to channel between Russell Island and Guadalcanal Island. 0143 with *Cape Esperance* bearing 131 true, distant 18.5 miles, proceeded to the SSE, making radical changes to avoid torpedoes. 0200 made contact with *Gwin* and *Benham*. 0216 proceeded on general southerly course to open sea. 0320 changed course to 140 true, 105 psc and changed speed to 23 knots. No material casualties, same to communications system, and light upperwork damaged by concussion of own gun fire. No personnel casualties. Expended rounds of ammunition as follows: 16"-117, 5"-478 common/62 star shell, 1".10-none, 20 mm-none. Average steam 590; average RPM 174.0.

R.P. Hunter, Lieutenant Commander, USN

Courtesy of William Paul Weidert.

NOTICE OF SEPARATION FROM U. S. NAVAL SERVICE
NAVPERS-553 (REV. 8-45)

1. SERIAL OR FILE NO. / RANK AND CLASSIFICATION: 634 05 14 / SF2C(T) / CCL-292 / 1045-292-8

2. NAME: BROWN JR. JOHN A.

3. RATE AND CLASS / PERMANENT ADDRESS FOR MAILING PURPOSES: USNR HON(COGD)10-13 / 2708 MONTGOMERY AVE. ASHLAND, KY.

5. PLACE OF SEPARATION: USN, PERS SEP CEN, UNIT 8, GT. LAKES, ILL.

6. CHARACTER OF SEPARATION: HONORABLE

7. ADDRESS FROM WHICH EMPLOYMENT WILL BE SOUGHT: SAME

8. RACE: W **9. SEX:** M **10. MARITAL STATUS:** S **11. U.S. CITIZEN:** YES

12. DATE AND PLACE OF BIRTH: 11/24/24, CATLETTSBURG, KY.

13. REGISTERED: NO **14. SELECTIVE SERVICE BOARD OF REGISTRATION:** NONE

15. HOME ADDRESS AT TIME OF ENTRY INTO SERVICE: 349-37TH ST., ASHLAND, KY.

16. MEANS OF ENTRY: [X] ENLISTED — DATE 12/17/41

17. DATE OF ENTRY INTO ACTIVE SERVICE: 12/17/41

18. NET SERVICE (FOR PAY PURPOSES): 3/9/27

19. PLACE OF ENTRY INTO ACTIVE SERVICE: NRS, LOUISVILLE, KY.

20. QUALIFICATIONS, CERTIFICATES HELD, ETC.: SEE RATING DESCRIPTION BOOKLET SHIPFITTER SECOND CLASS (T)USNR

21. RATINGS HELD: AS, SF2C.

22. FOREIGN AND/OR SEA SERVICE WORLD WAR II: [X] YES

23. SERVICE SCHOOLS COMPLETED: NONE

24. SERVICE (VESSELS AND STATIONS SERVED ON): USNTS, GT. LAKES, ILL. / USS WASHINGTON (BB56)

25. KIND OF INSURANCE: N
26. EFFECTIVE MONTH OF ALLOTMENT DISCONTINUANCE: Oct
27. MO. NEXT PREMIUM DUE: None
28. AMOUNT OF PREMIUM DUE EACH MONTH: 3.20
29. INTENTION OF VETERAN TO CONTINUE INS.: YES

30. TOTAL PAYMENT UPON DISCHARGE: $120.63
31. TRAVEL OR MILEAGE ALLOWANCE INCLUDED IN TOTAL PAYMENT: $22.75
32. INITIAL MUSTERING OUT PAY: 100.00
33. NAME OF DISBURSING OFFICER: F. A. SHAREK 520 026

34. REMARKS:
AMERICAN DEFENSE THEATER)
GOOD CONDUCT)
ASIATIC PACIFIC) 15 STARS
EUROPEAN AFRICAN)
PHILIPPINE LIBERATION)

35. SIGNATURE (BY DIRECTION OF COMMANDING OFFICER): FOR H. T. HAMBLEN, LT., USNR.

36. NAME AND ADDRESS OF LAST EMPLOYER: N.Y.A. ASHLAND, KY.

37. DATES OF LAST EMPL'MT: FROM JAN. 41 TO DEC. 41

38. MAIN CIVILIAN OCCUPATION AND D.O.T. NO.: ?

39. JOB PREFERENCE: STEAM HEATING AND PLUMBING

40. PREFERENCE FOR ADDITIONAL TRAINING: YES

41. NON-SERVICE EDU. (YRS. SUCCESSFULLY COMPLETED): GRAM. 8 / H.S. 2 / COLL. —
42. DEGREES: —
43. MAJOR COURSE OR FIELD: GENERAL
44. VOCATIONAL OR TRADE COURSES: WELDING (ACTY) 4 MOS.

45. RIGHT INDEX FINGERPRINT

46. OFF DUTY EDUCATIONAL COURSES COMPLETED: NONE

FOR CONVENIENCE, A CERTIFICATE OF ELIGIBILITY NO. 2459195 HAS BEEN ISSUED BY THE VETERANS ADMINISTRATION TO BE USED FOR THE FUTURE REQUEST OF ANY PROPERTY OR INSURANCE BENEFIT UNDER TITLE III OF THE SERVICEMEN'S READJUSTMENT ACT OF 1944, AS AMENDED, THAT MAY BE AVAILABLE TO THE PERSON TO WHOM SUCH CERTIFICATE WAS ISSUED.

47. DATE OF SEPARATION: 10-13-45

48. SIGNATURE: John Anderson Brown, Jr.

Commanding Officer, 1941-45

Capt. H.H.J. Benson	May 15, 1941-July 25, 1942
Capt. G.B. Davis	July 25, 1942-April 27, 1943
Capt. J.E. Maher	April 27, 1943-April 23, 1944
Capt. T.R. Cooley	April 23, 1944-Nov. 16, 1944
Capt. R.F. Good	Nov. 16, 1944-June 5,1945
Capt. F.X. McInerney	June 5,1945-

Campaign and Battle Stars, 1941-45
(Reference, Assistant Vice Chief of Naval Operations)

Russian Convoy Operations
Capture and Defense of Guadalcanal
Guadalcanal (Third Savo)
Consolidation of Solomon Island (Southern Solomons)
Gilbert Islands Operations
Bismarck Archipelago Operations (Kavieng)
Marshall Islands Operations (Kwajalein, Majuro)
Marianas Operations (Bonins, Marianas, Western Pacific,
  Battle of Philippine Sea, Guam, Palau, Yap, Ulithi)
Western Caroline Island Operations (Southern Palaus, Philippine Islands)
Leyte Operations (Okinawa, Northern Luzon, Visayas, Luzon)
Luzon Operations (Formosa, Luzon, China, Nansei Shoto)
Iwo Jima Operation (Honshu, Nansei Shoto)
Okinawa Gunto Operation

References and Further Reading

Baker, R.W., etal. *History of the USS Washington, 1941-46*. New York: Robert W. Kelly Publishing, 1946.
Brown, J.A. Personal Diary, Dec. 15, 1942-June 23, 1945.
D'Albas, A. *Death of a Navy*. New York: Devin-Adair, 1957.
Fairbanks, D. *A Hell of a War*. New York: St. Martin's Press, 1993.
Friedman, N. *U.S. Battleships*. Annapolis: Naval Institute Press, 1985.
Hammel, E. *Guadalcanal: Decision at Sea*. New York: Crown Publishers, 1988.
Irving, D. *The Destruction of Convoy PQ-17*. New York: St. Martin's Press, 1989.
Jernigan, E.J. *Tin Can Man*. Arlington: Vandamere Press, 1993.
Mooney, J.L., ed. *Dictionary of American Naval Fighting Shops*, vol. VIII. Washington, DC: Naval Historical Center, 1981.
Morison, S.E. *The Two Ocean War*. Boston: Atlantic Monthly, 1963.
Musicant, I. *Battleship at War: The Epic Story of the USS Washington*. New York: Avon Books, 1986.
Newcomb, R. *Iwo Jima*. New York: Holt, Rinehart and Winston, 1965.
Perry, H.A. "U.S. Battleships in World War 2," *American Legion Magazine*. September 1973, 10-15, 38-42.
Phillips, Nelson, "USS *Washington*, BB-56," *Sea Classics*, April 1988, 12-17.
Pratt, Fletcher. "The Ship that Liked to Shoot," *Saga*. n.d., 25-71.
Roscoe, T. *US Destroyer Operations in World War II*. Annapolis: Naval Institute Press, 1953.
Tucker, F. "With Men of USS *Washington* in World War II," *The Daily Press*. Newport News, Hampton, VA, July 4, 1965, 5-6.

Unless cited otherwise, all material was provided by the USS Washington (B-56) Reunion Group, Inc.

The Authors

Chuck and David Melson worked on this project for Turner Publishing and the USS *Washington* Reunion Group. Chuck was a naval services historian and a veteran of the US Marine Corps. He has written award winning histories of World War II, Vietnam, and the Persian Gulf. David has a long interest in naval vessels and aircraft that began with a childhood spent at Camp Pendleton and the US Naval Academy. His previous projects include work on the Solomon's Campaign and he is currently attending St. John's College.

1. Martie Zad, "Discovery Sails Tale of Battleships," *TV Week*, 8-14 June 1997, 4.
2. Jernigan, *Tin Can Man*, 46.
3. Fairbanks, *A Hell of a War*, 102.
4. Jernigan, *Tin Can Man*, 33.
5. Pratt, "The Ship that Loved to Shoot," *Saga*, 25.
6. Mooney, *Fighting Ships* VII, 129.
7. Fairbanks, *A Hell of a War*, 101.
8. Baker, etal., *USS Washington*, 28.
9. Mooney, *Fighting Ships*, 130.
10. Baker, etal., *USS Washington*, 37-38.
11. Baker, etal., *USS Washington*, 37-38.
12. Morison, *Two Ocean War*. 205.
13. Brown, Diary, 14 November 1942.
14. Baker, etal., *USS Washington*, 37-38.
15. Baker, etal., *USS Washington*, 40.
16. Mooney, *Fighting Ships*, 131.
17. Baker, etal., *USS Washington*, 45.
18. Baker, etal., *USS Washington*, 46-47.
19. Mooney, *Fighting Ships*, 131.
20. Tucker, "With Men of USS *Washington*." *Daily Press,* 5-6.
21. Baker, etal., *USS Washington*, 57.
22. Mooney, *Fighting Ships*, 132.
23. Baker, etal., *USS Washington*, 60.
24. Baker, etal., *USS Washington*, 79.
25. Pratt, "The Ship that Liked to Shoot," *Saga*, 25.

Special sea detail aboard the USS Washington.

USS WASHINGTON SPECIAL STORIES

SPECIAL STORIES

The Sinking of HMS Punjabi
K.A. Tipper

The time was 1545 on May 1, 1942. Kenneth Tipper, a telegraphist on the 1850-ton Tribal Class destroyer HMS *Punjabi,* was in the main wireless cabin just 15 minutes prior to going on watch in the cabin aft where he listened on high-frequency direction-finding equipment for Morse Code signals from marauding battleships like the *Tirpitz.*

The *Punjabi* was one of a screen of destroyers guarding US and British capital ships in a group covering Convoy P.Q. 15 on its way to Russia.

At 1545 on that unforgettable day, what had been a fairly uneventful trip turned into a nightmare. Suddenly, there was a tremendous crash, the *Punjabi* heeled sharply over on its side, and all the ship's lights went out. The immediate thought was that the ship had been torpedoed, but it later turned out that the *Punjabi* had been rammed and cut in two by the battleship HMS *King George V,* flagship of the Commander-in-Chief Home Fleet, Admiral Sir John Tovey.

In thick fog, the paths of the 35,000-ton battleship and the destroyer crossed. A court of inquiry later established that *Punjabi* had been well inside her station, following the destroyer HMS *Inglefield.* Soon after the fog came down, the leading destroyer sent out a signal to look out for a floating mine. To avoid the mine, *Punjabi* had turned to starboard and in so doing cut across the track of the battleship.

Ken Tipper and his shipmates scrambled over tilting decks to get to the upper deck in time to see the stern of their ship blown up by depth charges. The telegraphist Ken would have relieved one of those killed in the collision. It later transpired that by a miracle the majority of the crew survived - 206 men lived through one of the most bizarre events of WWII, picked up from the icy waters by the destroyers HMS *Martin* and *Marne.*

The scene on deck was chaotic, and when the order came to abandon ship it was very self-evident that it was every man for himself. The forward part of the ship, where most of the crew were located at the time of the collision, was listing badly and was obviously not going to stay afloat much longer. Four days' sailing north from Iceland had brought the fleet deep into the Arctic Ocean, and the water was icy cold and certain death for anyone swimming in it for many minutes. The ruptured fuel tanks of the *Punjabi* had laid a heavy film of fuel oil on the water and the decision of whether to wait on the sinking ship for help or jump in the freezing water was becoming one of life or death. The choice became obvious, and Tipper and most of his shipmates slid down the sloping side of the *Punjabi* into the water, and they were immediately coated with a thick covering of fuel oil. That oil, says Ken, probably saved his life, for he ws sitting in freezing water up to his waist on an overloaded Carley Float (life raft), for a long time before they managed to scramble up ropes to the deck of HMS *Martin,* which, together with HMS *Marne,* was responsible for picking up the survivors.

Before they abandoned ship, Tipper and his shipmates had seen the horrifying sight of the aircraft carrier HMS *Victorious,* followed by the USS *Washington,* bearing down on them out of the fog. Both these huge ships just managed to avoid colliding with the stricken destroyer, the after part of which slid to the bottom some 45 minutes after she was rammed.

Aboard the *Martin,* the survivors showered in an effort to get the slimy fuel oil off their bodies, and were given oddly assorted clothing by the crew. "I could smell that oil for many years after the war," says Ken, who also recalls seeing several members of *Punjabi's* crew, who survived the sinking but succumbed to the killing cold of the sea, being buried at sea. He vividly remembers one of them, a fellow telegraphist named Arthur Stiff, going over the side of the *Martin* wrapped in a Union Jack. "Stiffy, as we called him, had already survived two sinkings," he says, "Stiffy was swimming in the sea close to our life rafts, and we called him to come over and hang on to it. He refused, saying he would be OK, but it turned out third time unlucky for him."

The final count was 49 members of the crew died in the collision, seven of them officers,

The H.M.S. Punjabi was rammed aft where flag is shown flying.

2nd Division aboard USS Washington BB56.

Christmas Day

A head on view of the mighty Washington showing turrets one and two. January 1946.

"V" Division - August 1944.

whose wardroom was directly in the path of the bow of the battleship.

The sinking of the *Punjabi* was to set off an amazing set of coincidences in Ken Tipper's life. The first one was that the survivors were transferred to the *King George V* in Iceland for the trip back to Scapa Flow, the Home Fleet's base. While on board the battleship, Ken saw a sailor emerging from a hatchway on the main deck and recognized him as a fellow-employee of the newspaper where they worked in Birmingham. In fact, they worked in the same office! Both took a while to recover from the shock of seeing each other, and marveled over the fact that one's ship had sunk the others.

On the trip back to Scapa Flow, the *King George V* was listing badly due to a gaping hole in its bow. Tipper recalls being scared to spend too much time below decks on the battleship, but remembers nothing else about his time on the *Punjabi*'s nemesis.

The survivors returned to their home depots of Portsmouth and Devonport, were kitted out, and sent on survivor's leave. Their families were not notified for security reasons, and Tipper recalls his oldest sister's amazement when she saw him getting off a tram (street car) at the stop across from their house.

Returning to his depot, Tipper was reunited with a pal from *Punjabi* who had been on a hospital ship with appendicitis when the destroyer was sunk. They were both sent to the same ship for their next assignment, and served together for the rest of the war.

In 1957 the Tipper family emigrated to Florida, and in July, 1973, were living in Coconut Creek, north of Fort Lauderdale. Ken was reading the local paper and to his surprise saw that the reunion group of the USS *Washington* was holding its bi-annual meeting at a hotel in Fort Lauderdale. He called the hotel and asked for the organizer of the reunion, and that's how he came to meet John "Brownie" Brown. "Brownie" was equally amazed that nearby lived a survivor of the ship they last saw broken in two and sinking in the Arctic Ocean. He immediately invited Ken down to their hotel and they had a lively get-together, those American sailors and the "Limey", recounting their memories of that day in May, 1942.

"Brownie" and Ken stayed in touch, and at the reunion in Reno, NV, in 1989, Ken received his certificate of honorary membership in the BB-56 reunion group.

DEATH RIDE
by Robert G. Clark

While going to my battle station in turret one on the main deck, it was necessary to duck under the overhang to enter hatch opening. I looked to the starboard side and saw a Jap fighter plane going parallel with us. He was about 30 ft. off the water and about 50 ft. from us. The pilot's head was very visible. I watched him looking us over. At about the same time our 40mm and 20mm guns caught up with him, and he crashed in the water. There was one piece of the plane about a foot square floating in the air for a few seconds, and then he was gone. I'll never forget the look on the face of this Jap pilot as if he were on a pleasure ride instead of a death ride.

BIBLE CLASS
by Frank E. Bullock

A group met for Bible study each evening while at sea and sometimes when in port. There were times when the group met with Bible study groups from other ships and in Pearl Harbor it met with the Bible study group from the submarine base. The picture of the group was taken in the library. All are identified except two. Left to right those pictured are: (standing) unidentified, Glen Lockwood, MoMM2/c; Vernon E. Ledbetter, S2/c; H.A. Adams, FC2/c; Stover, GM2/c; Unidentified; J.M. Buckner, SF3/c; (setting behind the table) Loer S1/c; Camendish, S1/c; Gustafson, EM3/c; J.P. McQueen, MM2/c; A.W. Malphrus, MM2/c; E.H. Barnaby, S2/c; Chaplain Lundquist, LT; Karl A. Parshall, PhM3/c; (Front row) Frank E. Bullock, MM2/c; B. Feist, Pfc.; J.W. Pack, S1/c.

Most of the time the study was led by one of the men who attended the class. A part of the time the study was led by the Chaplain. There were several others who also attended who are not pictured.

MY RENDEZVOUS WITH THE ADMIRAL
by Billy Bryant

Being abreast of mount no. 1, the Admiral had the shipfitters build a storm shelter outside his door. I was standing AA watch as a hot caseman on Mt. 1. That was a cold North Atlantic day and a hot day for me. It was my duties to keep everyone clear. The mount started training inboard, and then the guns started depressing. I got on the phone but to no avail. Well, I guess this is where we could apply Murphy's Law—I'll never forget the rest. Me and those twin barrels were suddenly looking face to face with Admiral Wilcox for the first time and the last time. No, the guns didn't fire, but there were some hot times around that mount. My many thanks to the young officer who made my day. He said the phones were faulty.

MANY THANKS TO LT R.P. HUNTER
by Billy Bryant

After 18 months of holystoning the decks, side cleaning and other special details, I knew that wasn't my vision as a naval career man. After many "chits" for transfer were denied, I guess Lt. Hunter was convinced I was seriously unhappy with old Siggy, so he offered to put me in turret 2 as a GM striker. Yes Sir! I said. My belated thanks to you, Admiral R.P. Hunter.

A FEW REMEMBRANCES DURING W.W. II
by James B. Bias

One day while returning to port, we were all assembled on deck, when all of a sudden the port side anchor chain broke loose. We were lucky no one was hurt, talk about moving fast.

After ramming the *Indiana* we returned to Pearl Harbor for temporary repairs. We went ashore to the commissary to drink beer. We got off early and took up all the seats. The Marines came in after their training and were not to happy to see that all their usual seats were taken by us sailors. Fifteen minutes before closing four Marines picked a fight with me. One pushed me then the fight was on. The Shore Patrol broke it up and shoved my buddy and me outside. By that time someone had shouted "fight" and a lot of Marines came running, as their barracks were close by. Two Marines grabbed my arms and four Marines beat the hell out of me. I returned to the ship and word spread around the ship what the Marines had done to me. Everyone on the ship lined up on deck to go repay the Marines for what they had done to me, but the Officer of the Day closed the gang plank. It turned out my brother was in the Marines there but was working when all this occurred. I went to see him two days later and he could not recognize me. He wanted to get a few of his buddies to go after the guys who beat me but I told him not to.

REMEMBRANCE
by Paul W. Anderson

There are many shipmates, places, things and occurrences that touched my life aboard the USS *Washington*. But of all of the ones that standout in my mind today is one that could have ended her service early in the war, with the *Washington* meeting the same fate as HMS *Hood*.

Left to Right standing: unidentified, Glen Lockwood, MoMM2c; Vernon E. Ledbetter, S2c; H.A. Adams, FC2c; Stover, GM2c; unidentified, J.M. Buckner, SF3c (Sitting behind table) Loer, Slc; Camenish, Slc; Gustafson, EM3c; J.P. McQueen, MM2c; A.W. Malphrus, MM2c; E.H. Barnaby, S2c; Chap. Lundquist, Lt., Karl A. Parshall, Phmc; (Front Row) Frank E. Bullock, MM2c; B. Feist, Pfc.; J.W. Pack, Slc.

2nd Division on BB56

Sergeant Harry James on the USS Washington.

However after the emergency was over, the events that took place was quite comical to me.

This event took place in turret two, I don't recall why we were loading H.E. projectiles with proximity fuse unless we were firing target or bombardment. I was primerman on gun one, when the gun captain turned on the hoist to bring a projectile into loading position. The hoist jammed and hoisted the projectile straight up. Seeing this the gun crew abandoned the turret in the bat of an eye.

By the time I could climb up the gun deck from the primerman's platform the hoist had stopped, and I must say, "God was merciful that day" as the nose of the fuse was so close to the top of the turret, I doubt if you could slide a sheet of paper between them. When the crew returned I was standing by the projectile laughing, and ask "Where in the H@## did you think you were going?"

If my memory hasn't failed me the high explosive 16" projectile was about 1800 pounds of HE and steel balls which could have resiled back to the magazine which would have been a major disaster.

THE COLDEST WORKING PARTY
A.C. Anderson

In March 1942 my ship, the new battleship *Washington,* was anchored in Casco Bay, the harbor of Portland, ME, for a little over two weeks. While there I had my first experience with really cold weather. It was early Spring in South Carolina where I was from, but in Maine it was just like the dead of winter. Everything was covered with snow, and it was so cold no duties could be performed on the ship's weatherdecks without wearing heavy foul-weather gear. You really couldn't put on enough clothing to keep warm.

In the Navy everything except the men's regular duties is done by details of men called "working parties". One night when my section had the duty a working party was my bad luck to be a member of it. As usual nobody told us where we were going or what for, just to put on foul-weather gear. We mustered at the after gangway, got into a motor whaleboat and after about a twenty minute freezing cold ride, we arrived at the net tender (it opened and closed the torpedo net for ships to enter and leave the harbor).

On boarding the tender we were shown a watch-list assigning us to take turns, throughout the night, standing guard on the forecastle of the little ship. Armed with a Springfield rifle and a .45 automatic sidearm, we had to watch the harbor entrance for enemy submarines and, presumably, any other kind of ship. With an ice-like wind that felt like it was coming directly from the North Pole blowing snow across the deck, it was so cold one could only take a half-hour of it at a time. During my off-watch periods I never did really get warmed up before it was time to relieve the watch again.

We didn't have any place to sleep except just lying on the deck, so a lot of our time off we sat around and talked. That's when I learned this had been going on for some time; it was just the first time the *Washington's* turn had come to send men for it. I don't know if our ship drew that duty again or not, if so I had the good fortune not to be put on it.

With the benefit of hindsight what we were doing might seem ridiculous, but not if you can remember the times. German submarines were sinking ships all over the Atlantic and up and down our East Coast, so the prevailing wisdom was to take every precaution and not leave anything to chance.

Of course, if we had seen a submarine approach there wouldn't have been anything the guard could do except notify the Officer of the Deck so he could report to the proper authority. The small arms we carried would have been useless, and we weren't expected to use them; the only reason for carrying them was that they were standard equipment for sailors on guard duty anywhere.

When we got back to our ship after that miserable and seemingly endless night, I had never appreciated my warm sleeping compartment so much. I realized then that though I'd been aboard for a fairly short time, I was already starting to think of the *Washington* as my home away from home. For all practical purpose it was home. I ate, slept, worked and stood my watches aboard her; everything except liberty and leave.

For some reason this episode sticks in my mind better than any other one while in the navy, and I wonder if I'm the only one still alive who was on the deep-freeze working party. O'Neal T. Price from Alabama is the only other man I can remember who was on it with me.

NOTES FROM ADMIRAL GOOD SPEECH IN NORFOLK, VA JULY 1967
by Brownie

The day I stood for the last time on *Washington's* bridge, watched the Commission pennant she had flown so proudly be hauled down and the mothball tag go on, was the most nostalgic of my career.

I would like to recall some of the experiences we shared-and risk the charge that when you start thinking in the past, you have had it for the future. Many of you, and first hand at that, know *Washington's* early history better than I do. Commissioned 15 May, 1941, she was in action in the Atlantic within weeks. Transferred to the Pacific, she distinguished herself at the Battle of Savo Island and later in the fast carrier task force and in support of the invasions of Iwo Jima and Okinawa.

To my thinking, it was this period from 1943 to 1945 that the fast battleship really demonstrated its value and versatility. Let us take a look at what these magnificent ships did, not as special missions but as continuing, every day tasks that were a part of war as it had to be fought at that time, and at *Washington's* part in each such task.

First and quite possibly most important was anti-aircraft defense of the carriers in the Third and Fifth Fleet fast carrier task forces. *Washington* could bring up to 13 five inch guns to bear on a single aircraft target or divide 20 guns amongst as many as four targets simultaneously. The rate of fire could be and at times was over 400 rounds a minute. I recall vividly one Japanese "Snooper" plane shot down by *Washington* (the only ship firing) at 0200 on a dark night. The ammunition expenditure was 226 rounds in 42 seconds. With the five inch backed up by the 40 and 20 millimeter automatics the battleships gave the carriers the gun defense they could not provide themselves and still fly aircraft. True, we saw carriers hit with loss of life and severe damage. True, too, we destroyed nearly ten times as many attackers as reached their targets. What makes this accomplishment the more outstanding is that most of our victims were kamikazes, the first "guided missiles" ever used in warfare. And these missiles had human,not computerized, intelligence for final guidance, a feature not yet matched by the most sophisticated electronics.

Next consider shore bombardment and fire support of ground troops. *Washington* did not take part in the shore bombardment of the Japanese home islands; the closest we got to Tokyo was 74 miles. Instead, *Washington* and her sister *North Carolina* were detached and sent to support the Marine assault on Iwo Jima. *Washington* reached her assigned firing station with six minutes to spare after a 36 hour run at more than 1 1/2 knots above her designed speed and in the first 80 minutes of the assault delivered 600 rounds of 16 inch high capacity with pinpoint accuracy. So effective was this fire that the Marines who captured Japanese No. 2 airfield said later; "We went in standing up" after two days of "call fire" we went into close support in relief of two destroyers which had run out of ammunition. This was a job for the five inch battery and for nine straight hours that Marines got everything they asked for. When the destroyers returned and resumed their mission, *Washington* took off to rejoin the fast carriers, 100 miles off shore. We caught up with them about 2 a.m. of a pitch black night, and caught hell for being late! If ship's could shrug, *Washington* would have. She had been in there pitching.

In the third place, *Washington* and the other fast battleships made it possible for the destroy-

SECTION "D"
AT THE REQUEST OF

M. *Wm Deeter*

THE COMMANDANT, U. S. NAVY YARD, PHILADELPHIA
INVITES

M. *Kenneth Dolan*

to be present at the
LAUNCHING CEREMONY
of the
U. S. S. WASHINGTON

This card admits one person to the Navy Yard to Section "D", provided it is presented at the Navy Yard gate prior to 9:30 a.m. Daylight Saving Time on the day of the launching.

NON-TRANSFERABLE   NO CAMERAS ALLOWED

LAUNCHING

BATTLESHIP

U. S. S. WASHINGTON

JUNE 1, 1940

NAVY YARD PHILADELPHIA

REAR ADMIRAL A. E. WATSON, USN., COMMANDANT
CAPTAIN A. J. CHANTRY, JR. (CC) USN., MANAGER

SPONSOR

MISS VIRGINIA MARSHALL

OF
SPOKANE, WASHINGTON

DIRECT DESCENDANT OF
JOHN MARSHALL, CHIEF JUSTICE, U.S. SUPREME COURT 1801-1835

DESCRIPTION OF SHIP

STANDARD DISPLACEMENT - 35,000 TONS
LENGTH - WATER LINE - - - 703 FEET
BEAM - - - - - - - - 108 FEET
MAIN BATTERY - - - - 9 - 16" GUNS

ANNOUNCED BY

PHILADELPHIA NAVY YARD DEVELOPMENT ASS'N.

Portside of the superstructure including the scoreboard. U.S.S. Washington March 1946. (Courtesy of Roland

M Division - 1st Row: Holland, Newton, Dutton, June, Shepherd, Coffee, McCune. 2nd Row: Winters, Krumme Ewing Turner, Branciere, Jones, McNeil, Jukes. 3rd Row: Tait, Horton, Silver, Com. Strother, Lt. Strother, Raines, Pardo. 4th Row: Fialka, Ferrovecchio, Briltz, Walton, Albano, Pettingill, Philips, Little, Froempter. 5th Row: Handy, Szalack, Lappin, Cozzolino, Steorts, Allcorn, Onkst, Shoun, Bert, Toothill. (Courtesy of Michael

ers to stay in the task force screens. The battleships kept them in fuel, ammunition and fueled them when their own supplies were exhausted. Members of *Washington's* crew painted a huge sign reading, "Cougar Service Station, If we got it you can have it" and displayed it from the lower bridge rail whenever destroyers came alongside to replenish. One request was for "140,000 gallons of fuel, 7 tons of provisions, 86 pairs of shoes and 6 saxophone reeds" She got them all. Next time the same destroyer came alongside, her home talent orchestra put on a serenade while two lads, clad solely in new shoes and grass skirts, did a hula on her director platform. The grass skirts did not come from *Washington,* but the encouraging cries of "Take it off" admittedly did.

Washington's band was excused from watch it its pet five inch mount whenever we fueled destroyers or fueled ourselves from tankers in order to provide some music for those who had none. The band hung out its own sign, "You name it, we'll play it," On one occasion while *Washington* was fueling from the tanker *Tomahawk,* the band played "Deep in the Heart of Texas" and nothing else, for more than three hours. That's how we learned that *Tomahawk* was manned by a crew of Texas Reservists from the skipper down. Lt. Cmdr. L.B. Johnson, should have done his naval service in her.

Rounding out the virtues of the fast battleships in war is tremendous endurance and power of survival. *South Dakota* absorbed gun damage at Savo that would have destroyed lesser ships. *North Carolina* carried a Japanese torpedo and 7,000 tons of salt water out of the Battle of Santa Cruz at 25 knots. Both these and many others came out fighting. *Washington* was never seriously hit, a terrific tribute to her fighting ability. In addition, *Washington* holds the endurance record for the entire war; namely, 80 days and four hours without having a boiler off the line or an anchor out of the hawse pipe. During this time she steamed a total of more than 34,000 miles at an average speed of almost 21 knots, and shot at enemy aircraft on 69 of the 80 days. The crew averaged more than 10 hours out of each 24 at battle stations and certainly disproved the old adage that when the Navy changed from sailing ships to steam, they "changed from wooden ships and iron men to iron ships and wooden men" There was plenty steel in *Washington,* it was walking on two feet per billet.

These, then are the reasons the remaining battleships should be reactivated. Short of the employment of nuclear weapons, they can do more, and do it better, and keep it up longer than any other unused asset we have.

I hope you will not regard my recounting these anecdotes of *Washington* and her sailors as being frivolous. Far from it. My intention has been, through them, to pass on to you an image of men in action, to ask you to share with me my own abiding faith in the United States, its Navy and its people.

I cannot believe that men who fought *Washington* so patriotically, so bravely and so successfully, and without losing their sense of humor, could father and grandfather two generations of moronic cowards. There is nothing wrong with our current crop of teenagers that five minutes each in the Ship's Service barber shop won't cure. There is everything right with them when they stop playing games and shoulder the same responsibilities of American citizenship you *Washington* veterans carried so capably a quarter century ago.

So long as *Washington's* spirit survives in them, we will lose no wars and the history of the greatest of free nations will grow ever brighter. *Washington* veterans I salute you. Honored Guests: Thanks for listening. Mr. Chairman: Relieve the Watch.

SMOKE WATCH
by Ray Mason

We were steaming up Savo Strait (Iron Bottom Sound) The Japanese Naval Forces were to bombard Henderson Field at Guadalcanal and land troops. November 14-15 1942. We engaged them in battle at midnight.

I was assigned to Sky Control by Lt. Cmdr. R.J. Simpson for smoke watch. He instructed me to station myself so I could watch the smoke stacks for any excess smoke. *Life* magazine photographer Scherzel was with me and he mounted four cameras on the rail around sky control to photograph the battle action. The main battery of nine 16" guns fired at exactly 12 midnight and the concussion from the guns stripped our clothes off and disintegrated the cameras.

My ears were ringing so bad that when I picked up the ear phones and put them back on, all I could hear was a roaring and occasionally what sounded like a cat screaming when his tail was caught under a rocking chair. I found out later it was Lt. Cmdr. Simpson screaming for me to report to him on main control as to any damage. It took a few days for my hearing to return to normal.

The Japanese battleship *Kirishima* was sunk. The nice thing about our being there that night was the fact that we saved my nephews life. He was on Guadalcanal with the First Marine Division. He wrote my brother that seeing us there that night was the best thing that ever happened to him. He retired after twentyfour years in the Marine Corps, and he passed away in 1983.

Despite all the bad times we had, there was a few amusing incidents, such as the night we were expecting a torpedo attack. We had been issued night rations for the midwatch. Lt. Cmdr. Simpson was at main control in #3 engine room. The rations that night was a gallon can of pork and beans and lunch meat. The Chief on watch had the messenger to put the beans on the throttle and heat them up. He neglected to tell the messenger who was new, that he should punch a hole in the top of the can to let the steam escape.

I was in the engine room on the throttle watch and heard Mr. Simpson screaming that we had been hit with a torpedo. Actually, it was the beans that had blown up, painting the engine room with red and brown from the sauce and beans. I don't know if they ever got all that goo off the overhead and other places in the engine room. All in all the old 56 was a good ship was a bunch of real shipmates.

A GOLDEN ANNIVERSARY TRIBUTE TO THE USS *WASHINGTON* (BB-56)
by Billy Bryant

"PRIDE OF THE NAVY"

It happened in Philadelphia
aboard this Mighty Battleship
Her name
USS *Washington* - BB-56

From the sidewalks of New York
to the Farms of the South
Her crew became good buddies
from then on out

When the Japs attacked Pearl Harbor
They knew what they had to do
It was the beginning
of World War II

You couldn't buy their loyalty
Their friendship or their love
They gave it all freely
to you and God above

2nd. Division on BB56.

Left To Right: Lt. (jg) S.K. Turner, Ens. Wm. Bentinick-Smith, Lt. J.R. Burwell, Lt. W.S. Mackay, Ens, G.R. Greeley, Lt. Crd. H.J. Campbell (Ship's Comm. Officer), Lt. W.E. Wisthoff, Lt. E.J.F. Maslanka, Ems. M.A. Oreck. (Courtesy of Richard Greeley.)

L to R Back Row: Harold Mitchell, George Griffiths, Sgt. Robertson. Front Row: Cpl. Emil A. Zeits and Jake Foster.

-Chorus -
She was the pride of the Navy
Mother of her crew
She'll always be remembered
by those she dearly knew

From the great wide Atlantic
to the blue Pacific shores
She prowled across the ocean
in search of her foes

She was long, wide and full of pride
known quite well by all
She was the combination
to the great Pacific War

When it came to liberty
They were always a little shy
But three beers in Mog Mog
Was like having apple pie

Maybe it was God's will
to put that horseshoe in her keel
She earned all those fifteen stars
Riding on Tojo's heels

-Chorus-

When the War was over
they went on their separate ways
None shall be forgotten
Even after five decades.

OFF GUADALCANAL, 3RD BATTLE OF SAVO ISLAND
by E.W. Bronson, November 15, 1942

'twas a dark night at Guadalcanal
The ship's stood into the bay
Four "tincans" and two big boats,
For the foe in waiting lay.

All in line they came, off Savo's shore.
Ship's black, and deadly with hate.
The lookouts cried, they'd seen the prey
Standing in from the sea to their fate.

"Commence firing," the Admiral said,
the word passed to and fro.
With a roar of doom,
We opened up on the unsuspecting foe.

Not a scratch received, so we turned around
And started to go back through,
This time the foe was set for us,
Two cans were shot through and through.
The others were hit, one fatally, But, they kept on their fire,
The wagons were raising hell, blindly, it seemed they'd never tire
One can got home with the battleboats,
The others lie 'neath the foam,
Still I wouldn't trade all the ship's we sank,
For one of those little homes.

THE MYSTERY OF THE MISSING MAN
by Arthur Widder, Jr.

On the morning of March 27, 1942, a USN task force, Rear Admiral John W. Wilcox, Jr., commanding, zigzagged through the wintry North Atlantic bound for rendezvous at Scapa Flow off the North Coast of Scotland. In steaming position along with the admiral's flagship, the 45,000 tons *Washington,* were another battleship, the aircraft *Wasp,* two cruisers and eight destroyers.

With five of its battleships lying on the bottom at Pearl Harbor and three others damaged, this was the strongest force the Navy would be able to muster for some time.

Only a year before in these same northern waters the British had lost the pride of their fleet, the battle cruiser *Hood,* so the first salve of the German battleship *Bismark.* Though the *Bismark* had been sunk a few days later there were still other German warships, including the *Bismark's* sister ship, the *Tirpitz,* skulking in the Norwegian fiords, a constant threat to convoys bound for England. Danger to the task force lurked anywhere.

On the *Washington's* bridge, Lieutenant (jg) William Fargo, officer of the deck, peered ahead into the snow and freezing spray, alert for air attack, torpedo sighting, or what might be.

Under the great battlewagon's bridge, the barrels of forward 16-inch guns were glazed with rime ice. Waves slammed her bow, coursed her forecastle and streamed through her scuppers.

On the fantail in the lee of the after turret, a lookout shivering in his foul-weather gear swept the gray waves and churning wake with hand-shaded eyes as the forenoon watch were on.

According to the flagship's log, it was 10:31 when the heart-stopping cry suddenly came: "Man overboard!"

Almost immediately, a telephone talker reported that the fantail lookout could see a man in the water. Captain H.H.J. Benson was on the bridge in a moment and the *Washington,* bound by radio silence, signaled the grim message by the whistle and flags.

At once, two destroyers broke from position and closed toward the flagship's wake. The cruiser *Tuscaloosa,* in the murk a thousand yards astern, signaled that a man could be seen in the water "swimming strongly" toward a life ring. A few minutes later the destroyer *Livermore* reported sighting the man. But the moving ship was unable to recover him in the heaving seas. And there was no stopping in wartime.

Despite the foul weather, visibility had closed to 1,500 yards, the *Wasp* launched four scouting planes to search the areas. They could find no one.

Aboard the *Washington,* meanwhile, from skipper to seaman ran the question: who is missing?

The roll of every officer and man of the crew of 2,000 was called. And to the bridge came the astounding report that every single man of the *Washington's* crew was accounted for!

There must be a mistake somewhere. True, nobody had seen him fall, but there could be no question that a man had gone overboard. In all, six men had actually seen him struggling in the water. The *Tuscaloosa* and *Livermore* had seen him.

Captain Benson ordered a new roll call taken. This time he directed officers to sight each man in his charge as his name came up on the roster.

Minutes passed as the flagship bulled on through the sea and weather. The missing man, whoever he was, was long-since lost now. But who was he?

The officers' muster reports reached the bridge and were passed to the captain. Still not a man of the *Washington's* crew was missing.

Although there was obviously some error, the report must be submitted to the admiral. An officer took it to his cabin. The Marine sentry on duty outside opened the door.

Only the steady sighting of the ventilator blowers could be heard. The cabin was empty.

The answer to the puzzle became clear, since only one man was not carried on the ship's muster rolls, the missing man was Admiral Wilcox himself, the only U.S. admiral ever lost overboard at sea.

Exactly how Admiral Wilcox came to plunge to his death remains unknown. He is presumed to have been the victim of some incredibly rare accident.

Originally printed in *Coronet* March, 1957.

AN EXERPT FROM A SHIP'S LOG FIRST PRINTED MARCH 5, 1947
by Robert T. Shaffer, Shipfitter 1/c R Division

The details of the following story are based on an actual happening, and have never before been related. It is a tale of tragedy at sea, and of the heroism displayed by men thrown together in a common lot by the fortunes of war.

The setting is in the "Graveyard of the Atlantic", that frigid gray expanse of the North Atlantic in the land of the midnight sun, a hundred miles south of the polar ice packs. The time, July 1942, six months after our entry in the Second World War. Already this part of the Atlantic had become the final resting place for thousands of Allied seamen and their ship's, the victims of marauding German U-boats, surface ship's and aircraft. Our task force, under the command of Admiral George Giffen, USN consisted of the battleship *Washington*, cruisers *Tuscaloosa*, *Wichita* and the British *Devonshire*. We were escorted by ten destroyers to act as anti-submarine and anti-aircraft patrol.

The duties of the task force consisted of protecting the convoys of relatively unarmed merchant ship's that had to run the gauntlet of German submarines, aircraft, and occasionally, surface ship's. Our position was west of the coast of Norway and was such that our forces would absorb the first impact of any thrusting at the convoy.

The ever present threat to any convoy of the Nazi cruiser *Prinz Eugen* and the mighty battleship *Von Tirpitz,* sister ship of the ill-fated *Bismark,* was foremost in our minds. It was the prime reason for our most powerful battleship, the *Washington,* operating in the area. The Nazi ship's were based at Trondheim, Norway approximately half the distance of the convoy route from Iceland to Murmansk, Russia. The possibility of their making a foray on the convoy was only too evident.

At six o'clock, the morning of May 1, 1942 while on such a convoy run, we received the electrifying news that our fears had been realized. Planes had spotted the Nazi ships with destroyer escort, steaming westward from Trondheim Fiord to the open sea. Immediately condition zebra was set, meaning that all watertight compartments were secured. We expectantly awaited further developments at our battle stations.

Meanwhile, fog had settled to such an extent that visibility was very poor. The ship's had to close in to within a few hundred yards of each other, and needless to say, skillful navigation was a necessity at all times. At three o'clock in the afternoon, we were joined by a large British force. Led by the battleship *King George V*, with the flag of Admiral John Tovey, of the British Home Fleet, at her foremast, the force included the battle cruiser *Renown*, the carrier *Victorious*, the cruisers, *Kent, Glasglow, Tanganyika,* and the *Belfast* and nine of Britains crack tribal class destroyers.

We were reassured by the addition of the new force. The fog had become so thick by now, that fog horns were the only way we had of knowing our positions. At three thirty, our destroyers relayed the startling news that contact had been made. Suddenly, several heavy underwater explosions occurred in the vicinity of our ship, and the vessel shuddered violently from the concussion. We were thrown off our feet and onto the deck by the terrific force. Most of us at our repair stations below deck figured that surely we had been torpedoed. The turning and twisting of the ship, as if trying to escape those missiles of death, gave credence to our thoughts. A few more explosions sounded beneath the ship. Then all was quiet.

At four o'clock, the clear signal was given. We went topside to see what happened. Upon our arrival on deck, we received a pleasant surprise. The fog had cleared, and the sun was shining brightly. It was altogether different from the bleak day we had last seen before going below deck.

Our momentary joy was replaced by sorrow however, at a sight which met our eyes. To our port, lying on her side and slowly sinking was the crack British destroyer *Punjabi*. The ship was broken in half, and her crew was in the water trying to swim clear. Life rings and lines were thrown in the water in an effort to aid the unfortunate men. British and American ship's alike, braved the peril of being torpedoed, by stopping to pick up members of the crew.

Details of the tragedy were related to us by members of our ship's crew stationed topside during general quarters. In the fog, the *King*

Machine shop crew: First Row L to R: Caruso, Sherbert, Leach. Second Row: Steel Cargel, Horvath, Third row: Dmoch, Zubrod, Cybulsky, Clark, Coolman. (Courtesy of Thomas M. Coolman.)

The U.S.S. Washington (BB56) Visual Signal Gang (CS Div.) In Khaki uniform, second row, second from right of 4 Khaki Uniforms: Lt. S.K. Turner (USNR), ship's signals officer, to Lt. Turner's left, in Khaki, Chief Signalman Edward Soles USN. Others unidentified.

The U.S.S. Washington H. Division during the years of 1943-1944.

George V had made a ninety degree turn to starboard, and in doing so, had rammed the *Punjabi* amidships, breaking her in half. Only very skillful maneuvering by Captain Benson, had prevented our ship from colliding with the *Punjabi* in her death throes. The explosions, which we had mistaken for torpedo hits, were the *Punjabi's* depth charges exploding as the stern portion of the ship sank.

The loss of life on the destroyer was very heavy. Most of the men died in the frigid water before they could be rescued. The *King George V* was so badly damaged that she had to make port soon afterwards.

At six o'clock in the evening, we received the welcome news of the damaging of the Nazi cruiser *Prinz Eugen*. She had been struck by torpedoes from planes operating off the carrier *Victorious*, and she and the *Von Tirpitz* were steaming under forced draft back to the cover of Trondheim Fiord.

Our fears were now replaced by confidence. It was an exciting day, with only the tragic sinking of the *Punjabi* to mar the day. All of us slept soundly that night.

Recipe for a Sailor

Take one civilian, slightly green
Stir from bunk at early hour
Soak in shower daily
dress in blue jacket
Mix with others of his kind and
Grate on chief's nerves
Toughen with boot camp
Add liberal portions of beans and soup
Let stand on watch
Bake in 110 degree temperature
Let cool below zero
Season with courage and loyalty
Top with pride. . . and
Garnish with decorations
Serves 300 million people

Scuttlebutt: Why We Call A Ship A "She"

We always call a ship a "she" and not without reason,
For she displays a well-shaped knee regardless of the season,
She scorns the man whose heart is faint, and does not give him pity,
And like a girl she needs the paint, to keep her looking pretty.
For love she'll brace the ocean vast, be she a battleship or cruiser,
But if you fail to tie her fast you're sure to lose her,
Be firm with her and she'll behave, when clouds are dark above you,
And let her take a water wave, prize her, and she'll love you,
For such she'll take the roughest seas, and angry waves that crowd her,
And in a brand new coat of paint, no dame looks any prouder.
The ship is like a dame at that, she's feminine and swanky,
You'll find the one that's broad and fat, is

"Zero" ship's Mascot. (Courtesy of I.A. Quinn.)

never mean and cranky.
On ships and dames we pin our hopes, we fondle them and dandle them,
And every man must know his ropes, or else he cannot handle them.
Yes, ship's are ladylike indeed, for take them all together.
The ones that show a lot of speed, can't stand the roughest weather,
And that's why we call a ship a "she"
ANON.

"What is A Sailor"

Between the innocence of babyhood and the dignity of manhood, we find the delightful creature called a "sailor". Sailors come in an assortment of sizes, shapes, weights, and colors. A very important requirement is that they have at least one arm and two fingers to pick up a coffee cup, beer bottle, or liberty card. All sailors have the same creed. To spend as much time every hour of every day trying to discover new ways of getting out of working parties, standing watches, harassing the chief, looking for out-of-the-way-places in which to nap, where the chance of getting caught is slight and dreaming up good reasons why he should have special liberty on Friday or Monday. They protest to loud noises after taps when they have not been a member of the liberty party, but when they are, they can't understand why everything is so quiet at midnight and they try to do something about it.

Sailors are found everywhere; on and in water, in dark streets and alley-ways, in fast moving cars, bars, night clubs, popping in and out of port holes, and swinging from ropes and ladders. Many times they aren't aware they've been in these places until informed by someone of higher authority.

Girls love them, soldiers and marines hate them, cooks ignore them, the legal officer and St. Christopher protects them.

All sailors are truth with their fingers crossed, wisdom with cigarettes in their socks, beauty and pride in uniform, (which quite often is owned jointly between him and a buddy, from his skivvies on out). He's the hero of the past and promise of the future, with a girl on each arm. A sailor is a composite. He has the energy of a small sized atomic bomb, the speed of a jet when necessary, the curiosity of a cat, the superstition of a gypsy, the lungs of an auctioneer, the imagination of Walt Disney, the appetite of a lumberjack, the digestion of a whale, the slyness of a fox and the shyness of a ———? Well, I guess he's not too shy after all. All sailors likes girls, strong drinks, girls, nightclubs, girls, pictures of girls, movies, girls, mailcall, girls, payday, girls, poker and dice games, and water in its natural sources. He's not much on standing watches, beans for breakfast, shining shoes, hair cuts, shaving, shots, or boatswain mates, who have a never ending supply of paint, brushes, swabs, brooms, and chipping irons. His favorite songs are "Dixie", "Yankee Doodle", "The Eyes of Texas", "Anchors Aweigh", and "Roll Me Over in the Clover". A sailor is a sentimental creature. He is enchanted by sunrise and the playing of taps. He will always salute the flag, but will shift whatever he is carrying to his right hand or duck down a passageway to avoid saluting an officer. He will give his last dollar toward a party for an orphanage, or try to sneak a stray animal aboard a ship and defy anyone to report it. If you are a part time possessor of one of these astounding, magical, creatures, no matter if it's your husband, son, brother, or sweetheart, you will live for the moment you look out of the window and see a figure clad in the familiar attire of the men of the sea come bounding down the sidewalk with his boyish grin spanning his face from ear to ear. You may get him off the ship once in a while, but you know he can't stay along. Then comes the interminable wait for the mail man and the piece of paper which turns your mind to butter when you open it and read "Hi Darling". You can lock him out of your house, but not out of your heart, He's your thoughts, hopes, plans, yes, he's your Sailor.

A Personal Experience While On the USS Washington
by Samuel E. Maione

I was on liberty the weekend of the Pearl Harbor attack and got back to Norfolk too late to catch the last liberty boat. When I arrived on the pier another shipmate was also there waiting for the mail boat to make the ship. Being cold we went to the cafe at the end of the pier for coffee. Later, as we headed back to the landing, we passed a man and woman parked in a car. The passenger door was open obscuring the woman sitting sidewise facing out. When we passed behind the car I looked back and saw that the woman had a camera in lap. She was obviously taking pictures of the ships in the harbor and tied up along the wharves. Since we had just entered a state of war. I knew this was wrong and said to the other sailor that we should confiscate the film. In spite of his repeated objections that "We had no authority" I went up to the car and told them that we would have to take the film. As I reached for the camera she broke open the back and I had to pull the film out in two rolls to try to save some of the pictures. Then, to keep it out of the light I held it in my peacoat pocket. They immediately whipped the car around and high tailed it out of there but we managed to get a part of the license number.

Aboard ship I gave the film to the OD and had to make out a written report on the incident. The next day the Exec's yeoman looked me up and told me that Commander Ayrault was very pleased and might grant the request for the school I had in since I first came aboard and found out that I could not strike for the rate I wanted. I never heard another word about it for which I felt very slighted not to have at least been informed of the results. One good thing did come of it though, I was not placed on report for being overleave.

The Fork in The Road
by David H. Lippman

The 1st Battle of Guadalcanal spelled the difference between victory and defeat for the United States in the Pacific waters of Guadalcanal. At a cost of five ships and thousands of lives, the U.S. Navy had blunted Japan's drive to break the Guadalcanal stalemate.

Three months of bitter air-ground-sea action in the Solomon Islands had resulted in a stalemate. Both the Americans and the Japanese were short of ships. Their troops on Guadalcanal, the island prize of the campaign, were exhausted. Yamamoto was now taking the offensive, and his battleships and destroyers were a powerful force.

Yamamoto acted swiftly, firing Abe and sending south a convoy of 8,000 Japanese troops under Vice Adm. Gunichi Mikawa. And the survivors of Abe's group, headed by the battleship *Kirishima*, regrouped under Vice Adm. Nobutake Kondo, Abe's replacement.

Kondo, however, was little better than Abe. He was described as an "English sort of officer," very gentlemanly, and good with his staff, but better suited for training command than battle.

Nonetheless, Kondo was on hand and senior, so he took over, adding the two tough cruisers of his Cruiser Division Four, flagship *Atago* and *Takao*. One light cruiser, *Nagara,* and six destroyers would escort this group, called the Emergency Bombardment Force. The mission was simple: sweep Ironbottom Sound off Guadalcanal on the night of the 14th, shell the airfield, cover the convoy arrival, then high-tail it home before dawn of the 15th.

The Americans knew the enemy moves, thanks to their cryptographers. But Vice Adm. William F. Halsey, the aggressive commander of the Southwest Pacific Theater, had virtually no ships to hurl at Kondo. All his cruisers and destroyers had been used up in the Friday 13th battle. The carrier *Enterprise* was still only partially repaired after being damaged at the Battle of Santa Cruz, but her 78 planes could screen Guadalcanal by day. The problem would be a night surface action.

All that was left for Halsey's use were two fast, new, battleships, USS *South Dakota* and USS *Washington*. Naval War College doctrine forbade the use of battleships in a tightly confined space such as Ironbottom Sound, just north of Guadalcanal, but Halsey knew that wars were won at sea, not in a textbook. He ordered the dreadnoughts committed.

Commanding the two battlewagons was Rear Adm. Willis A. "Ching Chong" Lee, a chain-smoking, approachable, bespectacled gunnery expert who relieved tension on the bridge by reading lurid novels or swapping sailor stories with the enlisted men standing watch.

Lee was mostly business, though. With *Washington* Captain Glenn Davis and gunnery officer Lt. Cdr. Edwin Hooper, he sat up many nights discussing gunnery problems, taking a mathematical approach. Lee also used more prac-

The Boxing Club.

tical tools. He tested every gunnery-book rule with exercises and ordered gunnery drills under odd conditions—turret firing with relief crews, anything that might simulate the freakishness of battle.

Washington and *South Dakota* technically were outstanding ships: 35,000 ton displacements, able to race at 28 knots, armed with 16-inch guns. But *South Dakota,* despite her fiery Capt. Thomas L. Gatch, had a reputation in the fleet as a jinx ship because of her habit of getting into collisions and suffering mechanical breakdowns at inopportune times. One breakdown had resulted in *South Dakota's* nearly colliding with the carrier *Enterprise.*

Washington, a tightly run ship, had fewer problems and sported the new SG radar. But Hooper, the gunnery officer, had noted when the radar was installed that the antenna had a blind arc of 80 degrees aft. He pointed this out to his shipboard seniors, but no changes were made.

The big ships started moving as early as November 11. Halsey cut orders for *Washington* and *South Dakota* to sail that day, escorting *Enterprise* to Guadalcanal. At 8:30 a.m., *Washington's* bullhorn summoned the special sea and anchor details to their stations, and just as the accommodation ladder was secured, a harbor craft sped up and deposited on *Washington's* deck a panting Ltjg. Bartlett H. Stoodley, freshly assigned to the battlewagon. The executive officer, Cdr. Arthur Ayrault, wasted no time with formalities. Stoodley was immediately given a damage control party to command.

That night, all hell broke loose in Ironbottom Sound. Next morning, Halsey realized he was down to his last trump card, the two battleships, 300 miles south of Guadalcanal. At noon, Halsey told Lee that he was to head a new unit, Task Force 64, and warned him to be ready for a flank-speed run to Guadalcanal. At 7:15 p.m., *Enterprise* blinkered *Washington* the message: "To Commander TF 64: Proceed north with both battleships and your four destroyers at best speed."

Assigned to escort the two dreadnoughts were four tin cans (destroyers), *Walke, Benham, Preston* and *Gwin.* None had ever operated together before. They were chosen because they had the most fuel remaining in their bunkers. All were of different classes and different divisions. Cdr. Thomas Fraser, *Walke's* skipper, now headed a provisional destroyer squadron.

Command difficulties would hamper the big ships, too. Even though *South Dakota* and *Washington* were administratively Battleship Division 6, they had never before operated together. But there was no time to think about those issues just then. Everyone aboard *Washington* was excited. Officers and crew knew they would finally see some action.

Washington revved up to 26 knots, while navigator Lt. Cdr. Ed Schanze set a base course of 0 degrees true, straight north. On the bridge, Lee did some sums, then radioed bad news to Halsey: his ships could not be in position until 8 a.m. on the 14.

After dinner, *Washington's* officers remained in the wardroom and Lee and Davis briefed their men on the upcoming battle. Lee covered everything; gunnery, damage control, navigation, even feeding the men at general quar-

Patrol identification L to R: Bottom Row: third from left; E.S. Schanle. Second Row: Earl M. Lee, eighth from left Harry Nessly. Top Row: Gale Cuff, forth from left Martin. Identified by Harry Nessly. (Courtesy of Iris C. Lee.)

Joe Harding aboard the U.S.S. Washington in 1944.

ters. Davis fretted over navigating in Ironbottom Sound, but navigator Schanze was calm.

Meanwhile, Rear Adm. Raizo Tanaka's 23-ship convoy headed south. Early on the 14th, they were attacked by planes from *Enterprise.* No hits.

Tanaka blandly noted that "prospects looked poor for the operation," but he plodded on toward Guadalcanal. His destroyers were so cluttered with troops that he could not fight a battle. His only chance of landing the remainder of the convoy depended on Kondo's ability to clear Ironbottom Sound.

Kondo was steaming south to meet the light cruiser *Sendai.* On *Atago,* Kondo would directly lead a bombardment unit with *Atago, Takao* and *Kirishima,* his heaviest ships. A screening unit of the light cruiser *Nagara* and six destroyers under Rear Adm. Satsuma Kimura would protect the big ships. A sweeping unit of *Sendai* and three destroyers would comb the Savo waters for enemy ships. Kondo's plan was simple, blast through Guadalcanal and pummel the airfield. As soon as Ironbottom Sound was secure, Tanaka would land his transports. Meanwhile, Japanese reconnaissance planes picked up Lee's task force steaming toward Guadalcanal and mistakenly identified the battleships as cruisers.

Lee's sailors were having a busy day. *Washington* went to general quarters at 5:40 a.m., and her guns were ready in six minutes. Lt. Ray Hunter was officer of the deck, but he was to turn that duty over to navigator Schanze. At the last minute Davis intervened. He wanted the more-experienced Hunter to stay on the bridge, and Schanze to man the navigating table.

The task force stayed at general quarters all day, closing in on Guadalcanal. Radioman Chet Cox listened in on the continuing air-sea battle. Lee decided to wait, patiently staying 100 miles south of Guadalcanal. He noted his ships had only operated together for 34 hours of a high-speed run. Accordingly, he deployed a six-ship column: *Walke, Benham, Preston, Gwin, Washington* and *South Dakota,* with the battlewagons 5,000 yards behind the tin cans.

Both sides were bringing their favored weapons into this battle. The American edge was in their new battleships, equipped with the latest SG radar, 16-inch guns, thick armor, and an admiral who understand the use of radar and big guns.

The biggest guns the Japanese had were 14-inchers on *Kirishima,* a battleship that, while fast (28 knots), was also old (build in 1914). But Kondo was attacking by night with well-trained crews, lookouts whose eyesight outranged American radar, and 90 Long Lance torpedoes, the finest in the world.

At dusk Lee ordered his ships to approach Guadalcanal. *Washington's* Davis told his crew: "We are going into an action area. We have no great certainty what forces we will encounter. We might be ambushed. A disaster of some sort may come upon us. But whatever it is we are going into, I hope to bring all of you back alive. Good luck to all of us."

The grim words settled down on *Washington's* 1,500-man crew. In the secondary battery fire control, Ens. Hal Berc later said: "We had gone through a million drills, but who knew what a naval action was really about? When the captain finished his speech, there was a general sense of exhiliration. No one despaired."

At 7:20, Lee ordered Task Force 64 to head northeast, to run past the western end of Guadalcanal. Up in *Washington's* foretop Lt. Cdr. Harry Seely, main battery spotting officer, peered through massive lenses into the gathering dusk. At 7:45, lookouts saw gunfire flashes to port. Seely looked on and saw Tanaka's transports and escorts in the distance, fighting off the last air attacks of the day.

Lee steamed northeast, passed Savo Island on the starboard side and turned east. From there on, Halsey's orders stopped and Lee's initiative took over. The night was beautiful, moonlit, warm, and the sea was dead calm. Lt. Stoodley said the ship seemed to "slide through the sea as though in heavy oil."

As Lee's ships sped through the night, his radio operators heard American radio traffic. PT boats were reporting Lee's moves in plain English, blaring, "There goes two big ones, but, I don't know who they are" The PT boats swung in to attack Lee's ships.

Lee personally got on the TBS voice radio and called Guadalcanal, asking that the PT boats be ordered to pull out. Guadalcanal, however, didn't believe Lee was who he claimed to be.

Lee bellowed his Annapolis nickname: "This is Ching Chong China Lee! Chinese, catchee? Refer your boss about Ching Lee. Call off your boys!" Lee's temper did the job. Guadalcanal answered, "Identity established. We are not after you."

At the precise moment that Lee turned east, Kondo's ships swept in behind Task Force 64 and broke into three units. Kimura swung off in his flagship *Nagara,* while Hashimoto in *Sendai* did the same. Just as the convoy split, lookouts on the destroyer *Shikanami* spotted enemy ships bearing 200 degrees just west of south. *Uranami* lookouts had them in sight, too, and identified them as "new-type" cruisers." Hashimoto took his ships clockwise around Savo, with one destroyer, *Ayanami,* heading counterclockwise to sweep for enemy vessels.

At 10:31, *Atago,* Kondo's flagship, picked up the enemy. By 11 p.m., Kondo had a flurry of reports. At 11:07, *Sendai* flashed that the Americans were heading due west, south of Savo.

Kondo, sure that the enemy comprised four destroyers and two cruisers, ordered his light forces to attack first so that his battleship could shell Guadalcanal. Kondo was afraid that *Kirishima* would, as *Hiei* had, fall victim to enemy light forces. More important, his battleship was loaded with Type 3 14-inch anti-aircraft shells, excellent for shelling airfields, but useless for hitting armored warships. Kondo swung his ships around in a countermarch just north of Savo, back to the west.

So three Japanese daggers moved south. Kimura's group, headed by *Nagara,* to the west of Savo, *Ayanami* on her own west of Savo, and Hashimoto's group, headed by *Sendai,* east of Savo. They knew the Americans were there. They did not know the Americans had battleships.

The battleship crews were not napping. *Washington* gun boss Walsh sat ready in the upper conning tower and ordered his gunners to load their 16-inch weapons. The book said it could be done in 30 seconds. *Washington's* gun crew did it in 14.

At 11 p.m., *Washington's* radar located a

4th Division Gunner's. (Courtesy of Walter R. Krause.)

Front Row L to R: Hughs, unidentified, Kegaris, Ramey. Middle Row: Maxwell, Garcia, unidentified, Walsh, unidentified. : Back Row: Davis, Gordon, Woolsey, Quackenbush, Drewitz, Muehlenthaler. (Courtesy of Wilbur Drewitz.)

Officers of the Marine Detachment L to R: Capt Bob Knox, Capt. Joe Platt, 1stG Ted Abbey. 5 May 1943 aboard the USS Washington BB56 at sea.

Walter A. Palac in Hawaii 1942.

target bearing 340 true, broad on the starboard bow, 18,000 yards away. Lt. Hank Seely, in his spotting tower, eyed *Sendai* with his main director. On *Washington's* bridge, Ching Lee took a long drag on a Philip Morris and said to Davis, "Well, stand by, Glenn, here they come!"

At 11:17 *Washington's* bridge ordered, "Open fire when ready." The ship's electric bells rang twice, and blinding tongues of flame shot out of the main guns. Seconds later, the secondary 5-inchers opened up on the destroyer *Shikinami*.

Next, *South Dakota* fired on the same target. Her radiomen heard Japanese voices chattering on 13 stations. *South Dakota's* action report claimed that *Shikinami* sank instantly. That was not the case, however. Hashimoto's ships were unhurt. *Sendai* was straddled, so Hashimoto's made smoke and wheeled north, regrouping for a more favorable moment to attack.

"It looks like he's turned around and beat it." Davis said to Lee on *Washington's* bridge as they watched Hashimoto withdraw. Then Lee's destroyers raced in to attack.

Seely watched the tin cans clash. It looked to him like the entire east coast of Savo erupted with white blobs of light. Actually, the Japanese destroyers *Ayanami* and *Uranami* were firing, and behind them were a cruiser and five destroyers, headed straight for Lee's four tin cans.

The American destroyers lacked SG radar, night training and cohesion. *Walke* located *Ayanami*; *Benham* followed while *Preston* spotted *Nagara*. Soon all four ships were firing at *Nagara*.

Kimura's 5.5-inch guns, armed with flashless powder, hit back. He also fired torpedoes, but the range was too close. All missed.

Some Japanese shells did find their mark. *Preston* was heavily hit in the two firerooms, killing everyone there. The second stack toppled over into the searchlight platform, collapsing it onto the starboard torpedo tubes and igniting their contents. The area was soon a mass of blazing wreckage. The executive officer was killed, the forward guns jammed in train, and *Preston* began to settle into the sea.

Cdr. Max C. Stormes, *Preston's* skipper, ordered abandon ship at 11:36. A minute later, the ship rolled over on her starboard side, then hung with her bow in the air for 10 minutes before sinking. Gone were 117 men (45 percent of the crew) and her captain.

On *Washington*, Seaman Naaman Berman, standing next to Lee, was stunned at the speed with which *Preston* went down. Sailors on *Gwin* watched, too, but had little time to grieve, as their ship was hit at 11:32 in the aft engine room. Superheated steam drove out the crews. The concussion unlatched torpedo restraining links, and *Gwin's* fish slid harmlessly into the sea. Another shell hit her stern, splitting open two depth charges.

Shells hit *Walke* as her skipper, Cdr. Thomas E. Fraser, was swinging to launch torpedoes. At 11:38 she was hit by a Long Lance that exploded her No. 2 magazine and blew off the ship's bow. Power and communications failed, and the ship blazed fiercely. Fraser ordered abandon ship. Four rafts got away safely, but as *Walke* sank, her depth charges exploded, killing 80—including Fraser.

Berman, aboard *Washington*, saw *Walke* get hit. "I didn't realize what it was—just Boom, goodbye," he said later.

Another Long Lance blasted *Benham's* bow, ripping off a piece of it. The ship looped to escape gunfire, then staggered back in to action at 10 knots.

All four of Lee's destroyers were now out of the fight. He was down to his battleships. Lee swung in to attack, his ships racing by blazing hulks and shipwrecked crewmen floating in oily water.

Still, the destroyers' sacrifice had value. *Washington* found *Ayanami* and shelled her. More important, Fraser's tin cans took torpedoes Kimura had aimed at Lee's battleships. "It was beyond admiration," Lee wrote in his after-action report, "and it probably saved our bacon."

Washington and *South Dakota* raced along at 26 knots. In Repair 4-1 Shipfitter John Brown felt the concussions of *Walke's* depth charges going off.

On *South Dakota*, crews were patching minor holes from five-inch hits by *Ayanami* when at 11:33 the chief engineer tied down her circuit breakers, violating safety procedures. The system instantly went into series, and the big ship lost electrical power. Radar, fire control, turret motors, ammunition hoists, radios—everything went out, with her guns locked in train. Capt. Gatch wrote later: "The psychological effect on the officers and crew was most depressing. The absence of this gear gave all hands a feeling of being blindfolded." It was worse than that. *South Dakota* was facing 14 ships scattered across a 12-mile box on a dark night, amid spurious reports of enemy batteries on Savo and motor torpedo boats.

Washington was now the only intact ship left in the force. In fact, at that moment *Washington* was the entire U.S. Pacific Fleet. She was the only barrier between Kondo's ships and Guadalcanal. If this one ship did not stop 14 Japanese ships right then and there, America might lose the war.

On *Washington's* bridge, Lt. Ray Hunter still had the conn. He had just heard that *South Dakota* had gone off the air and had seen *Walke* and *Preston* "blow sky high." Dead ahead lay their burning wreckage, while hundreds of men were swimming in the water and Japanese ships were racing in.

Hunter had to do something. The course he took now could decide the war. "Come left," he said, and *Washington* straightened out on a course parallel to the one on which she was

45

steaming. *Washington's* rudder change put the burning destroyers between her and the enemy, preventing her from being silhouetted by their fires.

The move made the Japanese momentarily cease fire. Lacking radar, they could not spot *Washington* behind the fires. Kondo had to figure out his next move.

Meanwhile, *Washington* raced through burning seas. Everyone could see dozens of men in the water clinging to floating wreckage. Flag Lieutenant Raymond Thompson said, "Seeing that burning, sinking ship as it passed so close aboard, and realizing that there was nothing I, or anyone, could do about it, was a devastating experience."

Cdr. Ayrault, *Washington's* executive officer, clambered down ladders, ran to Bart Stoodley's damage-control post, and ordered Stoodley to cut loose life rafts. That saved a lot of lives. But the men in the water had some fight left in them. One was heard to scream, "Get after them, *Washington*!"

Everyone wondered why *South Dakota*, whose electrical problems had her virtually paralyzed, was plodding along silently behind. She did not follow *Washington* when the flagship turned left, but sailed in front of the flaming destroyers, presenting a perfect silhouette. The Japanese reacted quickly, illuminating *South Dakota* with searchlights. *Nagara* and four tin cans raced in for a torpedo attack. They fired at 4,000 yards, but miraculously none hit.

At 11:36, a three-minute eternity, *South Dakota* restored partial power and opened fire on *Nagara*. The first salvo set three planes on the Japanese cruiser's quarterdeck on fire. The next salvo snuffed out the blaze and sent the planes into the sea.

Washington opened up on the enemy searchlights. But there were dozens of blips on the radar screen, most of them Savo Island, making tracking difficult.

At 11:42, *South Dakota*, still having problems, fired a salvo from her No. 3 turret that set fire to one of her Kingfisher seaplanes. Once again the battleship was illuminated. Damage control crews, including a 12-year-old sailor named Calvin Graham, he had falsified his age to join the Navy, quelled the blaze.

Meanwhile, Kondo's battleship and two cruisers were still marking time north of Savo. Kondo, fearing a repetition of the Friday 13th chaos, held his ships back. His convoy was coming behind them. All Japan needed to win the war was one good shove.

Lee, meanwhile, made his moves. He put *Washington* on course 282 at 11:35, then detached the battered *Gwin* and *Benham* to retire; the wounded destroyers were a hindrance.

Now Kondo moved. *Takao* sighted *Washington,* and *Atago's* lookout said the enemy vessel "looked like a battleship." Kondo disagreed, but now he figured it was time to shell the airfield. At 11:54 he set course 130, right for Guadalcanal and *Washington*.

Washington's SG radar had picked up Kondo's force and was tracking it as it came in. *South Dakota* was not doing so well. Her radar had gone out again. When it came back on, it picked up Kondo forward of her starboard beam just three miles away. Kondo saw *South Dakota,* too, at 11:58, but even now he still did not believe it was a battleship.

At 11:40, *Washington* located Kondo's two lead destroyers, two cruisers and *Kirishima*. The firing solution was sent to the guns, but just as the firing circuits were to be closed, Walsh yelled, "Check fire!"

Walsh was afraid radar had picked out *South Dakota* instead of *Kirishima*. The problem was

First Class G.M. was a fellow by the name of Doke from Geo I believe.

the location of the SG radar. The 80-degree blind arc left a gap precisely where *South Dakota* was. *Washington's* gunners had to wait.

Down in repair 4-1, Johnny Brown broke out a jug that tonight held illegal raisin jack. Everyone had a swig.

Lee's ships were now 11 miles west of Savo. Kondo launched torpedoes at *South Dakota*, but none hit. At precisely midnight, the beginning of November 15, *Atago's* main searchlight picked out *South Dakota*. Kondo and his staff trained binoculars and studied the battleship's distinctive pyramid foremast.

Kondo finally believed he was facing America's newest battleship. All Japanese ships aimed at *South Dakota*, and soon a variety of shells of many calibers were flying at her. So were a large number of torpedoes, but once again, the Americans were lucky and the torpedoes all missed. *South Dakota's* Type B armor plate defeated a 14-inch shell, but 26 hits landed on her superstructure. Many rounds failed to explode. Other incoming shells were Type 3 ammunition, which could not penetrate *South Dakota's* armor. But damage was done, nonetheless. The shells cut up *South Dakota's* radar and communications cables, shattering radar plot and disabling gun directors. Four of six fire-control radars were destroyed.

Dakota was in little danger of sinking, but she was virtually useless. Worse, her captain had lost touch with *Washington*. Lee wrote later that the effect of the shelling was to "render one of our new battleships deaf, dumb, blind and impotent."

Washington watched all this as the quarter moon vanished, leaving behind darkness. *Washington* was still tracking the questionable target. It could not be *South Dakota*, could it? Then the target lit her searchlights, illuminating *South Dakota* and revealing herself as *Kirishima*. The Japanese ship was 8,400 yards away on the starboard beam. "Body-punching range," Seely called it.

In seconds, *Washington's* main battery plot had a solution from the SG radar, which was functioning perfectly. At precisely midnight, *Washington* fired a nine-gun salvo that straddled *Kirishima*. A minute later *Washington's* third salvo landed fair and square amidships, causing massive explosions.

Kirishima and *Washington* exchanged fire. Hooper fed the fire-control data into his range finders, and shells were hurled at the Japanese dreadnought. "Fire control and battery functioned as smoothly as though she were engaged in a well-rehearsed target practice," Lee wrote later.

Kirishima was covered with shells. Seely watched as three of the four main 14-inch turrets were knocked out and a "dull red glow amidships began to brighten considerably." At 12:07 a.m., *Washington* fired the last of 75 16-inch rounds. The shells disabled two of *Kirishima's* main turrets, started fires, jammed the rudder, and drilled waterline holes. *Kirishima* started flooding and began circling to port, coughing out gusts of smoke.

Lee was still worried about the location of *South Dakota*. That unhappy ship was still in *Washington's* blind arc. Lee planned to head north and attack the transports.

The destruction of *Kirishima* caught Kondo by surprise. He had been convinced that *South Dakota* was being sunk and was alone. Shelling Henderson Field was impossible. *Atago* and *Takao* were damaged. Kondo ordered three destroyers to remove *Kirishima's* crew. The rest of Kondo's ship's raced off to pursue *Washington*.

South Dakota now had a moment to breathe. Her executive officer, Cdr. A.E. Uehlinger, was surrounded by fires in Battle II, the alternate conning tower. For a time it seemed they were trapped, but determined shipmates doused the fires and closed open steam lines. With 39 dead and 59 wounded, Capt. Gatch realized this ship was in no shape for battle. He withdrew at 1 a.m., "to the great relief of the Task Force commander," wrote Lee.

Davis was less charitable in his report of the action: "Retired? Hell (*South Dakota*) just left the action. We didn't know anything about it, and we didn't see or hear from her until morning."

Meanwhile, Kondo raced after *Washington*. At 12:11 a.m., he spotted the American ship, and at 12:13 he fired eight torpedoes at 4,000 yards, all of which missed, and then swung 300 degrees to face *Washington* broadside. Lee was now fighting six ships single-handed. His only advantage was *Washington* herself, fast powerful, undamaged, well-protected and well crewed. Lee swung on course 340 at 12:20 to continue the battle.

Shells were now flying at *Washington*. LTJG Bob Macklin watched "six white-hot shells as they left the enemy turrets. They seemed to float slowly toward us, picking up speed as they came, becoming bright red as they drew closer. Remarkably, we didn't quail at the prospect of being hit, but rather the shots were subjected to professional criticism."

Seely watched "between the blinding flashes of our secondary guns, splashes close aboard, which from their size could only have been made by large-caliber projectiles. By their second salvo I could see it was the usual Jap pattern: over=short=on; I awaited the arrival of their third salvo with considerable interest."

But Kondo was running out of power and time. He ordered Kimura and Hashimoto to attack, but Hashimoto was far astern of the westward-moving battle, and Kimura was racing to catch up. The only ships left were Tanaka's destroyers *Oyashio* and *Kagero*, racing down from the north. Kondo swung his own ships on *Washington* at 24 knots but saw the American coming back, right for him and Tanaka's transports. Cautious and timid, worn down from the loss of his battleship, Kondo then pulled back to cover the transports and made smoke.

On *Washington*, Lee watched the gray smoke mass arise ahead. He figured nothing could be gained from attacking the transports now. In any case, he had delayed the Japanese so long that the transports would have to arrive by daylight, when American air power could savage them. He had one ship left. Best not to push his incredible luck any further. He ordered *Washington* to withdraw.

The ship turned 180 degrees to starboard at 26 knots and raced toward more Japanese destroyers, *Kagero* and *Oyashio* to starboard and Kimura's ships to port. The Japanese had poor firing positions, but they launched torpedos anyway. One exploded, sending up a 200-foot-high water mushroom just behind *Washington*.

To the north, Kondo decided he had had enough. He ordered a general disengagement to the north.

Kirishima, however, was still afloat. Like *Hiei* the previous day, her boilers and engines still worked, but seawater had sloshed into her steering machinery compartments. The rudder was jammed at 10 degrees starboard.

Capt. Sani Iwabuchi fought to save *Kirishima*, but the flooding defied control. Fire ripped through the magazines. Iwabuchi flooded them, but that only worsened things. Orders to evacuate the engine room came too late, and the firemen were stranded there. *Nagara* tried to tow the big ship home.

It was a familiar situation for the cruiser. The last time *Nagara* had been required to tow an ailing flagship had been at Midway, when she tried to tow the damaged carrier *Akagi*, which sank anyway. Now *Kirishima* limped behind *Nagara*, but the dreadnaught kept listing to starboard. Iwabuchi summoned the crew to the bow for what was now becoming a familiar ritual in the Imperial Japanese Navy, transferring the emperor's portrait, in this case to destroyer *Asagumo*. At 3:35 a.m., *Kirishima* sank several miles northwest of Savo Island, the second battleship Japan had lost in two days and the first enemy ship sunk by an American battleship since the Spanish-American War. *Kirishima's* final explosions were watched with great interest by a horde of shipwrecked *Preston* and *Walke* sailors, still awaiting rescue.

Another Japanese victim was dying nearby, the destroyer *Ayanami*. Forty of the destroyer's crew had been killed, and most of *Ayanami's* remaining crew boarded *Uranami*, but 30 of them, including *Ayanami's* captain, took a boat to Guadalcanal. *Ayanami* sank sometime after 2 a.m. after two explosions.

Another destroyer was ailing too, the American *Benham*, which was staggering home. *Benham's* hull was badly fractured. Her crew lightened the ship forward and tried to repair the damage. At 3 a.m., her skipper, Lt. Cdr. John B. Taylor, evacuated the ship's forward half to reduce strain on the keel. Taylor radioed his situation to Lee.

Lee ordered *Benham* and her escort, *Gwin*, to Espirito Santo, but gave Taylor permission to act as to abandoning *Benham*. All morning Taylor nursed his ship toward home, but by mid-afternoon, it was too much. *Gwin* evacuated *Benham* and tried to sink her, an attempt that only served to demonstrate the weakness of the American Mark XZ torpedo. One exploded prematurely, the second missed ahead, the third ran erratically. *Gwin* shelled *Benham* until a 5-inch round hit *Benham's* magazines at 7:35 p.m. and sank her.

Washington was heading home, too. At 4 a.m., a weary Ray Hunter was relieved of the deck after 24 hours straight as officer of the deck, but the ship was still at general quarters, so he stayed on the bridge. At 6:49 a.m. when the ship secured from general quarters, Hunter staggered down to his bunk.

Crewman came out on deck and found expended 5-inch shell casings lying all over the decks. Hal Berc rubbed his eyes in the morning

47

First Division, deck crew.

sunlight, caught the sight of dawn rays glancing off Old Glory, fluttering from the mainmast, and felt proud. The only hit the ship had taken was a 5-inch shellhole in the air search radar.

At 9:51, Lee's lookouts spotted *South Dakota* coming up, leaking oil and signaling "We are not effective." She took station ahead of *Washington,* and her leaking oil entered *Washington's* evaporators, polluting *Washington's* water lines for months. That evening, three destroyers arrived to shepherd the big ships home.

The battle was still not over. Kondo ordered Tanaka to get his transports to their anchorage and beach them. Tanaka complied, but Mikawa objected, saying beaching would not make landing troops more difficult. During the pre-dawn hours of November 15, discussions between the admirals filled Japanese airwaves. In the end, Yamamoto himself endorsed the beaching plan. At 4 a.m. four transports ran aground. At 4:30 a.m., Tanaka took his destroyers home. Most were jammed with soldiers from the earlier battles.

The maneuvers were watched by shipwrecked *Walke* and *Preston* US sailors, still awaiting rescue. At 5:55 a.m., they watched as seven dive bombers attacked the beach transports. Ten minutes later, planes from *Enterprise* came in, blasting transports and unloaded gear.

Finally the US destroyer *Meade* turned up and raked the freighters for 42 minutes, starting fires on all four. After that, *Meade* pulled 266 *Walke* and *Preston* survivors out of the drink.

Meade missed two survivors from *Walke,* Seaman Dale E. Land and Machinist's Mate Harold Taylor. After two days and nights in the water they reached Guadalcanal, but behind Japanese lines. They trekked eastward, stealing food from Japanese bivouacs. After finding a Japanese rifle and ammunition bandolier, they took up a sideline of sniping, killing a number of Japanese. Taylor lost his life in the struggle to survive, but Land, who staggered to within shouting distance of US lines was picked up, delirious, with a temperature of 106 degrees did survive from his ordeal.

Radio commentators on both sides were delirious, too, as they claimed victory. Japan's claims were immense: eight cruisers, five destroyers, and two battleships damaged. This alleged triumph cost Japan one battleship, one destroyer and three damaged cruisers, with damage to seven transports.

Japan's Domei News Agency crowed: "The American naval debacle in the Solomon area signified land hostilities on Guadalcanal have passed the decisive stage, having sent to the sea bottom, 10,000 officers and men, more than half it's battleships, almost all aircraft carriers, more than half its cruisers. The United States can no longer hope to carry out a large-scale counteroffensive against Japan." This report was posted on *Washington* bulletin boards and resulted in laughter.

The United States reported sinking one battleship, five cruisers and five destroyers in exchange for two light cruisers and six destroyers. After the battle, when Lee and Gatch discussed the after-action report, Gatch asked Lee to confirm some outrageous battle claims by *South Dakota.* Lee was astounded at the request and refused.

But *South Dakota* got most of the credit for the outcome of the battle. The ship went to New York for repairs, and Gatch described his ship's role to *The Saturday Evening Post,* which published the story of *"Battleship X",* a code name given because the Navy did not want *South Dakota's* name in print, a book about the incident followed, infuriating *Washington* sailors.

While all the claims made at the time were highly inflated, 242 Americans and 249 Japanese did perish in the Third Naval Base of Savo Island. The United States lost three replaceable destroyers, while Japan lost an irreplaceable battleship and a destroyer.

Also lost was Kondo's career. He claimed two battleship sinkings, but not everyone swallowed Kondo's gun-decked report. Yamamoto and his staff looked at the mounting toll of ships and men and recommended the unthinkable to the emperor, withdrawal from Guadalcanal. Kondo was fired.

The Japanese post-mortem also outlined other problems during the battle. One was all the torpedo misses, which were the result of poor firing angles. The failure to sink *South Dakota* was caused by Kondo's ships being armed with contact-fused Type 3 shells instead of armor-piercing shot. Then, too, Kondo had divided his forces (a mistake since the time of Xerxes) and refused to believe his own lookouts when they identified the American battleships. A more aggressive Japanese leader might have won that night.

There was second-guessing on the American side, too. After the battle, Lee's planning and execution kept Task Force 64 together. The battle never disintegrated into a brawl like the one the previous night.

The American weaknesses were many, however: the heterogeneous nature of the destroyer force; poor American torpedos; appalling work on *South Dakota* that made America's lastest battleship a menace only to herself; and the gap in *Washington's* radar coverage. Lee wrote: "We realized then that it should not be forgotten now, that our superiority was due almost entirely to our possession of radar. Certainly we have no edge on the Japs in experience, skill, training or performance of personnel."

He did not list some other things that went right, like his own effective handling of the crisis and appreciation of radar, and *Washington's* superb crew.

Still, *Washington* and *South Dakota* sailors fought pitched battles in bars over credit for the night's honors. Actually, the question of who deserved the credit was immaterial. There were plenty of heroes.

One thing was clear after the battle. The Japanese had sent a convoy loaded with an entire infantry division of 12,000 men and equipment to Guadalcanal, enough to turn the tide of battle. Only 2,000 soldiers, 260 cases of ammunition and 1,500 bags of rice (a four day supply) got ashore, after much punishment. The Americans shattered the convoy, sank two battleships, and put ashore 5,500 men and tons of supplies. The Americans had gained the edge on Guadalcanal, would clear the island, start climbing up the Solomons ladder and win the war.

Heavy thoughts of this nature did not strike *Washington's* crew on November 16. Captain Davis delcared "holiday routine" that day; no drills, and when work was done, the crew trooped down to enjoy ice cream sodas and watch Errol Flynn an Ronald Reagan in Santa Fe Trail.

At noon on November 17, general quarters sounded for entering Noumea and *Washington* moored at 2:20 p.m. in nine fathoms of water at the end of 360 feet of anchor chain. The officer of the deck laconically noted in his log the tanker *E.J. Henry* came alongside at 5:59 p.m. to provide fuel.

A few hundred miles away, a Japanese staff officer was also penning a report, an appreciation of the Pacific war situation just before the two battles of Guadalcanal, which read, "It must be said that the success or failure in recapturing Guadalcanal Island, and the vital naval battle related to it, is the fork in the road which lead to victory for them or us."

The fork in the road had been reached. After *Washington* headed south from Ironbottom Sound on the morning of November 15, it was clear which way the war would go.

David Lippman is on active duty with the USN. Further reading: *Pacific Turning Point: The Solomons Campaign 1942-1943,* and *The Lost Ships at Guadalcanal* by Robert D. Ballard, and *Guadalcanal* by Richard Frank.

Brandt and Chasin Story 1997

This is an interpretation of a story told jointly by two former USS *Washington* shipmates tht never met each other till I introduced them at the 16th reunion in 1983 at San Mateo, CA. Brandt said a sack of potatoes were in the bargain agreement and Chasin said it was a basket of fruit. Ray Brandt told me the story in the hotel restaurant and Nathan Chasin was in the lobby and I began to tell Chasin what Brandt related to me, Chasin was shaking his head as I talked and I asked, "was it you he was talking about" and he said, "yes." This is the uncut version from Chasin's letter to me, both are now deceased, so please take this word as is. John A. Brown, SF2/c R Division.

Sorry in hearing in the passing of Ray Brandt, who originated the story of trading potatoes for a bandmaster. Since we are on the potato story, I want to correct it a bit. It wasn't a trade since Captain Wyatt of the USS *Aldabaran* always brings baskets of fresh fruit to COM SER PAC officers when the ship gets into New Caledonia where the flagship *"Bull" Halsey* was located, also COM SER PAC was also there, so let me start at the beginning of the story.

I was first class when I put the *Washington* in commission and after being aboard a few months, Cdr. Dell told me that Damage Control needed me. As you know the war started and I stood watches with Lt. Cdr. Wilkinson in the main damage control station, situated in the double bottom of the ship. When we went to Scapa Flow and operated with the British Fleet, I was sent to their fire fighting school and it was very interesting, how the British fought the shipboard fires. As you know we came back to New York and loaded up with new anti-aircraft guns and lots of 16 inch shells and left for the South Pacific. I continued in damage control, working with Lt. Cdr. Wilkinson and Chief Warrant Officer Dyer. In November 1942 the Bandmaster rate opened up and I didn't qualify, because, I was supposed to hold first class for two years to qualify So, I told my tale of woe to Cdr. Dell who took me to the Executive Officer Ayrault, who had to get the Captain Benson to approve wiring BuPers to waive the two year requirement and let me take the exam. To make this short, I made Chief and was the junior chief. Edwards, Egan and others had 16 to 18 years of service, I had 14 years service after the third battle of Savo Island, the many Chief Bandmasters was sent back to the States.

A Unit called MOB4 wanted a bandmaster so, being the junior bandmaster I was sent to MOB4, the other guys didn't want it, because no one knew where it was. It turned out to be a mobile operating in Aukland, New Zealand. It was good duty on the base, this was a hospital unit with drafted doctors who were specialists in their field. The Co. A, Capt. Robbins bought up all the instruments in town, wanted a bandmaster to form a band, many pharmacists had musical training in high school, so, I got the Co. A band, we would go down to the docks and play while the wounded marines were taken to our hospital. We also played concerts on the base. The duty was super, I had my own room, had a pharmacists mate 2nd class clean up the room for one bottle of liquor I received from the mess, it only cost me $1.60 for one bottle and I was allowed two bottles a month.

My trouble started when the CO put me in charge of the stations laundry. I had about 25 New Zealand women working in the laundry. The laundry operated 24 hours a day. The CO said the laundry was losing money. We had to pay the women in N.Z. money which was about $16.00 a week and after having the job a few weeks, I found out why the place was losing money, it seems the midnight shift was not doing their work, they had parties with the sailors and as you well know a hospital needs a lot of sheets, so, I used my head and thought this out, it was easy, I offered one of the women, who was big and brawny a (10) shilling bonus weekly and take charge, that's $1.60 more in American money and she sure got the work out, after six weeks with the new setup and we had a large profit. I went to the CO and requested $100.00 a month for being manager of the laundry. I was fired on the spot. Navy regulations at the time was, enlisted men working for ship service, which included the laundry, were to be paid. The CO appointed a commissioned officer to take charge, he did not have to pay him.

After the fracas, the CO wired COM SER PAC to have me transferred back to the *Washington*. I left New Zealand and after arriving in New Caledonia, I found a new set of orders, sending me to the USS *Aldabaran*. The CO of the ship goes ashore to COM SER PAC for orders. He goes between San Francisco and the Islands, carrying goodies such as hundreds of cases of beer, loads of fresh eggs, as you know powdered eggs are not that good. The CO also brings to the top brass, many goodies such as nylon hose, which at that time was very hard to get. Our ship was a converted refrigerated cargo ship taken over by the Matson Lines. "So" this particular

Laundry Crew.

Band #121.

day the CO was taken over to COM SER PAC, a basket of fruit and wanted a bandmaster to form a band on the USS *Aldabaran*. I was available. The best part of this was the ship was leaving for San Francisco, and I was on board. When I got on board, I was given a large stateroom with one bunk. I was assigned to the Captain's office, no division officer gave me orders, only the Captain. I made all the division officers unhappy because I would pull their men off their duties and have rehearsals. My musicians were seamen, store keepers, boatswain mates etc., all had a bit of experience playing in high school bands. Some of the guys could read music, some didn't, they were willing so we worked hard, after a few weeks of rehearsing I found out the captain came from Georgia, so, I got on my knees and sang "Dixie" to the gang, I almost got tears in my eyes, hoping the guys would learn that melody, I finally got the gang to play "Dixie" and one day while on topside rehearsing the group, I saw the captain on the bridge and I played "Dixie", the skipper came down and complimented the gang and he told me to plan on playing for a ship's dance at the Palace Hotel in San Francisco. The duty was good, I didn't care for the long trips from San Francisco to the South Pacific. We were torpedo bait for the Jap subs, we didn't have any guns and we didn't go too fast to avoid the subs. After a few trips to the South Pacific, Captain Wyatt was promoted to Rear Admiral and was transferred to a heavy cruiser, he wanted me to go with him as his bandmaster, he offered me the job as his flag lieutenant which meant a commission as a junior grade lieutenant.

Which at that time, meant staying on active duty for 30 years which I didn't want. I also didn't want to stay at sea, so I asked the skipper to get me a set of orders to go to the music school in San Diego, this he did and I went to the school and here again I formed a band that qualified to play weekly over NBC radio with the top talent in music. I directed the band for 1 1/2 years and to make this short retired from the Navy. After retirement, took over a local band with 12 members, spent 38 years with last band and had 75 members, some were professional people, doctors, lawyers, engineers, school music teachers, in fact we had almost all professions, one guy played a trumpet, who owned a electronics company with millions in sales.

Exerpts from a memo by Robert L. Holland, manager of Peninsula Symponic Band:

The main reason for this memo is to make an announcement of historical importance to the band. The afternoon of December 8, I received a phone call from Nate Chasin. He stated that he had written a note to adult education principal Henry Page tendering his resignation from the band effective immediately. This action was a signal for Mr. Page to appoint a permanent successor. Nate's retirement marks the end of 38 years of faithful service to our band.

As some of you know, Nate retired as a chief warrant officer from the US Navy after a 22 year career. This is a total of 60 year experience with bands. He was a graduate of US Navy Conservatory of Music and studied extensively in several conducting clinics. He took clarinet lessons from Rudolph Schmitt, a noted musician with the San Francisco Symphony. Nate saw combat duty in major naval battles in the South Pacific and North Atlantic campaigns during World War II. During the war he conducted a Navy coast-to-coast radio show over NBC originating in Chicago called "Sky High". Nate has a standing invitation from us to play his clarinet for life in the band where he can best utilize his vast knowledge of the instrument.

Nathan Chasin, Mus. 1/c R. Division, member USS *Washington* (BB-56) Reunion Group became deceased in 1996 and was honored October 4, 1996, Wilmington, NC.

April 17, 1984

To: Ivan Musicant
3701 Glendale Terrace
Minneapolis, Minnesota 55410

We left Portland, Maine, on about March 12, 1942, I'm not quite sure of the dates, three days out to sea, in real heavy weather, we were called to man overboard. We all went to our man overboard stations, went up to the boat deck and stood by the boats. Capt. Benson came out on the wing of the bridge and hollered down, "Put that boat back into the skids. We're not going to lose six men for one man." Henceforth, we were all called to our division spaces and muster was taken. No one seemed to be missing. So they called a second muster, and still everyone was reported present. about that time a marine sentry went running up to the bridge yelling, "The Admiral is missing." Henceforth, they signaled over to the aircraft carrier, the USS *Wasp*, which was accompanying us along with the cruisers, the USS *Tuscaloosa* and the USS *Wichita*. They launched an SPD to search for the missing person believed to be the Admiral Wilcox, and they circled and circled and circled, but did not spot anyone. The SPD-2 tried to land on the deck of the USS *Wasp* and as she was right over the flight deck she cut her engines to land and missed the flight deck completely. We lost the lieutenant and the radio man 2nd. It was later confirmed to us that it was really Admiral Wilcox who was missing. He went over the side of the ship between the 5 inch mount which is located down on the main deck and the life line. There is space enough there for a person to get through because the mount needs that to train around.

It was just about then that we learned that our destination was Scapa Flow, Scotland, and that we were going to convoy ships to Murmansk, Russia, and we would patrol between Tronheim, Norway, and the streams of merchant ships that were going up around through the Arctic circle down and around into Murmansk, Russia. One of the things that upset Admiral Wilcox more than anything else, as I heard through a signalman, through a quartermaster, as you know the scuttlebutt on ships, that one of the orders was to seek out, find and sink the *Von Turpitz*.

Approximately five days after leaving Portland, Maine, we arrived in Scapa Flow, Scotland, amidst some of the largest displays of barrage balloons and large concentrations of ships in and around the Scapa Flow area. "Washing-Machine Charlie" was the name of a German plane that used to fly over at high altitude. We often times watched the anti-aircraft batteries on shore trying to hit these planes, but they were flying so high. Very seldom did we ever train out and attempt to shoot at these planes. We often times would go out and maneuver with the British home fleet and we took on some of their personnel so that we knew their signals and their radio signals. These men were berthed in a compartment just behind the first division in which I was berthed. We got to meet some of the English sailors who had already been fighting in this war for three to four years prior to us getting there. They were very, very much amazed at the newness and the facilities that we had aboard our ships in the US Navy verus their ships. I remember, one time, when they first saw our shower facilities with the beautiful stainless steel decks. They were just ecstatic that we had such facilities aboard our ships.

The dates and times of these convoys to Murmansk, Russia, were all documented in a log

I kept, which we were not supposed to keep, but I did keep. When I left the US Navy in 1948, I had that log with me, but a young lady that I was keeping company with some many years ago by the name of Winnefred Steinhelber, who lived in New Rochelle, NY, and Mount Vernon, NY, has all of these records and the dates of the ships in which we operated with. If I had that log with me now, I would be able to give you a more accurate account of the various convoys that we took to Murmansk, Russia.

The cold was unbearable in through the Arctic Circle. The darkness which protected us most of the time was most helpful. German Wolfpacks operated constantly. We were constantly at battle stations, and so forth, because of the continual harrassment by the German submarines that were concentrated in those sea lanes between Iceland and Scapa Flow to Murmansk.

A Coxson aboard our ship, and I can't quite remember his name, came up with a little verse and ditty which could be appropriate at this time:
From Iceland to Murmansk
From Murmansk to Scapa Flow
Wherever the convoy goes
You'll find the task force
It's on the right course
A worrisome thing to lead
You to sing the blues in the night.

One of the accounts that you asked me about in your letter was the ramming of the *Punjabi,* the destroyer, in the British navy. I recall this incident very well because at that time I was just a seaman second class in the 1st Division aboard the USS *Washington.* At the time of the ramming of the *Punjabi,* myself and another seaman, J.J. Brown, were standing fog watch on the bow of the ship. We were following HMS *King George V.* We could not see the *King George* at all, but we were keeping our bow right on a towing sparr. The towing sparr is towed by the ship forward of you and it throws up this big cockcomb sea spray. By us being able to keep our nose right abreast of the towing sparr we could avoid collisions and we would know the maneuvers of the *King George V.* Well, all of a sudden, there was submarine contact. In the English navy, their destroyers, start blowing their whistles and then start maneuvering. Then we heard this ungodly crash. We didn't know whether it was a torpedo or what. I was standing up on the bow with the headset earphones on still calling up the position of the towing sparr to the bow of our ship. Commander Dell was the officer of the deck at the time. We were standing watch-n-watch, so a commander is the officer of the deck on watch-n-watch. I was giving the position of the towing sparr up to the bridge when all of a sudden there is two parts of the destroyer. The forward part of the destroyer was the largest part. It was floating pretty good and there were a lot of men hanging on to the forward part of the destroyer. It was pretty well intact. Their water tight integrity was holding. Just as our bow got to the after part of the destroyer, *Punjabi,* their depth charges started going off and everything was blowing into the air, fuel oil, arms, legs and bodies, and the depth charges were going off under our ship and the engineers down in the lower berthing space were coming up topside thinking that surely were hit or something happened to us. When the explosions of the depth charges occurred, I yanked the phone line out of the jack as I was going back towards the barbett of no. 1 turret. But now I had to go back on to the bow and start relaying the information as fast as I could; so I held the phone lines together with my fingers and communications were still going up to the bridge, but by this time there was so much confusion with all of the ships and so forth, we were able to maneuver and get clear of all of the debris of the ship. There was no damage to our double bottoms and none of our seams gave way and we held our water tight integrity, kept on our position and continued with the convoys to the prearranged location in Murmansk and Archangel where we were heading.

The USS *Tuscaloosa* took the forward part of the *Punjabi* alongside, lashed her to and removed most of her crew and somehow managed to get the forward portion. I don't know where they took her to, but there were able to save the forward part of the *Punjabi.*

We later heard that Commander Dell received the Victoria Cross from the British for maneuvering the USS *Washington* through the pieces of the *Punjabi* without causing any further damage to ship or crew.

The other piece of information that you asked for in the letter that you wrote to me was about the King's visit to the USS *Washington* with the Queen of England. My recollection of that was, the first part I remember, was the Queen came up the gang plank first and that she asked for Douglas. Douglas Fairbanks was a lieutenant aboard the *Washington* at the time. He came through the ranks and that was the last time that we saw the Queen Mother. King George wanted to visit all portions of the ship and he was going around the ship with Captian Benson and Chief Boatswain Scarborrough, who was the chief master at arms on the USS *Washington.* I remember one conversation with the King and Chief Master at Arms Scarborrough. They got to an area of the ship where we burned all of our trash and everything aboard ship and the King asked what was that compartment. Chief Scarborrough said that this was the incinerator aboard the ship. The King said, "My gosh, your incinerator is cleaner than our ship." He was a very naval looking person. He had his navy uniform on and the gold braids on his hat, his epelets and so forth. He looked every bit the part of an English seaman. I believe, just by looking at the man that he truly loved the sea and navies.

In July, we went back to Reykjavik, Iceland, we took aboard as much gold as I have ever seen in my life. The marines brought it aboard ship and we stored it in our refrigerator lockers. It was just bullion after bullion. It took four men, two on each side, carrying these big bullion bars, as I said they were stored in our refrigerator lockers. We made a beehive from Reykjavik to New York. We did it at 30-31 knots all the way. We did not use any zig-zag course whatsoever, and I remember the destroyers coming along side and they would keep up with us as long as they could. Then they would drop off and we would get some other destroyer coming alongside. We maintained the speed straight into New York. In New York, we had some repairs done to some of the

From the Foc'sle of the BB56.

turrets and the roller barrings that were damaged from the heavy seas in the North Atlantic and so forth etc. Captain Benson was relieved of the command aboard the USS *Washington* and we received another great captain, Captain Glenn A. Davis. I happened to be close to the bridge one day and he came out on to the bridge. He looked forward and aft and he said, "With this ship, I will make history."

That will be the other part of the story when you tell me you need the story about the Pacific and Admiral Willis Lee Jr. coming aboard the *Washington* and the battles of Savo Island.

I am gunners mate 1/c John Stolecki USN Serial No. 224-38-54

Spot I's Comments on Night Action, November 15, 1942:
by H.W. Seeley, Lt. Cmdr, USN, Spot I Officer

1. General

(a) Such facts as the apparent failure to detect our presence, generous use of S.L., etc., would indicate that Japs do not have radar - or, if so, that it is not satisfactory.

(b) As far as I could see, the Japs used no starshell illumination.

(c) Jap SL seem to have about twice the effective range of ours, produced excellent illumination, and were well controlled.

(d) For reasons best known to the Japs, none of their S.L. (total of 8-12 reported) stayed turned on very long.

(e) Jap rate of fire of small caliber guns was high but not as high as our 5". Fire of their large guns was slow, deliberate and as far as we were concerned inaccurate (*South Dakota* will not agree with this).

(f) Japs apparently use two distinct types of powder, one giving off a bright white light and the other a dull orange flash of small radius.

(g) No richochets, own or enemy, were noticed.

(h) Enemy must either have been at battle stations or manned them with extreme alacrity as return fire was extremely prompt.

(i) Continued use of smoke screen tactics by Japs seems to bear out lack of radar. They did not fire from behind screens.

(j) Their smoke screens were quickly and excellently laid (by stack smoke) and the best possible use was made of these screens.

(k) Every Jap ship we tracked seemed to be making 26 knots. (our own standard speed!).

(l) Only two cases, were reported of Jap ships retaining any kind of formation: (a) the 3DD's reported in Phase 1, and (b) the group of freighters we tracked in phase 2 and 3.

(m) Although the phone circuits were clogged with reports of torpedo attacks, trailing DD's and MTB wakes, neither Spots 1 or 2 (who looked carefully from the director tops through 7-50 binoculars) were able to detect evidence of any.

(n) Japs appeared willing to "slug it out" when necessary.

(o) Later indications are that they were using AP projectiles with possibly some common. Apparently many of their large caliber projectiles failed to explode. Their penetration, however, was good.

2. Own Men and Equipment

(a) Though we had been at G.Q. stations since 0530 the previous morning there was nothing to indicate that personnel were so fatigued as to malfunction in any way.

(b) There was no indication of fear or excessive nervousness even though the men on my station had every reason to believe they were watching major caliber guns firing at us at 11,000 yards and on at least two occasions had reason to believe the ship had been hit.

(c) Real worry was caused only by the continued spreading of the word that we might be firing on the *South Dakota*.

(d) Passing of the caution to brace yourself for torpedo hit was annoying especially to those who had to keep on with their operating any way.

(e) To the best of my knowledge the fire control equipment, including radars, was used expertly by all concerned and proved itself in all case to be a fine system.

(f) With two minor exceptions, there were no MB fire control casualties.

(g) Talkers, in general, seem to have done a very creditable job.

(h) Radars proved themselves accurate and invaluable, although radar spotting was disappointing by its absence.

3. Gripes. (Some of these may have readily available answers - but we didn't know 'em then when it counted.)

(a) Our general mission was never announced. I personally assumed it was to "break up enemy landing operations" - which is pretty general.

(b) Although it was apparent the next day that the info. was aboard ship, we didn't get the news about the specific number and types of ships we could expect.

(c) We could have used some general directives as to what types of targets the main battery would fire on should they become available - would we knowingly fire on DD's which were not attacking if they were the only targets?

(d) Tactical consideration: Could we assume our force would remain in formation as far as practicable - or was it natural to assume that if one unit became involved it would be left behind? The whereabouts of the *South Dakota* apparently colored the results of the entire engagement - from our viewpoint.

(e) Could we have been told we would fight a hit and run type of action.

(f) Did we know that the possibility of a serious torpedo attack outweighed all other considerations including destruction of enemy heavy units?

(g) Failure to allow us to complete destruction of enemy BB, & failure to open fire on other targets, particularly the freighter group, undoubtedly caused considerable/nervousness & irritation - sufficient possibly to have interfered with fully effective fire later on.

(h) Many erroneous reports of contacts, especially by lookout and sky control, required time and trouble to refute and frequently broke up our tracking of what we fondly hoped were legitimate targets; and also filled up the phone circuit.

(i) Failure to invariably use "true" and "relative", and to give ranges and type of target (when available) caused delay, confusion and unnecessary talking.

(j) A lack of appreciation of our mission (See Grip #1) caused the sky control officer to make the statement that as long as the main battery was firing so would the secondary, but that he wasn't going to open fire or ask to if the main battery was not. This appears to be a far cry from the decentralized group control we could have. Or were we more intent on remaining concealed than in destroying enemy ships. I didn't know.

(k) It was a little embarrassing to cease firing twice and watch the enemy continue firing at us; morale did not improve at this point.

4. Recommendations

(a) In order to cut down on confusion of targets, delays due to talker relay, errors and omissions due to third or fourth hand information, it is strongly recommended that the Gunnery Officer (in a night engagement, at least) be with the Captain on the bridge.

(b) That the Ass't. Gunnery Officer - in Conn if desired - handle the mass of minor reports which continually cloud the main issue.

(c) That more latitude be given the A.G.O. (in Conn), Sky Control Officer, & Group Control Officers in opening fire. Or, that their instructions for a particular engagement be specific and detailed where possible.

(d) That more dependency be placed on SG & CXAM reports and less on FD reports. FC & FD radars are not well adapted to searching, and operators are not nearly as well trained in general searching as are SG personnel. Could the A.G.O. or radar officer receive, filter and coordinate all such reports? Lookouts likewise duplicate reports.

4. Special Comments on Enemy Forces

(a) Number, types, tactics — ships and planes.

No enemy aircraft were involved in the engagement.

A definite statement of the number and types of enemy surface vessels present is not practicable. Reconnaissance units reported November 14 the following ships in the general area: 3BB, 8-12 cruisers, 12 or more DD, 4 AK and 5 transports. A compilation of evidence deduced from visual and radar observations; size of guns as indicated by gun flashes, explosions and splashes; target speeds; density of fire, etc. indicates the following:

(1) East of Savo Island:

5-8 ships. Probable types and numbers: 1BB, 2-3CA(CL), 3DD.

(2) South of Savo Island:

6-10 ships

Probably most of these were DD although a burning transport was reported by several observers in this area—possibly MTB's.

(3) West of Savo Island:

9-12 ships

Probable types are: 1BB, 3CA(CL), 3DD, 5 unidentified (possibly 1 MTB transport or converted cruisers and 4 AK).

A recapitulation of the above estimates would indicate the following probable totals: from 18 to 32 ships broken down into units as follows:

2BB, 8CA-CL, 10DD, 5 unidentified: Total 25; of these, possible four ships were first observed East of Savo, and later rejoined the force West of the Island. If such were the case, a grand total of approximately 21 enemy ships were in the immediate area during the engagement. No MTB were actually sighted although the wakes of MTB were reported by several observers.

Tactics

It seems probable that Japanese ships were using Savo Island to prevent detection by radar or silhouette effect. During the approach and initial phase of the engagement the radars were unable to resolve the ships on the South side of Savo from the island. These ships could not be seen until they moved away from Savo.

The four heavy ships Northwest of Savo Island were apparently attempting to cut off the retirement of our ships. It is believed that they lost track of this ship when we ceased firing on the vessels bordering Savo, and that they reversed course 12 minutes later. The next five targets which the *Washington* tracked were to the Northward of this group and were possibly being screened by it.

Searchlights in groups of two were used many times, but were left on for only short periods. This illumination proved very effective. No real effort was made by the Japanese to use starshells.

(b) Communications, homing, RDF. No comments.

(c) Use of smoke, camouflage, deception.

Throughout the entire engagement the Japanese made extensive use of smoke screen tactics. These screens were rapidly and proficiently layed and very effectively used to hide subsequent movements of the ships so screened. However no difficulty was found in continuing to track these ships by radar. Smoke screens were probably used to (a) cover ships which were caught unprepared when firing was commenced: (b) cover non-combatant ships such as the AK; (c) cover retirement of damaged ships. From our viewpoint the chief effectiveness of the use of smoke lay in preventing more positive identification of enemy vessels.

Camouflage: None observed.

Deception: It is believed the Japanese used radar deception whenever possible by lying in close to land.

(d) Effectiveness of Gunnery:

This ship was fired on only sporadically. No hits were sustained and the nearest miss noted was the splash of a major caliber shell about 150 yards on the port quarter. The fact that the *Washington* was never illuminated by searchlight undoubtedly resulted in our comparative security. No estimate of the effectiveness of Japanese surface gunnery as pertains directly to this ship is therefore made. Observers who witnessed other ships of our force under concentrated fire reported the Japanese gunnery to be both accurate and effective. There is every reason to believe the Japanese ships were not equipped with radar. However, the enemy made excellent use of their searchlights, and during the brief interval in which any of our ships was illuminated the Japanese batteries were rapidly brought to bear and firing commenced.

It was apparent that the Japanese were using a type of flashless powder which contrasted sharply with the bright and blinding flashes of our own guns. The vividness of the flashes or both our 5" and 16" not only had a marked tendency to blind aloft personnel but also undoubtedly provided the Japanese with comparatively good points of aim.

Although many "torpedo" tracks were reported near this ship, no torpedoes were seen to explode nor is there any other definite confirmation of torpedoes having been launched against the *Washington*.

(e) Estimated Material & Personnel Casualties:

Material: 1 CA or CL sunk & 1CA damaged by this ship.

1 BB damaged badly or sunk.

1 CL left burning.

In addition to the above, the damaging or sinking of several small ships (DD or CL) is considered probable. Those enemy ships were lying close to the eastern shore of Savo were at first considered to be shore batteries and were taken under fire by *Washington* 5" mounts for about nine minutes. Fire was shifted as each successive "shore batteries" ceased firing.

On two occasions *Washington* 5" and *South Dakota* fired on the same target and the damage caused by the 5" firing is not estimated although hits were definitely obtained.

Personnel: No estimate is made. It is believed that no Japanese survivors were picked up.

Night Engagement
Nov. 14-15, 1942.

Phase 1: About 008, Spot 1 received word of radar contact of enemy ships; the director was trained on the designated bearing and two targets were shortly picked up by our radar (Radar 3). Radar tracking was commenced at once and a good solution quickly obtained. In the meantime both the pointer and trainer reported that they could see the ships optically. Spot 1 was unable to see the targets through the 26-power rangerfinder glass but eventually picked them up by using 7-50 binoculars out the top hatch. Control designated the right hand ship as the target, and later asked if this were the larger of the two; Spot 1 replied in the affirmative. The target was on our stbd hand, between this ship and Savo Island, range about 18,000 yards, target angle about 080 degrees. It was long, quite low with small free board, flush deck and no bulky superstructure, appearing to be a light cruiser of the *Tenryu* class. It did not appear to have spotted us, though it is quite possible she had been lying in close to the island, had seen us come inside (South of) Savo, and was trying to sneak out without being seen. She did not open fire on us or attempt to illuminate but did lay an effective smoke screen. We commenced fire about 0012 with normal set up, i.e., collective fire, director 1 controlling in train, director 4 in elevation, Spot 1 spotting; slow fire. After the second salvo, control ordered rapid fire, firing on one turret ready light. Spot 1 followed tracer of the first salvo but was unable to see the splash or target due to glare of salvo 2. Radar 3 operator caught the splash and was able to report the splash as over. Secondary battery opened fire at a nearby group of ships (range 12000 yards) at this time and visual sighting of target or splashes became impossible due to almost continuous gun flash. About the time our second salvo landed, Radar 3 lost the target entirely and was never again able to pick it up, although splashes continued to show on the screen.

Some 8-10 salvos were fired before cease firing was given about 0020. No definite estimate of damage to this target could be made. We did not attempt any sort of illumination on this target. Main battery picked up target on bearing 356 true at 0026, ship was on fire from secondary battery hits; was ordered to pick up shore battery on left end of island and commence firing but due to continuous gun flash and intermittent point of aim were unable to get on battery. At about 0038 Spot 1 saw a ship ahead blow up and burst into flames; it was a mass of fire as we passed her close aboard to starboard, about 0041, and exploding ammunition (possible .50 caliber or 20mm) could be heard. During this initial phase, our DDs up ahead were observed firing heavily at the shore batteries; the *South Dakota* was also seen on our starboard quarter firing at an enemy ship (or ships) which turned on two searchlights briefly. Shore installations from one end of the island to the other maintained a heavy rate of fire - Spot 1 estimated guns ranged from 40mm to 5 or 6 inch; the larger guns made a bright white flash on firing. A bright white light was reported turned on, on Guadalcanal, in line with our DD and Savo shore batteries when the latter opened up. It is believed

Scout Patrol Plane

possible that this was used to help line up the shore batteries on targets, or possibly to silhouette targets. No large splashes were observed near us during the first phase but many tracers were visible at all times. The air between our ship and Savo Island was literally full of shells. A fire was started on North end of the island by 5" fire and was still burning when we left the area.

All batteries ceased firing and we stood out of the channel SW of Savo - Spot 1 lost track of our DDs and the *South Dakota* at this time. It is possible that some of the enemy ships made for the north channel and the *South Dakota* followed; or that she just continued the engagement inside.

Phase 2: On rounding the southern end of Savo, about 0044, Radar 3 picked up a target, a good solution was soon obtained entirely by radar and we received word to open fire, but before the first salvo could be fired Control gave "Cease Fire". (Apparently this contact was believed at first to be the *South Dakota*). An enemy ship on our port quarter opened fire on us and I asked Spot 2 to keep his eye peeled and recommend divided fire if he thought advisable. A large splash (about 150 feet high) was observed 200 yards off our port quarter. We continued tracking and about 0058 commenced firing. First salvo was unobserved by either visual or radar, but second salvo was a hit and explosions illuminated some of ship's superstructure. Secondary battery illuminated with starshells and next salvo could be seen to land squarely amidships causing large, bright explosions which showed a tall heavy superstructure and large stack indicative of a battleship. Enemy also opened fire on us, firing from three turrets which appeared about equally spaced along main deck. The flashes from her guns were not bright, subsided quickly and were yellowish in color - possibly using some form of flashless power (or flash hiders?) Additional splashes from our turrets were easily seen to fall over about 300, on and short about 400 yds. Ship was burning in superstructure and still firing. At about 0102 fire was checked apparently to assure that target was not *South Dakota* during which period she fired two 3-turret salvos at us which landed 800-1000 yards short of our starboard bow. Fire was resumed but starshells dropped short and burned in water cutting out view of the target. Sky control was asked to fuse out starshells, which was done. Another full salvo was seen to hit the target and explode before cease firing was given. Enemy ship fired two more single turret (after turret) salvos after we ceased firing. Radar spots could not be obtained; possibly because splash signal merged with that of the BB. Group one continued tracking this ship (which was easily visible due to the superstructure fire) for some considerable period of time and repeatedly request permission to resume fire, making a final request when target range was about 20,000 yards and fire was fading. Although a number of salvos were clearly seen to splash - splashes appearing gray and white - the orange dye was not at all in evidence. Deflection was excellent (one spot of left 2 mils being made), and both range and deflection patterns were very small. It is believed that this ship was hit by at least 8 16-inch shells and was seriously damaged.

Phase 3: At 0114 picked up and tracked target on port quarter but could not get permission to open fire. Considerable number of ships were in this attack and firing and searchlight flashes were visible at one time or another in every sector. Two additional targets were tracked at ranges less than 14,000 yards. Picked up visually five ships in close formation at about 10,000 yards and commenced tracking, using radar ranges and optical train. Spot 1 could see outline of ships quite plainly using 7-50 binoculars and identified same as a number of freighters led by a man-of-war (probably a converted merchantman). A good rangekeeper solution was quickly obtained but permission to open fire could not be gotten although it was repeatedly requested. Spot 1 could distinctly see smoke screen being laid. Order to open fire on this group was never given although it was in sight and tracked for a considerable period of time. (possibly 25-30 minutes).

For the next hour or so several targets were picked up, tracked and dropped while the ship maneuvered to avoid reported torpedoes: Spot 1 made special efforts to pick up torpedo tracks but could see none although as many as 2-3 at a time were reported. Numerous false reports of objects by Sky Control were also investigated during this period. No MTB wakes were ever seen.

On passing out of this area on southerly course about 0300, a bright glare could be seen near the north end of Guadalcanal with occasional flares as tho' explosions were occurring.

HOMEWARD BOUND
by Granville E. Stuart

The temporary repairs were made to the ship after the collision with the *Indiana*, and we headed back to Pearl Harbor for more repairs.

The Signal gang and the Quartermaster gang got together to make a homeward bound pennant, this being a tradition with the Navy when a ship has been away from home for a long time.

In a short time the pennant was completed and ready to be hoisted to the main mast. It would be hoisted to the main mast where the commission pennant normally flew. When it came time to hoist the pennant up what a big surprise when we found the halyard that the pennant was connected to was gone, it had been burned off from the heat of the two smoke stacks. Now came the question, how do we get the pennant up where it was supposed to be?

After some discussion we found out that what we needed was someone to climb the mast and string up a new halyard. We had to have a volunteer to climb the mast and string up a new halyard for the homeward bound pennant. To this day I don't know why I volunteered to climb that mast, it was only 129 feet above the deck. Now that we had a person to make like a monkey, we had to get the power cut on the radio antennas, otherwise a person climbing through that area might just get fried to the bone. After some debate the captain said he would stand on the bridge, and when I got close to that area he would have all the power cut off to the antenna's and that he would be the only one to have it turned back on, he asked that I get the job done as soon as possible because we wouldn't have a radio until I got back down.

The pennant was rolled up and tied in a bundle, I went to the bottom of the mast, connected one end of the halyard to my belt, I don't remember who was with me but I'm sure it was someone from the QM gang who would play out the halyard. I took a nice long breath, took hold of the rungs of the ladder looked up and step by step began my trip to the top of the mast. I reached the area which was even with the smoke stacks it was easy, but then when I reached the area the ladder was black with suet from the smoke stacks. I had to make sure that I had a good grip on the ladder so I wouldn't lose my hold and find the deck below. Once I got to the yard arm I had to climb out and over it. I was at the point of standing on the yard arm when I realized something, the pulley that the halyard was to go in was at the end of a two inch pipe that extended about eight feet above the mast running lights. Now this would mean that I would have to stand on top of the running lights and reach up and feed the halyard through the pulley. I did this with my arm wrapped around the pipe, I stepped back down onto the yard arm which was much wider and gave me more room to stand with a lot better balance.

I now proceeded to pull up the remainder of the halyard, with the bundle of pennant attached to the other end of the halyard. I tied one end of the halyard to the pennant, then the other end of the halyard to the pennant, now all that was left was to untie the string around the pennant, and give it a big heave out into the wind; I think that was one of the greatest moments in my life when the pennant flew out over the water.

The pennant was about eight inches wide at the top, about one inch at the small end. It was 179 feet long. Blue field with seven stars, one red and one white stripe. What a wonderful feeling to be going home, the United States of America, our pennant flying proudly, homeward bound.

by Dick A. Shepherd

In boot camp I was in sick bay for Cat fever (what ever that was) and missed rifle practice. They said I got it from practicing on the plastic bugle. My trumpet arrived from home, two days later. I played the trumpet for the other boots for over two hours. Was not accepted for bugling.

Shipped to Shoemaker, California where I arrived broke. We were told to bring no money back from leave, as we would get paid when we got back. Didn't get paid as you couldn't get paid while in transit.

On May 13, 1943 I arrived aboard the USS *Washington* broke.

Before the service I was a machinist and tool & die maker. I tried to get into that division, but was turned down. (I had my own successful family company after the service until 1990). The ship was having trouble with the vaporizers for making fresh water. There were three of them and one was always down. While visiting the machine shop they were repairing one. When I saw how they were fixing it I pointed out what they were doing wrong. They took my suggestion and after each one was corrected there was

U.S.S. Washington. Painted by CQM Herbie Francis in 1961 for Shipmate Sam Scalzo.

very little trouble thereafter. Maybe I was too smart to join that division.

At one time I was in charge of cleaning and painting the signal bridge. I didn't like the way the chains on the ladder draped so I tightened them as much as I could. Well the next time the five inch and 16 inch battery let loose these chains split and went all over the place. They never found out who or what caused this to happen.

I was transferred to Division R and started standing bugle watch on the quarter deck November 23 during the day and in the air conditioned damage control room at night. Buglers duties, aboard ship, are to keep the bell polished and the officers of the deck quarters clean. During the war you can't have a shiny bell so it is painted, so a stern division painted it and we kept our mouth shut. Division 1 to use the Officers of the Deck quarters to store their refueling gear in it so they wouldn't have to bring it up from below. We agreed as long as they would always keep it clean in port or anchorage. This gave the buglers nothing to do but practice. We also got to eat early mess because we are to wait an hour before playing. How, at home, when we played for dances we always had food and drink on the band stand and ate all the time.

The buglers got so bored, at times, that we offered to paint the Damage Control Room. We latched down all doors and sprayed the room. But with the latches paint dust still spread through to several compartments. The worst was the telephone exchange which was right next to the Damage Control Room. What a mess. We were cleared of all damages and other had to clean up the mess.

One hot night the officer in charge of Damage Control asked me to go to the gedunk and get all of us some ice cream. Well while I was gone they called down for general quarters. Because I was gone the officer tried to blow general quarters. He didn't know how to sound that call so he just blew what ever he could. Later some crew members asked me what it was. They thought it was anti-aircraft. Fortunately, being at night latches are closed and the bridge couldn't, hear it.

While in South Hampton, England, being the top ranked bugler, I had to stay aboard to sound attention for the First Lord (like our Secretary of the Navy) who was coming aboard. A member of the band always played mess call for the officers mess. They all wanted to go ashore so they asked me if I would do it for one of them. Of course I would. They told me it was different than the mess call the bugler would use. It was playing about eight bars of an appropriate tune. Usually the officers are already in or at their seat. When it came time I really blasted the tune and scared the wits out of them. It seems the band forgot to tell me it was to be played very very soft.

Being on the bridge during the day I got to know the Admiral, Captain and others up there. At one time Admiral Lee asked if I would join his group and be the bugler.

I still play the trumpet in several bands and am bugler for Lincoln Post 13 burials. Playing for a burial in a late January, I usually play taps facing the service and turn around and play taps as an echo. It was so cold the spit froze in the bugle. This reminded me of the time we sailed up the Hudson River during a bad blizzard to anchor at a New York City pier. The bugle froze up then and I had to keep running in and out of the bridge to thaw it out. Some of the calls didn't come out to clear, but then most of the officers were in the bridge and didn't realize the bad notes.

When the Chaplains new organ arrived I offered to buy the old one. I paid $25 for it. There was a nice little air conditioned hole right off of the Damage Control Room. The room was large enough that the organ would fit with a couple of chairs. I used to spend a lot of time practicing in there. It was a pump organ so I did get a little exercise. When I was told I was to be discharged and had to be off in a hour I was in such a hurry that I left my gear that was below deck and the organ aboard. I often wish I still had it as I've been the secretary and vice-president of the Western Reserve Theatre Organ Society for 18 years and could sure have fun with it now.

I was talking with one of my high school classmates who was in the Marines, talking about the service, and he said he bet that I never head of Mog-Mog. The next Sunday at church I showed where I had listed having recreation on Mog-Mog.

by Cdr. C.R. Knowlton

After repairs from damage done by explosion of HMS *Punjabi* by KG5 off the coast of Norway, the new PP1 radar SG was installed by Raytheon Company. As a radar officer, I protested position of antenna in front of the tower structure, limiting the loss of about 60 degrees relative astern of the ship. No change was made as we were due at Guadalcanal. I was ordered by RADM Willis Lee to be his radar advisor. We were off the western end of Guadalcanal with DDs and USS *Enterprise*. I read the flashing message from ADM Spruance, detaching the *Washington, South Dakota* and four DD's (*Gwin, Preston, Walke* and *Benham*) with the most fuel to proceed to point "X" (Savo Island). After reaching north of Savo, RADM Lee put the four DDs ahead of us in column at 1000 yard intervals. We changed course to about 180 degrees between Florida and Savo Islands when I heard course change to Corpen 9 about five miles from Honaira, Guadalcanal. I operated the SG radar myself. Upon execution of Corpen 9 (new course 270 degrees) the first place I looked at the SG screen was the 60 degree blank space. The SG now showed two ships following us at about 18,000 yards. RADM Lee and staff came to radar plot. After everyone expressed opinions RADM Lee said to me, "Now what do you think these two echoes are?" I said, "two ships". He immediately ordered target designation and ordered all ships to fire. The two ships retired to the northeast. This started the battle. All firing was from our starboard side. The *Preston* and *Walke* were sunk. The *Benham* sunk on retiring, and the *Gwin* was damaged. The *South Dakota*, which was about 3,000 yards astern of us, was damaged and was silhouetted by the burning destroyers, whereas we passed in the back of the destroyers.

I was busy giving target designations, one of which was the battleship *Kirishima*. On radar, I watched our 16" shells and the *Kirishima's* shells pass each other. As we were leaving. I detected what were three Japs DDs coming up on our starboard. We were at flank speed. RADM Lee told me later that we had only old charts of the New Georgia Reefs and had to turn south, before hitting a reef. From the JA talkers reports the 3 DDs fired many torpedoes at us. None hit us. I saw them retire north after we turned south to the Coral Sea. RADM Lee told me about 2 a.m. that we had sunk the *Kirishima*. He also said to me, "You must be tired". We saw the USS *South Dakota* ahead of us the next morning, she had sustained extensive damage.

BETTY GOES BYE-BYE
by Wilbur Drewitz

I remember well the occasion of a particular air attack. It was dusk, and while at my battle station as a loader on the starboard stern aft 40mm quad, a Betty torpedo bomber came up our wake. Initially, everyone was firing at a decoy plane on our port side, between us and a carrier, going in the opposite direction. Once we saw the plane coming up our wake, we commenced firing on it. We could see the torpedo door bay was open, and could see the torpedo, but seemingly it was stuck, thank goodness! The plane now started to ascend and could have easily kamikazed into our fantail, but luck was again on our side. By now we could see the pilot was apparently dead and slouched over the controls and the co-pilot now fired his 20mm guns at our quad. One round ricocheted into our steel protection guard and the piece of shrapnel entered into our gunner's (J.D. Hill) buttocks. (He later refused the Purple Heart). The plane now flew over our heads and we could almost touch it. It gradually veered to starboard and miraculously missed crashing into the side of us. By now it was losing altitude quickly and exploded into a ball of fire, sinking very fast.

HEAT OF THE MOMENT
by William R. Hippard

After the Bremerton Navy Yard overhaul in 1945 we were headed south for California, the executive officer pulled a surprise inspection of the main engine rooms. At the start of the inspection in #1 engine room word was secretly passed, over sound powered phones, to the other engine rooms. For some reason the ventilation systems shut down to a bare minimum. With boilers and steam lines containing 850 degree superheated steam the engine rooms soon got very hot. The men standing watch in the succeeding engine rooms were dripping wet with perspiration. The exec. didn't realize or know that temperature conditions weren't normal.

The heat didn't slow the old boy down he completed his inspection of all four main engine rooms chewing me out all the way. Thank goodness he never found out of the attempt to get him to cut short his inspection.

LOST ON AN ISLAND
by Michael J. Ferrovecchio

We were anchored out from one of the islands in the Pacific and they let some of us go ashore for some recreation.

My shipmate Albert Fialka, who has passed away, and I decided to go hunting. We had only one gun between us. We saw these very large colorful chickens, but couldn't get close enough to get a shot. We decided we would have one person stand while the other made a sweep around and try to drive the game towards the one which the gun. I noticed a mud hole with wild pig tracks, then I saw it again, and then a third time, I realized I was lost. I climbed the highest tree and when I looked out all I could see were the tops of the trees. I found a trail and decided I would follow it and see if it would come to some village. I followed the trail and it kept getting dimmer, finally it disappeared. I turned and headed back on the same trail, there along the trail Al was sitting waiting for me. "What took you so long?" he said. I said I was lost. I'll never forget that experience of being lost.

TIDBITS
by Alfred B.K. Rodrigues

Many of the activities conducted aboard ship were transacted without the knowledge of the proper authorities. To relieve the daily stress and boredom of being at sea or anchored in some ungodly named atoll, a few enterprising sailors would find means to enhance the routine. Before I relate a few interesting anecdotes let me describe my duties aboard ship.

As one of the chief storekeepers my responsibilities included the storage and maintenance of all the dry provision storerooms. Was also in charge of the ships store, gedunk stand, clothing and small stores, the alcohol locker and the beer storeroom. We normally would have 1,000 cases of beer on board for liberty parties.

It was no secret that some scheming young men who knew how to prepare spirits had their stills or is it distilleries operating in dark corners of the ship. Most of the brews they concocted would knock you for a loop.

Accountability for the provisions in the storerooms was lax. Whenever a friend of a friend would ask me for a gallon of raisins or any kind of fruit I would always oblige. I assumed that they were sharing these fruits with shipmates within their division. Many months went by before I realized what was going on. One of the friends brought me a sample of what I recall they called swipe. Do not know how much proof it was but it did not take long for me to feel giddy. From then on whenever I gave anything away I insisted on a sample of the finished product.

Whenever one of my storekeepers needed to get supplies for the galley they would come to me for the keys to the storerooms. It was more convenient than having to sign for it in the supply office. Months after my transfer I met a shipmate who told me that they used to have big poker games in those provision storerooms. Only then did I understand why the cooks always asked for supplies at unusual hours. I also learned that the storekeeper took a cut from every pot for providing the space to gamble.

Cdr. Kohlas the supply officer gave me a standing order about a specific brand of cigarettes. This was the brand that Admiral Lee CombatPac smoked and he was a chain smoker. Some of us named him Smoky Lee. I think the supply officer was jesting when he told me that I would not be chief very long if we ever ran out of the Pall Mall cigarettes. I was still a chief petty officer when I got transferred.

Like the rest of the crew the chiefs experienced the same boredom from the early morning GQs one hour before sunrise and the four on and eight off *Natches* during battle condition one. So on Christmas and new years and other special occasions we broke out the pure alcohol. With some orange juice and ice we released our tensions. We were fortunate to have reliable, trustworthy chiefs who never got out of hand or revealed the source of their gratuity.

When not working or standing watches the most entertaining times I enjoyed was playing poker in the chiefs quarters. We would start playing after the dinner table was cleared and very often continued until GQ sounded in the morning.

Until I was stationed on the USS *Washington* I had never been to the United States. Hawaii was a territory when World War II began. My first state was Washington. After our collision with the *Indiana*. I came from a town of less than 2,000 people. In fact the *Washington* had more people on guard than my hometown. So I really was not street wise like most of the crew on some anyway. I was like a country hick but learned fast.

3RD BATTLE OF SAVO ISLAND
by Raymond Serenson

November 14-15, 1942, just past 2400 hours on November 15 myself and other shipmates were ordered to place life rafts over the side, because the first two destroyers had taken hit from the Japs, first DD split in half, second DD damaged, unknown how bad at the time. Moon was bright, I saw some foliage from the beach (shore) leaves were large that I could see from deck of USS *Washington* at this time, ordered to take cover inside ship. Went forward to area just below #2 turret, 16 inch. Every time turrets were fired, a hatch door would spring open. We would try to dog (lock) hatch closed. Repeated this many times. After winning this battle, one Jap battleship sunk, we headed out of Savo Island to launch a Kingfisher aircraft for search of area, we got a bleap on radar. It was a bogie ship. No I.D. received. Aircraft spotters ship and notified its ours. It was the USS *South Dakota* which was in battle with us in Savo Island. Radar damage, also superstructure damage. It returned to the States for repairs, she was called the Battle X for some bond drives stateside.

1st Row: Fialka, Putton, Pettingill, Tait, Silver, Holland, Klieman, Yausohn, Cozzolind. 2nd Row: Whitehouse, Froempter, Newton, Waller, Shoen, Cross, Kovack, Omiela, Malvick, Kirkam. 3rd Row: Reigrut, Handy, Moore, Ferrovecchio, Tepper, Alvarez, Parmenter, Poist, McCune, Maris, Maclosky, Lambert, Maguire. (Courtesy of Michael Ferrovecchio.)

THE THIRD BATTLE OF SAVO ISLAND (GUADALCANAL)
by H.W. Seely

In early November 1942 it became increasingly evident that the struggler for control of the island of Guadalcanal was of major importance to the success of the South Pacific campaign - both to the Japanese and to the Allies. Our ground forces were making satisfactory progress on the island, but our air and sea forces had been drastically reduced in a series of air and surface engagements. Consequently, when intelligence sources revealed that the Japs were preparing a large scale reinforcement effort, heavily protected by a major surface force, we had available to combat the landing only two new battleships, four destroyers and a few motor torpedo boats. Air support consisted of a small number of fighters on Guadalcanal.

The meager information obtainable on 13 November predicted the Jap landing force should arrive off Guadalcanal during the night of 14-15 November. The fightable GS ships at that time were anchored in Noumea, New Caledonia, replenishing fuel and supplies. Admiral Halsey, CinC, South Pacific, immediately ordered Vice-Adm. W.E. Lee to proceed with the battleships *Washington* and *South Dakota* and four destroyers, so as to arrive at an intercepting position west of Guadalcanal about midnight the 14-15 November. Admiral Lee's "aim" was to prevent Jap reinforcement of Guadalcanal.

Task Group 38.4 as the group was designated, departed Noumea and approached the southwest coast of Guadalcanal the evening of November 14 after an uneventful trip. However, repeated requests to the Army for air cover had been of no avail and it was feared we might have been spotted by a Jap snooper, thus leading to severe repercussions in the form of air and possibly submarine attacks during the approach.

Excitement throughout the *Washington* grew intense as the long evening wore on and our approach to the intercepting point came closer. Men remained at, or near, their battle stations even though "General Quarters" had not been sounded. Eventually, complete darkness set in, only to be erased, all too soon, by a bright full moon. The sea was glassy, with not even a whisper of wind to ripple the surface.

Savo Island is a small dot three miles in diameter located about four miles north of the western tip of Guadalcanal. Other islands to the north and east serve to form a nearly land-locked harbor with Guadalcanal the southern boundary. This sea area had already become known as "Iron Bottom Bay" because of the number of Jap and Allied ships sunk there.

As main battery spotter, my action station was in the foretop some 110 feet above the sea. As a result, from a temporary vantage point on top of the 16-inch turret director, the outline of Savo Island was clearly visible in the moonlight as we approached at midnight. The smell of tropical flowers was heavy in the air and the absolute stillness of an apparently perfect autumn night was broken only by occasional rifle shots from the front of Guadalcanal. The crew spoke in whispers, or not at all - the intensity was gripping. The entire ship's company knew that, if we hadn't arrived too late, we were in for the bitterest sort of showdown.

Our source was in column, the four destroyers leading, followed by the *Washington* and *South Dakota*. As we moved slowly up the west coast of Savo, some eight miles distant, it was apparent that our radars would have difficulty picking up ships because of the strong land signals coming in from every direction.

It was, therefore, not entirely unexpected that there remained no evidence of a sea-going enemy as we rounded the northern tip of Savo and turned east into Iron Bottom Bay. Nor was there any break in the stillness as the Task Group was directed to turn south down the east coast of the island. However, at this juncture American voices were heard over the voice radio definitely indicating that our ships had been spotted by friendly forces who had mistaken us for Japs and that we were about to be attacked by our own motor torpedo boats. Admiral Lee promptly grabbed a microphone, called General Vandergrift by his first name after identifying himself as "Chink" Lee (both having served in China waters together) asked the General to call off his "dogs". Seconds later, instructions were heard going out to the motor torpedo boats that the forces they were preparing to attack were friendly. An awkward situation was thereby narrowly averted.

A few moments later our surface radar reported a contact on the starboard quarter of the *Washington*. Almost simultaneously, the *South Dakota* reported a similar contact. My director was immediately trained to the reported bearing, and at a distance of some eight nautical miles we were able to distinguish the hazy outline of a four-stack Jap cruiser. In half a minute a solution to the problem was reported by "Plot" and I requested permission to open fire. Authority was soon granted to all ships to commence firing and the battleships cut loose seconds thereafter. After three salvos from our 16-inch guns, the cruiser could no longer be seen nor could an echo be obtained on the radar scope. Firing ceased and the *South Dakota* reported seeing the cruiser roll over and sink.

This initial phase appeared satisfactorily completed, but only for a matter of minutes. As if controlled by a master switch and with no warning, the entire east coast line of Savo suddenly became dotted with white blobs of light which were all too evidently the accompaniment of heavy gun fire. We tried vainly to separate ship and shore radar echoes to no avail and finally commenced fire, using the shore line as a target in the hope of retaliating, at least in minor measure.

While this decidedly unsatisfactory melee was proceeding, three of our four leading destroyers received simultaneous torpedo hits. Two sank almost immediately, the third broke in two and disgorged thousands of gallons of intensely burning fuel oil. As the *Washington* neared this enormous funeral, pyre, dozens of the men could clearly be seen clinging to the floating wreckage in the midst of the blazing inferno. The screams of anguish and the smell of burning flesh were appalling. The *Washington* altered course slightly (away from the Jap force) to avoid the burning wreckage, unable to assist in any way. Our "aim" was to prevent enemy reinforcements from landing on Guadalcanal at any cost, but the sight of those burning men, almost scraping alongside our ship, is never to be forgotten. Those who succeeded in surviving the flames spent terrifying hours being attacked by sharks. The survivors were few.

THE BEGINNING
by Roland E. Buse

Some time in June as well as I remember, our Civil War troop train came into the Seattle area, much of my boot company men were with me and we were put up in the "receiving station" which is also called receiving barracks and every morning we were "mustered" and names of men who were to go aboard "their ships" were announced. The rest of us were put on "make work" working partners and all of us goofed off as much as we could get away with.

Getting fed here was a big thing in itself as we seemed to spend much of the day just waiting in the "Chow-line" that was because there just was so many of us.

Each night we'd go down to the "Beer Hall" to help our friend's celebrate their being assigned to a ship.

Each morning more and more men got ships, of all of these they were assigned to the *Washington*.

Day after day this went on, and at that point in time I figured one ship I wouldn't get was the *Washington*. I was really surprised one day, most of my boot company men were now gone, when my name was called out to go to the *Washington*.

Now this was in the Bremerton Navy Yard and the *Washington* was up in dry dock, undergoing a very big major overhaul because she had just finished a 14 month cruise in the Pacific and as such was just "worn out"

Each day we had a eight hour work day stocking our ship, a very real working party.

Also we got at least a eight hour fire watch, being next to either a "yard bird" welder or a man using a cutting torch. Yard birds were civilian worker's who were closing all the work to get our ship back into the war.

On the "fire watches" we always had a very large warm jacket, not to wear, but to use as a bed to sleep on, because when we come off watch we went back on the working party.

If we complained to our officer about being "over worked" we got a "pep talk" which said there's a war going on and we got to get this ship back into the water to invade Japan.

When we talked to any of the sailors who, had been in combat the conversation went like this. We said, hey we'd never see combat because the war in Europe is over and Japan is just about done. The reply was always the same, the war against Japan has not yet started. Sure we sank their entire navy but that was for small islands all over the Pacific now we are going after their own islands, Japan itself and now they are showing us how they can really fight.

Just to prove that they were right, all one had to do was walk down the "waterfront" and see most of our aircraft carriers in for bomb damage alone by kamikazes, alone in the first, won battle of Okinawa.

Yes we got Okinawa but the Japs sent most of our ships back to the states for repairs.

So I'd call all that a mixed bag.

Our life went on like this for all of July and part of August.

While all of this was going on, a bus would pull up to the ship on a Sunday loaded with our shipmates, they would get off and another equal number of men would board the bus to go for a ride. That ride was to Pacific beach gunnery school near Alberdeen Oregon.

This went on for some time until one day it was my turn to get on the bus.

When we got to this school, we'd learn all about what type of gun that we'd be assigned to in combat from what ever ship that we came from.

Mine was a bofor's 40mm anti-aircraft gun. This school had all kinds of small guns: 3 inches, 4 inches, 20mm-40mm and so on.

All day we'd study, some times fire, then at night, night practice.

This went on Sunday, Monday, Tuesday, then on Wednesday in the middle of the day, over the loud speaker, the order came for everyone to go outside for a short speech.

The speech was from the base Chaplain. It was very short, only two words. The war is over. Japan has surrendered.

Now back to the classroom. We did work just as hard as ever and on Sunday back on the bus to our ship.

What a difference, no more "double" working parties. The yard birds only worked during the days, but in a few days from then as I remember our ship was back in the water, and on a cruise through Puget Sound and out to sea.

Funny thing about this I was very busy doing some painting on the deck and didn't notice that no matter where I walked on the deck I couldn't see land. I figure that was because of very quiet waters, I never had any "motion" discomfort like seasickness.

We went down the Pacific Coast, to the Los Angeles Area of Southern California.

Several eventful things on this anchored off the coast of Long Beach. We watched from a distance. Life on the amusement park and wishing that we were there.

Landing crafts were used to take us ashore for liberty and whether we had any money or not - hey a sailor always goes ashore on liberty. This was nice because there was a lot to ask around there.

My good friend Ed Campbell who was from Ardmore, AL had a Uncle who, while being like Ed Campbell and myself a very poor person, who now lived and worked there.

We (Ed and I) spent an entire evening just riding around and looking at things his Uncle showed to us. I'll never forget how nice this all was.

Amazing things how beautiful the entire area was, the clear blue skies and clean air not at all how you see things out there these days.

Going down towards Panama the sun shone hotter and our necks got sort of sunburned.

We tied up on the Pacific side of Panama and went ashore one or more times on liberty before going through the Panama Canal.

While in the Los Angeles area we went back and forth out to sea to bombard a island which worked to us like a large lump of clay out there.

As I remember, there would have been about 10 days of this gunnery practice, like if we were still at war.

While on liberty we could buy things that we couldn't buy in the states like silk stockings and I bought some for my brothers' wives and they were very glad to get something that because of war time rationing they hadn't been able to buy since 1941.

While many of the fellows bought rum to drink, I don't remember buying only for myself but I suppose I had some, also Milwaukee beer brewed in Panama, also bananas which we never saw in the states during the war, 25 cents bought you more than you could eat.

Actually being in the canal zone was much like being in the states but the rest of Panama was a different world.

Going through the canal, it looked like the ship just about fit in there.

Looking out on the north side we saw the rusted out machinery abandoned by the French engineer. I believe his name was De Le Gyrtz, who dug out the Suez Canal in Egypt.

Whenever we got in the Atlantic side I looked back to watch our sister ship the USS *North Carolina* coming through the canal and that was a site I'll never forget. How rather high mountain peaks one on each side of the ship.

We cruised through the Caribbean sea up the Atlantic coast to the Philly Navy Yard. Our objective to be there for the Navy Day celebration, which at that time was quite a holiday at least in the Navy.

Life and liberty in Philly was just great, the people very friendly, and on one or more times, while on liberty we crossed the river threre to go on liberty in Camden, New Jersey.

When the war ended in May in Europe the army men wanted to go home, but for the most part, the answer was, "hey, there's still a big war going on in the Pacific."

After VJ Day, and they still weren't getting home, the soldier said, "it took us three years to get here, I suppose it will take us three years to get home."

To this the Navy said you will be home for Christmas.

The *Washington* and several other ships were then committed to the "Magic Carpet" that was to make it all happen.

When we got to Philly, for the most part we had full combat crew, about 2400 men, well they took most of them off leaving about 800 men to run the ship.

Sometime in mid November, we left Philly for South Hampton England.

On the trip over there one event I'll never forget, sometime during WWII, President Roosevelt moved up Thanksgiving Day one week, and we 800 men celebrated Thanksgiving Day with full holiday chow; turkey, ham, and all the very best.

Then we got into South Hampton and one half of the crew got liberty to go to London and I suppose other things in England of interest.

I myself and many others went on to London, and saw the King's Palace and many other places of interest, then back to our ship, along with 1600 army men, to New York City.

While going back we again celebrated Thanksgiving because many states celebrated it that day, including, I believe Wisconsin, because we were Republicans and did not agree with FDR

Admiral Lee aboard the USS Washington.

on his idea when Thanksgiving Day should really be.

Crossing the Atlantic was more or less uneventful, and we went into the very heart of New York City.

I suppose we were in New York for a few days, but not to many and it was back to England for more soldiers.

Again as I remember the trip was rather uneventful. We had maybe one day of liberty and I stayed in the South Hampton that day and looked over the sights of this poor bombed out city.

At one time I went into a pub and had one more bitters which to me lived up to its name, which was no where as good as our Milwaukee beer. While sitting there I asked an Englishman sitting next to me, "hey how did this town get so bombed out?" But according to him, I best remember him saying, was a lot of the damage came during the 1940 Blitz, but even much more from the V-1 Buzz Bombs.

At one time I stood near the ship watching the army men boarding our ship for their trip home.

I even heard one soldier saying to another, it looks like they are putting us down in the basement.

Shortly after we were again out to sea, headed home, we ran into a storm. It was said, as this storm was getting worse the other ships left us; saying this storm was going to get too bad to keep on going, but our captain said, I got a battleship and we can get through anything.

The waves came over the entire main deck and no one was allowed "top side"

However one or more men were out there and one man was washed overboard.

It was said that the captain ordered the ship to go back to look for this sailor and they found him, and of course took him back on board, something the "old salts" said would not have been done in war time combat conditions.

We hit into a big wave and all the time the ship would just "shudder" and seemed to for some minutes sort of stand still.

Other times the ship would rock to either one side or the other, causing the men to say, "hey can we walk up the bulk head, or the walls of the compartments are called."

Water kept coming into the ship from the ventilator and caused quite a bit of flooding.

It was so bad in my sleeping compartment that one morning I woke up to find my shoes floating right next to me as I slept in a bottom bunk.

I guess the worst thing for us in this storm was the food, the lack of it.

Because of the rough weather our cooks could not cook anything and we were reduced to just eating sandwiches which were really rationed, meaning we didn't get too many per meal.

Although I was normally in the 4th Div. at the beginning of our trip to England I was assigned for mess duty, and this job was to work where all of our trays and forks, knives and so on were washed between each meal. This was a very busy job getting everything on this washed between each meal.

In the navy any type of KP is considered a privilege including this job, which also meant every night liberty while in port.

I guess everyone of us sailors were hungry but worse for us young guys, I myself was 18 years old then.

Because of this prolonged hunger one of my friends, Melvin Morton, also one of the younger men, with a very big appetite, came to my sleeping compartment one night thinking that because of my KP assignment I could get him some extra food, which I could have done under normal conditions. Now I had to tell him, I can't get enough to eat myself, the only thing that you can do is to go to the "mess" compartment where the raw carrots, in big 50 lb bags were temporarily stored. All of us were swiping these carrots and I often wondered how many of these big bags were emptied.

These carrots were brought aboard just before we left Philly, and we never had the time to put them where they really were supposed to be.

The soldiers in one way were better off then than we were. It seems that they from time to time on the move always were able to stow away some extra rations and it seemed like all of them had some of these.

On this one thing I'll never forget, while walking through a "army" compartment, a soldier said to me, hey sailor, you hungry. I said you damn right I am, and he tossed a boxed ration to me which I quickly opened and started to "gobble it" up. I don't remember what it was, but I thanked him for it, and I said this is really good, and he said to me, you wouldn't think so if you had to eat them for three years.

One funny thing about this bad storm was, the bad conditions bothered and worried the "old saltz" much more than us guys fresh out of boot camp and that was because the fact that these fellows had been through so much and so many storms of one kind or another, they had never been in one this bad.

I believe that might have been the first time in my life where I said either to myself, to others or both, what is the difference between being ignorant, and being brave?

I mean I had such great confidence in our ship, its officers and even ourselves, that except for some discomfort I really wasn't worried at all.

As we got closer to the states the water calmed down, and we got into New York City, which meant seeing our army buddies go off, hopefully back to their homes, and to us to give half the crew a Christmas leave, meaning that all of us got to go home, one half for Christmas, the other half for New Year. I got to go home for New Year.

Boy what a time that was. My family, friends, and everyone were glad to see me, and everyone else treated me like a conquering hero.

An example, if I went into a tavern to get a drink, almost any one there would like to buy me one. Also walking on the street just about anyone not only would offer you a ride but offer to take you to where you wanted to go.

I think that I had about a weeks leave and a one day delayed train ride back to New York and my ships, and I never was punished for coming back one day late, as one officer told me, they most likely over looked it for a lot of reasons, just one being bad weather.

A short time after we were back in New York we shipped over to Boston.

I'll always remember Boston as a friendly city mostly because most of the people living there had some thing to do with being at sea.

A place where merchant seaman were regarded as heroes.

Sometime in March or April of 1946 we went on a cruise down the Atlantic and through Chesapeake Bay to anchor off Annapolis a most holy city.

First of all I believe we had a Admiral on board and he simply wanted to go to Annapolis, never mind taking a train or driving a car there, take a battleship.

I say most holy city because it was a city made up of only naval cadets and naval officers.

When we went ashore for liberty we had to ride some way out of Annapolis to either Baltimore or Washington, DC.

I don't remember how I got to Washington, DC, but I suppose it was either a taxi cab or bus. If any enlisted sailor was caught in Annapolis without leave papers showing that he actually was home on leave there he'd be arrested by the shore patrol.

Of course the same rule I suppose applied to a sailor on liberty, but one would need more than a liberty card.

Any way liberty in Washington, DC was a most interesting place. Our fascinating countries capitol, there was so much to see. The white House, home of President Harry S. Truman, the Jefferson, Lincoln, Washington monuments and so much more including a sort of side visit to Mt. Vernon, home of George Washington.

This really was a trip that I'll never forget. One reason being not too many Americans could afford to go visit their countries capitol in the 1940s. Quite a time later, going in and out of Chesapeake Bay, I feel that Chesapeake Bay is just one big overgrown marsh.

There is a channel cut through the center of it in which all ships must travel, marked with buoys. Everyone staying out of this channel is sure to run aground.

A trip up the Atlantic coast and we were back in Boston.

The odd thing about, after the trip to Annapolis was like some kind of "time warp" You had winter in Boston, then went into spring, then back into winter.

Being back in Boston was pretty much uneventful except for two things, one is to each night, even late at night to read who was to get off the ship for discharge.

The other things was a great big birthday party given to I guess everybody to celebrate, I believe the commissioning of the ship.

One night in May I came aboard the ship and read who was getting off to get discharged and near the bottom of the list was my name. I couldn't believe it. It meant getting up extra early after a hard night of liberty to pack my sea bag and go off to the Fargo building.

Now the Fargo building was just a very big whorehouse with a lot of bunk's in it. If you wanted to eat you had to go to another building and like any other receiving station, a long chow line. I don't remember ever eating there, I'd simply go back on board the *Washington,* where I knew my way around. I don't remember how many days I layed around in Boston waiting for a train ride out, but one night I remember running into this big birthday party which I guess would have been for officers as well as enlisted men.

The one thing that I'll always remember was being out on the street feeling no pain, and actually bumping into Mr. John Buse, and he too was not feeling any pain, put his arm around me and said, well if it ain't my long lost cousin.

Good thing there were no SP's around for it certainly was not the proper way for an enlisted man to be with an officer.

Now as to this officer, John Buse, one time very early on my boarding the *Washington,* I was summoned up to the JOD to meet a navy ensign.

Now as I kind of look back at this it must have been in port, because you have OD officer of the deck, which is a LT, the JOD is junior officer of the deck, an ensign.

The JOD has one enlisted man with him and this man summoned me to meet the JOD. The JOD asked me many personal questions, like where I was from, and a whole lot of other thinks, like who my father was and how long my family had been in America.

I told him my fathers family came from some small county in north central Europe which in about 1870 became Germany, so therefore I suppose I was of German descent.

He also asked about what year my ancestors came here, and I said I guess the early 1800s, because my father was born here in 1871. The he asked me if I had any questions of him? I said, yes, why did you ask me all those questions?

To this he said simply, You and I have the same last name. Now my ancestors also came from Germany 300 years or so anyway, I suppose before the Revolutionary War.

He then asked me on what side in the war did your family fight on? He meant the Civil War.

To this I said, as far as I know they didn't for some reason fight in the war and if they had it would have been with the North because of all the wars that my father ever talked about was the Civil War and he'd been "abolishinist", meaning he was very much against slavery.

He said that being from South Carolina his family had fought for the South.

From then on we sort of became friends and the men in my 4th Div. always said, here is a man we'd fight to go to hell with him. He's just that great. Meaning he was very well like by all the enlisted men. I will always remember him as one great guy.

After a few days in the Fargo building I got on a train to Great Lakes for discharge and home to Milwaukee and that is about it, like maybe May 20, 1946.

TURKEY DINNER
by Carl P. Parrett

Carl came aboard in New York after Zero became missing, and ship left for Southampton, England to transport soldiers to the United States December 1945.

The soldiers came aboard and we had the ship spotless. They felt that this was the branch of service to be with until we got to sea and got in a bad storm. The soldiers were told not to go topside, but, they went up anyway. They came back below like a bunch of drowned rats, along with being seasick. They divorced themselves from the Navy right away.

50 Caliber Machine Guns.

Some of the old-timers aboard said it was a worse storm than the typhoons that were in the Pacific. On this one occasion during the storm, they were to have turkey for dinner. Some of the hatches had been left open by the soldiers and the turkeys began to roll around on the mess hall deck. I can still remember those turkeys hitting one bulkhead and the ship would roll and the turkeys would slide across the deck in the other direction. Anyway, we had cold cuts that evening.

We averaged one knot per hour for three days. The captain opened up the throttle after we got out of the storm and we still made it into New York a couple of days before Christmas.

BATTLESHIP X
by Bud Gore, '39

Shipmate: Captain Paul Gray's "The Ill Fated Cruise of Battleship X" (*Shipmate*, December 1995) discusses at some length the Task Force 64 night action of 14-15 November 1942 off Guadalcanal. It is difficult to know where to start corrective surgery, but I think it might be helpful if I established some highly respected references:

From *The Encyclopedia Of Military History, 3500 B.C. To The Present*, R. Ernest Dupuy and Trevor N. Dupuy, Harper and Rowe, New York and Evanston, 1970.

"...The opponents met at close range in Ironbottom Sound, just south of Savo Island. Two of the American destroyers were quickly sunk and the other two put out of action. The two battleships, however, closed boldly with the Japanese, who concentrated their fire on *South Dakota,** causing an electrical power failure and putting her out of action for the rest of the engagement. Briefly, it was a battle between *Washington* and 14 Japanese warships. The odds were quickly lessened, however as (RAdm. Willis A.) Lee calmly concentrated *Washington's* radar-directed guns against *Kirishima*, leaving her and a destroyer in sinking condition. (Japanese VAdm. Nobutake) Kondo now withdrew. The naval battle of Guadalcanal was ended..."

From *History of United States Naval Operations in World War II*, Volume V, Samuel Eliot Morison, Little Brown, Boston.

"...again, and not for the last time, the Japanese taught the Americans a lesson in the use of torpedoes. *South Dakota* was lucky to escape alive. *Washington*, conned by Captain Glen Davis and directed by Admiral Lee with a skill and imperturbability worthy of her eponym, saved the day for the United States..."

From Guadalcanal, *The Definitive Account Of The Landmark Battle*, Richard B. Frank, Penguin Books, 1990.

"...Lee never allowed the action to degenerate into a nautical brawl, because he formulated a workable plan and then adhered to it, even after every ship in his task force except *Washington* was sunk or forced to retire... The tactical formation chosen by Lee permitted his destroyers to perform their screening function... And above all the skillful touch of Captain Davis at the conn of *Washington* and the performance of his crew. Regrettably, security concerns masked *Washington's* vital role and, instead, wholly disproportionate credit went to *South Dakota*, which went stateside for repairs..."

Incidentally, my wife brought the discrepancies in Captain Gray's article to my attention.

*The reason the Japanese focused their fire on *South Dakota*, well-known among *Washington* personnel from the time it happened, is documented in Dr. Frank's book. Captain Davis conned *Washington* to place the fiery stricken destroyers to starboard to keep his ship concealed... Unfortunately, *South Dakota* changed course to put the sinking vessels to port, which silhouetted her for the enemy...

South Pacific Report
Panama Canal WWII
August 1942
by John A. Brown, R. Div.

Brownie was a new boot, assigned to R. Division work force, however, each recruit was required to serve three months mess hallduty. My job was to carry dirty trays to the scullery and return clean trays to holding cabinets. I slept in a hammock in mess hall, we attended quarters, and were dressed in uniform of the day. As the ship was moving through the Panama Canal to the Pacific Ocean, and my work assignment completed, there was a period of free time. This particular day I went to the shipfitter shop and sat on a stool near the outside doorway reading the ship's news. Soon I heard voices then shouting. I looked toward the main deck and an officer was talking and motioning to someone above me, possibly the blacksmith shop, and words were being exchanged between the two persons. Not being any of my business, I turned and laid down on the work bench and continued reading. Soon the officer that was at quarters, on the main deck, came into our shop. He asked our Chief Siniard, who was the last person near doorway, I volunteered that I had been sitting there then moved to the bench. Officer, told Siniard to put Brownie on report. He said "what for, he hasn't done anything wrong." Officer replied, "Put him on report now or I will put you on report." Later we were both summoned to Executive Officer mast and Mr. Ayrault read off seven charges against me. He said I did not look like the type of person to violate these Navy rules. We both told the Executive Officer Ayrault, that we had no idea what the problem was or who with. Mr. Ayrault believed us and said take this charge sheet and have the accusing officer to release Brownie from these charges, that he was not the person involved in this dispute. Siniard and Brownie went to the officers stateroom and he balked about signing it. He said well after all he was out of uniform and not at quarters; I said, "but I" and the chief stepped on my foot to close down my anger at an officer with scrambled eggs on his cap. He probably never found out who he had the problem with. Case closed.

South Pacific - 1944
Island of Saipan and Tinian
by John A. Brown, R. Div.

Fellow shipmate, George Arnold, and I from the R. Division were on deck while ship was at anchor and watched the flares explode and light up the battle area and watched our troops being driven into the water. Boats appeared, picked them up and returned them to a safe area. We watched the native Japanese committing suicide and bodies floating to sea among debris. In later years, as a plumber on a federal housing development, my plumbing boss was Jack Schultz, a former Marine. He related how on Saipan, Marines were being killed by a sniper well-hidden, and when they located him he had been in the fallen smokestack of a sugar mill in the town of Garapan. I told him that the mill was our target and we destroyed it.

Also, a mysterious man was brought aboard the carrier with our command and related that he was the one trying to tell our forces where military installations were. I read a story on him in a *True* magazine later. The man was ordered to leave his base and refused. He stayed with the natives on Saipan and Tinian. He was sabotaging the Japanese. He finally came home and was with the Department of the Interior as a fire watcher in Utah, he was a true American hero, enough said.

South Pacific, Plane,
Potato, WWII
by John A. Brown, R. Div.

One day I was standing outside the carpenter shop and I noticed that the cloud cover was real low and a Japanese plane just dropped out of the clouds. It was close enough that the pilot and I stared at each other. Our ship was carrying several sacks of potatoes and later I thought, if I had a potato, I could have thrown it and hit the pilot. He was that close. Seeing our ship and possibly the American flag, he gunned the engine as he passed over the USS *Alabama*; their antiaircraft guns fired straight up, but missed him.

Our 20mm crews on watch duty requested permission to fire and were denied because the officer in their command did not see the plane. I watched the plane heading toward a carrier. I don't believe anyone ever got another shot at the plane as he left the area. This incident happened in a matter of seconds. Witnessed by Brownie.

South Pacific
Sharpe Discharge
by John A. Brown, R. Div.

Bernard Sharpe, Atlantic, *Iowa* plumber, was assigned to the shipfitter shop with the plumbing gang. He made every morning and afternoon sick calls in sick bay. So, we were denied his services and there were only six men to take care of this battleship. In repair one day while on duty, a plot was made up to give Bernard a medical discharge. Brownie engaged Sharpe in conversation in the carpenter shop when the phone rang. Schauer read from a prepared script and he bought the story. Sharpe, moved too quick for us and came to Brownie to write up his last 10 days of ailments. At sick bay he told the pharmist mate the story and he called the doctor and was told to tell the victim someone was pulling his leg. The doctor was asleep. Sharpe came to Brownie who was standing in the chow line and dragged, told him he knew who pulled this on him. Eventually, he found out, Schauer, Lowman, Hartsell, and for about a year later he confronted Brownie and we had a real good laugh. Years later, he would call Brownie and chuckle about it.

South Pacific, Merritt Ring,
WWII
by John A. Brown, R. Div.

Carl Riley CM1/c and Brownie were given a damage control assignment of replacing gaskets in the port holes. We went to the Executive Officer's office and checked out the key to the admiral's guest room. Carl opened the door and moved to the left toward a port hole; Brownie went to the right and as he passed a small table, he noticed a ring on it. He picked it up and tried it on his finger then walked over to show Carl. Carl remarked that maybe it was stolen. We looked inside the ring and it said USN Robert Merritt graduate of US Naval Academy. Being concerned that it might be stolen, Brownie returned it to the table and moved again toward a port hole. Carl called out to grab the ring and another person made a move to the ring, but Brownie beat him to it. The stateroom was unoccupied at the time, Flag was not on board.

We returned the key and gave the ring to a yeoman, and he said he would fill out a form describing the incident. Later, Brownie was required to attend an executive officers mast and was commended by Executive Officer Walsh who recommended that I appear at Captains Mast. Brownie was escorted to Captains Mast by the chief master at arms, line officers formed an aisle and the bugler announced the Captain approaching. Captain James Maher read the same document, commended me and said he could not award a medal for honesty; however, he would give a character and honesty recommendation when advancing in rate. Captain James Maher shook my hand for an estended amount of time. It was a beautiful day in my Navy career and life.

South Pacific Void
Distillery WWII
by John A. Brown, R. Div.

At one time my work assignment was the tool room on the third deck, doing the maintenance and issuing tools. One day I opened up the void beneath it and noticed that it was small and proceeded to clean it. I dumped fresh water in it then sugar and raisins. Result a nice raisin jack drink. On November 14-15, 1942 I had dropped a jug in it and my shipmates in Repair 4-1 checked it out, and it seemed to fortify our spirits and courage.

South Pacific Galley, WWII
by John A. Brown, R. Div.

George Arnold and Brownie were serving in the plumbing gang at this time. We were walking through the mess hall one day and observed a cook slicing a ham. I asked Geogre if he would like a ham sandwich and ordered two. The cook did not look to see who we were or even cared. So, we decided to educate the new first class cook on his first meal watch on our ship. We proceeded to the third deck and turned off both the cold and hot water to the galley. We then hurried to the shipfitter and carpenter shop and soon the phone rang for a plumber. We told the caller none was around. We saw the cook heading to our area and we went in the carpenter shop. Again, he was told they would convey his message. He said he only had 45 more minutes to have the meal ready. On leaving the cook went down one ladder and we followed down the other ladder. We approached the half door to galley and the cook called out "are you the plumbers." I said, "Yes." He said, "We have no water." We tried the faucets and sure enough, no water. I left to check and returned to third deck and opened the valves. I returned to the galley and bled air out of the lines and water service was restored. The cook thanked us and said if we ever needed a favor just let him know, and I replied, "How about fixing us two ham sandwiches," and he fixed us two real hefty ones. Education completed.

South Pacific, Lost Anchor WWII
by John A. Brown, R. Div.

The R. Division was assigned anchor duty and Brownie served in the anchor windlass room when ship anchored or left harbors. Chiefs and first class served topside and we talked by phone. Brownie's job was to set up the gear machinery to lock or unlock and a machinist mate ran the motor. This particular day I performed my duty and anchor chain started moving over my head, then it picked up speed and really went very fast. I ran to the brake and it was locked in place and would not turn. The machinist mate bailed out and I was alone. The sound was deafening and then the end came by and silence as the machinery stopped. Two officers came to the scuttle and looked down at me and did not identify themselves. I was on the phones calling, "topside-topside" and no one answered. On topside I was told our division men jumped behind the manager and someone went over the side; the chain hit the 20mm shields and disappeared. No one was injured.

Later, Brownie was on duty yoke patrol and manned the anchor windlass and Len Lewis, shippfitter first class, was working topside when the grapplin hook caught on the anchor, then the deck crews took over and retrieved the anchor and chain. They stretched it along the deck and chipped and repainted; it was restored to its original status and returned to the chain locker.

South Pacific Indiana Collision, WWII
by John A. Brown, R. Div.

Brownie, while serving on yoke patrol, R. Division would be required to work with the fueling crew to take fuel aboard and also dispense fuel to destroyers, cruisers, carriers if needed. I served the 8:00 p.m. to midnight shift and was relieved and went to bed. At about 0400, a message awakened the crew saying, "Stand by for collision," I jumped up and grabbed my clothes and shoes. I figured maybe a destroyer tangled with our lifeline and would be minor since I knew we had been fueling cans. Then, another voice said, "All hands stand by for collision to starboard." That's when I headed to port side, was in the passageway connecting where pay records were displayed, the ship hit very hard and I was knocked off my feet but uninjured. Ensign Dean, the R. Division officer and damage control, came into our berthing compartment calling for our men to go forward immediately to assist in damage area. At this time we, who were below decks, did not know what had happened or that it was the *Indiana*, that crossed our bow. We shored up the bulkheads as we had been trained to do, reinforcing those that were still intact. Some water came in and we manned pumps, bringing it under control. We stood watches there and it was scary. While searching the damaged area, we saw Lieutenant Turner with a steel beam across his head. He was deceased. I had seen him the day before in a mess hall teaching a class. Other stories will tell other parts of this incident.

South Pacific - Invisible Bug
by John A. Brown, R. Div.

Robert Shaffer and I were always dreaming up a way to entertain our shipmates. Very successful was a bug that we would suddenly catch and stretch it across the passageway and dare anyone to break it. Some mates went to their knees and crawled under. I pulled this trick in the carpenter shop one day and no one was laughing as usual. Two officers said maybe you ought to send Brownie to sick bay to be checked out, then everyone laughed as did I.

We invented another unseen bug described as yellow with black stripe on the back, long legs and antennas. In the R. Division passageway, we took a mop and broom and began swinging at the electrical cables as if we saw it. An officer came by and looked under the scuttlebutt and moved on. One shipmate wanted to be boosted up on top of a locker so the broom would reach a higher level. Shaffer and I backed into the division and watched as the audience moved on and left the fellow yelling for someone to help him down. We really enjoyed this. Bob returned to Ohio and I visited him several times and we enjoyed our fun stories. Bob is now deceased.

South Pacific Shark At Tonga Tabu September 1942
by John A. Brown, R. Div.

The *Washington* made runs to Guadalcanal on patrol for five weeks and carried out her assignments without a destroyer escort and alone from Tonga Tabu. One day while at the friendly island of Tonga Tabu, a motor launch left the ship with a swimming party; the coxswain anchored between the ship and island and the best swimmers dived over the side and swam toward the island. Not being a good swimmer, I stayed close by the launch. A shipmate stood up and pointed out a shark that appeared and shouted "Shark." I swam back and climbed back aboard and saw a long white shark that someone thought was a sand shark. Shipmates closest to the island were told to swim on it and ones close by to return to the launch. We proceeded to circle the island and finally found a small dock to retrieve our shipmates. We took a short walk and came upon the Queen of Tonga with native girls making baskets. She was very cordial and gave us tea and cookies. We returned to the ship, safe and unhurt, with a memory of a scary liberty in Tonga.

South Pacific, Porter Chicken
by John A. Brown, R. Div.

One day while working with the damage control department, we were air testing compartments and used duck seal to close up any cracks or holes in bulkheads, making them watertight.

On this day we were working in the freezer where frozen food was stored, a fellow shipmate from the R. Division (Ralph Porter of Pine Bluff, AR) came in and asked if he could have a chicken, and I told him he was on his own to do whatever. He put a couple of chickens in a sack and left. I came up the ladder and called out, "chicken thief, chicken thief" and you should have seen those long legs move. He laughed about it later and said I scared him so he ran.

North Atlantic, Admiral Wilcox March 27, 1942
by John A. Brown, R. Div.

Joe Reid, shipfitter first class, R. Division and Brownie, shipfitter striker, were assigned to repair plumbing in the admiral's head. No one was there when we went in and permission was granted. Joe returned to the shop as he needed a part to finish the job. I waited in the head and finally decided I would rather wait in passageway. With the tool tray in my right hand I proceeded in to the large room and there was Admiral Wilcox, pacing back and forth and smoking a cigarette. Finally, he seen me and wanted to know what I was doing in his quarters. I failed to salute him and told him we were working on the head. He said, "What do you want." I said, "Which door did I come in." He pointed and the door opened and there was Joe coming back in. He immediately saluted him and related why we were there. We finished the repair and left the quarters of Mr. Wilcox. Later, he disappeared, circumstances unknown. He was the first admiral to ever have been lost at sea.

A Reunion - 30 Years Later

Story by Charles "Chips" A. Herget, CCM, R. Div., USS Washington, now deceased. Chips wrote the book, Dear Shipmates, and this story is from his book.

Chips was ordered to the new construction, pre-commissioning and outfitting the USS *Washington* (BB-56) at Philadelphia, PA, May 1941. One of our commissioning crew members was a quartermaster. He was well-known and very popular throughout the ship. He was always ready to go ashore and usually managed to be included in the first liberty party. Whenever we hit port, his destination was the first bar. He was a good sociable drinker, but after a few drinks usually got sleepy (caused no doubt from standing too many mid-watches) and passed out. When it came time to return to the ship those still capable would practically carry this shipmate back aboard. This task often fell to a boatswain's mate, one of his drinking partners and a very close friend. However, after a few too many times, it was decided something should be done to cure the QM of this "passing out" habit.

During our visit to San Juan, Puerto Rico, our shipmate passed out and fell asleep face down. When the time came to arouse him for his return to the ship, it was discovered that while asleep someone had neatly cut the "stern sheets" out of his trousers. In order to cover his nakedness, it was necessary to remove his jumper and use the sleeves as tie string to drape it as an apron, covering his rear. It was an embarrassing situation, but it had a very effective and sobering effect. To my knowledge our shipmate, thereafter, managed to remain in a more or less sober upright posture, with sufficient propulsion power to navigate a return course to the ship.

Almost 30 years later at a ship's reunion, I asked the QM if he ever learned who it was that cut the "stern sheets" out of his trousers. He answered that a few years later, he was told it was the Fourth Division BM. He asked if he was still living and I answered yes and said I expected him to attend. He said he would be looking forward to meeting him. I took a position near the door, so I could check those arriving. I had recently met the BM and he lived not too far from me and worked in Philadelphia. He was a member of the Fleet Reserve Association, hence we met occasionally. When he arrived at the entrance door, I approached him and said, "I have someone here who's anxious to meet you and please don't mention your name, I am curious to see if he recognizes you or you he." I escorted the BM over to where the QM was sitting, addressing him by his Christian name (which few knew him by). I said "John, do you recognize this fellow?" He stood up and stared for a moment then answered no. I said "Well before I introduce you two old shipmates, I want you to shake hands." As they shook hands I said, "John, this is that old drinking partner of yours, that Fourth Division Boatswain's Mate whom you asked about. They hadn't laid eyes on each other in 28 years. Both had remained in the Navy and had completed 30 years service shortly after WWII. Both had served continuously at sea during the conflict and had some horrendous experiences. They had a grand reunion, and this time it was the BM who passed out and the QM who saw to it that his old shipmate got home okay, with his "stern sheets" intact.

WWI To Pearl And Midway

Following is a page from, The United States Navy 200 Years, by Edward L. Beach, Captain, USN (Ret.) 1986.

Not quite a year after Pearl Harbor, the new *Washington* achieved a first for American battleships in a ship-to-ship engagement with the Japanese *Kirishima*. It was the first time an American battlewagon had engaged and defeated an enemy of the same class since the classic battle between the *Monitor* and *Merrimack*. For a comparison of the opposing ships, however, it is only fair to note that *Kirishima* mounted eight 14-inch guns and had been built in 1915 (with extensive modernization later upping her speed to a reported 30 knots), and that she had within the hour put our very newest battleship, the *South Dakota*, out of action with disabling, though superficial, damage.

Her initial antagonist were two: *Washington* and *South Dakota*, completed in 1941 and 1942 respectively, each with nine 16-inch guns and 27 knots speed. *Kirishima*, supported by two heavy cruisers and two destroyers, came upon the *South Dakota*, which had become separated from her consort, and achieved early hits. Unfortunately, the injuries were to *South Dakota's* fire-control equipment, without which she could not aim her guns accurately, and this forced her to leave the combat area. The *Washington*, however, superbly trained and thoroughly shaken down, was arguably the most efficient surface warship in our Navy at that moment. She had recently been fitted with a new radar fire-control set in which her crew and the admiral on board, Willis A. Lee, had great confidence. Now berefit of supporting cruisers or destroyers (which had retired with the *South Dakota*), *Washington* determined to press the action to a decision and took on the entire Japanese force. Her guns flamed with speed and precision, and within seven minutes she pumped out 72 rounds of 16-inch shells aimed at *Kirishima* and 107 rounds of 5-inch aimed at the vessels accompanying her. How many hits the *Kirishima* received is unknown, for she was so badly damaged that she could no longer maneuver, and the Japanese admiral ordered her sunk by her remaining consorts.

But these battles in the Guadalcanal area, where most of the early ship-to-ship fighting took place, were not fleet actions of the traditional kind. They were individual single-ship or small squadron actions, more reminiscent of the Civil War sea fights or those of 1812 than of Jutland or any other of the famous battles of past epochs.

The main batteries of cruisers and battleships also received radar fire control. Electronic certainty was substituted for increasingly difficult long-range spotting of the fall of shot. It was this that enabled the *Washington* to demolish the *Kirishima* off Savo Island with the war not quite a year old.

Zero

Memoir Article on "Zero" ship's mascot, USS Washington (BB-56) served in 1st Division, WWII, by Edward J. McGuire, BM1/c.

Zero was residing with an Hawaiian family at Nanakula Beach, where we were sent for R&R, and proceeded to follow one Boyd Smith, BM2/c, 1st Division from Rocky Mount, NC back to the ship. Smith, was transferred later in 1943 to Stateside.

James Peadrick S1/c was in charge of Zero, Peadrick was permanent captain of the head and, therefore, nearly always available to care for Zero, and, needless to say, a strong bond developed between them. Peadrick was usually known as "Poop deck" or "Pappy," and his home was somewhere in the vicinity of Myrtle Beach, SC.

Zero lived a happy life on board. As he got older he would on occasion try to make love to a shoe or anything else left lying around. Like most dogs he would not mess in his own area and quickly learned where the dividing line was on the forecastle between the 1st and 2nd Divisions, which my fellow shipmate Ray Gough, BM1/c 2nd Division did not appreciate, but no fights developed over this.

Zero obtained numerous articles of war from shipmates who wanted to be a part of his life. He had his own custom made boatswain pipe which was obtained from one of the men in the R. Division. He had me make a pipe lanyard for him so that he could send a miniature pipe and lanyard to his young son and in return he made a small pipe for Zero. Zero, also, had a very sharp looking breast harness with his name engraved on it. The harness was made by one of the men in the 7th Division. Zero, also had a dress blue uniform, coxswain badge and all with his campaign ribbons and battle stars on it. I don't know who made the uniform, but whoever did make it, did a great job.

Zero went on liberty in many ports: Honolulu, Seattle, Panama, Philadelphia and New York, where he was treated first class. In one of the "Big Apple's" top restaurants, he was greeted like Halsey himself, even had his own VIP chair at our table and had his picture taken. I have one of these pictures at my home in the Upper Peninsula of Michigan.

What finally happened to Zero is what happened to most of us after the war. The ship was about to leave its pier on the Hudson River and proceed to South Hampton, England for a load of Army troops for their return home, when Zero just walked down the gangway to start his search for a mate. The OD and the rest of the quarter deck crew were new and just watched him go. Admiral Cooley was very concerned along with many others and contracted Walter Winchell. His broadcast informed the public about Zero being AWOL and offered a reward. We made our trip to England and back riding out a terrific storm with waves 50 feet straight up. All ship's turned back to England including the carrier, *Lake Champlain*, who lost a rudder, but our ship pushed on. Upon our arrival in New York, the ship was greeted by loads of reporters and camera men and people with dogs, black ones, white ones, tan ones, brown ones, all looking for the reward. Zero was never found, but he was a good sailor and I imagine some of his Hawaiian blood line is still around the Big Apple. This is the straight poop.

Warship Still On Guard

by Rex Smith

Ships are but boards, William Shakespeare-Upton.

The walls of the battleship USS *Washington*, which helped support American forces in the Pacific during WWII, are now shielding scientists at Brookhaven National Laboratory from lethal radioactive beams.

The *Washington* fought Japanese ships in the South Pacific, sinking the *Kirishima* and *Ayanami* at 3rd Battle of Savo Island, capture of Guadalcanal in 1942 to Okinawa in 1945. She earned 15 Battle Stars after 38 months overseas.

The ship was protected by armor of foot thick steel. When it was sold for scrap in 1960, pieces of the unusually thick hull were sold to the Brookhaven Laboratory in New York.

Now the steel is used to shield scientists and workers from beams of radioactive particles produced in an experiment. "We stop the beam from radiating people in the area by hitting it into a tremodous amount of steel," explained Bob Marascia, a Brookhaven engineer who designed the experiment.

The armor stands alongside anchors that Marascia believes held the submarine nets protecting American harbors during the war. The anchors and battleship walls create a steel barrier 20 feet thick, backed up by a 4-foot wall of dense concrete.

"It would be unbelievably expensive to buy steel of this thickness," Marascia said, "It's reused constantly."

RESCUE AT OKINAWA WWII

The following news story account was sent to the USS Washington Reunion Group, by former naval aviator, John C. Marlin, Elgin, IL, who served on the USS Essex and also served on the USS Washington (BB-56) for 24 hours. He is a member of the Reunion Group and will be in attendance in Mobile, AL. His war time name was Marcinkoska.

From: Fleet Home Town Distributor Center, America Fore Building, Chicago, IL. For immediate release: Editors are reminded that any man mentioned in this story may have become a casualty between the time the story was written and the editor receives it.

ABOARD A FAST BATTLESHIP OF THE CARRIER TASK FORCE

A youthful Corsair pilot is alive and safe today, thanks to the skill, courage and the opportune appearance of Lieutenant William E. Lemos, USN of Providence, RI. Senior aviator of this battleship and a past master at the controls of his Kingfisher seaplane.

The Corsair pilot is Ensign John Marcinkoska, USNR, of Murphysboro, IL, who found himself on a rubber liferaft, drifting toward an enemy shore, just 10 days after coming out to the combat zone. He had been in a flight of Corsair fighters making a late strike on enemy targets. He encountered heavy anti-aircraft fire which shattered an oil line and his motor conked out. He had made a successful water landing four or five miles from land. After he had been in the water 15 minutes, Lieutenant Lemos passed high overhead, returning to his ship from a long trip with urgent mail and photographs. Seeing the great splotch of dye-marker the Ensign had put in the water, he dropped down to investigate. Lieutenant Lemos had no rescue equipment. He had no radio and no gasoline gauges, these having been knocked out by a hard landing shortly before. The sea was rough with 10 foot crests and a 25-knot wind blowing Ensign Marcinkoska steadily toward enemy territory.

All the conditions were against a successful rescue. However, Lieutenant Lemos picked his moment and made a landing only 75 feet from the raft. With only a 10-foot piece of cotton line he had used for lashing mail bags, Lieutenant Lemos and rear seaman, Henry G. Offney, aviation radioman second class, Baltimore, MD, hauled the drenched fighter pilot aboard. Ensign Marcinkoska returned to his carrier the next day.

Lieutenant Lemos graduated from the US Naval Academy in 1941, serving two years aboard the sister ship, USS North Carolina before his flight training at Pensacola, FL. He is the son of Mr. and Mrs. Albert Lemos, Riverside, RI. His wife and his year old son live in Amherst, MA, while he is on duty at sea. Lieutenant Lemos received the Air Medal for his low altitude flights over Iwo Jima.

MAN OVERBOARD!

by Winston Jordan

When the cry went up on board the battleship *Washington*, no one knew who the "man overboard" was, and after they discovered who it was, they puzzled over how it could have happened.

"Man overboard!" The young gunner screamed. Moments before, his hands had tightened on the splinter shield of the gun he was braced against. About 20 feet from the ship, rising on a long, gray swell, was a man face down in the water, being swiftly left astern. In that instant, while the man was atop the wave, Seaman Second Class M.D. Stanford thought he saw an arm rise in an effort to swim.

"Man overboard!" he called again, running aft, pointing toward the wake. Others took up the cry.

The ship was the USS *Washington* (BB-56), flagship of Rear Admiral John Walter Wilcox Jr., Commander, Battleships, Atlantic Fleet, and Commander, Task Force 39. It was 1030, Friday, March 27, 1942.

Admiral Wilcox was leading Task Force 39 from Casco Bay, ME to Scapa Flow, where it would operate as part of the British Home Fleet. The 45,000-ton Washington was at the right front of the formation, acting as guide. Splitting the battleship's wake, 1,000 yards astern, was the heavy cruiser, *Tuscaloosa* (CA-37). Approximately 1,500 yards off the *Washington's* port beam was the *Wichita* (CA-45), which flew the two-starred flag of Rear Admiral Robert C. Giffen, Commander, Cruiser Division Seven. The carrier *Wasp* (CV-7) was 1,000 yards astern of the *Wichita*. Eight destroyers formed a semicircular screen beginning slightly forward of the *Wasp's* port beam, and reaching to slightly forward of the *Tuscaloos's* starboard beam. They were: the *Wainwright* (DD-419), *Lang* (DD-399), *Sterett* (DD-407), *Wilson* (DD-408), *Plunkett* (DD-431), *Madison* (DD-425), *Livemore* (DD-429) and *Ellyson* (DD-454).

The North Atlantic was cold and mean that morning. Task Force 39 had zigzagged all night, smashing its way at 18 knots through a quartering sea state six from the northwest. The water was 36° Fahrenheit. Snow and occasional rain reduced visibility to less than a mile. A chilling 24- to 30-knot wind whipped from the north, northwest, and green water swept across the main deck. In the captain's night order book, on the bridge, Captain H.H.J. Benson left this note: "While seas are coming over the decks keep men off the forecastle, port side main deck, and main deck aft."

Around 0830, on the morning of the 27th, Captain John L. Hall Jr., chief of staff and aide to Rear Admiral Wilcox, was in the *Washington's* flag plot. Captain Benson called to inform Hall that the ship was taking water over the main deck aft and endangering one of the aircraft. He asked permission to change course to starboard for about 30 minutes to secure it. Hall told Admiral Wilcox, suggesting two 20° course changes to bring them to 130°. They would remain at 18 knots and, after the plane was secured, resume zigzagging on the base course of 090°. The Admiral approved and at 1013 the task force ceased zigzagging and steadied on 130°.

The deck and aviation divisions set about securing their areas. The order to stay clear of the main deck was lifted while the ship was on 130°.

Admiral Wilcox walked aft to where the plane was being secured. "How are things going?" he asked Lieutenant (jg) Thomas Washington.

"Everything's fine, sir." Washington replied. "The plane isn't damaged. Just the spare float." The Admiral nodded and walked forward of Turret 3, crossing to the port side.

Chief Boatswain Earl Brown was inspecting the work of the men securing the main deck port side when the Admiral approached.

"Attention on deck!" called Brown, saluting.

"Have your men carry on, bosun," Wilcox said. "I see you have the ship well lashed down." Then he looked forward and said, "Is there a ladder leading to the upper deck?"

Brown told the Admiral that the ladder was located on the port side, forward of five-inch gun mount number two. The time was about 1000 or 1015 as Wilcox left Brown and his men.

The officer-of-the-deck for the 8-12 forenoon watch was Lieutenant (jg) William B. Fargo. Captain Benson was also on the bridge. At 1015 Captain Hall called down and asked Benson how long it would be before he was ready to return to base course. "Less than five minutes," said Benson. Hall informed the Admiral in his cabin by phone. The Admiral said, "Fine."

Hall turned to the flag lieutenant, "Hoist a signal, divisions column left, to true course 110°."

As Hall was talking, the sound-powered talker on the navigation bridge rushed to the officer-of-deck. "Man overboard, port side, sir!"

"Break the five flag!" shouted Fargo, "Sound the whistle! Release the life buoys!" The time was 1031.

In flag plot, Captain Hall heard the call over the communophone. "I was trying to get the Admiral," he would say later, "to tell him we were ready to return to base course, and to inform him of the man overboard. I was unable to raise him. I called ComDesRon 8 over the TBS and directed him to send the nearest destroyer to pick up the man. I then ordered the flag lieutenant to go down to the Admiral's cabin and report to him in person, and to inform him that everything was being done to save the man that could be done under the prevailing conditions."

Lieutenant Fargo had the word passed to muster the crew at quarters, below decks, and for all those who had seen the man in the water to report to the bridge.

On the *Washington's* main deck aft, Aviation Machinist's Mate Third Class John Sciarra saw the body in the water. It looked as if the *Tuscaloosa* would run the man down. The cruiser made a quick turn to port followed by a quick turn back to starboard and dropped two buoys that fell very close to the man.

Fargo called for another muster. No one was missing.

On board the *Tuscaloosa*, Captain N.C. Gillette and his executive officer, Captain P.M. Thornton, saw the man when he was 100 feet from the bow. Only Gillette's quick action kept them from hitting him.

Marine Captain J.M. McMasters and Coxswain J.E. Schmidt saw the man when he was about even with the *Tuscaloosa's* bridge. They heard him cry out for a buoy or raft, but could not be certain of his words. He was swimming, apparently trying to get away from the ship's side. He was about 15 feet from one of the buoys.

The following are excerpts from the *Washington's* TBS (voice) radio log, with enciphered calls decoded. There is constant static. Some signals are very weak. Many repeats are requested and have been deleted.

No time noted. ComDesRon 8 from CTF 39.

Man overboard from *Washington*. Direct nearest destroyer to rescue him. CTF 39 from ComDesRon 8.

Wilco

Wilson from *Tuscaloosa*

Man is in vicinity of our buoy.

Pick him up.

On board the *Washington*, the flag lieutenant reported to Captain Hall that he could not find the Admiral. Captain Hall told him to check the bathroom and have others check the sick bay, dental office and barber ship. The Admiral's entire staff began searching everywhere.

Captain Hall said later, "It began to be most alarming to me that the Admiral could not be found. I directed the commander of the screen to send another destroyer to join in the search and asked *Wasp* if conditions permitted launching planes to assist. I then called Captain Benson and told him my belief that it might be the Admiral overboard. The Captain and I discussed the necessity of coding a report to ComCruDiv 7, and decided to send a visual message in plain language to expedite."

Continued from the *Washington's* TBS radio log:

No time noted. *Wasp* from CTF 39. Would it be practicable some scouts assist *Ellyson* in locating buoy?

Wasp affirmative.

1450Z ComDesRon 8 from CTF 39.

Send another one of your people to assist in the search.

1503Z *Tuscaloosa* from *Ellyson*. Go ahead.

Tuscaloosa Ellyson is calling you.

Tuscaloosa go ahead.

Tuscaloosa said go ahead.

We are in between the two buoys. ...there is no man.

1505Z ComCruDiv 7 to all ships on circuit.

ComCruDiv 7 has tactical command.

At 1113 Admiral Giffen reversed the course of the formation by flag hoist, ordering ships right 180°. Speed was slowed to 10 knots as the ships passed through the area in which Admiral Wilcox had been lost.

Continued from the Washington's TBS radio log:

1550Z ComCruDiv 7 from *Livermore*.

Have man in sight floating face down toward us. Report man in sight.

1558Z ComCruDiv 7 from *Livermore*.

Go ahead.

Div 7 from *Livermore*. Livermore from ComDesRon 8. ComCruDiv 7 told you to go ahead. Have man in sight face down.

...CruDiv 7

Can you pick up using grapnel?

1600Z ComDesRon 8 from *Livermore*.

We have lost sight of man. Will go closer.

ComDesRon 8 from ComCruDiv 7.

Body is within 100 yards of *Livermore*. Please give our planes AC by light.

1607Z *Livermore* from *Wasp*.

Crash in water abeam of *Wasp*. Crash plane.

1611Z ComDesRon 8 from *Madison*.

Going toward place where plane crashed.

Wasp from ComCruDiv 7. Please coach destroyer in recovery.

1615Z *Madison* from *Wasp*. You are on spot now.

Madison see four smoke bombs and yellow object, nothing else.

1620Z *Wasp* from ComDesRon 8.

Do you think any advantage to further search?

Wasp wait.

ComDesRon 8 from *Wasp*. Are you positive you have observed whole area of crash?

ComDesRon 8 affirm.

1624Z from ComDesRon 8. Reform screen.

1626Z *Livermore* from *Washington*. Did you recover body?

...from Livermore. Body was not recovered.

1655Z No signals.

The snow had worsened as Task Force 39 returned to base course 090° and continued on its way to war. Long gray swells stretched astern, stormy and foreboding. Ahead, the way was dark, cold, and just as grim.

Late on the afternoon of the 27th, on Admiral Giffen's orders, a board of investigation was convened on board the *Washington* to investigate completely and report upon the circumstances attending Admiral Wilcox's loss at sea. The board met in closed sessions over the next seven days and examined 43 witnesses. Six of the witnesses saw a body in the water, but no one saw anyone fall overboard. All agreed on one thing. The man was bald.

The last person to see the Admiral was his orderly, Marine Private First Class Charles R. Nettle. The time was about five minutes before the alarm sounded. For 15 minutes Nettle watched from the passageway as the Admiral paced back and forth in his cabin. When the alarm sounded, Nettle looked into the cabin but did not see the Admiral.

Marine Private First Class Carrol V. Simmons Jr., told the board:

"I was standing safety watch this morning, 8 to 12, outside mount 9, I saw the Admiral come between the boats and mount 9 walking aft on the superstructure deck. He walked by me and made an attempt to go to the main deck by the ladder, and he changed his mind and started walking back again. In fact he made three attempts to go down the ladder and on the third attempt he did go to the main deck. As he reached the main deck, he stood there for a minute, then walked around the 20mm gun encasement, then walked aft on the main deck. Then he started between the superstructure and turret 3 on the port side. He changed his mind again and started walking aft. At that time, I saw him stop and talk to what I think is one of the pilots. I didn't see him after that."

William Tillett, apprentice seaman, saw the Admiral on the morning of the 27th. "He walked around, and looked like he was sad about something."

Commander Alfred R. Harris, Dental Corps, told the board that the Admiral had visited the dental office the night of the 26th and mentioned that it was important for all hands to be extremely cautious on topside. The dentist made the following additional statement after questioning: "I consider the Admiral a perfectly normal individual; there was no question in my mind but what the Admiral was a perfectly normal individual the last time I saw him. I have known the Admiral for four years, and there was no change in his actions at all."

Commander Lloyd L. Edmisten, Medical Corps, however, made the following statement: "From my professional observations of Admiral Wilcox, I believe he had certain eccentricities not common to officers of his grade, but to the best of my knowledge and belief he was of sound mind and had no physical impairments."

If any of these statements had an impact on the board it is not indicated in the record. The board did not interview members of the Admiral's family to see if he suffered from depression or any other personal problems.

The board was faced with a unique problem in an unfamiliar wartime situation. Its members did their job and were not about to ruffle any feathers where a flag officer was concerned. But one thing no one ever brought up was the possibility of seasickness. The *Washington* had been at sea for only 24 hours. But it had been a very rough 24 hours. Did the Admiral have his sea legs?

During the investigation, Chief Boatswain Brown said, "My first reaction in greeting the Admiral was that he seemed quite white and without color in his face." At the end of the examination the board asked Brown if he would like to make any further statement, and he added: "One thing I would like to mention is that the Admiral's appearance at the time of my conversation caused me to think and wonder why he was so pale and white."

Commander Thomas M. Dell, the

Washington's first lieutenant and damage control officer, said: "After the accident, I made an inspection of the life lines on the port side of the main deck, and found them all to e in proper order excepting one short section of the upper life line aft of Number 8 mount which was down. I do not consider the fact that this small section was down created a great hazard. In the vicinity of the 5-inch mounts, the life lines are not continous, and stop short of the mounts on both sides. In order to make room for the mount to turn, it is necessary that a small space between the life line stanchion and the mount be left. Chains secured to the stanchions with a hook on the other end to snap on the mount are provided, but operating under war conditions as we are, it is manifestly impracticable to keep these small sections of chain snapped into place. Even if they were hooked into place, the first time the mount was trained, they would be carried away, as time is not available for the crew inside to jump out and take them down every time it is necessary to train."

If the Admiral had been suffering from seasickness, could he have rushed to the rail only to find himself plunging into the sea?

On Thursday, 2 April, the board met in final session and rendered the following Finding of Facts:

Item 17: The loss at sea of Rear Admiral Wilcox was not caused in any manner by the intent, fault, negligence, or inefficiency of any person or persons in the naval service or connected therewith.

Item 18: Rear Admiral John W. Wilcox, Jr., USN, was at the time of his loss at sea on Friday, March 27, 1942, on duty assigned by proper authority. The board from the evidence before it, is of the opionion that John Wilcox Jr., late rear admiral, USN, died on March 27, 1942, in the line of duty and not as the result of his own misconduct.

LOOKING BACK
by Paul Stillwell

Half a century after WWII, Vice Admiral Willis A. "Ching" Lee is best known for one surface battle he fought and two he did not. The battle he fought (and won) was a desperate night action in November 1942, his makeshift force of two battleships and four destroyers matched against Japanese heavy bombarment ships in the crowded waters between Savo Island and Guadalcanal in the Solomon Islands. Three of the four US destroyers were lost as a result of the action, but the Japanese bombardment of Guadalcanal was thwarted. That battle was essentially the turning point that led toward US victory at Guadalcanal.

From then until Spring 1945, Ching Lee remained on the front line as the senior US battleship admiral in the war against Japan. For years both US and Japanese war plans had anticipated a climactic surface gun battle. Lee was the man poised to be in command of the US battle line because of his tactical expertise, including a better understanding than many of his contemporaries of how to use the capabilities of still-new radar in battle.

In June 1944, US amphibious forces invaded Saipan in the Mariana Islands. The commanders of US forces expected that this was too big a challenge for the Japanese to ignore. For the most part, the Japanese had been husbanding their major combatants since late 1942 as a fleet in being. But now they would be forced to come out and fight.

On board the *Lexington* (CV-16), flagship of Commander Task Force 58, Commodore Arleigh Burke was chief of staff to Vice Admiral Marc Mitscher. He got Mitscher to send a message to Lee, on board the battleship *Washington* (BB-45), trying to prod him into going after the Japanese and seeking a gun battle. Lee declined, remembering the confusion and disarray of the night battle in the Solomons. As his flag lieutenant, Gil Aertsen, explained years later, Lee reasoned also that he would again have a patchwork team, because his fast battlesips had been integrated into the carrier screens to provide anti-aircraft protection. As a result, his ships had not been able to hold tactical maneuvers together to practice for battle and were not as ready as he would have liked. Admiral Raymond Spruance, in overall command of the Fifth Fleet, endorsed Lee's cautious decision, because he was concerned about an end-run attack on Saipan if Lee's ships went off to seek battle. It is likly that Lee felt a more propitious opportunity for a surface action would arise later, and then he would be able to bag the Japanese heavies.

That opportunity did indeed come along in the Fall of 1944, during the Battle of Leyte Gulf. The story has been told so many times that only a brief summary is necessary. A Japanese surface force under Vice Admiral Takeo Kurita was mauled by carrier planes in the Sibuyan Sea as it headed east toward San Bernardino Strait on 24 October. Admiral William Halsey, Commander Third Fleet, announced his intent to take the carriers and supporting the ships of Task Force 38 on an aggressive charge northward in response to the sighting of Japanese carriers. Actually, the Japanese carriers were decoys, specifically intended to lure the US forces away and leave San Bernardino Strait unprotected so Kurita's ships could get through and attack US invasion forces off Leyte.

Aerial reconnaissance initially indicated that Kurita was headed back west, away from the strait, and presumably no longer a threat. A later report, during the night, said that the Japanese ships had again turned east toward San Bernardino. Lee wanted to stay behind as Commander Task Force 34 so that his battleships could pick off the Japanese as they emerged through the strait. When the later sighting report came in, Lee sent a message calling it to the attention of Admiral Halsey in his flagship, the *New Jersey* (BB-62). Lee's aide, Aertsen, remembered that the only response was an acknowledging "Roger."

Nor was Lee successful when he tried to press the issue. Thus his ships were still a part of Task Force 38 when it steamed north to face the Japanese carriers. En route, reports came of Kurita's damaging attacks on the destroyers and escort carriers that were off Samar in the absence of Lee's battleships. Halsey then turned around and headed south, without wading in to attack the force of decoy carriers. Lee's battleships arrived too late to go against Kurita's force. Years later, Admiral Thomas Kinkaid said he could imagine the frustration experienced by Lee, a Naval Academy classmate of his, at having steamed 300 miles north, 300 miles south, and not having been able to fire a shot from either direction.

Vice Admiral Willis A. Lee was eager to engage the Japanese in the Philippines for both strategic and tactical reasons. In June he would have had to fight in the open sea at night, probably a melee situation. In the Philippines it was likely that he would have the tactical advantage of crossing the enemy's T, an ideal position for surface gunnery, as Kurita's ships came out of San Bernardino. A more aggressive, less cautious commander might have steamed west to fight the enemy on 19 June. A more fortunate commander might have encountered greater flexability on the part of Halsey about forming Task Force 34 on the night of 24 October. Thus it was that the combination of Lee's judgement and the circumstances of war denied him the opportunity to command the battle line in the great surface action for which he had prepared all his professional life.

THE BUCKET
Submitted by J.L. Slaughter, B Div., state of Texas

After over 50 years since I entered the US Navy, I now feel free to reveal the following story:

I entered the Navy on 9 September 1939. I was only 18 years old at the time, that's why I considered it such an honor to be issued this very important piece of equipment. This equipment came with written instructions, plus the drill CPO also gave lectures and oral instructions on how to use this piece of equipment.

Upon completing boot camp I was allowed to take this very special piece of GI equipment with me to my next assignment, the USS *Indianapolis*, a 1932 heavy cruiser with an 8" main battery. The *Indianapolis* was a very modern ship that had taken President Franklin D. Roosevelt on a world cruise.

I went on the *"Indy"* in Vallejo, CA and was assigned to the "B" Division, Boiler Division. I soon found out I wasn't the only one who had this very important piece of equipment. In fact every sailor in the B Division had one exactly like mine. Naturally, they had much more experience with theirs than I had, they kept theirs shined with Bright Works Polish and even had their name on a bronze plate, and a rack to put them in, and locked up. This equipment was so personal that no one was allowed to use another's equipment.

This equipment had many, many uses. Most important of all I suppose was it's ability to deodorize. I don't believe we could have stood to stay below decks if it had not been for this wonderful piece of equipment.

Since it's been over 50 years, I'm still reluctant to reveal its true identity. But, here it goes. It was our "bucket" yes a bucket. This was our most important piece of equipment. Since the Indiana*polis* had no fresh water shower, only salt water, to take a bath we could draw one bucket of water, put it under the steam to heat it, wash and soap up. Then we could draw another bucket to rinse of with. We used the same process to wash our clothes. No laundry. So you can see

67

how important our bucket was. After a four hour watch in the fire room at 120° we sure needed to be deodorized.

My bucket served many other functions as well. I used it a lot in the recreation department. My first class water tender in #1 forearm (boiler room) was a big husky man named Duke. He kinda took me under his wing and he was going to show me how to play poker. I didn't tell him my dad and I had played poker for matches for years. He soon learned I wasn't the sucker he had expected. This was another place this fine piece of GI equipment came in handy. We played poker in the forearm and naturally there were no chairs. You guessed it. We used our buckets. First we sat on the open end until we got a big ring on our butts, then we would turn em over and sit on the other end. Everything turned out OK unless the ship's doctor pulled a surprise physical exam. Then you had some explaining to do about the big and little circles on your butt. Buckets were a wonderful piece of equipment.

The *Indianapolis* went to Pearl Harbor in January 1940 to tie up at 10-10 dock. We were assigned the Flagship of the Hawaiian Detachment. We stayed at sea seven days and seven days in port. This never happened to me but, some of the sailors found their bucket came in handy when they had too much to drink, or too much raw fish or Chinese food. Their bucket was always closer than the head (John) and often used it. I left the *Indy* in March 1941.

I was transferred back to the States to put the USS *Washington* (BB-56) in commission. I cried for two hours, for all it was a chance to go home to the newest, biggest and best ship in the Navy, being built in the Philiadelphia Navy Yard. Yes, of course, I took my bucket with me. Upon arriving in Philadelphia I stayed in the Navy Yard barracks for a couple of months. The crew of the *Washington* had been hand-picked to serve on this newest and best ship in the US Navy and the world.

When she was ready to go to sea we were moved aboard and much to my surprise there were no bucket racks. Where was I going to keep my bucket? I began to inquire around and found this ship had a laundry and fresh water showers, so there was really not much use for a bucket. After all this time together, it seemed like it was time to part. It took some time to get used to being witout it, but having clothes washed for you, and showers with plenty of hot water, did have certain advantages.

THE BATTLE OF US AIRCRAFT CARRIER
by John Brown

Admiral Lee, the commander of the US Battleship Squadron, was ordered by the US Government to stop the Japanese Battleship Squadron from attacking and destroying the Guadalcanal Airport; therefore, they were standing by south of Guadalcanal. In spite of the continuous attacks of the US squadron on the 14th, Admiral Lee's squadron found out that a group of Japanese cargo ships, guarded by a destroyer and cruiser, were going toward Guadalcanal Island. Also Admiral Lee found out on the same day that the Japanese main battle force was spotted at 14:00, 15 miles north of Guadalcanal Island, moving down to the south. From this Japanese tactic, Admiral Lee judged the Japanese were going to attack the Guadalcanal Airport the night of the 14th, followed by entering Guadalcanal Island by a group of aircraft carriers. Therefore, early that evening Admiral Lee's squadron left the place where they were standing by, and started moving along the west shore of Guadalcanal Island. The steaming order of the ships were, first four destroyers followed by the battleship, *Washington* and last the *South Dakota*; they steamed in a vertical line. These four destroyers were selected in the order of which one had the largest amount of fuel still left in the tank even though none had a commander on the board.

Japanese spy aircraft searched all afternoon. One spotted and reported, "two cruisers and four destroyers were moving to the north," (this was Admiral Lee's squadron).

At first Admiral Lee decided to destroy the Japanese airport and then attacked a group of cargo ships. As Admiral Lee could not find the Japanese battleship on the way back from the west side of Savo Island, he ordered a change of direction to the east at 19:00. Looking at Savo Island on the right side, he went inside of the water pass. At 20:52 while changing direction to the west, the radar of the *Washington* caught the target, nine miles northwest, confirmed visually at 21:12. The *South Dakota* also saw her. Under the 16 star bullet light the US started to fire main gun at 21:17. Instead of firing back, the Japanese battleship spread smoke and retreated to the north.

During this firing, the front destroyer spotted the Japanese destroyer *Ayanami* going to the west, south of Savo Island at 21:12. The US destroyer made a warning sound and started to fire. Other US destroyers started firing also. One destroyer kept firing star light bullets to the target. Soon after that, Japanese destroyer escorts and four destroyers from the south of Savo Island entering from the west and the US started firing. The other three US desroyers targeted the Japanese destroyers and started to fire; however, the Japanese destroyers fired vigorously at the US destroyer. While the US destroyer was target of Japanese destroyer, the US battleship tried to rescue the US destroyer by firing the second gun to the Japanese destroyer. However, the *Washington's* radar could not recognize the Japanese ship among many of the other targets. Meantime, the electricity of the *South Dakota* was completely destroyed by the attack of Japanese bullets at 21:33 and it became impossible to use the radar system.

During this battle, at 21:38, torpedoes which the Japanese destroyer fired started hitting US destroyers. Because of both Japanese gun and torpedoes, all four US destroyers lost the capability to battle without firing even one torpedo.

As a result of the first battle with *Ayanami*, the first US destroyer caught fire and was hit by many bullets and one torpedo from the Japanese destroyer escort *Nagara*. The first US destroyer was sunk a little after 21:34.

The second US destroyer's bow was hit by Japanese torpedo during the battle at 21:38; her speed was reduced to five knots and she tried to go to the *Cape Esperance*, however, she sunk at 13:37 on the 15th after she became unable to maneuver. The third US destroyer sunk also at 21:36, after being hit by many bullets from *Nagara* during the battle. The last US destroyer was running at reduced speed and was left alone at the war zone after taking a shell in the machine room and rudder.

Admiral Lee ordered a retreat at 21:48 after realizing that he could no longer use destroyers. He also gave the order to change direction slightly to the north. To avoid the US destroyers fire on the sea, the *South Dakota* changed direction and got lost from the flag ship completely. At this time, the *South Dakota's* electricity was repaired; however, without complete radar screen she was again attacked by the Japanese main force. The Japanese main force fired torpedo under the illumination of a searchlight. Even though none of the torpedoes hit the *South Dakota*, many of Japanese destroyers' 36 miles gun targeted and hit her. As she was damaged on the deck and caught fire, the captain of the *South Dakota* decided to retreat with full speed while battling against Japanese main force with all available weapons.

Meantime, by changing direction slightly to the north, the Wa*shing*ton was searching for the big battleship with radar. It was difficult to distinguish between enemy or friendly ships; therefore, she was waiting to fire. However, because of the Japanese searchlight, it was clear which was her target. At 22:00, and at a distance of 8,400 yards, the *Washington* started to fire her main gun. Since Japanese main force was targeting the *South Dakota*, the *Washington* did not get hit much by Japanese and was able to fire effectively. Soon, the *Kirishima* caught fire and recognized rudder was destroyed.

As the *South Dakota* had lost communication and also lost position, Admiral Lee ordered the *Washington* to change direction to northwest to assist the *South Dakota*. He ordered again at 22:20, to make a heading of 340 degrees to induce the Japanese force to the north. The Japanese force moved to the north, and started retreating the Japanese force after spreading the smoke. Admiral Lee made Japanese cargo ship to enter the Guadalcanal delayed. He also ordered to right turn around and retreat at 22:32, realizing the *South Dakota* was saved and out of danger. While retreating, the Japanese destroyer came after the *Washington* and fired torpedoes; but they exploded in the after wave of the *Washington*. The *South Dakota* went back to the US after being hit 48 times and virtually destroyed by big guns.

Arrival of the USS Washington into New York in July of 1942.

Admiral William F. Bull Halsey

USS WASHINGTON
BIOGRAPHIES

USS WASHINGTON MEMBERS

THEODORE H. "TED" ABBEY, COL, born March 21, 1921, Atlanta, GA, enlisted in the USMC while a student at Georgia Tech. Called to active duty Jan. 31, 1942, to attend Candidate's Class and Reserve Officers Class at Quantico, VA.

Reported to the USS *Washington* July 29, 1942, a second lieutenant fresh out of Sea School, Portsmouth, VA.

Remained on board until June 27, 1945. During these months served as a company officer and finally commanding officer of the Marine detachment. The Marines were a part of the gunnery division manning two 5" mounts and the controlling fire control director. Participated in all engagements from Guadalcanal to Iwo Jima. Most vivid memory was of the night battle off Savo Island Nov. 14-15, 1942, when as searchlight control officer had a great view of the sinking of a Jap battleship.

Released from active duty March 27, 1946. Later promoted to colonel USMCR and now lives in Atlanta.

ELTON RAY ADAMS, CWO4, born Aug. 13, 1921, Terre Haute, IN, joined the USN Aug. 26, 1940. Assigned to the USS *Washington* May 15, 1941, signal bridge, signalman second class.

While at sea he participated in all naval action including the collision with *Indiana*. (He left the ship soon after in the spring of 1944.)

His memorable experiences: There was a skirmish with a Japanese plane. He stuck his head over the signal bridge shield at the wrong time and found himself looking into the business end of a 5" twin mount. Before he could move the guns fired and he was deaf for three days. His ears still ring.

Adams was discharged in August 1967 (after 27 years service).

He has two sons, twin daughters, two step-sons, one step-daughter, 16 grandchildren and two great-grandchildren. He and his wife live in central Florida on four acres in the woods.

ALBERT C. ANDERSON SR., born Aug. 22, 1924, Marion, SC, enlisted in the USN Aug. 26, 1941, graduated boot camp at Norfolk, VA Oct. 7, 1941.

Was then assigned to the USS *Washington* (BB-56) which was soon escorting convoys to Murmansk, Russia, while based at the British naval anchorage at Scapa Flow, Scotland.

After several months convoy duty the ship returned to the States for overhaul at the New York Navy Yard, leaving in August 1942 for the South Pacific via the Panama Canal, with a stop at Tongatabu, arriving Noumea, New Caledonia in late September or early October 1942.

In one of the battles for Guadalcanal (Third Savo) the *Washington* sank the Japanese battleship *Kirishima* and destroyer *Ayanami*, not taking a single hit itself.

After this and other Pacific actions, the ship was ordered to the Puget Sound Navy Yard for replacement of the bow which had been badly damaged in a collision with the USS *Indiana*. After going on leave and to trade school, Anderson and his fiancee, Frances McBride of Shenandoah, VA, were married. He was then assigned to the USS *Farragut*, also in the Pacific, there completing his enlistment.

After the war, in September 1945, he went to work for Merck & Co., Inc., manufacturer of pharmaceuticals, retiring Oct. 1, 1983, after 38 years. After retiring Anderson and Frances moved from Harrisonburg, VA to their present home in Burleson, TX. They have a son, a daughter, a grandson, two granddaughters and a great-grandson.

PAUL W. ANDERSON, BM/2-DO, born Oct. 19, 1924, Jefferson County, KY, joined the USN Dec. 17, 1941, and boarded the USS *Washington* Jan. 13, 1942, off Key West, FL, and assigned to the 2nd Div.

He served aboard the *Washington* until after Japan's surrender Aug. 15, 1945. His memorable experiences were many. *Washington's* first plane shot down, he was on a 20mm next to 5" mount two (they should have issued them a mouth piece and earplugs). He doesn't recall if the number of torpedoes fired at the *Washington* in the 3rd Battle of Savo Islands were recorded, but swears he hit the deck of the powder magazine in turret two 27 times. The lost anchor was probably one of the most chaotic moments in the *Washington's* history. On entering port all hands at quarters, the starboard anchor was dropped. As coxswain he had the 2nd Div. at quarters but noticed the chain markers and as the danger markers appeared called out, "CLEAR THE DECK, IT'S COMING OUT" [end of chain], as he dove over the lifeline onto the billboard with the spare anchor. BM Gough stopped a disaster by preventing the dropping of the port anchor into a mass of men who dove or jumped overboard to escape the sweeping chain.

He departed the ship in Bremerton in September 1945 for shipping—over leave and reassignment. He later served aboard the USS *Navasota, Wyoming,* and *Orion*. He was discharged March 10, 1949, but served in the USNR, USAFR and retired from USCGR as chief warrant officer 4 with 35 years service. Retired lieutenant, Louisville Police Department, now runs a private detective agency in Somerset, KY.

He has three sons: Donald, Ronald and Gerry; and two daughters, Denise and Lynnl, by a previous marriage. Now married to Mildred Beasley Howson and has two step-sons, Charles and Michael, and eight grandchildren.

WILLIAM T. ANDERSON, LCDR, born Dec. 14, 1916, Orlando, FL, joined the USN in September 1936. Boot camp at Norfolk, VA. Spent four years on WWI destroyer DD-156. Transferred to Philadelphia, PA in March 1941 to *Washington* BB-56 until April 19, 1943. Went to Diesel School and changed rate to MoMM to PC 1246. Commissioned ensign in August

1944. Nine months later was engineering officer on APDs, DMS, DD and DDR, two and one-half years, Ship's Parts Control Center, Mechanicsburg, PA. His last assignment was with repair office, destroyer tender *Yosemite* AD-19. Anderson retired in August 1979 as lieutenant commander, USN.

He has two sons and one daughter.

LAURENCE ARTS, CM1, born July 5, 1913, Tony, WI, joined the USN Feb. 23, 1942, as mechanic third class at Great Lakes Naval Training Station.

He was assigned to the USS *Washington* during the last part of April 1942 at a receiving station in Washington, D.C.

He went aboard the USS *Washington* in July 1942 at the Brooklyn Navy Yard.

While on leave from the ship in April 1944 he got married to the girl back home.

In May he left the ship at Pearl Harbor with scarlet fever and went to the Base Eight Hospital in Oahu.

He got back to the ship in October 1944.

He left the ship for discharge as mechanic first class at Bremerton, WA Aug. 31, 1945, and was discharged at Great Lakes Naval Training Station Sept. 19, 1945.

Back home in Wisconsin he finished his last year of college. He taught agriculture, science and math at a local high school for 14 years. He then worked for the Farmer's Home Administration, a federal agency that made loans to farmers and for individual housing, for 18 years.

He purchased a 120+ acre dairy farm in 1947 and added 160 more acres through the years. He milked from 24 to 45 cows for many years.

The family increased to two boys and two girls, seven grandchildren and two great-grandchildren.

He sold the farm in 1979 and retired on a hobby farm in north central Wisconsin near Ladysmith.

ROBERT T. AUGHTON, SN1, born Nov. 21, 1924, Detroit, MI, joined the USN Dec. 17, 1941. He was assigned to the USS *Washington* Jan. 13, 1942, and served with 1st Div. and 8th Div. While at sea he was aboard for all major actions. Also the Murmansk Run, third battle of Savo Island, 57 air attacks and sinking of the *Kirishima* and *Ayanami*.

All of his experiences were memorable.

Aughton was awarded 15 Battle Stars, American Theater Medal, Asiatic-Pacific Campaign Medal, European and African Campaign Medal, Philippine

Liberation Medal, Philippine Independence Medal, Philippine Presidential Unit Citation and WWII Victory Medal.

He was discharged Dec. 21, 1945, as seaman first class.

He married the former Merriann Adams of Los Angeles, CA June 21, 1952. They have one son, John Adam. Aughton retired from the Long Beach Police Department (California) after 32 years service.

MELVIN D. AVANT, S1/C, born Nov. 12, 1923, Kannapolis, NC, son of Henry and Ola Mae Avant. Volunteered for the USN Feb. 20, 1941, and was assigned to the USS *Washington* BB-56 in May 1941.

Stood gun watches in 5" 38 mounts, his job was hot casement.

Avant was awarded the American Area Campaign Medal, European African Campaign Medal (1), Asiatic-Pacific Campaign Medal (12), American Defense Service Medal, Philippine Liberation Medal (2), and WWII Victory Medal.

Served in North Atlantic and South Pacific. He was discharged Oct. 24, 1946.

He and his wife, June, live in Umatilla, FL.

CHARLTON B. BARFIELD, born in Columbia, SC, joined the USN Feb. 22, 1941. Assigned to the USS *Washington* BB-56, May 15, 1941-Oct. 31, 1944. Served on 1st Div. Deck and Turret No. 1. Barfield retired in 1960.

EUGENE H. BARNABY, born April 19, 1922, Grand Rapids, MI. Joined the USN Dec. 18, 1941. Boot camp: Great Lakes (Navy Pier), Chicago. Boarded the USS *Washington* in the Gulf Jan. 13, 1942, with Co. 20 B, Great Lakes. Was aboard during all major action.

Some of his most memorable experiences included: being on Man Overboard Watch seated on the found of the starboard catapult, when the destroyer *Hailey*, in trying to abort its fueling approach, backed down taking the catapult with her and dumping the kingfisher on deck about three feet from his head. Also, he was on surface lookout when the *Washington* collided with the *Indiana*. Due to zero visibility and darkened ships, there were only about 150 yards between the ships, when the *Indiana* hove into view and the *Washington* broadsided her.

Left the *Washington* at Bremerton, WA in August 1945 for Fleet Air Alameda, CA, then to Jacksonville Naval AS, after that to Naval AS, Deland, FL. From there to Great Lakes, IL for discharge Oct. 2, 1945.

Served in the Merchant Marines in 1949, and USNR again in 1955-59 as airman first, and aviation machinist's mate third.

He was married to Ellen Morrison Feb. 21, 1948, in Detroit, MI. They have five children and seven grandchildren.

Returned to California in 1949 to Cal Fliers School of Aeronautics and received his A&E license. Worked for Western Airlines and North American Aviation on the flight line then worked as a tech writer for north American and Douglas.

Moved back to Michigan in 1961 to work for 34 years as a partner in the family trucking business. Retired in 1995.

WAYNE HAMPTON BARNETT, BM 2/C, born July 24, 1922, Williamstown, SC. Joined the USN Feb. 24, 1941, had boot camp at Norfolk, VA and went aboard the USS *Washington* May 15, 1941. He served with the 6th Div.

Barnett was awarded six Battle Stars and was discharged April 15, 1946.

His most memorable moment was taking part in the battle that sank Japanese battlewagon and other ships in that battle.

Has been married to his wife, Mary, for 51 years and they have one daughter and two granddaughters. Worked 34 years for the H.K. Porter Co. Barnett is presently retired.

ROGER G. BAYLOR, CPL, born March 7, 1925, Georgetown, IN. Joined the USMC Sept. 28, 1942. Transferred to 10th Replacement Bn., South Pacific; assigned to USS *Washington* in January 1943 with 7th Div. Served on board until July 1945 as a gun striker and shellman on the 5-inch guns.

Participated in all major action while on board, including Saipan, Iwo Jima and Okinawa. Memorable experiences were the collision with USS *Indiana* and the encounter with the typhoon December 1944.

Honorably discharged Oct. 4, 1945, with rank of corporal. Remained in USMCR, returned to active duty in Korean War in August 1950-August 1951, as a sergeant with D Co., 16th Inf., Camp Pendleton, CA.

Worked as a farmer, route foreman for Bowman Dairy and for Pierce Electric Co. until retirement in 1987. Married the former Bettye Sue Allen June 27, 1955, and has one son, Roger A.

VERNON J. BAYS, born Feb. 21, 1923, Eccles, WV, joined the USN Dec. 20, 1940, and was assigned to the USS *Washington* in March 1941. Station/job while on ship was carpenter mate, damage control. He achieved the rank of damage control mate first class.

While at sea he participated in the Murmansk/Archangle runs; third battle of Savo Island; collision with USS *Indiana* and many bombardments and numerous air attacks.

His memorable experiences include: (1) Atlantic convoys receiving Bluenose Certificate April 30, 1942. (2) The loss of Adm. Wilcox March 27, 1942. (3) The loss of the HMS *Punjabi* May 1, 1942. He was on 01 level and watched half of ship and numerous men float by him. (4) Their first burial at sea - two seamen, their cause of death unknown. (5) Entering Pearl Harbor after the Japanese attacked and seeing the men with cutting torches retrieving the dead and knowing they were the only capital ship left in the South Pacific. (6) Receiving his subpoena and summons extraordinary and finally becoming a shellback - a story in this. (7) The third battle of Savo Islands Nov. 15, 1942 - his battle station was directly behind #2 turret on the main deck and someone had left the door improperly dogged down. They tied two lines to it and fought the door all night not knowing whether the Japs would sink them or the concussion from their 16" guns would. Was he scared? Hell, yes! (8) The bombing of Nauru in December 1942 - they bombarded this island two or three times with 5" guns. The mystery was how could they get their radio towers back up so quickly. (9) The bombardment of Kwajalein. (10) The collision between the USS *Washington* and the USS *Indiana* - their admiral's orders were to change course and for some unknown reason the USS *Indiana* failed to do so and the results were disastrous! (11) The ship returned to Pearl Harbor for temporary bow work and they returned to Seattle, WA after 34 months of continuous combat.

He was transferred from the USS *Washington* to Seattle, WA. He and other crew members were in need of R&R. He was told he could put in for two air stations near his home. He put in for Bainbridge, MD and Jacksonville, FL - orders came in for Norman, OK. He was in charge of four crash crews and was told he would get nine months flight for flying four hours a month. He was even more scared of flying with the cadets than he was in Guadalcanal - if this was R&R he did not want any more!

He was honorably discharged from the USN personnel separation center as a carpenter mate first class USN Norman, OK Feb. 23, 1946.

He stayed in the USNR and was recalled to active service July 4, 1950. His rating by this time was changed from CM 1/c to DCW 1/c. He was sent to Little Creek, VA and was told he could send for his family in a month. One week later he got his orders to report aboard the USS *Missouri* BB-63. He knew he was in for more R&R.

The rest of his story is written about his duties aboard the USS *Missouri* and his commendation on board hand delivered to him in sickbay personally by Capt. Duke.

He knows that he owes all his training and experience to the members of the USS *Washington* - they were trained well!

LLOYD PAUL BEARD, QMED, served in the USNR from Oct. 2, 1943-December 1945 (active). He was sent to San Diego, CA for boot camp. Served aboard the USS *Washington* BB-56 as fireman, #1 fireroom, firing boilers. After discharge he taught school for 20 years as teacher, coach and principal.

From 1966-85 he served on merchant ships for Merchant Marines for 20 years. Beard retired as QMED.

PAUL C. BEATTY, EM 1/C, born Aug. 17, 1917, Ironton, OH, joined the USN in January 1942. He was assigned to the USS *Washington* as damage control electrician, interior communication.

While at sea his duties included the North Atlantic and Pacific. Beatty was awarded 15 Battle Stars.

He was discharged in October 1945.

73

Beatty and his wife, Jean G., have one daughter, Cynthia B. Benedetti; and two grandchildren, Danny and Teresa. He is presently retired.

MELVIN E. BECKSTRAND, CSK, born April 19, 1919, joined the USN in November 1941. He was assigned to the USS *Washington* in January 1942. Station/job on ship: Spare parts (CSK). He served aboard the USS *Washington* for two and one-half years and on the USS *Kwajalein* for one and one-half years.

Beckstrand was discharged in October 1945. He was awarded Battle Stars and ribbons.

He and his wife, Marie, have two children, Bradley and Sandra. Beckstrand is presently farming and ranching.

ALLEN HENRY BELL, born Aug. 14, 1922, Pelzer, SC, joined the USN Feb. 5, 1941. After boot camp in Norfolk, VA he was assigned to the USS *Washington*, 1st Div., May 15, 1941, and was gunners mate second class in turret 1. He participated in all the battles on the ship until March 1944.

Honorably discharged Sept. 14, 1960, he was employed with Union Camp Corp. until Feb. 1, 1986, when he retired and enjoyed his favorite hobbies, hunting and fishing.

Married Mary Anna Rowland Jan. 31, 1945. They have one daughter, Martha, two granddaughters and one grandson. Bell died Sept. 26, 1993, and is buried in Sedley, VA.

HOWARD H.J. BENSON, born Oct. 8, 1888, Baltimore, MD, the son of Adm. William S. Benson and Mary A. Benson. Graduated from the USNA in June 1909.

Served on battleship *Vermont* until April 1912 when ordered to submarine flotilla. In July 1913 he fitted out and commanded submarine H-2.

From January 1916-July 1917 he had duty at Navy Yard, Washington, D.C. and Navy Department. Then duty in connection with steam fishing vessels for distant patrol duty, served as aide to commander Patrol Forces 3 and 4, and command of *Guinevere*, *Noma Corona*, *Roe* and duty on the destroyer *Sigourney*. After return to US he commanded the destroyers *Buchanan*, *Yarnall* and *Howard*.

From September 1920-June 1922 was instructor at the USNA, then commanded destroyer *S.P. Lee*. In October 1922 he was assigned to battleship *Tennessee* and served as first lieutenant and then navigator until March 1925.

After two years in the Hydrographic Office, Navy Dept., he commanded the destroyer *Sloat* from May 1927-1929. He attended the Naval War College at Newport from 1929-May 1930, senior course.

Reported as executive officer in the department of navigation, USNA. Headed the department from Feb. 6, 1932-July 25, 1932. Became commanding officer of the oil tanker *Sapelo* and a month later assigned as executive officer of the battleship *Tennessee*. On May 4, 1934, he assumed command of the *Tennessee* and proceeded to Culebra and New York City. At New York the fleet was reviewed by President Roosevelt.

Attended the Army War College, Washington, D.C. June 1934-June 1935, then assigned to the Shore Establishment Div., Navy Dept.

In June 1936 he returned to sea duty commanding submarine tender *Holland* and in July assumed command of station ship at the USNA. He remained there until March 1941, when he reported for fitting out of USS *Washington*, and assumed command of *Washington* May 15, 1941.

Under his command *Washington* operated from Scapa Flow with the British Home Fleet guarding convoys between Iceland and Russia against possible action by German Battle Fleet.

Benson was detached from command of *Washington* in July 1942. He served as chief of staff of Seventh Naval District and Gulf Sea Frontier. He retired from active duty Nov. 1, 1946, as commodore.

Benson was awarded the Navy Cross (WWI), the Legion of Merit (WWII), Victory Medal, Patrol Clasp (WWI), second Nicaraguan Campaign Medal, American Defense Service Medal w/Fleet Clasp, American Campaign Medal, EAME Campaign Medal and WWII Victory Medal. He has also been awarded the Order of the Southern Cross and diploma from Brazil and the Oak Leaf Emblem for Distinguished Service.

JAMES B. BIAS, born Sept. 14, 1923, Logan, WV, joined the USN Feb. 17, 1941, and was assigned to the USS *Washington* as a gunners mate on turret #2 in May 1941.

He saw all action for 34 months including the Battle of Savo Nov. 14, 1942, while receiving 14 Battle Stars, American Theater, Good Conduct, Asiatic-Pacific, European & African, American Defense and WWII Victory Medals.

He remembers as a 17-year-old relaxing on the deck looking at the clouds, they suddenly parted and a Jap plane appeared and he saw the Rising Sun painted on the wings. All of a sudden all Hell broke out as the fleet fired at the plane.

One day while in Pearl Harbor he decided to get a shave. The barber was a young Japanese girl who used a razor that had JAPAN stamped on it. As she ran the blade over his neck all he could think about was getting out of there.

After achieving the rank of first class he was discharged Nov. 19, 1946. He is now a retired mechanic living in southern San Francisco, CA.

He married the former Hazel Campton in 1945 and was happily married for 51 years until her passing on Nov. 2, 1996. They have four married sons and nine grandchildren.

AMADEUS VON BIBLE, TEL 1/C, born Nov. 2, 1910, Kirklin, IN, joined the USN in May 1929 and was assigned to the USS *Washington* in the spring of 1941. He served as MUS 1/c and then TEL 1/c. Action while at sea: Convoy to Russia, South Pacific to 1944.

He was awarded the American Defense Medal, American Theatre Medal and WWII Victory Medal. He was discharged in March 1952.

After his USN career he spent 20 years with the postal service. He and his wife, Elsie, had three children: Ruth, Roland and Frederic. He passed away Sept. 9, 1990.

POWERTAN BLANCHETT, born April 7, 1924, Nancemond County, VA was among the original roster of the USS *Washington* where he served as mess attendant. He served aboard the *Washington* for her shakedown cruise. Believes they were the first battleship to be refueled while underway. On the rough voyage to Rekejavik, they lost two seamen and their captain. A turret became inoperable. Experts were flown from Philadelphia to make repairs.

At Scapa Flow, President Roosevelt's son, King George, and Douglass Fairbanks, Jr. toured their ship. As they left Scapa Flow, the battleship *King George* ran into another British ship, a "tin can." As the doomed ship sank, the depth charges were exploding. Few survivors were saved. Joining Task Force 39, the *Washington* escorted convoys to Russia. His battle station in those scary days was many many decks below. He left the *Washington*, attended Fleet Service School and became an officer's cook. Service aboard the *Claxton*, *Engstrom*, OBQ, Adak, the Vallejo Naval Base and finally honorable discharge at Shoemaker, CA Oct. 12, 1945.

He and his wife, Sarajane, have five sons and two daughters. Blanchett is a retired teamster.

JOHN H. BOGHOSIAN, EM 2/C, born Jan. 3, 1923, St. Louis, MO, joined the USN Sept. 17, 1943, and was assigned to the USS *Washington* in May 1944. He served on 16" gun, turret #3, as electrician.

His memorable experiences: Dry docking in AB&D-2 and passing through the Panama Canal in 1945. Remembering the USS *Franklin* come back to life, after the kamikaze attack and steam back to Pearl Harbor under her own power for repairs.

Action while at sea included the bombardment of Saipan, battle of the Philippine Sea, Palau, Okinawa, Iwo Jima, Taiwan, Luzon and the battle of Leyte Gulf. He was called back into service in 1951 for the Korean War, and served aboard the USS *Earl K. Olson* DE-765.

Boghosian was awarded the American Campaign Medal, Asiatic-Pacific Campaign Medal, EAME Campaign Medal, Victory Medal, Philippine Liberation Medal and Korean Campaign Medal.

He married the former, Ann Aslanian, April 15, 1950. They have one daughter, Linda Schmitt; one son, Paul; and five grandsons. Boghosian was employed as a radio electrician in 1953 and retired as a flight test buyer in 1987 from McDonnell Douglas Aircraft.

He and Ann are enjoying their retirement with their grandchildren, visiting their friends, dining out often and traveling now and then.

OLIVER L. "BO" BOHANNON, SR., SF 3/C, born Dec. 3, 1923, Louisville, KY, Jefferson County, joined the USN Dec. 17, 1941, at age 18. He was assigned to the USS *Washington* BB-56 Jan. 13, 1942, as seaman the first year, then the R Div. Shipfitter Shop. He was on board ship for all major action—Murmansk Run, third battle of Savo Island, collision with USS *Indiana*—bombardments and air attacks.

His memorable experiences: The sinking of the *Kirishima* and *Ayanami*.

After discharge as 3rd class shipfitter Nov. 5, 1945, he re-enlisted for six years June 30, 1946, as shipfitter 3/c. After 22 years he was discharged from naval service Dec. 27, 1962, as chief shipfitter. May 3, 1966, he worked at the Portsmouth Naval Shipyard, Portsmouth, VA as a pipefitter WG-10 5th step. After 21 years of civil service he retired May 1, 1987.

He married the late Germaine B. Hassison, from Fall River, MA. They had four sons, one daughter, two grandsons and three granddaughters. They made their home at Virginia Beach, VA.

HOMER WILSON BOHNSACK, WT1/c, born April 22, 1918, Detroit, MI and joined the USN Oct. 19, 1939. Assigned to USS *Washington* in 1941 and stationed in boiler room.

Also served in USS *Badger*, *Blueridge* and *Siboney* (CVE-112) and saw action in Philippines, Guadalcanal and Leyte Gulf. His memorable experience was being anchored off-shore during a hurricane aboard the destroyer *Badger*.

Discharged Nov. 16, 1945. His awards and decorations include the Asiatic-Pacific w/5 stars, WWII Victory Medal, Philippine Liberation w/star, European Theater w/star, American Defense w/star and Presidential Citation.

Married 55 years and has three married children. He is a retired electrical engineer, Los Angeles, Dept. of Water & Power.

ROBERT L. BOST, COXSWAIN, born March 20, 1925, Napoleon, OH, joined the USN May 15, 1942, and was assigned to the USS *Washington* in July 1942. He was assigned as sail locker on ship.

His memorable experience: Knocked overboard when they lost their anchor.

Bost participated in the entire Pacific Campaign. He was awarded the Asiatic-Pacific Campaign Medal, Good Conduct Medal, WWII Victory Medal, etc. Discharged March 24, 1946.

He and his wife, Evelyn, have five children. Presently retired as locomotive engineer.

LINFORD BOYD JR., born May 14, 1924, Ecorse, MI, joined the USN Dec. 17, 1941. Short training at Navy Pier, Chicago, then left for Key West, FL. Assigned to USS *Washington* in Gulf of Mexico in January 1942. Served in American Theatre, European Theater w/1 star, Asiatic-Pacific Campaign w/12 stars, Philippine Liberation w/2 stars and Guam w/1 star. Main assignment was 20mm gunner.

His memorable experiences: Refueling and taking on supplies at sea and the battle of Savo Island. Discharged Oct. 13, 1945.

He married the former Doris Shelt March 17, 1946, and has two children and two grandchildren. He started his student trips on DT&I, Flat Rock, MI Oct. 19, 1945. Promoted to locomotive engineer Aug. 30, 1949. Served 41 years and six months.

S. ANTHONY BRADEN, SN 2/C, born Sylvester Ratajczak, Dec. 13, 1925, Cleveland, OH. He joined the USN Feb. 16, 1943, and served his entire enlistment aboard the USS *Washington*. He was discharged Jan. 27, 1946, as seaman second class.

He received the Asiatic-Pacific Campaign Medal w/9 Battle Stars, the Victory Medal, American Theater Medal, and Philippine Liberation Medal w/2 Battle Stars.

After his discharge he changed his name to S. Anthony Braden.

He has two children, David F. and Jennifer T.; and two grandchildren, Adam J. and Emily K. Braden passed away Jan. 31, 1997. *Submitted by Rita T. Braden.*

JOHN LOUIS BRANCIERE, MM 1/C, born May 28, 1920, Vicksburg, MS, enlisted in the USN Nov. 20, 1940. His job was machinist's mate stationed in the engine room deep within the battleship. He earned rank of machinist's mate 1/c.

His most memorable event: The sinking of the Japanese battleship *Kirishima* Oct. 3, 1946. The USS *Washington* was tied up to the dock at Bayonne, NJ. The last of her sailors left the battleship forever.

Branciere was honorably discharged Nov. 19, 1946. He was the first WWII veteran to become a member of William T. Gifford Post No. 2572 of Vicksburg, MS.

While in the USN John married Mary Alpe April 2, 1945. They have three children, five grandchildren and two great-grandchildren.

He retired from Agrico Chemical Co., Donaldsonville, LA. After retirement he returned to his hometown, Vicksburg, MS. On Saturday, July 14, 1990, Branciere died. He is buried in Vicksburg.

BEA BRANTLEY, SN 1/C, born Feb. 26, 1922, (Buffalo Bill's birthday), Liberty County, TX. He joined the USN in Houston, TX Feb. 26, 1942. He first saw the USS *Washington* on TV as she was launched at the 1940 World's Fair in New York. Three years later, he was assigned to the greatest battleship to ever sail the ocean blue. He boarded the *Washington* in 1943 at Pearl Harbor and was assigned in I Div., as a lookout.

One of his most memorable times was as he watched the USS *Washington's* 16 guns bombard Iwo Jima. His idols were the great Adm. Willis A. Lee of Kentucky and the great Capt. Good.

During his time on the *Washington* he rated nine Battle Stars including Good Conduct and other various medals. Brantley was honorably discharged as seaman first class at Camp Wallace, TX Oct. 11, 1945.

He is a retired rancher and guard from Union Carbide. He married the former Margaret Romero Nov. 24, 1956, who is now deceased. They have five children: Faith, Joan, Michael, Dorllyn and Lanette. He now enjoys his free time with his 13 grandchildren and little dog, Poncho, who reminds him of his shipmate, Zero.

JAMES F. BRESKE, EM 1/C, born Oct. 4, 1920, Milwaukee, WI, joined the USN in May 1944 and was assigned to the USS *Washington* in January 1945. He was stationed at power distribution.

His memorable experience: Going aboard the ship for the first time.

Boot camp at Great Lakes. Action at sea included Iwo Jima, Taiwan and Okinawa.

Breske was awarded Campaign Medals and Asiatic and American Defense Medal. Discharged Jan. 7, 1946.

He married the former Beverly Marger Oct. 11, 1941, (she passed away in August 1991). They have three daughters and one son. Retired in January 1986 as an electrical foreman. Spent the majority of his working career as an electrician.

ALBERT BRIGHTWELL, Damage Controlman 2/C, born Oct. 1, 1924, Louisville, KY, joined the USN Dec. 16, 1941, Naval Training Center, Great Lakes, IL. He boarded the USS *Washington* in January 1942 in the Gulf of Mexico. Left BB-56 Aug. 2, 1945.

Served aboard the USS *Juneau* from Feb. 23, 1948-Jan. 25, 1951.

Received American Theatre Medal, Asiatic-Pacific Campaign Medal, WWII Victory Medal, EAME Campaign Medal, Philippine Liberation Medal, Navy Occupation Medal and Good Conduct Medal.

His most memorable experience: Watching their aircraft carrier being sunk at Guadalcanal and witnessing kamikaze attacks.

Received honorable discharge Jan. 25, 1951.

Employed 34 years as meter reader for Indiana Gas Co. Married the former Evon Nalley Sept. 15, 1951. He has three sons: Albert Jr., Joseph and Bruce; and six grandchildren.

CHARLES BLANE BRINKLEY, CDR, born Dec. 12, 1908, Glen Alpine, NC, joined the USN Oct. 3, 1926, and was assigned to the USS *Washington* May 15, 1941. He served with E Div. as chief warrant to lieutenant commander. Detached from USS *Washington* Feb. 15, 1945. Retired Oct. 1, 1954.

He received all medals awarded to the USS *Washington* personnel and China Fleet (1948-49).

He married the former Joyce Luster (deceased in 1989). They have two sons, LtCol. C.B. Jr. and Prof. John L. Cdr. Brinkley passed away Dec. 26, 1986.

EDWARD M. BROWN, RM 2/C, born Aug. 4, 1920, DeWitt, AR, joined the USN May 29, 1942, and was assigned to the USS *Washington* in August 1942 in New York. Stationed in radio communications, made second class there. He was assigned to the flag and was a part of it until he received 31 points which made him eligible for shore duty stateside.

His first and most memorable experience: The night action Nov. 15, 1942, when the *Washington* sank the battleship off Savo Island. Also finding his brother on Manus Island when they went in to a floating dry dock to have their bow replaced and he went ashore there.

Discharged Nov. 6, 1945. Awarded the Philippine Liberation Ribbon w/2 stars, American Area Service Ribbon, WWII Victory Medal, and Asiatic-Pacific Service Ribbon w/8 stars.

He is a semi-retired real estate broker. He and his wife have been married for 50+ years. They have five children and nine grandchildren. His son, Randy, served and was wounded two times in Vietnam.

JOHN A. BROWN, born Nov. 24, 1924, Catlettsburg, KY, joined the USN Dec. 17, 1941-Oct. 13, 1945. He served aboard the USS *Washington* BB-56 from Jan. 13, 1942-Sept. 30, 1945, as shipfitter second class, shipfitter shop, damage control, plumbing gang, fresh water king. Saw all major action by ship.

Awarded the Asiatic-Pacific Campaign Medal, two Philippine awards, Good Conduct Medal, 38 months overseas, 15 Battle Stars. Participated in sinking of *Kirishima* and *Ayanami*, Third Battle of Savo Island Nov. 14-15, 1942, 57 air attacks, 10 island bombardments, 12 planes shot down. Discharged Oct. 13, 1945.

Married the former Gladys Bowling April 25, 1946. They have two sons, Richard M. and Donald Keith; two granddaughters, Deborah and Lori Nicole; two grandsons, Jeremy and Shane; and two great-granddaughters, Megan Nichole and Holly Layne.

Organized USS *Washington* BB-56 Reunion Group 1948, Associate Unit 1989, Out of State Kentucky Veterans, instrumental in obtaining 242 million in veterans bonus for 424,000 men, women and children. Served as president.

In service with Reunion Group Executive Director for 50 years, Shaklee, Watkins, Athletic Boosters, Police Academy, Kentucky Colonel, portal chief OSU stadium, life member VFW, Kiwanis, Buckeye Sideliners, retired plumber Local 189, served May 10, 1946-October 1986. Assisted in books, *Battleship at War, Memories & Memorials, Lost Ships at Guadalcanal* and USS *Washington* history book.

MELVIN F. BROWN, EM 2/C, born Sept. 18, 1925, Tribune, KS, joined the USN Jan. 8, 1942. He was assigned to the USS *Washington* from October 1942-November 1946. Station/job on ship: E Div., light locker and batter locker.

His memorable experiences: Battle of Savo, Iwo Jima, passing through Panama Canal and various other battles of the South Pacific.

Actions while at sea included all of the above, plus the encounter of the USS *Washington* and the transport of troops from the European Theatre.

He was awarded 15 Battle Stars, Good Conduct Medal and WWII Victory Medal. Discharged Jan. 18, 1946.

He married the former Margaret "Teenie" Bland July 1, 1951, Fort Scott, KS. They have one son, Terry; one daughter, Tammy; and three grandchildren: Toby, William and Megan. Semi-retired after owning and operating a truck line for 33 years.

JAMES BILLY BRYANT, GMC, born Aug. 25, 1923, Carbon Hill, AL, joined the USN Jan. 27, 1941. After boot camp in Norfolk, assigned to USS *Washington* May 1, 1941. He served turret #2 until Aug. 1, 1945, he then sent to GM School in D.C. Decided on a naval career and served aboard the USS *Duluth*, Tsingtao, China, Ammo. Depot, Guam, PACRESFLT San Francisco, USS *Pittsburgh*, MCB-10 Guam and instructed at the GM School, Great Lakes his last three years prior to retirement Sept. 16, 1960, with the rating of GMC.

In addition to *Washington* medals he was awarded a Command Commendation, Good Conduct Medal w/5 stars, Expert Pistol, Expert Rifle, China Service Medal and various occupational medals.

Upon retirement, lived in Waterford, CA for 15 years. Moved to west Tennessee in 1975 and has been active in real estate sales and related businesses many years. Married the former Leona Hinton many plus years ago and they have three children and four grandchildren. Now retired again, and lives on the Tennessee River near Camden.

ROBERT O. BUCHHOLZ, YN 2/C, born Jan. 30, 1922, Detroit, MI, joined the USN July 14, 1943, and was assigned to the USS *Washington* in March 1944. Served as intelligence yeoman in captain's office and admiral's tanker at GQ.

His memorable experiences: (1) Riding out two typhoons and looking and listening for survivors of destroyers caught dead in the water and breaking up. (2) Witnessing the carrier directly in front of them being destroyed by three Jap bombers. (3) Watching the 16" shells being fired 15 miles or so onto Okinawa. (4) Seeing a Japanese torpedo bomber being shot down by their 40mm quads a scant 50 yards away on his run to their starboard side. (5) Watching a Jap plane being shot down by a 20mm gunner on the signal bridge and the admiral remarking that the gunner just earned the Bronze Star. (6) Seeing his first hit by a kamikaze (on the *Lexington*) and cursing the war. (7) Watching the unfurling of the battle flag, which at the time, appeared to be at least a third of the ship's length. (8) While nearing dry dock, a boat load of nurses in swimsuits passing on the starboard and their loud speakers ordering half of the crew back to the portside.

Buchholz was awarded the American Campaign Medal, Asiatic-Pacific Campaign Medal w/7 stars, Philippine Liberation Medal w/2 stars, Asian Occupation Service Medal, Victory Medal and Letter of Commendation. He was discharged Feb. 4, 1946.

He married the former Fran Dodsworth Aug. 10, 1946. They have two sons, two daughters and seven grandchildren. Retired from J.L. Hudson Co., finance division.

SYLVESTER M. BUDZINSKI, born Aug. 21, 1924, Webster, MA, joined the USN June 7, 1943, and was assigned to Newport Naval Training Station in Newport, RI. He attended Gunnery School and Fire Fighter School at the Naval Training Station.

On Aug. 18, 1943, he was assigned to the USS *Alabama* BB-60; transferred to the USS *Washington* BB-56 Sept. 22, 1943.

Was aboard for all major action in the Pacific, including the collision with the USS *Indiana*, typhoon and many bombardments and air attacks.

The most memorable experience was being made a coxswain of the captain's gig #3 motor whale boat and ready boat; and being lowered into the water while the battleship was still underway to rescue downed aircraft flyers and pilots.

On Feb. 18, 1946, he was discharged. He received 15 Battle Stars, European Theater Medal, Good Conduct Medal, Asiatic-Pacific Campaign Medal, WWII Victory Medal, Expert Rifle Ribbon, Philippine Liberation Ribbon, Naval Occupation Medal, and Philippine Presidential Unit Citation Medal.

He is retired, owned and operated his own meat market for several years; later worked as a senior storekeeper in the purchasing department at Woic City Hospital. He is a member of the USS *Washington's* Reunion Group. He married the former Mary Ferro July 3, 1948. They have two children, Elaine and Brian; one grandson; and three granddaughters.

FRANK E. BULLOCK, MM 2/C, born Aug. 3, 1921, Nodaway, MO, joined the USN May 28, 1942, and was assigned to the USS *Washington* Aug. 1, 1942. He was stationed in the evaporator room and transferred to refrigeration and air conditioning.

He was on board in all actions from August 1942-September 1945.

His most memorable experiences: The time spent in the Bible Study classes which met each evening while at sea and the sinking of the *Kirishima* and *Ayanami*. He also enjoyed visiting with church leaders on Efate Island.

He left the ship at the end of September 1945 and was discharged Oct. 12, 1945, with the rate of machinist's mate second class. He received 14 Battle Stars. He served in the American area, Asiatic-Pacific area, and Philippine Liberation. Bullock received the Good Conduct Award.

He is a retired Southern Baptist Home Missionary. He married the former Rosella Hayden July 1, 1945. They have three daughters, eight grandchildren and three great-grandchildren.

BILL LYNN BUNDY, SN 1/C, born Aug. 3, 1924, Alexandria, MN, joined the USN Dec. 17, 1941, and was assigned to the USS *Washington* Dec. 20, 1941. Assigned to 2nd Div. turret #2 for surface attack, and as gunner on 20mm for air attack. Served aboard the USS *Washington* until his discharge Nov. 6, 1945.

Received 13 Battle Stars, EAME Campaign Medal and Asiatic-Pacific Campaign Medal.

Following the war Bundy was in law enforcement for 30 years, first as an officer, then as an instructor at the Alexandria Area Tech. College.

He married the former Irene Korkowski Nov. 28, 1946. They have one daughter and one granddaughter.

ROY F. BURNS, MM 1/C, born July 15, 1921, Tranquility, OH, Adam County, joined the USN Dec. 17, 1941, and was assigned to the USS *Washington* Jan. 13, 1942. Station/job on ship: #2 Engine Room. Action while at sea included Murmansk, third battle of Savo, *Indiana* collision, Asiatic, European and American Campaigns, Philippine Liberation, African, 57 air attacks.

His memorable experiences: Met his brother on the islands and the sinking of the *Kirishima* and *Ayanami*.

Burns was discharged Oct. 13, 1945. He was awarded 15 stars and Good Conduct Medal.

He and his wife of 65 years have two daughters, three sons, and four grandchildren. After suffering two strokes he is not doing anything.

ROLAND E. BUSE, SN 2/C, born March 6, 1927, Milwaukee, WI, joined the USN in February 1945 and was assigned to the USS *Washington* in June 1945. Station/job on ship: 4th Div. He was discharged May 20, 1946, as seaman second class.

His memorable experiences: Magic Carpet Service twice to England and back.

He is presently retired.

ANGELO H. "ANDY" BUTERA, Pharmacist's Mate 3/C, born May 21, 1925, San Jose, CA, joined the USN Sept. 11, 1943, and was assigned to the USS *Washington* Jan. 21, 1944. Station/job on ship: Dental Tech. "H" Div. Discharged April 2, 1946, as pharmacist's mate third class.

Action while at sea included Asiatic-Pacific, American Area, Philippine Liberation and Victory.

His memorable experience: Being in the Navy.

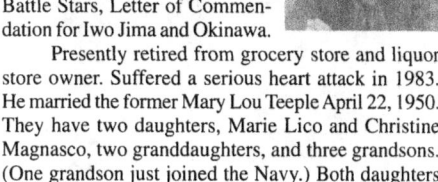

Butera was awarded eight Battle Stars, Letter of Commendation for Iwo Jima and Okinawa.

Presently retired from grocery store and liquor store owner. Suffered a serious heart attack in 1983. He married the former Mary Lou Teeple April 22, 1950. They have two daughters, Marie Lico and Christine Magnasco, two granddaughters, and three grandsons. (One grandson just joined the Navy.) Both daughters are associate members of the USS *Washington*.

ROBERT P. BYERS, BM 3/C, born April 24, 1924, Chicago, IL, joined the USN Dec. 16, 1941, and was assigned to the USS *Washington* Jan. 14, 1942.

Was aboard for all major action including Murmansk Run, third battle of Savo Island, collision with the USS *Indiana*, many bombardments, and 57 air attacks. He remembered Zero and his antics, the sinking of the Japanese battleship, and was so proud that not one sailor aboard died in the war.

Was discharged Oct. 13, 1945, as boatswain's mate third class. Would have been eligible for all Battle Stars and medals the crew of the ship rated. Re-enlisted in the Navy Dec. 16, 1946. Served on the *Wasp, Midway* and *O'Hare*, and shore duty at Point Mugu, CA; Guam; and Oak Harbor, WA. Discharged Sept. 18, 1961. Worked for seven years in civil service and 18 years at the Iowa State Men's Reformatory in Anamosa, IA.

Married the former Ina Boyles Aug. 4, 1953. They have four children: Barbara, Shirley, William and Carol; three grandchildren; and two step-grandchildren. Byers died of cancer Feb. 5, 1995.

MONROE E. BYRD, born July 21, 1924, enlisted in the USN in 1941, served aboard USS *Washington* May 17, 1941-Aug. 25, 1945, covering all operations of WWII.

His battle stations were all in the 5" battery system from the upper handling room to the mount and then sky director. Served in the 8th and 5th Divs.

Discharged in 1946. Immediately started a 40 year railroad career in communications and signals.

Memorable experience: While patrolling around the *Washington* after dark Dec. 7, 1941, in a whale boat they heard a faint voice demanding identification coming from the stern of the carrier *Hornet*. On approach, there stood a Marine detachment armed with rifles and 50 caliber machine guns aimed at them. After identification, they were informed that on the next pass they would have been fired upon! No other ships had been informed of their patrol, consequently they were about to become some of the first WWII casualties.

JOHN CADWALADER, owes his career in the USN to Adm. John Wilcox who was a family friend. Wilcox helped Cadwalader get his commission, and later got him attached to his staff when he became commander Battleships Atlantic with his flag on the *Washington*. After they were underway for Scapa Flow Wilcox showed him a set of plans of the *Bismarck* prepared by the British from information provided by German prisoners picked up after she was sunk. *Bismarck* was a sister ship of the *Tirpitz* who they might soon be fighting, and from studying these plans the admiral was convinced that the *Washington* was the better ship. It was clear from Wilcox's enthusiasm that he would welcome a chance to prove it and his loss overboard soon afterwards was a terrible tragedy.

When they reached Scapa his staff was broken up, and he was ordered to the ship, where he remained through their service with the British, then to the Pacific and Guadalcanal. From his battle station on the foremast he had a fine view of their shells crashing into the *Kirishima*. Next he went to the states to commission the *Monterey*, CVL 26, and then to a lot of action from the Gilberts to Okinawa, during which the *Monterey* and *Washington* were often in the same task force or group, so he was still in company with his former shipmates. They shared two things in common: neither ship had any injury from the enemy, but both had a near disaster caused by the stupidity of an admiral, *Washington* a collision and *Monterey* a near loss from steaming into the eye of a typhoon.

He had 17 more years in the USN, but none better than his tour in the *Washington*.

HUGO A. CAMPANELLI, SN 2/C, born Dec. 7, 1923, joined the USN in January 1942. Got on board the USS 56 in Brooklyn Navy Yard in June 1942. He served with the 4th Div. as deck hand. Participated in action at Guadalcanal.

He was a casualty in Pearl Harbor when they were in dry dock in 1943. A hatch aft of turret three fell on his head. He was taken to the Naval Hospital in Pearl Harbor. He thanks God he was able to recuperate over a few years.

Was medically discharged in February 1944.

Campanelli has been married for 53 years. They have two sons and one daughter. Presently retired after working for GM Motors.

LUTHER E. CAMPBELL, PhM 2/C, born April 10, 1914, Mason, TX, joined the USN Jan. 8, 1944, and was assigned to the USS *Washington* April 5, 1945. Station/job on ship: Sickbay, hospital and office.

His memorable experience was assisting in rescue of overboard shipmate in Atlantic during storm in December 1946.

Action while at sea included Okinawa and Iwo Jima. Campbell was honorably discharged Jan. 2, 1946.

Presently widowed. Was chief deputy and sheriff of Mason County, TX; owner of insurance agency; and tax accountant. He also enjoyed ranching. Campbell is presently retired.

JOHN THOMAS CANTY, born Dec. 21, 1936, the son of Thomas J. Canty, medical officer, USS *Washington*. Married the former Phyllis Lockwood, July 7,

77

1962, daughter of VAdm. Charles A. Lockwood, commander, Submarines Pacific under Adm. C.W. Nimitz.

Canty has five children: Hilary, Thomas, Meredith, Edward and Andrew; and seven grandchildren. He passed away April 22, 1997.

EARL E. CARGILL, MoMM 2/C, born Jan. 19, 1921, Pontiac, MI, joined the USN April 14, 1942, and was assigned to the USS *Washington* in June 1942. Station/job on ship: Worked as machinist in machine shop and worked on diesels in aft space.

His memorable experience: When they hit the USS *Indiana*. Cargill participated in all major campaigns.

He was awarded the American Campaign Medal, Asiatic-Pacific Campaign Medal, Philippine Liberation Medal, Good Conduct Medal and WWII Victory Medal.

He was discharged Dec. 4, 1945.

Cargill was married May 11, 1946, and has three children and five grandchildren. He is still working as a journeyman tool and die maker.

JAMES GORDON CATLETT, born Oct. 20, 1923, raised in a small town named Glensboro, KY with one sister, Louise. After high school he enlisted in the USMC at Louisville, KY Jan. 22, 1943.

He had sea duty on the USS *Washington* July 27, 1943-Sept. 5, 1945. Had special qualification as AA machine gun crewman and received a medal for rifle expert in March 1943. He was discharged at Camp LeJeune, NC Oct. 2, 1945.

After service he married the former Betty Perkins (50 years), had two children (Jane and Gordon), and seven grandchildren. He owned and operated a bulldozer and later served as Anderson County judge-executive for three terms (12 years).

He died at the age of 73, Feb. 14, 1997. *Submitted by Betty Catlett.*

JOHN T. "J.T." CAUDELL, Ship's Cook 1/C, born May 8, 1919, Habersham County, GA, joined the USN April 25, 1941, and was assigned to the USS *Washington*. He was stationed in ship's mess hall.

Discharged April 25, 1947, as ship's cook first class. Received four medals: American Defense, American Area Campaign, Asiatic-Pacific Campaign and WWII Victory Medal.

While anchored at Portland, ME in March 1942, the USS *Washington* and USS *North Carolina* were sending liberty parties to shore by motor launch.

After a long night on the town, they returned to the dock to catch a boat back to the ship. It was past midnight and foggy as all get out. After a long ride back to the ship, they went below deck ready to hit the "sack." The only problem, someone was in his bunk. Caudell was about to throw him out, when they passed the word for all *Washington* sailors to lay up to the quarter deck. In the fog, their coxswain had taken them to the wrong ship!

He married the former Stella Boyko, from Lac La Biche, Alberta Canada March 14, 1947. After his discharge he was employed as a steel fitter for an Atlanta construction company until 1953. He was co-owner of a cafe in Baldwin, GA from 1953-63. In 1963 until his semi-retirement in 1976 he and his brother-in-law owned and operated an agricultural business and feed mill in Cornelia, GA. During his semi-retirement, he worked at the ASCS office in Habersham County, GA until 1980. He was employed as a courier for Habersham Bank, Cornelia, GA, until his death in January 1992.

He is survived by his wife, daughter (Margaret), son (Larry) and stepdaughter (Lorraine), two grandsons, one step-granddaughter, and one great-granddaughter.

FRANCIS ROY CHERRY, FC 3/C, born July 21, 1921, Ogden, UT, joined the USN Sept. 4, 1943, with boot camp in Farragut, ID. Attended Type "A" School at Lake Union Seattle, WA. Joined the *Washington* in Bremerton, WA after the bow was repaired. Served in 40 & 20mm shop, sky control, talker on watch, main director #1, and worked GQ station. Ranking: fire control third class(T) SV6 USNR.

Some memories include dry docking in ABSD-2 Manus Island, passing through the Panama Canal and the typhoon. In the director, saw three waves of Marines wiped out in Iwo Jima, kamikaze attack on aircraft carrier and the whole saga off USS *Franklin*.

Medals awarded during service include Philippine Liberation Medal w/2 stars, Asiatic-Pacific Campaign Medal w/6 stars, Victory Medal and American Area Medal.

Currently retired after 36 years with Utah Power and Light. Married Laura D. Cherry in 1941. They have four children, 20 grandchildren and 12 great-grandchildren.

DONALD ALFRED CLARK, BTC, born Oct. 10, 1921, Frazee, MN, enlisted in the USN Nov. 7, 1939. He was assigned to BB-56 Feb. 2, 1941, as boiler fireman. Left the ship in November 1944 for new construction as boilerman first class.

His memorable experiences: when Adm. Wilcox was lost overboard in February 1942. North Atlantic - King George V cut a destroyer in half. (Punjabi) stern, sunk on their portside. Nine depth charges went off. Was on watch in forward mach-space. Scary!!!

Action while at sea included Torpedo Junction, North Atlantic and Pacific.

Clark was awarded 13 medals. He served on seven ships. Honorably discharged in October 1959 as chief boilerman.

Married the former Evelyn Cooke Feb. 12, 1942. They had two sons, Donald Jr. and George M. In 1989 he remarried to Twila Handcock. Retired from LA Airport as senior BOE (building operating engineer) Oct. 10, 1979.

He used to think USS stood for United States ship. But after duty on seven ships found USS meant underway - Saturday and Sunday. Amen!

ROBERT G. CLARK, born Jan. 9, 1924, Berkley, MI, enlisted in the USN Feb. 25, 1941, in Port Jervis, NY; boot camp Newport, RI. Assigned to the USS *Washington* May 15, 1941, in 1st Div.; made boilerman first class and reassigned to 5th Div. as leading petty officer. Left *Washington* short time before decommissioning. Discharged for 89 days of 90 and re-enlisted for shore duty in Atlantic City, NY.

Married the former Irene Boller Feb. 17, 1948. They have two daughters and four grandchildren.

Served aboard USS *Robert L. Wilson* (DD-847); USS *Massey* (DD-778) and USS *Sierra* (AD-18). Made BMC. Shore duty Norfolk, VA at Shore Patrol Hq. Went to A/C and Refrigeration Night School for two and one-half years, and worked for Civil Service 16 years in A/C & Refrigeration shop. Made leadingman supervisor; retired and started his own business for 14 years.

JACK RICHARD CLEMENS, born Dec. 7, 1925, in Des Moines, IA. Enlisted in the Navy Oct. 19, 1943. He was assigned to the USS *Washington* in February of 1944. As a loader on anti-aircraft guns, he participated in eight major engagements in the Pacific.

His medals include the American Campaign, Asiatic-Pacific Campaign, EAME Campaign, Liberty, Philippine Independence and WWII. He was honorably discharged April 4, 1946.

He married Marie Miller June 22, 1946 and worked in different areas of the telephone industry. From 1963-82, he and Marie owned and operated the Webb-Dickens Telephone Co. in Webb, IA. They had one son, two daughters and three grandchildren. Marie Died April 12, 1995 and Jack died Dec. 9, 1996.

WILLIAM NELSON "BILL" CLINGER, CPL, born Oct. 5, 1917, Columbus, OH, son of Nelson and Janet Burke Clinger. Volunteered for the USMC in January 1943 because he wanted to fight the Japanese. Was assigned a berth on the USS *Washington*, July 12, 1943. He stood various gun watches from 20mm to the 5-inch mark 38 director. Cpl. Clinger found it ironical that he was prepared for landings on the Pacific Islands, however, the only island on which he landed was Pegerian Island on the Majuro Atoll. There he served on the firing squad at funeral services for Lt. Turner who was killed in the USS *Washington*-USS *Indiana* collision.

Following the war Clinger attended Optometry School in Chicago and practiced optometry for many years. He enjoyed the *Washington* reunions, especially liked to recall the Covington reunion he helped host. Adm. Lee was honored at that reunion.

He married the former Doris Davis Sept. 12, 1942, has two daughters, three grandchildren and two great-grandchildren.

THOMAS GAETANO COLASANTO, born Nov. 20, 1927, Brooklyn, NY, graduated Machine and Metal Trade School, New York. Enlisted in the USN Nov. 1, 1945, and reported to boot camp at Camp Perry, Williamsburg, VA on Nov. 2, 1945. Boarded the USS *Washington* at South Boston Navy Yard. Was assigned to the R Div. They picked up midshipmen from Anapolis Naval Academy, and as part of their ship board training, took them on cruises to the Caribbean, Guantanamo Bay, Cuba and Colon Panama.

One memorable experience he had was one night during gunnery practice, he was relieved of damage control watch and decided to have a smoke top side. Not realizing the main battery 16-inch guns were ready to fire broad side. The impact of all three turrets firing knocked him down up against the life lines. This caused him momentarily to lose his vision. When his sight returned he crawled on his belly to the hatch, back to safety, below deck.

Another memorable experience was when the ship was in dry dock at the Brooklyn Navy Yard he walked under the hull. The ship was being decommissioned. The saddest experience was being towed by 12 tug boats to Bayonne, NJ to join the moth ball fleet.

He received the WWII Victory Medal, and was honorably discharged Oct. 31, 1947. Married the former Dorothy Motola, has four children: Patricia, Steven, Thomas and Dominick; five grandchildren; and one great-grandson. Since 1949 he has operated and owned Able Welding Co. For two consecutive years, 1995-97, has been the commander of the George Washington Memorial Post 1872 in Brooklyn, NY. He is active in community services and various charities. He is currently on the board of directors of the Ben-Bay Kiwanis Club.

For several years he has enjoyed the USS *Washington* reunions where he met some interesting people, and enjoyed hearing their stories about their services on the USS *Washington*. Hopes to see them soon. They look forward to the next reunion.

ROBERT A. COLBY, CAPT, born Nov. 18, 1909, Buffalo, NY, was commissioned as a lieutenant (junior grade), USN, March 18, 1940. Served aboard USS *Elliott* in the Caribbean until transferred to BB-56 July 13, 1941. In Iceland he fractured a leg while mountain climbing. Dr. Prevost carried him down the mountain to an Icelandic home and eventually a British ambulance got him to the ship. In 48 hours Drs. Canty and Prevost had him in a walking cast and working. He was aboard for the Murmansk run, the Punjabi incident, and the King's visit. After the historic Savo Island battle in the Pacific he was detached Dec. 28, 1942, Noumea, NC for transportation to USNH Memphis for duty. He later served aboard USS *Intrepid* and at NAS Honolulu; USNTTC Jacksonville; NDS Bethesda (eight years); Yokosuka Japan; and AFIP Washington, D.C. Promoted to captain July 1, 1955. Received the Legion of Merit March 1, 1957, for professional accomplishments. Was physically retired June 30, 1960.

He wed the former Mary Sherman July 3, 1936. They are still celebrating. They live in southern Florida and have two sons, Charles and John, and three grandchildren.

CLAUDE C. COLLINS, MM 2/C, born June 5, 1919, Corbin, KY, joined the USN Nov. 18, 1940, and was assigned to the USS *Washington* March 15, 1941.

Station/job on ship: All system on 150 lb. line. Action while at sea included everything the *Washington* took part in. His memorable experiences: Sinking of *Kirishima* and *Ayanami* and all the other battles.

Awarded the Good Conduct Medal twice. Collins was discharged Jan. 6, 1947.

He has one son, one grandson and two granddaughters. Presently retired.

RAYMOND W. COLLINS, SN 1/C, born March 21, 1928, Mt. Vernon, MD, joined the USN March 20, 1946, and was assigned to the USS *Washington* about June 1, 1946.

Station/job on ship: 5th Div., C-R Div. Action while at sea included cruises to Caribbean, Cuba, Panama, and Southern Drill Grounds. Discharged Jan. 21, 1948.

He was very proud to serve on the USS *Washington*. He missed all the real action, but wishes he could have been there, through all of it.

He remembers a few good times. They picked up 600 midshipmen from Annapolis, steamed down the coast to Cuba and Panama and who could ever forget that party, on the beach at Guantanamo Bay. All the memories he has of the *Washington* are good. He really loved that ship. The only sad thing he remembers was having to paint that beautiful teak deck, with him, being in the paint gang, just happened to be the unlucky one to be the last man off. He painted himself right off the ship, sad to say, that was the last time he saw the BB-56.

Married the former Thelma V. Ward Dec. 31, 1955. They have one son, two grandchildren, and three great-great-grandchildren. Collins is presently retired.

THOMAS M. COOLMAN, CMM, born Jan. 22, 1920, Thorntown, IN, enlisted in the USN in August 1940 in Detroit, MI. Assigned to the USS *Washington* May 15, 1941. Discharged from the USS *Washington* and the USN in August 1946 as chief machinist mate, spending five years and three months in the machine shop. He received all of the service medals and battle stars the USS *Washington* was awarded.

He has worked various jobs including owning a hardware store. He has spent the last 15 years running his own machine shop. Has been married to Beverly for 55 years and they have two children, a boy and a girl, and five grandchildren.

WALTER COPELAND, served with the USMC aboard the USS *Washington* from May 1941-Nov. 22,

1942. He was a member of the Marine detachment when *Washington* was commissioned. While stationed in Philadelphia he became engaged to a lovely girl, whom he later married. They have two children and three grandchildren.

After serving two years aboard *Washington* he was transferred to the Fleet Marine Force, reporting to 1st Marine Div., later to Guadalcanal.

While aboard *Washington* he had the honor of being orderly to King George of England. Later transferred to Adm. Wilcox, USN staff, serving with Robert Montgomery and Douglas Fairbanks Jr.

While in the Pacific they engaged the Japanese navy at Savo Island on the night of Nov. 14-15, 1942.

He later was rotated to the USA where he very quickly married the young lady that had been waiting for his return.

Discharged in January 1945 (medical) and returned to civilian life a real misfit. Upon returning to civilian life he became interested in the food business. Pursuing his line of thought in that field he became a distributor of imported gourmet foods, staying in that field for 30 years when he retired.

In retrospect he's had a ball. He made friends while in the service and they remain friends today. No regrets. Best of luck and good health to you all.

JOHN A COTÉ, RM 2/C, born Jan. 19, 1925, Stamford, TX, joined the USN July 13, 1943. Completed Radio School and boarded BB-56 C R Div. in February 1944. Stood eight hour watches sending/receiving voice/Morse code traffic. Battle station was on bridge which offered good close-up of action. Earned nine Battle Stars.

When returning from England with soldiers a seaman was washed overboard in a storm. He was spotted by a lookout and rescued. The ship's press station sent a description of the event to New York for publication.

Coté was honorably discharged March 13, 1946. He married the former Katie Swain May 4, 1954. They have four children.

NOBLE WILLIAM COULAM, RM 1/C(T), born Feb. 6, 1919, Polo, MO, joined the USN Feb. 14, 1942, (enlisted Feb. 2, 1942). Direct from naval training at Great Lakes, IL to USS *Washington* in May 1942.

Station/job on ship: Radar (Naval Training School, fire control). In 1945 he transferred to Pearl Harbor and taught radar.

His memorable experiences: "Qualified shellback," Guadalcanal, Southern Solomons, Gilbert Islands, Marshall Islands, Kavieng Strike, Marianas, Peleliu, Anguar, Central Philippines, Luzon, Okinawa, Iwo Jima, Taiwan, and Leyte Gulf.

Awarded the American Campaign Medal, Asiatic-Pacific Campaign Ribbon w/4 stars and Philippine Liberation Medal w/2 stars. Honorably discharged Oct. 21, 1945.

He married the former Anna Lee Ash March 21, 1944. They have two sons, David William and Robert Frederick; one granddaughter; and one grandson.

Worked 43 years for Sherwin-Williams Paint Co. and was a real estate representative.

ELMER R. COX, YN 2/C, born March 29, 1925, Muncie, IN. On July 7, 1943, assigned to Co. 1045, Great Lakes Naval Training Station. After completing basic training he was shipped to Bainbridge, MD for 16 weeks Class "A" Storekeeper's School and he reported aboard the USS *Washington* in February 1944.

The day he reported he was assigned to the executive officer's office and he stayed there until he was discharged in Boston May 5, 1946, as yeoman second class.

Retired in 1985 after 39 years of railroading. He is widowed after 41 years of marriage to the former Irene Patterson. He was active in politics and civic affairs all his life and a member of the reunion group since the late '50s.

ROBERT F. CRAFT, Rdm1/c, born Dec. 29, 1923, Assumption, IL, joined the USN Jan. 27, 1942, and was assigned to the USS *Washington* Aug. 18, 1942. Station/job on ship: CIC radar operator.

Action while at sea included Guadalcanal through Iwo Jima.

His memorable experiences: November 14-15, 1942, action; Feb. 1, 1944, collision; numerous air raids and bombardments; number of ships from the Canal to Iwo Jima operations.

Discharged Oct. 29, 1954. Received all awards earned by BB-56 as a crew member and Meritorious Mast on USS *Tarawa*.

Retired from Railway Mail Service and independent grocery business, nine years as school board member and seven years as mayor.

Has been married to Pat for 48 years. They have six grown children and six grandchildren.

CLARENCE CLIFFORD CRIDER, EM 2/C, born March 9, 1920, Harlan, KY, joined the USN Sept. 13, 1939. Served aboard the USS *Milwaukee*, transferred to the USS *Washington* in April 1941. He was a member of the original crew assigned to the Electrical Div.

He was aboard for Murmansk runs, third battle of Savo Island and all major action including the collision with the *Indiana*, until Feb. 25, 1944. He then served aboard the USS *Howard W. Gilmore*, until February 1945 when he was transferred to the Navy Electrical School in Virginia for six months. His most outstanding memory was the sinking of the *Kirishima*. He was discharged Oct. 8, 1945, as electrician's mate second class. Received American Theater, Good Conduct, Asiatic-Pacific, European and African Campaign Medals.

He worked at the Philadelphia Navy Yard, graduated college and seminary and was ordained a Baptist minister Nov. 20, 1959.

He married the former Anna Marie Jordan in Philadelphia, PA Jan. 26, 1946. He had two daughters, Diane and Patricia (deceased in 1984); one son, Clifford; three grandsons; four granddaughters; and three great-grandchildren.

The Lord called him home Nov. 26, 1993. *Submitted by Anna Marie Crider.*

ROBERT LEON CROSS, born Sept. 29, 1925, Brimson, MO, joined the USN Dec. 17, 1943. After boot camp at Farragut, ID was assigned to the USS *Washington* at Bremerton, WA in March 1944. A member of the 2nd Div. as seaman first class his entire term of duty. Left the ship at Philadelphia in November 1945 for duty on the USS *Hullandia* at San Diego.

Most memorable was seeing the carrier *Franklin* heavily damaged and other carriers hit by kamikaze. The storm in the south China Sea that caused the ship to take a number of 25 degree lists nearing the 28 degree maximum. Zero, their mascot, was everyone's friend.

Honorably discharged April 23, 1946. Received the American Area Ribbon, Victory Medal, Asiatic-Pacific w/4 stars and Philippine Liberation w/2 stars. GQ stations varied from powderman in #2 16-inch and 5-inch turret or loader on a 20mm.

Completed college in 1950, joined inactive USAR unit in June 1949. Unit activated in September 1950. Honorably discharged in June 1952.

Employed with Ford Motor Company Aircraft Div. for six years, the US Atomic Energy Commission and subsidiaries for 32 years. Retired at age 65 Jan. 1, 1991.

Married the former Norma F. Brown in August 1947. They have a son, Steven; a daughter, Cathy; two granddaughters; and two grandsons.

Other events: (1) While refueling a cruiser on the starboard side it lost power. Before the 10-inch hawser could be cut free the cruiser was drawn into their side. Their ship maintained speed. The cruiser's port anchor raked off several stanchions, their sea plane and its catapult. Their only prize was the cruiser's port anchor on their fantail.

(2) A damaged kamikaze over shot a carrier and missed their fantail about 50 feet. He hit the water and exploded just beyond their starboard side. Cross can still see the pilot through the closed canopy. He was looking straight ahead. Cross could see him from elbow level up. He was in full uniform including cap.

(3) One day, while at sea, he was on a work detail to receive 50 cases of boneless beef. It soon became obvious that all cases were spoiled and not fit for use. He never forgot thinking about just how good those hamburgers would have tasted.

(4) Several of them noticed dark specks in some slices of bread. Some tried to pick out those specks that were visible, after learning that bugs had invaded the flour supply. The specks were so numerous that success was impossible. They enjoyed more chipped beef gravy on the shingle than usual for many days.

(5) During mid dusk one evening, while at GQ, the fleet learned that an enemy plane had been sighted a great distance forward on course toward them. Soon, a Jap Betty Torpedo bomber was sighted at very low level aligned toward a carrier. Much fire power downed it early and its mission scratched. However, it was later reported that their cross fire had killed six crewmen on another ship.

SAM CUCINOTTA, GM 3/C, born Feb. 19, 1924, Reading, PA joined the USN April 22, 1942, and was assigned to the USS *Washington* Sept. 20, 1943. Station/job on ship: Gunner's mate.

Action while at sea included naval bombardments, many air attacks, and collision with USS *Indiana*.

His memorable experience: Being able to serve under Adm. Willis Lee.

Discharged Nov. 30, 1945. Cucinotta was awarded nine Battle Stars in Pacific and European and African Campaign Medals.

Presently retired research technician, senior warden of Chandler Lodge 227 (Masonic Temple). He has been married for 40 years and has five great granddaughters and one great son.

LAURENCE EVERETT CUFFEL, born Aug. 1, 1916, Brooklyn, NY, enlisted in the USN Nov. 21, 1934, Portland, OR. Assigned to the USS *Washington* E Div., CWT, May 15, 1941-Feb. 28, 1943.

Cuffel served on the USS *West Virginia* and USS *Minneapolis*, prior to the USS *Washington*. Later the USS *McCord*, USS *Marquette* and USS *John W. Thomason*. Transferred to USN Recruiting, Great Falls, MT, USN Recruiting Klamath Falls, OR.

Medals and awards: Good Conduct, American Defense, American Area Medal, Asiatic-Pacific Area Medal, European-African, WWII Victory Medal, China Service Medal, National Service Defense Medal, Korean Service Medal, United Nations Medal, Philippine Liberation Ribbon. Total stars earned 18. Honorably discharged April 1, 1957. Attended Southern Oregon and Oregon State colleges. He was self-employed.

On March 27, 1970, he married the former Mary Wells at Kingsley AB in Klamath Falls, OR. Cuffel died Sept. 16, 1994. *Submitted by Mary Cuffel.*

RUSSELL CUSICK, SN 1/C, born Nov. 15, 1924, St. Paul, MN, joined the USN Dec. 12, 1941, and was assigned to the USS *Washington* Jan. 13, 1942.

Station/job on ship: Stationed on USS *Washington* 3rd Div. upper power car operator, trainer turret 3 after three years changed to C R Div., GQ station fire fighter and put antenna up if knocked down.

His memorable experiences: Diving off top of aircraft crane - just ONCE! Removing Japanese bodies around ship with whale boat at Saipan.

Action while at sea included Guadalcanal third battle. He was awarded 15 Battle Stars and seven ribbons. Discharged Oct. 13, 1945.

Married the former Dorothy Jones June 30, 1945, the best thing he ever did. They have 10 children, five boys and five girls; 16 grandchildren; and one great-grandchild. Presently working in an outboard motor shop and fishing.

GLENN B. DAVIS SR., VADM, born in Norwalk, OH, graduated from the USNA in 1913. He served in the Atlantic during WWI. Studied ordnance engineering and chemical warfare. Also commanded a destroyer and was executive officer of the *Philadelphia*.

When the US entered WWII Adm. Davis was assistant chief of the Bureau of Ordnance. In July 1942 he took command of the *Washington* and sailed her in Guadalcanal. The *Washington* became engaged in the bitter fight off Savo Island on the night of Nov. 14-15, 1942.

In April 1943 he was named commander of Battleship Div. Eight. He led the division against the enemy at Truk and during carrier raids on Saipan, Tinian, Guam and in other legendary battles of the Pacific war. He returned to the mainland in March 1945. His postwar assignments included tours as superintendent of the Naval Gun Factory in Washington, and commandant of the Potomac River Naval Command. His last assignment was as commandant of the Sixth Naval District in Charleston, SC. He retired from active duty in 1953.

His WWII medals included two Legions of Merit and the Navy Cross.

He first married the former Ruth Manahan who died in 1955. He later married Marguerite Evans Willis who also is deceased. He has one son, Glenn B. Jr.; a stepson, Stanley Willis; three grandchildren; and eight great-grandchildren.

He became an executive in the shipping industry, including president of the Isthmian Steamship Co. and board chairman of Isthmian Lines Inc. before retiring a second time in 1958. Davis passed away Sept. 9, 1984.

CHARLES B. DAY, LCDR (R), born April 1, 1892, Evanston, IL, graduated from Northwestern University in 1914 with a degree in mechanical engineering. He was ordered to active duty from Naval Reserve Force Oct. 1, 1917. He served as ensign and then lieutenant (jg) with the Atlantic Fleet during WWI aboard the USS *Maine* and USS *Cummings*. From 1919-34 he served as gunner and chief gunner on expeditionary duty and aboard the USS *New Mexico, Saratoga,* and *Colorado*.
From 1934-36 he taught ordnance and gunnery at the USNA. His next duty assignment was aboard USS *San Francisco* as an ordnance officer from 1936-38. From 1938-40 at the Great Lakes Naval Training Station he taught ordnance. In December 1940 he was assigned to the Philadelphia Naval Shipyard as an ordnance gunner for "connection and fitting out" of the battleship USS *Washington*. His duties aboard the USS *Washington* was as Ordnance J.W.&D.O. As member of the crew on the *Washington*, he served overseas in the North Atlantic (Iceland, Scapa Flow and Murmansk) on convoy duty and in the South Pacific (New Caledonia, Espiritu Santo, Noumea, Guadalcanal and Coral Sea) battling the Japanese Fleet. During his service on the *Washington*, Chief Gunner Day kept a diary of the ship's activities, infrastructure and combat. On June 15, 1942, Chief Gunner Day was promoted to lieutenant. In May 1943 Lt. Day was assigned, as a gunnery officer, to the US Naval Station at Astoria, OR. On Nov. 25, 1947, Lcdr. Day retired from the USN.

Awards include the Presidential Unit Citation w/ Gold Star, Croix de Guerre (France), WWI Victory Medal w/star, Haitian Campaign Medal, second Nicaraguan Campaign Medal, Yangtze Service Medal, American Defense Service Medal w/Fleet Clasp and "A" (combat prior to WWII), American Campaign Medal, EAME Campaign Medal w/star, Asiatic-Pacific Campaign Medal w/3 stars and WWII Victory Medal.

DUANE C. DAY, born April 6, 1922, Kearney, NE, joined the USN in September 1942 and was assigned to the USS *Washington* in December 1942.

Station/job on ship: Signalman third class. Ac-

tion while at sea included all that happened from September 1942-December 1945. Day was discharged in December 1945.

His memorable experiences: Was aboard USS *Washington* for three years, was in Task Force 58 in collision with USS *Indiana*. He was sleeping on top side of the deck, was too hot below. His division officer, Lt. Turner, was killed. They buried him on an island over there. Then they went back to Pearl, cut the bow off, temporarily fixed it up, until they could go to Bremerton, WA.

He married Dora in 1984. Day has two sons, two daughters, and one grandson. Presently retired from Eaton Corp.

WILLIAM J. DEAS, born Oct. 13, 1922, Shelby County, TN, joined the service in February 1941 and was assigned to the USS *Washington* in April 1941. Station/job on ship: Port boat crane, 1st loader 1.1 gun. Participated on patrol in North Atlantic. Deas was discharged in June 1947.

He is presently retired.

MARIANO DECANO, CM 3/C, was assigned to the USS *Washington* in the carpenter shop, R Div. He was awarded five medals and 15 Battle Stars. Decano died Dec. 14, 1989.

RAYMOND J. DeMANN, born March 12, 1925, Pittsburgh, PA, joined the USN April 7, 1943. After boot camp at Sampson, NY, sent to Treasure Island, San Francisco, then was shipped out to Pearl Harbor. Spent a week at Pearl and was assigned to USS *Washington*, 4th Div., Battlestation, 40mm located at the fantail. Duties - ram boat crane and the aviation crane. Leading seaman studying for coxswain when war ended.

Most memorable experiences were crossing the date line, their collision with the USS *Indiana*, Iwo Jima, air attacks, kamikaze, Panama Canal. Was in all battles after their ship returned from Guadalcanal.

Honorably discharged Feb. 27, 1946, with five Battle Stars, Asiatic-Pacific Ribbon, Good Conduct Medal, American Defense Medal, and Philippine Liberation Medal.

Married Angelina and has one daughter, Jacqueline; two grandchildren, Angela and Christopher. Retired going to Florida for the winter and enjoying all kinds of sports, dancing, line dancing. Employed as a meatcutter then got degree and was a food service instructor in a technical school.

GEORGE BRUNS DENNIS, FC 3/C, born Sept. 24, 1920, Macbeth, SC, joined the USN Dec. 19, 1940, and was assigned to the USS *Washington* April 11, 1941.

Station/job on ship: Fire control #1 turret, Crows Nest. Participated in all action through 1944.

Memorable experiences: Crossing the International Dateline, sinking of the Japanese battleship *Kirishima* and destroyer *Ayanami*. Plank owners group, first men assigned before commission of ship.

Discharged Feb. 1, 1947. Dennis was awarded the Philippine Liberation Medal w/2 stars, Asiatic-Pacific Medal w/10 stars, American Area Medal, African European Medal w/1 star, American Defense Medal, WWII Victory Medal and Good Conduct Medal.

He married the former Ruth Barden Sept. 8, 1946. They have three children, seven grandchildren and nine great-grandchildren. He is a retired firefighter and presently lives in Macbeth, SC.

RUSSELL B. DeWITT, GM 2/C, born Jan. 16, 1924, Jackson, MI, joined the USN Feb. 11, 1941, and was assigned to the USS *Washington* in April 1941. Station/job on ship: Right gun, rammerman.

He participated in all action up to January 1945 and was discharged Nov. 11, 1945.

His memorable experiences: Transferred at sea to oil tanker *Kankakee* and *Indiana* collision.

He and his wife, Jeane, have 12 children. Presently retired after 38 years with Consumers Power Co. where he served as vice president of nuclear operations.

HARRY C. DOUGLAS, born Nov. 3, 1921, Warroad, MN, joined the USMC in July 1942. Trained in San Diego, shipped out to the South Pacific 1st Marine Amphibious Corp. He vividly remembers the first night patrol on a lonely stretch of beach. The *Washington* needed three replacements in the Marine Detachment. He started in the 5.38 mount #1 where he spent the Christmas of 1942, 1943 and 1944 which covered much of the South Pacific Operation. There were several instances that strayed from the norm. Several times they had problems with faulty ammunition while firing. Backing the ammo out of the hot gun and getting it down to the main deck and over the side was a task with the 16" and 5" firing broadside. Another time when they were entering a lagoon for night anchorage the *Washington* was the last ship through the torpedo net. They assumed a small submarine followed them in and damaged one ship nearby. They were in a small boat searching for any source of the explosion. Were called in before night fall or any friendly fire. Unusual riding out the typhoon on their return to the Task Force after their new bow replacement.

Seeing their flag on Mount Suribachi **most memorable**, and the most disappointing was at Okinawa where his two friends that came aboard the *Washington* in 1942 were transferred out. Went down the South China coast to the Philippines and eventually home.

Douglas was honorably discharged Oct. 10,

1945. He was awarded the Good Conduct Medal, two Silver Campaign Stars, Bronze Campaign Star, Asiatic-Pacific Campaign Medal, Philippine Liberation Ribbon and Philippine Presidential Unit Citation.

He and his wife have one son. Douglas is presently retired.

DUANE C. DUKE, CAPT, while awaiting reassignment after the sinking of USS *Northhampton* (CA-26) at Guadalcanal Dec. 1, 1942, and a couple of months at COMSOPAC in Noumea, New Caledonia boarded the USS *Washington* (BB-56) in March 1943. His duty as an ensign was in the Radio Div. (CR) as a communications watch officer. With COMBATDIV 6 (Adm. Lee) aboard, the decoding and encoding of messages were very active.

With the collision of the *Washington* and the *Indiana* in 1944 he became the radio officer and assistant communications officer as well as the CR Div. officer.

Just after returning to Bremerton, WA in July 1945 he received orders to Adm. Good's staff (COMCRUDIV 6) as flag lieutenant which read to proceed immediately to his flagship overseas in the Pacific Theatre. Left the *Washington* in August 1945.

Retired from the USN in March 1975 as captain with 32 years longevity.

H. JAY "DURG" DURGAN, born July 20, 1918 in Muskegon, MI, the son of Clyde F. and Genevieve Durgan. He joined the USN in September 1939 and served aboard the USS *Arkansas* until he was assigned to the USS *Washington* in March 1941.

He was a baker first class and was assigned to CASU 37 in November 1943 at Hollister California Air Field, where he spent the remainder of the war years. He was discharged at Crows Landing, CA in September 1945.

Married Margaret McDermott Nov. 21, 1941 in Philadelphia, PA, and they have five sons, one daughter, 13 grandchildren and eight great-grandchildren.

He attended Los Angeles Chiropractic Collage on the GI Bill and practiced in Salinas, CA for 40 years. Retired in 1984 and now lives in Granite Bay, CA. His favorite pastime is playing the guitar with friends.

WILBUR CARY DUTTON, born May 26, 1920, Woods Cross Roads, VA, joined the service in August 1940 and was assigned to the USS *Washington* when put into commission. Station/job on ship: Machinist mate first class. Participated in every battle while at sea.

His memorable experiences: Made many friends and loved Zero, the mascot.

Dutton was discharged in September 1946. He earned many awards.

He was married April 27, 1946, and had one son and two daughters. Dutton passed away Nov. 21, 1979.

ANTHONY WILLIAM ELLIOTT, MM 3/C, born July 25, 1924, Albuquerque, NM, joined the USN Sept. 14, 1942, and was assigned to the USS *Washington* in April 1943.

Station/job on ship: #1 machine space, operate and maintain ship's engine and its auxiliaries, M Div. Participated in the Pacific operations from November 1943-May 1945. His memorable experiences: Equator crossing initiation July 13, 1943, and the *Washington-Indiana* collision.

He was awarded the WWII Victory Medal, Philippine Liberation Medal w/2 Bronze Stars, Good Conduct Medal and Asiatic-Pacific Area Medal w/9 stars. Elliott was discharged Jan. 13, 1946.

He is a retired mechanical engineer.

AUSTIN A.J. ELLIOTT, born June 20, 1924, Lawrence County, IN, enlisted in the USN in January 1942 and was assigned to the *Washington* in June 1942. On Aug. 23, 1942, left for the South Pacific. Was assigned to gunnery 3rd Div., turret #3 as a gun pointer. Participated in all major actions and the sinking of Japanese battleship *Kirishima*.

Authorized to wear Pacific Service Ribbon w/ 12 Bronze Stars, Philippine Liberation Ribbon w/2 Bronze Stars. He remembers the typhoons they were in October and November 1944.

He was married March 22, 1944. After 20 day leave went back for 18 months and was discharged Oct. 13, 1945.

He has three daughters, three sons-in-law, eight grandchildren, and six great-grandchildren. He and his wife have been married for 53 years. Retired in June 1988 and spends winters in Zapata, TX and summers in Indiana. God bless the USS *Washington* and crew.

GEORGE EARL EVANS JR., SN 2/C, born July 10, 1920, Richmond, VA, joined the USN Nov. 21, 1941, and was assigned to the USS *Washington* Dec. 11, 1941.

Station/job on ship: 2nd Div. Action while at sea included Murmansk run in 1942, Iceland, Scapa Flow, and South Pacific. He was injured in late 1942.

Memorable experiences: Being injured and left the BB-56 and going to USHS Solace to Fiji (Fantaw Project). Was stabilized and then back to Solace and the States. Was at Treasure Island Hospital until he could fly to Bethesda, MD (USNH) July 23, 1943. Was discharged on July 18, 1944, as 100% disabled.

Evans was awarded the American Theater Medal, Asiatic-Pacific Campaign Medal, European and African Campaign Medal.

He married the former Pearle Paulson, Y 3/c, Sept. 9, 1944. Evans passed away April 9, 1993. *Submitted by Pearle Evans.*

DOUGLAS E. FAIRBANKS JR., CAPT, born Dec. 9, 1909 in New York, NY, joined the USN in 1941 and was assigned to USS *Washington* March-April 1942. Served as flag lieutenant, Iceland and Scapa Flow, Scotland.

His memorable experiences includes writing "*A Hell of A War.*

Upon completion of training and passing examinations he was commissioned a lieutenant (jg), USNR, 1940-41. Proceeded through the ranks to full commander (1945). Released to inactive duty in Reserve (February 1946).

Served in United States Coastal (Atlantic) waters; North Atlantic and Arctic Oceans; Newfoundland; Norwegian and North Russian Coast; Mediterranean, Adriatic and Aegean Seas; Enlish Channel; North Africa (Morocco, Algeria, Tunisia, Egypt); Malta; Italy (Sicily, Sardinia, Salerno, Naples, Anzio, Ischia, Capri, Procida, Bari, Pontine, and South Italian group of Islands); Yugoslavia (Island of Vis and Dalmatian Coast); Corsica; Elba; Gibraltar; Greece; France; Great Britain.

He was awarded the Silver Star Medal, Legion of Merit, Distinguished Service Cross, Chevalier of the National Order of the Legion d'Honneur, Croix de Guerre w/Palm, Letter of Commendation, USNR Medal w/8 Stars,, American Defense Medal, American Theater Medal w/Star, EAME Campaign Medal w/6 Stars, USN Expert Pistol Shot Medal, Distinguished Public Service Award from the Navy League of the US presented by the Secretary of the navy, the Honorable John Dalton.

He married Lucille Le Suer (Joan Crawford) June 1924 and they were divorced in 1934; Mary Lee Epling April 22, 1939, died Sept. 14, 1988; Vera Lee Shelton, May 30, 1991.

He has children: Daphne Fairbanks, Victoria Fairbanks and Melissa Fairbanks and has grandchildren: Anthony Fairbanks-Weston, Natasha Fairbanks-Weston, Dominick Fairbanks-Weston, Barend Van Gerbig; Elizabeth Van Gerbig; Crystal Morant and Joseph Morant and great-grandchildren: Aislinn Fairbanks-Weston, Georgina Fairbanks-Weston and Benjamin Fairbanks-Weston. He is a retired actor, producer and writer.

WILLIAM B. FARGO, CAPT, born June 1916 in Oregon and was raised in Los Angeles. He attended UCLA and graduated 1939 from the Naval US Academy. His duty assignments include: 1939, *Arizona* (BB-36), junior watch and division officer; 1940, *Manley* APD-1, communications officer; 1941, *Washington* (BB-56), watch and F Div. officer, Secondary Battery, fire control officer, main battery spot one, air defense officer, finally first lieutenat; OOD when RADM Wilcox lost over the side. Last officer plankowner to leave the ship after 5 1/2 years. Ensign to lieutenant commander.

Attended US Naval Academy in 1946, companyh officer; 1948 *Richard B. Anderson* (DD-786), executive officer; 1950 COMSERVPAC, force gunnery officer; 1952 *Ozbourn* (DD-846), commanding officer (Korean War); 1954, *Roanoke* (CL-145), executive officer; 1959, Office of CNO, OP 90; 1961, *Platte* (AO-24), commanding officer; 1962, COMSERVGRU THREE, Japan, chief of staff; Commander Task Group 73.1, Vietnam; 1965, Fleet Training Center, San Diego; Commanding officer. 1969 retirement, started and operated Fargo Travel Service and Faraway Travel, San Diego for 18 years.

He was awarded the Legion of Merit, Combat V, Bronze Star, Combat V, Meritorious Service Medal, miscellaneous campaign area and foreign awards.

In 1941 he married Lucia Morgan who died in

1959. Later married Helen Boulton. He has three children: Thomas Fargo, VADM, USN, and COMFIFTH FLT, Bahrain; Barbara Fargo, attorney, San Jose, CA; Keith Fargo, CAPT (SC) USN, Naval Supply Center, San Diego, and five grandchildren.

He is happy to have had such a long, exciting, rewarding and satisfying service in the USN, shared with hundreds of close friends and fine shipmates.

FRANCIS F. FARNEY, MM2/C, born July 10, 1922, joined the service October 1941 and was assigned to the USS *Washington* Jan. 12, 1942, serving as mail man second class.

He participated in the Murmansk Runs and all Pacific action while at sea.

His memorable experiences include when they lost the Admiral at sea and all the Pacific actions.

Farney was discharged December 1945 and received 15 Battle Stars, and Good Conduct.

He is retired from Buick MT Div., GMC after 35 years service. He has one daughter and a grandson. His folks had five sons in the Navy in WWII. All were overseas and came home safe.

DELMAR LE VON FAULKS, born Sept. 7, 1925 in Corcoran, CA. Grew up at Fresno, CA later joining the USN Sept. 25, 1942.

He boarded the USS *Washington* (BB-56) late 1942 at Noumea, New Caledonia. His duty assignment was to CIC.

His battle station was the open bridge. He witnessed air and surface bombardment while on board, because his battle station was where he could see everything visual. He did not witness the collision of the USS *Washington* and the USS *Indiana* because he was sound asleep in his bunk, but he was rapidly awakened by the impact. He departed the USS *Washington* at Philadelphia for assignment to the USS *Barton* (DD-722) for Operation Crossroads atomic bomb testing (able) (Baker) at Bikini.

He witnessed the sinking of the Japanese battleship *Nagato* at Bikini and was 8,000 yards from target ship USS *Nevada*. The USS *Barton* (DD-722) was the closest ship to the atomic bomb blast.

One day as he was walking by the USAF recruiting office, they were serving the noon meal and he was hungry, but had no money to purchase a meal. He entered the AF recruiting office and they fed him a very appetizing meal. After the meal he departed with an assignment to Castle AFB, Meried, CA.

He is a veteran of WWII, Korea and Vietnam and retired from the USAF, Jan. 1, 1969.

He is proud to have served the US Armed Services. The only negative thing he has to say is that "war is hell."

It has been very rough on him during his retirement years. Lots of good fishing and fishing mostly at the base of the Grand Coulee Dam, WA. He catches lots of Bass, Trout and Walleye.

A very special lady, his wife of many years, Sula Christine Roseluis Faulks, died July 31, 1989. They had children, Patrick Daiward, Geri Starbuck, Mari Faulks, Debbie Bell, Jeffrey Faulks, Joseph Faulks, plus grandchildren and great-grandchildren.

His biggest disappointment in his life time occurred when they took the USS *Washington* (BB-56) off the Navy inventory, by dismantling it. It should have been preserved.

WILLIAM J. FEHN, S1/C, born June 25, 1922 in New York City, joined the USN, April 1943 and was assigned to the USS *Washington* June 1943, 3rd Div., S1c.

He served in all operations June 1943 to November 1945, stationed at powder room 16 inch, left shellman five inch, loader 20 mm.

His memorable experiences include crossing the line; special sea detail; fueling at sea; supplies, recovering patrol plane; typhoons.

Fehn was discharged November 1945 and was awarded the American Campaign, Asiatic-Pacific and Philippine Liberation Medals. He is a retired ironworker with Local 580 NYC.

He married Evelyn Comskey in November 1947 and they have two children, a boy and a girl, three grandchildren and one great-grandson.

MICHAEL J. FERROVECCHIO, CMM, born Dec. 8, 1919 in Brooklyn, NY, joined the USN, Nov. 15, 1939. He attended Group 3 Naval Service School, Class 2-40 in Norfolk, VA, and was assigned to the USS *Prairie* for a short while and then to the USS *Washington* before the ship was commissioned.

His job aboard the ship was in engine room #3, main control. He was on board for all major actions in the Pacific including the Murmansk runs. His enlistment of six years was over while they were in Philadelphia Navy Yard.

He was discharged Nov. 16, 1945 and attained the rank of chief machinist mate. Ferrovecchio received 15 Bronze Stars, the American Theater, Asiatic-Pacific, EAME and Good Conduct Medals.

He retired after 40 years as a wood pattern maker. His family includes his wife, Anita, a son, Michael Jr. and his daughter-in-law, Diane.

RAYMOND E. FORD, CAPT, born July 25, 1922, Laramie, WY, attended US Naval Academy 1940-43 and reported to USS *Washington* July 1943. Assigned to Gunnery Dept., 16 inch main battery fire control.

Participated in Gilberts, Marshalls, Nauru, Kwajalein and Marianas campaigns. Ford received his wings as naval aviator in 1945. Served as instructor flight instructor, NAS Corpus Christi. Served in VP-5, VR-24, VQ-2, and as CO AEWTULANT. US National Representative, NATO Allied Staff, Greece. US Naval Attache to Argentia. Chief, Intelligence Plans, DIA.

He was awarded the Secretary of the Navy Meritorious Service Medal, Commodore Cross of the Royal Order of George I, Greece; Order of Naval Merit, Argentina; Honorary Command Pilot Mexican Air Force; WWII, Pacific area (seven Battle Stars); Korea and Vietnam Service.

Retired June 1973. Following death of wife Ruth in 1979, he married Frances Pavel in 1982. They reside in Fort Collins, CO.

THOMAS F. FORHAN, COX, born Dec. 23, 1923 in Worcester, MA, joined the USN, March 4, 1941, age 17 and was assigned to BB-56, May 15, 1941. He served in 2nd Div., turret 2 and attained the rank of coxswain.

Most memorable experience includes being on deck watching a kamikaze plane hit the USS *Franklin*. He was at his battle station when BB-56 shot down 12 enemy planes and bombarded 10 enemy islands.

Received his 15 Battle Stars, EAME w/Bronze Star, Asiatic-Pacific, 12 Bronze Stars, Philippine Liberation, two Bronze Stars, American Defense, American Service Ribbons, Good Conduct. He was honorably discharged Dec. 24, 1946.

Forhan retired from Norton Company. He is married and has a daughter, Patricia, and grandson, Roger. Enjoys golf and is a member of Green Hill Golf Club in Worcester.

HENRY VIRGIL FORREST, SF2/C, born Dec. 24, 1921 in Jeffs, VA, joined the USN, March 14, 1941 and was assigned to USS *Washington*, May 4, 1941 as ship repairman.

Participated in all major battles and was present during its commissioning. Action in the North Atlantic included convoy duty from Hvalfjord, Iceland to Murmansk, Russia. First action in the Pacific, November 1942, was the night battle of Savo Island, which included the sinking of Japanese battleship *Kirishima*.

Forrest earned 15 Battle Stars from Asia to the Pacific area and two Stars, European. December of 1945, he suffered a broken arm during a storm of the Azores, with gales sweeping wide reaches of the Atlantic, while the *Washington* transported 1500 soldiers from Europe to New York.

He was honorably discharged May 12, 1947 and then recalled to serve on the USS *Markab* (AD-21). He was again discharged September 1955.

He married Rose Grande, March 21, 1944 and has two children and one grandchild. He retired in 1974 from Philadelphia Water Department and now works part time at a golf club and enjoys boating and fishing.

ROBERT J. FRASER, FC3/C, born Nov. 18, 1925 in Milwaukee, WI, joined the USN, Sept. 8, 1943 and was assigned to USS *Washington* May 1944, serving in fire control tower, maintaining FC equipment. He achieved the rank of FC3/c.

While at sea he participated in air strikes on Phil-

83

ippines, Taiwan, Japan, Battle of Leyte Gulf, bombardment of Iwo Jima, Okinawa and many air attacks.

His memorable experiences include typhoon of December 1944; seeing carriers *Franklin* and *Bunker Hill* burning; seeing a lady wave a big US Flag as they approached Bremerton on the day they arrived in US from the Pacific.

Fraser was discharged December 1946 and received six Battle Stars, Asiatic-Pacific, Philippine Liberation, American Theater, Good Conduct and Victory Medals.

He retired after working as civilian with Department of Defense and now does volunteer work. He married Mary Ann Killius June 1956 and they have one son, Tom and one grandson, Alex.

FRED A. FREEMAN, S1/C, born Dec. 11, 1924 in Detroit, MI, joined the USN, Dec. 17, 1941 and was assigned to USS *Washington*, Jan. 13, 1942, fuse setter, 5" and 40mm machine gun. While at sea he participated in action at Guadalcanal and Savo Island.

His memorable experiences include typhoon, Luzon December 1944. He was awarded the Army Good Conduct and Vietnam Medal.

He was discharged Oct. 13, 1945 in Chicago after serving four years in the USN (WWII); two years USN (Korea War) and 18 years US Army (Engineers). Retired with 24 years total service.

Freeman is married and has one daughter, from first wife and five stepchildren with present wife, Bertha, 19 grandchildren and two great-grandchildren.

CARL G. FROEHLICH, S1/C, born Jan. 19, 1913, joined the USN April 22, 1942 in Baltimore and joined the USS *Washington* in Brooklyn two months later. He was a longshoreman, running winch's, rigging booms and went into the Deck Div. No. 4 and was assigned as a boat crane operator. His battle station was a 40mm A.A. Quad, high in the superstructure.

His first day ashore in Honolulu while standing in line for a beer, they had an air alert and everybody headed out of town. All clear was sounded but his four hour pass was up. During the November 14-15 midnight naval battle, his battle station was told to take cover inside. Lying among the shelves of 40mm shells they could hear the Japs shells passing between their stacks. Later he was selected to operate the aircraft recovery crane, on the stern of the ship. He stayed there until the end of the war. Separated from service Oct. 14, 1945, Bainbridge, MD as S1/c.

ARTHUR OSCAR FROEMPTER, MMC, born Feb. 28, 1924 in Boston, MA, joined the USN March 14, 1941 and was assigned boot camp, Newport, RI. After leaving boot camp he was assigned to the USS *Washington* May 20, 1941, M Div. #3 engine room.

Action at sea includes all major actions: capture and defense of Guadalcanal, Gilbert Island operation, Marshall Island operation, Marianas operation, capture and occupation of Pelilieu and Anguar, battle of Leyte Gulf, Okinawa Jima, Formosa and Luzon raids, Iwo Jima occupation and supporting operation, bombardment of Okinawa Jima.

He was awarded the EAME Campaign Medal, Asiatic-Pacific Campaign Medal and the American Campaign Medal.

Froempter was discharged from the USS *Washington* Oct. 21, 1945 and from service Aug. 1, 1962. He retired as serviceman, Boston Gas Co. after 32 years, and died Jan. 3, 1997.

JOSEPH J. GALANTE, PO1/C born Jan. 8, 1925 in Philadelphia, joined the USN on Jan. 18, 1942 and was assigned to the USS *Washington* in March 1942. Stationed on 20mm machine gun, 9th Div. and achieved the rank of first class petty officer.

Served on the USS *Washington* for 43 months during the Asiatic-Pacific Campaign, and discharged Sept. 9, 1945 and received 15 Battle Stars.

His memorable experience includes the ship being attacked by Jap kamikaze planes.

He married Rita, Nov. 25, 1950 and they have two children, Joe Jr. and Rita and six grandchildren. He established his own business, (roofing and siding) and is now semi-retired.

His parents are immigrants from Italy. They raised a family of 12 children, eight boys and four girls. Six of the boys were in the Armed Forces, two in the Army, two in the USN and two in the Marines. His war stories are unending. He remembers playing checkers with Capt. Lee and the loyalty the men had for the *Washington*, each other and those wild shore leaves.

GROVER W. GALE, BM1/C, born Jan. 14, 1916 in Jacob, IL, joined the USN July 1939 and was assigned to the USS *Washington* May 15, 1951. He served with 2nd Div as BM1c and was aboard for all major action.

His memorable experience was the sinking of battleship *Kirishima*.

Gale was discharged July 15, 1947 and was recalled for Korea Oct. 5, 1950 and discharged Jan. 2, 1952 with 26 years service.

He married Helen W. Miller April 1, 1944 and they have two daughters, one son and one grandchild. He retired from United Cal Poly Bank in 1978. Gale passed away Sept. 18, 1994.

CHARLES F. GALLIGAN, PHM2/C, born July 6, 1925 in Pomona, CA, enlisted in the USN, June 25, 1942. After boot camp was sent to New Caledonia and assigned to USS *Washington* October 1942 in Dumbea Bay, Noumea, as a seaman second class, 5th

Div. He became a "corpsman striker" H Div., and eventually a Phm2/c.

Participated in the naval battle of November 1942 (Savo Island) Gilbert and Marshall Island campaigns and consolidation of the Northern Solomons.

The thing he remembers, to this day, is the smell of cordite in the ship, the morning after Savo; the massive, overwhelming assemblage of naval might that was present at Majuro Atoll when they arrived after the collision with the *Indiana*.

He received the Asiatic-Medal with Battle Stars and was eventually assigned to the USN Hospital Corona, CA; Seabee Bn. Dispensary, Port Hueneme, CA. He was honorably discharged from the naval service in May 1946.

He married Mary K., Fitzpatrick, Aug. 7, 1948. They have one son, Mark and one granddaughter, Danielle. He was employed by Chevron Corp. for 34 years in Southern California.

WILLIAM F. "BILL" GALVIN, FC3/C, born July 4, 1925, Boston, MA, enlisted in the USN Dec. 6, 1942, and attended boot camp at Newport, RI. He was assigned to the Fire Control Div. aboard the USS *Washington* in the summer of 1943.

While on board *Washington* his watch stations and battle stations were mostly second battery gun directors. He participated in all major action and earned nine Battle Stars. Galvin transferred from *Washington* to destroyer duty (*Bailey*) January 1946. Discharged July 1946 with an FC3/c rating.

He was recalled and served in Korea, destroyer duty (*Beatty*), earning two Battle Stars until discharged February 1952.

He is married and has six daughters: Carol, Brenda, Jean, June and Donna and Ellen, one granddaughter and five grandsons.

Employed as fire fighter at Boston, MA, 13 years; fuel oil company owner operator, 10 years; technical service manager and field engineer with General Binding Co., 21 years.

MARCEL L. GARCIA, F1/C, born June 1, 1995 in Jemes, NM, joined the USN Oct. 22 1943 in Santa Fe, NM, and went to boot camp in San Diego, CA. He attended Class A School for eight weeks, then served as security guard at Terminal Island prison camp for a month. Shipped to Pearl Harbor, HI where he boarded the USS *Washington* for a tour of duty from May 1944 to June 1945, serving as GQ #5 turret, 5' powder room loader # 3 Fireroom B Div. When they went to Seattle, WA for repairs the war ended. From there they sailed to Panama Canal and onto Philadelphia Navy Yard where he left the ship to go to Shoemaker, CA for his discharge on Dec. 26, 1945. After that he finished high school in Sante Fe.

His memorable experiences include kamikaze, explosion behind a fantail and he got wet.

He was awarded eight Battle Stars from South Pacific, American Defense, Good Conduct, Asiatic-Pacific w/6 Bronze Stars, and Philippine Liberation w/two stars

He married Margaret and they raised two boys and two girls. He worked at a sawmill for five years, auto electric service five years, then went to work at Kirtland AFB for 29 years as a mechanic until he retired in January 1986 as a ground support inspector.

JOHN FILLMORE GASKILL, BTC, born Feb. 18, 1916 in Wanchese, NC. Joined the USN Dec. 10, 1934. After recruit training at Norfolk, VA, he served in USS *Ranger, Colorado* and *Kilty*. Transferred to USS *Washington* pre-commission detail in February 1941.

Most memorable experiences was the night action Nov. 15, 1942 with the sinking of the Japanese battleship *Kirishima* and collision with USS *Indiana* in February 1944. He was in all actions in which the USS *Washington* participated.

He was awarded the American Defense, EAME and Asiatic-Pacific Theatre Campaign, Russian convoys, Liberation Philippine and Guam, Good Conduct.

Transferred November 1945 to shore duty, later serving in USS *Sierra, Wyandot* and *Antares*. Transferred to Fleet Reserve June 17, 1957, ending 22 1/2 years active service.

Employed by Vitro Engineering, US Army and Department of Defense. He retired in 1970. He married Dorothy Broderson May 16, 1938 and they have two daughters, Joan and Jean.

LEONARD GATH, EM2/C, born Oct. 19, 1920 in Rhode Island, joined the USN April 29, 1942 and was ssigned to the USS *Washington* August 1942, as electrician E5, turret no. 1. At sea he maintained all electrical in turret Nn. 1. Discharged Nov. 30, 1945 as EM2/c with 12 Battle Stars.

Attended Bowdoin College July 1946 to 1949 and received an AB degree. Attended Indiana University and received an MS degree in health and safety and Dir HS. He taught high school in Michigan 1952-58. In 1958 appointed to State University of New York at Cortland teaching Health and Safety, retiring in 1985, as associate professor.

He was inducted into the RI Aquatic Hall of Fame because he was New England diving champion, swim coach and official.

He and Louise O'Brien Gath have four children: James, Frances, Elizabeth and Thomas, all college graduates and eight grandchildren.

He and Louise summer in Cortland, NY and winter in sunny Florida.

BARTHOLOMEW R. GAUDIOSO, S1/C, born July 24, 1924 in Bronx, NY, joined the USN May 5, 1943 at Albany, NY. Attended boot camp in Sampson, NY, and was assigned to the USS *Washington* July 27, 1943, no. 3 turret, 3rd Div., powder room and 20mm gun during air attack.

His memorable experiences include going through Panama Canal; and shooting at torpedo Jap plane. He was awarded the American Theater Victory, Asiatic Ribbon w/nine stars and Philippine Ribbon w/2 Stars. He was discharged Feb. 5, 1945.

Guadioso is married to Gladys and they have seven children and 16 grandchildren. He is now a semi-retired business owner, (pet foods and supplies-retail and wholesale).

ROBERT CLYDE GEISINGER, WT3/C, born Feb. 1, 1921 was drafted into service Sept. 30, 1943. Attended boot camp Coeur D. Alene, Idaho, and attended eight weeks of engineer school at Great Lakes, IL.

Assigned to USS *Washington*, February 1944 as F1/c then promoted to watertender third class. Stood watch on #3 and 4 boilers and GQ. Stayed with ship until they brought troops back from England.

He was discharged and was called back to put AO-100 USS *Chickawan* in commission. He was discharged on March 31, 1946.

Geisinger drove a truck cross country from May 1946 to January of 1993. He is married and has eight children, 16 grandchildren and one great-granddaughter.

FRANK E. GENOVESE, SC2/C, born in Peninsula, OH, joined the USN Feb. 3, 1941. Put the USS *Washington* in commission and stationed as ship cook, achieving the rank of SC2/c. He was on board for all major action and served as original plank owner until the war ended in 1945.

His memorable experience includes the bombardment of Iwo Jima and watching the Marines land on Iwo Jima. He has a lot of respect for them.

He was discharged Sept. 10, 1945 and was awarded 15 Battle Stars, the American Defense Ribbon, Good Conduct Ribbon, American Theater Ribbon, Asiatic-Pacific Theater Ribbon, EAME Ribbon and Philippine Liberation Ribbon.

Genovese retired from Firestone with 30 years service, the last five years were spent in West Africa. He moved to Georgia and owns and operates a mobile home park with his wife Marion. They have been married 52 years and have sons, Robert and Jim, a daughter, Pam and a grandson, Jimmy.

JOSEPH J. GIANNINI, RDM3/C, born July 25, 1924 in Northampton, MA, joined the service April 12, 1943, and was assigned to USS *Washington* June 1943 and stationed as radar operator, achieving the rank of RDM3 class.

His action while at sea includes all major action from and including Operation Galvanic.

His memorable experiences include almost getting hit by a kamikaze. If a shipmate hadn't hit the kamikaze, the kamikaze would have hit Giannini.

He was discharged Feb. 3, 1946 and awarded the WWII Victory Medal, Philippine-Liberation Medal w/2 Stars, Asiatic-Pacific Theatre Medal w/11 Stars, American Theater Medal.

He married Theresa Panto, June 1, 1946 and they have four children: Joseph, Gail, Gary and Linda and six grandchildren.

JOHN HASKELL GIELE, SP(A)1/C, born Sept. 7, 1918, Dayton, OH, joined the USN Aug. 15, 1941, and was assigned to USS *Washington* December 1941, as bridge and main battery plot. He achieved the rank of SP(A) 1/2.

While at sea he participated in main battery gunnery, sinking Kirishima, etc.

His memorable experiences include North Atlantic duty with flag; Islands/battles in Pacific.

He was discharged Oct. 6, 1945 and received the usual end of war stuff.

Now retired as pistol range safety officer he is presently a fencing master/Coach. He has a son John Carr Giele, wife Jill and two granddaughters.

JAMES J. GLAVIANO, S1/C, born Nov. 26, 1915 in Hickory, LA joined the USN, Nov. 18, 1940 and was assigned to the USS *Washington* March 6, 1941, stationed in the paint and chemical storeroom, Supply Div.

He was aboard for the Murmansk runs and the third Battle of Savo which was his most memorable experience.

March 18, 1943 he was transferred to the Pacific Fleet Training Center, Pearl Harbor, HI. February 1945 he was discharged as storekeeper first class.

He received the Good Conduct Medal, American Campaign, Asiatic-Pacific Campaign, EAME Campaign Medal and WWII Victory.

March 1946 he was hired at the Naval Weapons Center, China Lake, CA. His brother was the first Navy combat sailor stationed there and recommended him as someone who knew supply.

He married Donna Frederick February 1948. Twenty-five years later he retired as an engineering technician. After retirement he purchased a 20-acre almond orchard in Biggs, CA, which he has tended for 21 years. He has three daugthers, five grandsons, four granddaughters, one great-granddaughter and one great-grandson.

GEORGE R. GREELEY, CAPT, born Jan. 18, 1918, Scranton, PA, received a BA degree from the University of Scranton in 1939. He enlisted in the USN in August 1941 and after midshipman training aboard

USS *Prairie State* (IX-15) was commissioned ensign USNR on Jan. 16, 1942.

He served in the new battleship USS *Washington* (BB-56) for two and one half years as a communications officer, first in the Atlantic where *Washington* was part of a US - British force covering allied convoys to North Russia, and later in the Pacific in 1942 during the capture and defense of Guadalcanal, and in the third battle of Savo Island, a night action in which *Washington* sank the Japanese battleship *Kirishima*. Later he participated in carrier task force operations against the Japanese in the Gilbert Islands, Marshall Islands and the Marianas campaigns.

Following WWII, Lt. Greeley transferred to the regular Navy, completed a one year course at the General Line School, and served tours of duty in USS *Wasp* (CV-18), USS *Shangri-La* (CV-38), and USS *Iowa* (BB-61). In 1948 he was designated a special duty officer (Communications) and served tours of duty as OIC, US Naval Radio Station, Dupont, SC; OIC, US Naval Communications Unit #33; and CO, US Naval Communications Station, Adak, AK. He has served in the Bureau of Naval Personnel; the office of the Chief of Naval Operations; as director, Naval Security Group (Atlantic) on the staff of CINCLANTFLT during a period including the Soviet-Cuban missile crisis of 1962; the Naval Security Group Command; and three tours with the National Security Agency. After 30 years of active duty, he retired from the USN in August 1971.

Among his decorations, Capt. Greeley wears two Joint Service Commendation Medals from CINCLANT and DIRSNA, the Navy Unit Commendation Ribbon, the Asiatic-Pacific Campaign Medal w/7 Battle Stars, and the EAME Campaign Medal w/ Battle Star.

He married Catherine Crowley of Scranton, PA in 1945. His dear wife died in 1983. Their two children are Patricia A. Collins and George R. Greeley Jr. He has six grandchildren and one great-grandson.

WARREN P. GREENE, EM1/C, born June 1, 1920 in Greensburg, TN, joined the USN, May 2, 1939, and assigned to the USS *Washington* May 1941.

He was stationed in after diesel room/after distrubution. His memorable experiences include re mfg. wt. electric fire pump motors and promoted to first class.

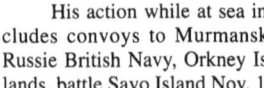

His action while at sea includes convoys to Murmansk, Russie British Navy, Orkney Islands, battle Savo Island Nov. 14-15, 1942.

He was awarded the Good Conduct Medal, American Defense and European Defense South Pacific.

Greene received a medical discharge May 2, 1944. He has four children, three girls and a boy. His wife is deceased. He is retired and now lives in Florida in the winter and Indiana in the summer.

ROBERT J. GRIBLER, MM3/C, born Nov. 29, 1918 in O'Fallon, IL, joined the USN Sept. 7, 1943. Sent to US Naval Training Station, Farragut, ID, Camp Hill, May 8, 1943 to Nov. 14, 1943. Sent to Great Lakes Naval Training Station and attended Engineering School eight weeks and then sent to Bremerton Navy Yard to go aboard USS *Washington*, Feb. 23, 1944, as member of A Div., boat shop. He was in the Pacific Operations, crossed the equator and took part in Iwo Jima, Okinawa operations.

His memorable experiences include crossing the equator and initiation ceremony; he'll never forget Polywog to shellback; going through the Panama Canal.

Awarded Victory Medal, Philippine Liberation w/2 Stars, Asiatic-Pacific w/6 Stars and the American Area.

Discharged Dec. 3, 1945 from Navy pier in Chicago After discharge he went to work. Retired as tool & die maker on October 1981. He and his wife Jane live in O'Fallon, IL. They have five grandchildren and four great-grandchildren. All the family lives in other states.

DONALD WINTERS GUIDICI, MMR3/C, born Jan. 8, 1928, enlisted in the USN at age 18, Jan. 10, 1946. Went to boot camp at San Diego, CA, then engineering school at Great Lakes, and refrigeration school at Norfolk, VA.

He was assigned to the USS *Washington*, A Div., ice machines and boarded her at Annapolis, MD, July 4, 1946. With the USS *North Carolina*, USS *Randolph*, (carrier) and several destroyers they made two midshipman cruises up the Atlantic Coast and to Cuba and Panama.

He was not an old veteran of the times when *Washington* was in its glory. He served as a fireman first class during its last days. He has many good memories of his service aboard her. Once three of them in the air conditioning gang were hiding in the compressor compartment on the bridge and were caught "goofing off" by Adm. Cooley and Capt McClnerney. They didn't put them on report!

In October 1946, most of the crew left their ship and Guidici was one of a skeleton crew that remained on board in Bayonne, NJ. Just before Navy Day he was transferred to Brooklyn Navy Yard.

The remainder of his two years enlistment was on the USS *Amphion* (AR-13). He was discharged as a MMR3/c in November 1947.

He is now a third generation cattle rancher in northern California. He has a wife, Doris and four grown children: David, Doug, Donna and Diane and one grandson, Nicholas Guidici.

JOHN S. HADSELL, LT, born Oct. 29, 1921, Berkeley, CA, attended Berkeley and Oakland schools. Enlisted Navy V-7; graduated University of California, Berkeley, 1943 and Midshipman's School Columbia University, NY, fall 1943.

Enroute to USS *Washington* married his childhood sweetheart Virginia Thompson. Served as ensign, lieutenant (jg) and lieutenant in 9th Div., January 1944 to November 1945, in all actions of the *Washington*, with usual medals.

His memorable moments include joining the *Washington* in Efate, January 1944; on watch in Sky Control at 0428, Jan. 31, 1944, when *Washington* collided with battleship *Indiana*; two overhauls Bremerton, WA; first following collision, second, on leave in Berkeley when A-bombs dropped through Panama Canal in October 1945; arrival in Philadelphia Navy Yard; leaving the Washington, November, 1945.

Career as Presbyterian minister; 17 years professor at San Francisco Theological Seminary, San Anselmo, CA; retired 1987. He has been married to Virginia for 53 years and has two daughters and four grandchildren. He and Virginia are living in Berkeley.

TROY F. "HALZIE" HALL, SC2, born Oct. 5, 1921 in Albertville, AL, enlisted Dec. 9, 1941 and joined the USN in January 1942.

He was assigned to USS *Washington* as machine gun turret/cook SC2, His memorable experiences include the Panama Canal passing and the sinking of *Kirishima* and *Ayanami*.

While at sea he participated in all battles. His units shot down enemy planes. The night of the collision with the *Indiana*, he had duty cooking in the galley, making some of that good old Navy meatloaf. Everything was stacked up on each side of the ovens and then, they weren't stacked up any more. There was raw meatloaf all over the galley floor. What a time he had cleaning up. That was a highlight of the whole darn war.

Hall was awarded the Asiatic-Pacific, EAME, American and WWII Victory.

He was honorably discharged Oct. 21, 1945 as SC3. He married Dec. 25, 1946 and was widowed in 1978. Hall married Wanda Watts, May 3, 1980. He began driving for Armour Meats Co., Dec. 20, 1951 and retired Jan. 1, 1981, Portland, OR.

JOSEPH VANCE HALYBURTON, SF3/C, born Oct. 7, 1925, Canton, NC, moved to Miami, FL in 1938. He had two brothers and one sister. He and his brothers all served in the USN. He received the Medal of Honor posthumously.

After school in Great Lakes in 1944, he was assigned to the USS *Washington*, in the shipfitter shop and served there until his discharge, March 1946.

He went to aircraft school and was employed at Pan American Airways. Recalled to the USN, 1950 and stationed in San Diego. Discharged in 1952.

He married Marian Gilmer in 1949 and they had two children, Dan and Donna. Continued employment with Pan Am in 1952 with a total of 40 years before retiring in 1987.

The USS *Halburton*, guided missile frigate was built in 1982 in honor of his brother Billy. The ship is based in Norfolk, VA. Joe and Marian moved to Flat Rock, NC in 1992. He died Aug. 20, 1994.

JAMES ALLEN HAMILTON, RDM3/C, born April 1, 1920 in St. Louis, MO, entered the service Dec. 31, 1943 in San Diego, CA, and was assigned to USS *Washington* as radarman and lookout.

He achieved the rank of radioman third class and served in the Pacific and returned troops for England while at sea.

His memorable experiences include seeing a Japanese attack plane on their port side, the pilot was in it.

Hamilton was discharged March 10, 1946. He is now retired. Traveled in the LP gas business. He has been married for 45 years to Elinor and they have two children, Jim and Christine and five grandchildren: Candiff, Sterling, Jamie, Blake and Missy.

STANLEY HAMMER, born Dec. 28, 1923 in New York City, joined the USN, Jan. 20, 1941. He received basic training at Newport, RI. Luckily he was hospitalized with "cat fever". Most of his fellow trainees were assigned to USS *Reuben James* and USS *Ellis*. Both ships were sunk in North Atlantic early in the war.

He joined the USS *Washington* as plank owner. He was part of its commissioning. Shared in all of the Lucky W's actions. Entitled to 16 Battle Stars, American Area, Victory Medal American Defense w/star; Philippine Liberation w/2 stars, European Theater Operations w/star; Asiatic Pacific w/12 and Good Conduct.

His most vivid memories include the battle of Guadalcanal; operating with British Fleet on Murmansk Run; kamikaze attack on USS *Franklin*; collision with *Indiana*.

He spent six weeks on USNH St. Albans late 1946. Reassigned to ELSM 446. Hammer was discharged at Norfolk on Dec. 29, 1946.

He left New York for California in 1955, went into own business in restaurant kitchen equipment field and retired in 1990. Married his high school girlfriend, Fran, July 1, 1945. They have a son, Robert, daughter, Carol and grandson Cody and granddaughter, Chelsea.

JODIE HAMRICK, JR., CQM, born at Wynne, AR, June 29, 1923, and was sworn into the USN, Jan. 10, 1940 at Nashville, TN and sent to Norfolk, VA for boot camp.

Upon completion of boot camp was assigned to the USS *California* for duty. In March 1941 he was transferred to the pre-commissioning detail for the USS *Washington* (BB-56) at the naval shipyard Philadelphia and for duty aboard when commissioned May 15, 1941.

When Adm. Willis A. Lee commander of battleships Pacific Fleet came aboard in 1942 and was transferred to his staff and remained with him until October 1944. At this time he was given a leave and transfer orders to stateside.

Upon completion of leave, returned to the West Coast and served on the following ships or stations during the rest of his naval career: USS *Pitt* (APA-223) in the invasion of Okinawa; Naval shipyard Philadelphia; fleet training center and underway training units at Long Beach and San Diego, CA, Guam, Subic Bay, Japan, USS *Conflict* (MSO-426); US Naval Gun Factory as tug master and river pilot; amphibious base, Virginia as tug master and harbor pilot; USS *Sagamore* (ATF-208) from which transferred to Fleet Reserve, Sept. 9, 1960.

He was awarded the Good Conduct, five awards; American Defense, Americal Theater, EAME, Asiatic-Pacific, 13 stars, WWII Victory, Korean, Navy Occupation, China Service, UN Medal and Philippine Liberation.

During leave in 1944 he married Miss Gertrude G. Muir of Philadelphia and had two children, a daughter and son. His family now consists of five grandchildren and two great-grandchildren.

Upon retirement in 1960 he settled in Philadelphia and worked in the Department of Labor and Industry for Commonwealth of Pennsylvania. He retired from state service in 1985 as a senior manager in the employment service.

DAVID ELMER HANDY, MM1, born June 3, 1923 in East Providence, RI, joined the USN, Feb. 6, 1941 and was assigned to the USS *Washington* May 15, 1941 at main control #3 engine room.

He participated in all major actions from 1941 to 1945 and received the American Area Ribbon, EAME Ribbon w/Bronze Star and Asiatic Pacific Ribbon w/12 Bronze Stars, Philippine Liberation Ribbon w/2 Bronze Stars, Good Conduct and American Theatre Ribbon.

Handy has two sons, Bruce and Craig and two granddaughters. He is now retired. He worked for 29 years for W.F. Culton Express.

DONALD ARTHUR HANSEN, born Nov. 22, 1922 in Flint, MI, enlisted in the USN, ten days after Pearl Harbor, about Dec. 18, 1941. He was assigned to the USS *Washington* and worked in sick bay. He participated in major actions and crossed the Arctic Circle. He later returned with the ship to the states and went to pharmacy school. As a hospital apprentice, Hansen then served on the LCI 475 and was in the Philippines.

He came home in 1945 and in August 1946, married Beverly Lind. They had three girls and one boy, Susan, Douglas, Rebecca, and Pamela. Beverly died of cancer at age 41 in 1965. He later married Shirley Justin who had three children and they had one son named after Don. He had become a registered pharmacist and had his own drug store. He and Shirley both died of cancer in 1992. She in January and he in March. *Submitted by his sister, Virginia (Hansen) Bertosso, Burton, MI.*

JOSEPH H. HARDING, BMCS, born April 22, 1919 in Evansville, MN, joined the USN, April 10, 1940 and attended boot camp in San Diego, CA.

He transferred to the *Cincinnati* for one year and then ransferred to new construction which was the *Washington* (BB-56). Transferred to the R Div. to the sail locker, to become a sail maker for the rest of the war; E-4, E-5 and E-6 on the *Washington*. He went through all the battles the *Washington* was in, including the collision at sea. During his time on the *Washington* as a seaman, he was in turret #1 as a powder man in the magazine. Went to R Div. and stood watches on the bridge and in damage control center.

January 31, 1946 after the war, he left the *Washington*. One year on shore duty at Great Lakes and four months at sea on the 863. Permanent shore duty for two years at Green Bay, WI as an instructor. Transferred to the *San Pabalo* (AGS-30) in the Oceanographic Div. for three and a half years. While on the *San Pabalo* was interviewed to be on the crew on the Presidents yacht, but had to turn it down due to his family. Transferred to the *Requisite*, which was a hydrographic ship, to do survey work. Shore duty in Glenview, IL, as chief in charge of electronic maintenance crew for two years. Transferred to the Pineapple Fleet in Hawaii. Served on the *Radford* as chief master arms for three years. Shore duty in Hawaii as harbor patrol and then transferred to the fleet post office as operation chief for the whole fleet under one officer and 28 men, for one year. Transferred to the degaussing stations as chief in charge. Transferred to shore duty at Millington, TN, as a brig warden. This is where he finished his Navy career. He was on the *Washington* when commissioned in Philadelphia, PA Navy Yard and served until it was semi decommissioned Jan. 31, 1946 at Boston, MA. He served 26+ years in the USN, plus inactive reserves for four years.

Harding received eight Good Conduct awards and all the medals the *Washington* was awarded. He was discharged July 29, 1966. After his Navy career was over he worked for Sears as a salesman for 13 years. He married Margaret Jerrek in 1946 and they have three children. He is now retired and resides in Northern Wisconsin.

ISAAC B. HARRISON, S2/C, born June 24, 1919 in Agricola, GA, joined the USN on Navy Day, Oct. 27, 1939 and attended boot camp at Norfolk, VA. Served on USS *Arkansas* during 1940.

He was a member of the original crew which was assigned to USS *Washington* in 1941 (plank owner). He served in S Div. as S2/c. Participated in major actions including escorting convoys from Scapa Flow, Scotland to Murmansk, Russia in 1942; Guadalcanal, Solomon Islands, Gilbert Island. He was transferred to USS *Salamaua* (CVE-96) (plank owner) in late January 1944 a few days before the collision of the *Washington* and the *Indiana*.

After five years of sea duty, was assigned in late 1944 to shore duty at Navy pre-flight school at St. Mary's College, CA and onorably discharged November 1945.

Employed at the US Post Office in Macon, GA for 31 years, retiring in January 1981. He married Betty Caldwell of Macon on April 27, 1947 and has one son, Terry, two granddaughters and two stepgrandchildren. He passed away Sept. 19, 1997.

ROBERT LEE HATCHER, SENIOR CHIEF BOATSWAIN, born Aug. 14, 1921 in Maryville, TN, joined the USN on Dec. 7, 1939 and was assigned to numerous ships including the *Melville*. He then was detached from the *Melville* to the USS *Washington* in April 1941.

He witnessed all major action including the sinking of the Japanese battleship, *Kirishima* and the destroyer *Ayanami*. He received 15 Battle Stars and numerous ribbons.

In 1978 he retired from the USN as senior chief boatswain. He now spends his time playing golf and fishing with his grandson.

He married Peggy Weist on Sept. 16, 1947 and has three wonderful daughters, four grandsons and one granddaughter.

PAUL W. HECHT, EM1/C, born Aug. 18, 1921 in Ridgeway, NC, worked as projectionist in a local theater and joined the USN, Nov. 24, 1941.

He was assigned to the USS *Washington* on Dec. 24, 1941 and placed in 4th Div. A few months later was transferred to the E Div. and put in charge of the movies. Transferred to Brooklyn Naval Hospital when the ship arrived in New York because of fractured hip.

He completed his six year enlistment by serving on two destroyers in the Pacific and was involved in seven invasions.

Hecht was discharged Nov. 30, 1947 as EM1/c, receiving eight Battle Stars, American Theater, Good Conduct, Asiatic-Pacific, EAME Campaign Medals and recently the Russian Great Patriotic War Medal for the Murmansk Run.

He is a retired television chief engineer, married to Edith Loyd, July 5, 1946. They have two daughters, Carol and Pamela and two granddaughters.

ROBERT B. "BOBBY" HENDRICKSON, R3/C, born April 6, 1924 in Ft. Worth, TX, joined the USN, Aug. 2, 1942 and was assigned to the USS *Washington* Jan. 21, 1943, serving as radar operator. He served 31 months and participated in 14 major engagements while at sea.

Hendrickson was discharged Nov. 29, 1945 and he died April 4, 1974.

ROYCE A. HERMAN, S1/C, born Dec. 22, 1925 in Helena, MT, joined the USN, Dec. 20, 1943 and was assigned to the USS *Washington* April 1944, as crane operator.

While at sea he participated in action in Saipan, Tinian, Guam, Iwo Jima, Kyushi and Okinawa. His memorable experiences include troop transport from England; Jap plane so close to ship you could see the pilot.

He was discharged April 18, 1946 and achieved the rank of S1/c. He was awarded the WWII Victory Medal, Asiatic-Pacific Area Campaign Medal w/6 Stars, American Area Campaign Medal, Philippine Liberation Medal w/2 Stars.

Herman married Audrey Hoisington July 20, 1947 and they had four sons, three grandsons and one granddaughter. He was a truck driver for Teamsters Local 190 and died Dec. 25, 1987.

RICHARD C. "DICK" HINZPETER, AOM3/C, born July 3, 1924 in Lake Geneva, WI, joined the USN Dec. 17, 1941 and was assigned to the USS *Washington* Jan. 13, 1942, 9th Div. and V Div.

He served in ship action from Jan. 13, 1942 to April 29, 1944 while at sea. His memorable experiences include the North Altantic; Russia; *King George* and *Punjabi* collision; Savo Island Battle and *Washington, Indiana*. He was discharged with the rank of AOM3/c Dec. 18, 1961. His most memorable experiences include being rated chief petty officer.

He married Annabelle Wittig, Oct. 1, 1946 and they have a daughter, Carol and two sons, Richard and Gary and nine granchildren and two great-granddaughtes. His wife Ann passed away Aug. 16, 1991. He is now retired and traveling.

WILLIAM R. HIPPARD JR., born May 31, 1922 in Coulterville, IL, enlisted in the USNR Sept. 22, 1942 and reported on board USS *Washington* Nov. 12, 1944, served as with Div. JO and JWO. General Quarters Station was #4 engine room.

His most memorable experience was seeing the night bombardment of Iwo and listening to the chaplains description, over the PA system of the kamikaze attack on the USS *Franklin*.

He was honorably discharged June 12, 1946 and received four Battle Stars with accompanying ribbons.

Hippard was employed by Republic Steel Corporation and Reynolds Metals Company in engineering and management assignments. He retired Feb. 1, 1988. He married Patsy Parker Aug. 8, 1953 and they have two daughters, one son and four grandchildren.

JAMES DONALD HITTLE, BRIG GEN, reported to USS *Washington* in Philadelphia Navy Yard, May 31, 1941. *Washington* was assigned to be part of British Home Fleet, Scapa Flow, Orkneys. Lost their Admiral at sea on way to join British Home Fleet. With duty platoon from *Washington,* put down mutiny on SS *Ironclad*. Sailed as covering force for PO 17. SS *Ironclad* was in convoy. Went to GQ for Von Terpitz off northern Norway. *Ironclad,* with skipper and new crew went north, painted ship white and proceeded to Murmansk. Capt. Moore, unbeknown to him that channel lights were off-set, piled up on rocks outside harbor. Later got another ship and participated in landings in North Africa. Detached USS *Washington* in Navy Yard Brooklyn and proceeded to Quantico, VA. Participated in latter operations in Guam. Was G-4 for Iwo Jima, 3rd Marine Div.

After active service in USMC Hittle was director, National Security and Foreign Affairs, VFW for eight years. Also columnist for *Navy Times;* served as correspondent. Mutual Broadcasting System; columnist Copley Newpapers; also director and founder D.C. National Bank. Served as senior vice president Pan American World Airways. Presently retired.

His decorations and medals include the Purple Heart, Legion of Merit w/combat V for Valor, Murmansk Commemoration, North China Medal, Asiatic-Pacific, North American and Atlantic, EAME, two awards City of Paris (Gold and Silver).

ROBERT HOFFER JR., born Sept. 5, 1923 in Raymond, WA, joined the USMC Feb. 8, 1943, and was assigned to the USS *Washington,* July 27, 1943, as a heavy antiaircraft gun crewman. He saw action in the Solomon Islands, Gilbert Islands, Marshall Islands, Saipan, Okinawa, Leyte, Luzon and Iwo Jima. On Oct. 3, 1945, he was honorably discharged as a corporal.

He was a co-owner of a service station with his brother. In 1947, he married Shirley Ford and they had three children: Kenneth, Nancy and Elaine. He was a member of the Raymond American Legion, the Pacific County #968 Veterans of Foreign Wars, and was an active 20 year member of the Willapa Lions Club. After his death, Aug. 15, 1979, the Lions Club renamed their park the Robert Hoffer Memorial Park.

POSEY L. HOLBROOK, born Feb. 16, 1924 in Birmingham, AL, joined the USN Feb. 17, 1941, attended boot camp, Norfolk, VA. Assigned to USS *Washington* May 22, 1941, 4th Div. Transferred to CR Div. November 1941.

He was aboard for all major action including Murmansk Runs, third Battle of Savo Island, collision with USS *Indiana,* many bombardments and many air attacks. His most memorable experiences include the battle of Savo Island and collision with USS *Indiana.*

December 1944 he transferred to Flag Allowance Vice Adm. Lee Com-Bat Ran 2. Moved to USS *South Dakota*. Returned to US for further assignments Com 7th ND Miami also Jacksonville, FL; Pensacola NRTC; Birmingham TAR. Retired from the USNR July 1967.

He was awarded the American Campaign Medal, EAME Campaign Medal, Asiatic-Pacific Medal, Philippine Liberation/Guam, Saipan, China Service and the Good Conduct Medal.

He married Bess Holbrook, Dec. 31, 1945 and they have three daughters: Juanita, Linda and Virginia and three grandsons: Jason, Steven and James Michael. Holbrook is now retired from the trucking industry and still an active square dance caller after 37 years.

WILLIAM C. HOLLAND, AMM3/C, born April 8, 1924 in Joliet, IL, joined the USN, June 2, 1943 and was assigned to the USS *Washington* February 1944. He was stationed in V Div. and achieved the rank of AMM3/c.

He was aboard for all engagements, campaigns and battles starting with the Bonins and Marianas (Saipan, Tinian, Rota and Guam) through the Okinawa Jima campaign and discharged Dec. 9, 1945.

His memorable experiences: went through typhoon of Dec. 17-19, 1944; 1st air attack, terrific noise made by their anti-aircraft guns; 1st kamikaze attack; the power of the 16" guns when they were fired for bombardment. He was awarded the American Theater Campaign Medal, Asiatic-Pacific Theater Campaign Medal w/2 Battle Stars, Philippine Independence Medal and the Philippine Presidential Unit Citation Ribbon.

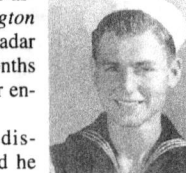

Holland retired as supervisor after 40 years with the Chicago Refinery of Union Oil Co., of California.

He married Beverley Evans, Aug. 11, 1945 and they have two daughters, Terrie and Gail, two grandsons, Jeffrey and Scott, two granddaughters, Janelle and Amy and two great-grandsons, Marc and Christopher.

MARTIN W. HOLLOWAY, SF2/C, born July 30, 1923 in Harnette Co., NC, the son of James Wesley and Ada Campbell Holloway. He joined the USN in December of 1940. After boot camp in Norfolk, VA assigned to the USS *Washington* and remained on the ship for four and a half years. Served in the 5th Div. and later in the (R) Div. and made shipfitter second class.

The most memorable experience was when the *Washington* crossed the equator for the first time, he was in sick bay. The second time the *Washington* crossed the equator, he got a special summons for hiding under the blankets of the sick bay, and he got an initiation he will never forget.

On Feb. 4, 1946, he went to Alabama and married Marcelle Hill and they've had 51 years together. He was discharged in December of 1946. Retired from Reynolds Metals Company as an electrician after 34 years. They have one daughter, Ladonice Wier, and two sons, Martin Jr. and Dewayne and eight grandchildren.

HAROLD E. HOLM, born Feb. 15, 1923 on a farm near Story City, IA, joined the USN, Sept. 30, 1942 and went to San Diego NTS in California.

He went aboard the USS *Washington* at New Caledonia Jan. 21, 1943 and was assigned to B Div., #3 fire room. He was asked to join the oil gang "Oil King" March 9, 1944.

His memorable experience includes the collision with USS *Indiana;* typhoons, bombardment of Iowa Jima and 79 continuous days at sea.

He was awarded the Asiatic-Pacific w/12 Stars, Philippine Liberation w/2 Stars, Good Conduct, Victory Ribbon and the American Area.

After his discharge on March 6, 1946 from the US Naval Hospital, Great Lakes, IL he returned to Story City, IA, and started farming, which he continued until retirement in 1986. He married Gladys Owenson in 1949 and had two sons, a daughter and four grandchildren. Gladys died in 1985 and he remarried Jean Kraemer in 1987. He and Jean are retired in Bella Vista, AR.

PAUL JOHN HOOVER, S1/C, remembers most what happened on the USS *Washington:* he was standing on the boat deck and his legs were spreading apart. He went to his division officer and told him the ship was breaking apart. Hoover showed the officer and the officer laughed and told him it was an expansion strip. At age 17 it was all new to him. The officer said if they didn't have it, the ship would break apart; When the GQ's alarm sounded, he ran to his 40mm and a Jap plane was along side the ship. The gunner in the plane was dead. The pilot had turned the plane into the side of the ship to commit suicide. The Marine on the 20mm

hit the plane and blew it up. Hoover hit the deck and thanked God for saving his life. He was discharged Feb. 7, 1946 with a Good Conduct Medal and 21 Battle Stars. He has been married 51 years and has four children, and is in good health.

CLAYDON D. HOUSEMAN, S1/C, born Oct. 25, 1924, in the town of Ridgeway, NY. He was drafted and joined the USN on April 12, 1943. After spending seven weeks at Sampson NTS he was shipped out to Pearl Harbor and assigned to the USS *Washington,* July 10, 1943, with 1st Div., special sea duty as a leadsman.

He remembers their collision with the USS *Indiana.* He was in the 16" handling room when the fire alarm sounded. He ran top side to his fire station, frame 1-10. It was dark and someone grabbed him and kept him from running off the bow. He sure would like to know who the shipmate was that saved him.

They were watching one of their task force on the horizon having an air attack, when all of a sudden there was a huge black plane with a red emblem flying along the side of the ship. It was so close you could see the pilot and the gunner. A Marine on a 20mm shot it down and you could see the holes the shells had made.

At Iwo Jima they were backed up about a mile off shore, they were in condition A. He was taking soundings on the fantail, there was no bottom at 65 fathoms. He looked up and saw a Jap tank coming down the beach toward their landing. He reported it and one of their 5" mounts took it out.

He was honorably discharged on Jan. 31, 1946 as a seaman first class. He received a Victory Medal, American Campaign, Asiatic-Pacific w/8 Stars and the Philippine Liberation w/2 Stars.

On April 27, 1946 he married Lorraine Wilson. He worked in construction for 31 years and retired as president of Houseman and Fisher Construction. They have a son, Mark and a daughter, Debra. They also have three wonderful grandchildren. He and Lorraine enjoy spending their time traveling, fishing, golfing and bowling.

HORALD MCRAY HUGHES, CDR, born Jan. 4, 1923, in New Bern, NC, enlisted Dec. 12, 1940, attending boot camp in Norfolk, VA. He reported to the USS *Washington* (BB-56), May 15, 1941, participating on the *Washington's* shakedown operation, before engaging in active war duty, March 1942.

He served as storekeeper on the USS *Washington,* until April 10, 1945. While on the USS *Washington,* he participated in all major actions.

His 30 year career also included seeing action in the Korean Conflict, Cuban Missile Crisis and Vietnam. He was honorably discharged Jan. 31, 1971. His distinguished career was marked by his rise from an enlisted man to a commander.

He was awarded the Navy Commendation Medal, Navy Good Conduct w/2 Stars, Navy Expeditionary Medal, China Service Ribbon (extended), American Defense Service Medal, American Area Ribbon, EAME Ribbon, Asiatic-Pacific Area Ribbon w/ 11 Stars, WWII Victory Medal, National Defense Service Medal w/Star, Korean Service Medal w/2 Stars, Armed Forces Expeditionary Medal, Vietnam Service Medal w/2 Stars, Philippine Presidential Unit Citation, Philippine Liberation Medal, United Nations Medal and the Republic of Vietnam Service Medal.

He went to work after retirement for 14 years with the city of Norfolk as city transportation manager, and then opened his own accounting firm, Security Accounting Associates.

He was married to the former, Dorothy Nelson for 51 years. They had two daughters, seven grandchildren and six great-grandchildren. Mac died Jan. 15, 1997 and is buried in Norfolk, VA. His wife Dorothy is also deceased.

RODNEY WM. HUGHES, CWO, born April 19, 1910 in Burnside, KY, first enlisted in the USN at Louisville, KY on April 10, 1935. Reenlisted as SK2c on Jan. 14, 1941 for duty in connection with outfitting and commissioning of the USS *Washington* (BB-56). Reported aboard May 15, 1941 the day of commissioning and assigned to duty in the pay office, paying the officers and crew twice a month. This duty was very much enjoyed as he became acquainted with many of the officers and crew, now fond memories.

His battle station was in the main battery plotting room during the Third Battle of Savo Island (Guadalcanal). Never to forget. Detached as a warrant officer after 31 months for duty ashore in the USA.

THOMAS INCH, FC/3, born Oct. 8, 1918 in Detroit, MI, joined the USN, May 10, 1944. Attended boot camp at Great Lakes; FC School at Treasure Island, San Francisco, CA. Sailed on *Admiral Coontz* to Ulithi. Assigned to the USS *Washington* Feb. 5, 1945 as S1/c. GQS was Sec/Plat, then SRY4 as MTCE/OPR. He made FC/3 May 1945.

A good time was a swim at Ulithi; action at Iwo and Okinawa plus the air raids on carriers; S/W kamikaze hit carrier; he has mixed feelings of crossing the equator; the ship in dry dock was awesome. Cruised the Philippines, Navy Yard Bremerton; gunnery Long Beach; Panama Canal; Philly Naval Yard; he left the ship for leave but went to Philly Hospital for hearing. After schooling he was discharged Dec. 18, 1945.

He went home to family and work. Now retired 15 years after 44 years working with Michigan Bell and living alone at his lake home.

AMON LEE JACKSON JR., born Sept. 23, 1926 in Galatia, a small town in Saline County of Southern Illinois. In 1929 his family moved to Anna, IL which continues to be his home.

Lee joined the USN on Sept. 15, 1944. He spent 16 weeks at boot camp at USNTC, Great Lakes, IL. After boot camp, he was sent to Cooks and Bakers School for 16 weeks in Bainbridge, MD. After graduating in the top five of his class, Lee was given the opportunity to choose his desired type of duty vessel, a battleship.

Having the luck of the Irish, he was sent to Bremerton, WA to serve on the USS *Washington*. He felt both proud and thrilled at his first glance of the magnificent battleship. He was assigned to the "S" Div. as a butcher. To this day, Lee still feels that serving on the USS *Washington* was one of the best times of his life.

On March 5, 1949, A.L. Jackson married Bonnie Rendlemen. The couple had three children: (daughters: Bonnie Lee and Janet and son Mike). There are three grandchildren. A.L.'s wife, Bonnie died in 1987.

He later married Eva (Graves) Parrott. He has stepsons, Terry and Rob and stepdaughter, Judy and three stepgrandchildren.

After serving in the USN, Jackson was employed at Bunny Bread Bakery in Anna, IL in the position of sales manager for 25 years before retiring. A.L. is currently employed as manager of the Lylera Lake Hunting Lodge in Southern Illinois.

GEORGE EARL JAMES, S1/C, born Feb. 24, 1921, Asheville, NC, joined the USN on Dec. 13, 1941. After boot camp, went aboard the USS *Washington*, Jan. 13, 1942, off the coast of Key West, FL, 6th Div., mount six as gun striker. He joined the British home fleet in 1942 and served four months. Sailed to the Pacific on Aug. 23, 1942. Participated in all major actions. He received 15 Battle Stars. A big thrill going from pollywog to shell back. He was discharged Oct. 15, 1945.

James is married to Margaret Pressley and they have two sons and two grandsons. He retired from A.B.F. Freight Systems in 1986.

HOWARD PAUL JENNINGS, CS1, born in Metter, GA Feb. 16, 1924, joined the USN, Feb. 18, 1943 and was assigned to the USS *Washington* June 18, 1946, serving as ships cook and achieving the rank of CS1. While at sea he was on tin cans and saw all his acton on USS *Purdy* 734. His most memorable experience was just being on the *Washington*. It was a thrill of a lifetime.

He was discharged Aug. 15, 1954 and received the American Theater Medal w/2 Stars, Asiatic-Pacific w/4 Stars, Good Conduct and the Unit Citation. He is now retired.

JOHN R. JOHNSON, WT2/C, born Aug. 29, 1922 in Chicago, IL, joined the USN, Sept. 10, 1943 and was assigned to the USS *Washington* when it got new bow in Bremerton. He was stationed with B Div. #2 fire room as WT2/c.

He received the Asiatic-Pacific w/6 Stars and the Philippine Liberation w/2 Stars. Johnson was discharged Dec. 4, 1945.

He married Marie C. Elliott Sept. 4, 1943 and they had two daughters, Carol and Kim and a son Elliott. They also had six grandchildren and eight great-grandchildren. His wife passed away Feb. 21, 1985 and he is now living in Sun City. He was employed as a carpenter for 45 years and is now retired.

CREIGHTON JONES, PFC, born April 9, 1925, in Little Springs, MS. He enlisted in the USMC on Aug. 20, 1943. After basic training he held the rank of PFC (L) (TA) and held weapons qualification as a rifle marksman. He was assigned to the USS *Washington* on May 12, 1944. He participated in actions at Marianas Islands, the attack on Philippine Island, raid on Manila Bay and the air strike against Okinawa Jima. Also air attacks against the Japanese Naval Fleet in San Bernardino Straits, Luzon Island and Palau Island. Creighton was an antiaircraft machine gun crewman. He was honorably discharged Oct. 27, 1945.

Employed by Johns-Manville for 33 years. Creighton married Daisy Joseph on May 11, 1946. They have two daughters, Ann and Theja and four granddaughters: Amanda, Halley, Cindy and Rikki.

Creighton died on Nov. 15, 1996 and is buried at Ozion Baptist Church in Franklin County, MS.

ELMO R. JONES, S1/C, born Aug. 14, 1920 in Ranger, TX, joined the USN Dec. 8, 1941 and was assigned to the USS *Washington* Jan. 4, 1942, as deck, leading seaman. He achieved the rank of S1/c.

While at sea he participated in all action the USS *Washington* was in. His memorable experiences include the Third Battle of Savo. He was discharged Sept. 17, 1945 and received 15 Battle Stars and all medals given to the USS *Washington*.

He married Helene Newell April 3, 1944. They have been married for 52 years. Jones is employed with the Molene Removal and Transportation Service.

WESLEY V. JOYNER, born June 20, 1920 in Fort Valley, GA, joined the USN Sept. 10, 1941 and was assigned to the USS *Washington*, boarding Jan. 10, 1943 out from Key West. Served in the 2nd Div. and was stationed in North #2 turret. Transferred from the USS *Washington* to gunnery in September 1944.

Following the war, he worked at Inland Container in Macon, GA until he retired in 1980. Wesley and his wife, Ruby, enjoy living on the farm. In recent years, they have also enjoyed attending the USS *Washington* reunions.

ABRAHAM JUNGNITSCH, CGM, born Feb. 12, 1920 in Page, ND, joined the USN Sept. 15, 1937 and was assigned to the USS *Washington*, March 1, 1941, as mount captain, 5" mount 1.

He served on the *Washington* from mid March 1941 to mid March 1943. Being a crew member of the *Washington* was the greatest adventure of his life. At the commissioning ceremony when the Honorable Frank Knox, Secretary of the Navy made the statement that the *Washington* was the most powerful ship in the world, they proved it on Nov. 15, 1942, by single-handedly trashing a Jap task force. He had one of the best gun crews and was very proud of the way they performed in time of battle. He was saddened to hear the *Washington* ended up in the scrap yard, for it more than did its duty to save the world from Hitler, Mussolini and Hirohito.

After he left the *Washington,* he was assigned to the USS *Meredith* (DD-726) and participated in the invasion of Normandy. He lost his ship there due to a mine, but not until they had put down a lot of Nazis.

He retired in 1957 as CGM. He is married to Vivian and they have five children. He is now 77 years old and retired.

JOSEPH KASUNICK, S1/C, born Oct. 27, 1925 in Elton, OH, was the second youngest of ten children. He was orphaned at the age of six. When he turned 15, he moved to Cleveland, OH and got a job with the New York Central Railroad (NYCRR). In February 1944, when he was 17, he enlisted in the USN. After boot camp at the Great Lakes Naval Base, he was assigned to the USS *Washington*.

He was in every major battle and received the Asiatic-Pacific Area Ribbon w/6 Bronze Stars and the Philippine Liberation Ribbon w/2 Bronze Stars.

On May 8, 1946 he was discharged and returned to Cleveland and his job at the railroad. In 1947, he met his soon to be bride, Rose Albertino. On May 24, 1948, they were married and on May 27, 1987, after 39 years of marriage, Joe passed away from heart disease. He left five children: Maryanne, Philip, Joseph, Judy and Fred and six grandchildren. He was very proud to be a part of the USS *Washington* and its colorful history.

ROBERT PETER KAROW, F2/C, born May 5, 1927 in Faribault, MN, joined the USN, April 24, 1945 and was assigned to the USS *Washington,* July 27, 1945 as fireman. He was discharged July 26, 1946. Married June Fredenburg, June 17, 1952 and had four children and five grandchildren. Karow died Aug. 28, 1996 and is buried in Ft. Snelling National Cemetery, Minneapolis, MN.

JOSEPH D. "JOE" KELLER, MM3/C, born May 5, 1926 in Williamsport, PA. He joined the USN June 1944 and was trained at Bainbridge, MD and then received basic engineering training at Gulfport, MS.

In January 1945 he boarded the USS *Washington* at Ulithi South Pacific Island and remained aboard until his discharge February 1946. As a MM3/c he served at Okinawa and Iwo Jima and also participated in Japan air strikes

The most memorable experience for him was participating in antiiaircraft firings and watching the kamikaze hits on the *Ticonderoga* and *Bunker Hill*, both within a few hours of each hit.

His awards include several Battle Stars, American Theater and Asiatic-Pacific Campaign Medals. His USN awards include several Battle Stars, American Theater and Asiatic-Pacific Campaign Medals.

After the USN he graduated with engineering honors from Syracuse University June 1951. He is a licensed professional engineer and owner of a consulting company. He has written a book and lectures internationally on electronics. He is also an inventor. He resides with his wife at Plantation, FL. Due to the great amount of five inch gun firing he lost his hearing and has been disabled through the VA since February 1946.

FRANK R. KENFIELD, of Dade City, FL, Oct. 5, 1924 joined the USN on his 17th birthday and attended boot camp at Norfolk then overland to Key West. Boarded USS *Washington* offshore Jan. 12, 1942 and was picked for Radio Gang (CR Div.). He made radioman third and second in 1943 and left December 1943 for new construction and commissioned USS *Wisconsin* April 1944.

Returning to Pacific transferred to Adm. Lee's flag as RM1 aboard USS *South Dakota* then under Adm. Shafroth and Adm. Denfield to USS *Alabama* then USS *Iowa*. Postwar sea duty with Vice Adm. Delaney on USS *St. Paul* then to USS *Springfield* finishing up to 8 1/2 years with shore duty Radio San Fran. Out in March 1950 but recalled for Korean War and 19 months at Radio Guam.

During and after college made career in transportation, port and chamber of commerce work in Amarillo, Dallas and Houston. Retired to Central Texas with 29 acres of woods and wild critters with civilization nearby in Waco, Bryan-College Station and Custin.

ROBERT E. KENNEDY, S1/C, born Sept. 5, 1917 in Detroit, MI, joined the USN Oct. 30, 1939 and was assigned to the USS *Washington* April 2, 1941, as 40mm gun stricker, 4th Div. crane operator. Action while at sea: Russian convoy, Guadalcanal, Savo Island, Iwo Jima, Okinawa, Japan; Nov. 15, 1942, sinking *Kirishima* and *Ayanami*. He was awarded the Asiatic-Pacific w/10 Bronze Stars, American Defense w/Star, EAME w/Star, WWII Victory Medal and Good Conduct.

Kennedy was discharged Dec. 15, 1947. He married Betty Carlson Jan. 26, 1962 and has two daughters, a son and three grandchildren. He is a retired engineer, Conrail Railroad.

JOHN WILLIAM KING, Y2C, born Feb. 9, 1917 in Detroit, MI, enlisted in the USN July 21, 1943 as part of Co. 1047. His basic training was at Great Lakes and from there he was assigned to Class A Storekeepers School in Bainbridge, MD. He boarded the USS *Washington* in Bremerton, WA in February 1944. He participated in the final 13 Pacific actions in which the *Washington* was engaged preceding the end of the war.

King transferred off the *Washington* in September 1945 in Long Beach, CA and was finally honorably discharged from Great Lakes Jan. 12, 1946.

He returned to Detroit and married Juanita Leavitt Aug. 10, 1946. They had one child, Karen and twin grandchildren, Colleen and Jay. He was employed as a credit manager for Sears Roebuck & Co. until retirement in 1982. He went to be with God Jan. 3, 1991.

C.R. KNOWLTON, CDH, born in Stonington, ME, Sept. 2, 1908, was commissioned an ensign February 1940, Boston, MA. Attended Bates College and received a BS, physics major, 1930. Employed as amateur radio operator with station WIATE since 1930; radio engineer, Delco Radio, 1938-39; Delco sales engineer, GM, 1940, US Naval Academy, Post Graduate School February to September 1941; USS *Washington* Sept. 1, 1941; Radiation Lab, Anacostia, MA, 1st radar class, December 1941.

He served as first radar officer, USS *Washington* CXAM-1, 1941, in battle station C-1-C. Besides being ships radar officer he was by his direction, Adm. W. Lee's, radar advisor. Knowlton was operating the SG radio and detected two ships following them, 18,000 yards, March 14, 2900. Admiral Lee ordered target designation and all ships to fire. This action started the battle.

After the war he returned as Eastern sales manager for the Delco Div. of GM. His wife passed away Feb. 25, 1988. They had four children.

He is confined as physically handicapped to a wheelchair. He has been very active in amateur radio, and has won five international radio contests.

ROMAN J. KORZELIK, born June 20, 1925 in Chicago, IL, joined the USN, Sept. 29, 1943. After boot camp in Farragut, ID and service school at Great Lakes, IL, was assigned to the USS *Washington* in March of 1944, No. 4 fireroom.

One of his memorable experiences was observing his 19th birthday at General Quarters during the Marianas "Turkey" shoot.

He was honorably discharged March 27, 1946. He received nine Battle Stars, American Theater, Asiatic-Pacific, Philippine Liberation, and WWII Victory Medals.

After discharge he went to school and studied accounting. Today he is a retired accountant. He married Marilyn Mueller in 1950 and they had two sons Joseph and Gary. Marilyn died in 1969. He remarried Alice Urba in 1973 and has two stepdaughters, Joyce and Susan and seven children call him Grandpa.

WALTER R. KRAUSE, GM3/C, born in Maspeth, NY, Aug. 21, 1923, joined the service Feb. 11, 1941. He was on board when the ship was commissioned in May of 1941.   Served at Scapa Flow when King George came aboard and participated in the Murmansk Run and became a "Blue Nose" at the Arctic Circle. He passed through the Panama Canal, saw action in the Gilbert and Marshall Islands, the bombardment of Nauru, but the most vivid recollections are of the Battle of Guadalcanal: "When those guns let loose, it really shook the hell out of them."

In 1944 Walter was transferred to the *Sitkoh Bay*, a "Kaiser Coffin," serving as a gunners mate third class. He was honorably discharged Oct. 4, 1945.

He was awarded the American Defense, American Theater Campaign, Asiatic-Pacific Theater Campaign, Campaign and WWII Victory and the Good Conduct.

Krause has been married for 50 years to Georgia Hicks. They have two children, Richard and Susan and two grandchildren, Jacqueline and Christopher and they enjoy retirement.

STANLEY J. KRAWCZYK, EM2/C, born Oct. 8, 1919 in Wilmington, DE, enlisted in USN September 1941. After boot training at Newport, RI, he joined the battleship USS *Washington* (BB-56) at Philadelphia Navy Yard. After doing convoy duty to Murmansk, Russia, the USS *Washington* entered the Pacific War in August 1945. In defense of Guadalcanal on the night of Nov. 14, 1942, "Third Battle of Savo" the USS *Washington* engaged a powerful Japanese force coming down the "Slot" and sank the Japanese battleship *Kirishima*. He stayed aboard the USS *Washington* through every major engagement in the Pacific War.

Krawczyk was honorably discharged October 1945 as EM2/c earning 13 Battle Stars and seven ribbons. He married Addie Laurenzi on Feb. 1, 1947 and they have one daughter, Marianne. He retired in 1980 as electrician from Delaware Memorial Bridge. His membership in VFW Post 7006, American Legion Post #30, Guadalcanal Campaign Veterans and USS Washington BB56 Reunion Group.

ELTON C. KROSCHEL, S1/C, born Sept. 17, 1925 in Del Norte, CO, joined the USN December 1943 and was assigned to USS *Washington* February 1944 as deck hand, S1/c. Action while at sea includes dwelling on sketchy poetic portraiture, patters that lend themselves to prose.

His remembered experiences: the accentuate of the *Iowa* class battleship of their painted patinas of antiquity-so striving to quell the envy of the North Carolina class battleships, battleships *North Carolina* and battleship *Washington*.

1943 winter boot camp at Farragut, ID then to Bremerton, WA, where the battleship *Washington* rested in dry dock, a new bow was being formed and fitted for that ship, not knowing this then.

Battleship *Indiana* collided with battleship *Washington* at the Marshall Island Crusade. In another dry dock was battleship *Nevada*, the *Nevada* of Pearl Harbor vintage. 1944, then underway leaving Puget Sound aboard USS *Washington*. So trained and polished of In the Arts of the Sea. Underway South Pacific bound.

He was discharged Dec. 20, 1945. He is married

to Nancy. They have three sons: Aaron, Ethan and Kenan and a daughter Sonja. Kroschel states that he is doing today, what he did while in service, "Sweeping and swabbing the deck."

DONALD KRUEGER, CM3, born Dec. 19, 1925 in Jamestown, ND, joined the USN Dec. 18, 1943 and was assigned to the USS *Washington* February 1944, in the carpenters shop as CM3. While at sea he participated in the Philippines, Okinawa Jima, Formosa and Luzon.

Memorable experiences include September 14 he was a polywog initiated into King Neptunes Reign and became a true shellback. Krueger was discharged April 18, 1946 and was awarded the American Area, Asiatic-Pacific, Philippine Liberation and WWII Victory Medal.

He was a postal clerk, now retired. Traveling, camping, playing a lot of golf. He is married to Alyce and they have three sons: Mike, David and Scott and four grandsons.

RAYMOND H. KRUEGER, EM2/C, born Jan. 20, 1925 in Chicago, IL, joined the USN, May 1, 1943 and was assigned to the USS *Washington* Oct. 31, 1943, serving in 1 and 2 engine room as EM2/c.

While at sea he was aboard for all major actions after Oct. 31, 1943. He went through the Panama Canal to the East Coast and made two trips to Southampton, England and New York.

His memorable experience includes the collision with the USS *Indiana* and the rescue at sea. Seaman were washed over board during Atlantic storm after struggling 55 minutes in bitter cold waters by the skillful maneuvering of ship.

Krueger was discharged March 30, 1946 and was awarded the American Area Campaign Medal, Asiatic-Pacific Area Campaign Medal w/9 Stars, Philippine Liberation Ribbon w/2 Stars and the Victory Medal.

He married his high school sweetheart, LaVerne Liska, April 20, 1946. He retired from Illinois Bell after 30 years service. He was the 5th District of Illinois Children & Youth Chairman for nine years with his wife (American Legion and American Legion Auxiliary).

CHARLES H. KUHN JR., born in Bethlehem, PA, June 14, 1920, enlisted in USNR, April 13, 1942. Following boot camp in Newport, RI, assigned to the USS *Washington*, where he was an FC3/c in I Div., with work station, watches and GQ in secondary plotting room. In February 1945 he transferred to advanced fire control school, San Diego, CA. Discharged Oct. 15, 1945, San Pedro, CA. Recalled Sept. 20, 1950 and served aboard USS *Carmick* (DMS-33) in Korean waters. Discharged June 11, 1955 in San Francisco, CA.

He married Elna A. Nyholm in San Diego, June 22, 1945. They have two sons and three grandsons. Graduated Moravian College, June 1949.

Kuhn was employed as comptroller Moravian College, 1952-61 and business manager, Susquehanna University, 1961-63. Director of business affairs, University of Pittsburg, 1963-82. Retired and residing in Stuart, FL.

AUGUST C. LAPEER, S1/C, born Aug. 1, 1923 in East Jordan, MI, joined the USN, July 1942 and was assigned to the USS *Washington* February 1943, serving as gunner, 9th Div. and U Div. 20mm. He achieved the rank of seaman first class. He participated in first action Gilbert Islands, November 1943 while at sea, and was aboard until the ship returned to the States after the *Kyusho* action July 1945.

His memorable experiences include firing on planes that hit *Yorktown* and *Franklin's* 20mm gunner.

Lapeer was discharged Jan. 9, 1946 and was awarded the American Theater, Asiatic-Pacific w/9 stars, Victory Bar, Good Conduct, Philippine Liberation and two Bronze Stars.

He married Isabell Fuller in 1947 and they have three sons, one daughter, 11 grandchildren and four great-grandchildren. Lapeer is presently retired. He is a past commander of VFW Post 2051 Petoskey and likes to travel.

MERLE A. LARSON, EM2/C, born Jan. 16, 1923 in Bremen, ND, joined the USN April 14, 1943 and achieved the rank of EM2/c. While at sea he participated in the battle of Saipan, Guam, Tinian, Iwo Jima, Okinawa and Philippine Sea.

He received five Battle Stars and the American Theater Ribbon and was discharged April 15, 1946.

Larson passed away November 1988. Since leaving the the USN he was in the grain elevator business. For close to 30 years he owned and operated "Merle A. Larson Inc.", a grain elevator in Washburn, ND. He is survived by his wife Ardeth of Bismarck, ND and had four sons: Doug, Dave, Dwight and Drew.

ANGELO LA VALLE, MM3/C, born April 23, 1924 in Syracuse, NY, joined the USN Oct. 5, 1943 and was assigned to the USS *Washington* Jan. 5, 1944, A Div. During General Quarters, he was in 16" powder room, later on the telephones for repair #1.

La Valle achieved the rank of MM3/c and was awarded the American Theater Medal, Asiatic-Pacific Medal w/5 Stars, Philippine Liberation Ribbon w/2 Stars, and the Victory Medal.

His memorable experiences including locating a man overboard in the Atlantic; midget Jap submarine in Eniwetok.

He was discharged May 26, 1946. Married and has one boy and two girls. Employed as general contractor from 1946-1996 and is now retired.

HAROLD RUMSEY LEACH, Y2/C, born May 8, 1918 at Marathon, NY, joined the USN April 28, 1942 as captain's OFC and achieved the rank of Y2/c.

While at sea he served in the South Pacific campaigns. His memorable experiences include a collision Feb. 1, 1944 with USS *Indiana* and their "zig-zag" courses to confuse and evade the Japanese.

He was discharged September 1945. Awards awarded for South Pacific action except while hospitalized on medical leave.

Leach has been employed for 20 years with Hathaway Bakeries and 25 years as insurance agent representing State Farm Insurance Companies. He married Katherine Potts June 30, 1945. They had three children: Paula, Brian and Vern and 12 grandchildren and three great-grandchildren.

PATRICK T. LEAK, HNC, born Nov. 10, 1924 in Philadelphia, PA. He joined the USN in June 1942, one day after high school graduation. He served under many commands with both the USMC and USN, during WWII, Korea and the following years. Throughout his USN career, he earned many awards of which he was very proud. As well as the USS *Washington*, he served aboard the hospital ship *Repose* and organized their reunion in Long Beach, CA.

His father, LT Leslie N. (Joe) Leak served 30 years in the USN, also in H Div., and was one of the survivors's from the USS *West Virginia* at Pearl Harbor, being listed in the book *A Day of Infamy*.

He met and married Stella in Christchurch, New Zealand on Jan. 21, 1960, while serving with Operation Deep Freeze in Antarctic. They had two children Kevin J. (May 23, 1964) and Debra A. (Oct. 13, 1966).

He retired from active duty in 1962 with the rank of HMC and worked for the US Post Office in Long Beach, CA until ill-health forced him to retire in 1981. He moved to Carson City, NV in 1985. Pat was called by the Supreme Commander Feb. 26, 1994.

ROBERT S. LEBAIR, LT, born May 23, 1923, Jeukintown, PA. July of 1942 entered Princeton University, Navy V-12 program July 1943. Commissioned ensign, Naval Midshipmen School, Columbia, October 1944. Three months Naval Communication School, Cambridge, MA assigned to USS *Washington* (BB-

56), bringing troops back from Europe, Magic Carpet duty. Released active duty July 1946 and completed undergraduate education at Princeton University June 1947. Duty during Korean War as an intelligence officer with communication duties on 7th Fleet Staff, Far East (served on USS *Wisconsin,* USS *Iowa,* and USS *Missouri*). Advanced to rank of lieutenant.

He was released from active duty February 1953 and was awarded the American Theater Ribbon, WWII Victory Ribbon, Korean Ribbon w/2 Stars, China Service Ribbon and the United Nations.

He has been married 47 years to Marie Frances Lebair. They have five children, (one daughter and four sons), and 11 grandchildren. Owner of air-conditioning and heating contracting firm. Currently retired doing volunteer work for Navy Marine Corps Relief Society and the Independent Seaport Museum in Philadelphia.

EARL MASON LEE, QMC1/C, born Feb. 28, 1923 in Ashland, KY, joined the USN March 16, 1942 and was assigned to USS *Washington* July 27, 1942 and aboard for most major action.

He left the USN after WWII but reenlisted several months later as a seaman with the goal of reaching E-9, which he attained in 1964 but remained in the USN to retire as SMCM with 30 years service.

Among his 11 medals and 16 Battle Stars are Philippine Presidential, Korean Presidential, Asiatic-Pacific and China Service.

His career included tours of duty on the Mullinax, Stormes, Henrico, Joy, PHIBERUP 2, DESRON 32, two years two shore duty in Washington, DC with the Armed Forces Police and several other ships.

He was married to Iris Hennen and the father of Anthony Lee and had two grandchildren and one stepson. He passed away Aug. 1, 1991 and buried with military honors in Norfolk, VA.

WILLIS A. LEE, VADM, born in Natlee, KY, May 11, 1888, the son of Willis Augustus Lee Sr. and Susan Arnold Lee. His father, known as "Pink Lee", was a lawyer and later a judge in Owen County, KY, and was the brother of Jefferson Davis Lee, the father of Isabel Lee Wilson.

Willis Augustus Lee was appointed to the US Naval Academy, Annapolis, MD, from his native state, Kentucky, in 1904. While a midshipman, he won his letter on the Rifle Team, qualifying as an expert rifleman, and was awarded the Gold Medal for small arms efficiency as a second classman. He was a member of the Naval Academy Rifle Team which participated in the National Rifle Match at Camp Perry, OH in 1907, winning the national individual match and the national pistol match. As a First Classman he had his name engraved on the cup presented by the Sons of the Revolution (General Society) for proficiency in great gun target practice or practical ordnance and gunnery. After two years at sea, which were then required by law after completing the four year course at the Naval Academy, he graduated on June 6, 1910 and was commissioned an ENS in the USN. He subsequently advanced in rank until he was appointed Vice Admiral on March 21, 1944.

Having completed the course at the Naval Academy in June 1908, he remained at the Academy as a member of the Navy Rifle Team during the summer. He then served on board the USS *Idaho* from October 1908 until May 1909. During the summer of 1909 he again served with the Navy Rifle Team at the Academy. In October of 1909 he assisted in assembling the crew of the USS *New Orleans* and served on board that cruiser from her commissioning, Nov. 15, 1909, until May 1910.

The USS *Helena* on the Asiatic Station was his next assignment where he served until his detachment from that cruiser in January 1913 to return to the US to take part in the National Rifle Match. In July he rejoined the battleship *Idaho,* and in December of 1914 was transferred to the USS *New Hampshire.*

While on that battleship he participated in the landing of forces engaged in the occupation of Vera Cruz, Mexico in 1914.

December 1915 he reported to the Union Tool Co., Chicago, IL, where he served for three years as Inspector of Ordnance. In November 1918, a few days after the signing of the Armistice of WWI, he joined the destroyer force based in Queenstown, Ireland, assigned to the USS *O'Brien.* December 21, 1918 he reported to headquarters of US Naval Forces at Brest, France and was assigned to the USS *Lea* in which he served until June 1919.

Upon his return to the US he again participated with the Naval Rifle Team at the National Matches. During this time he served as executive officer of the USS *Bushnell* flagship and tender of Submarine Div., Atlantic Fleet, from September 1919 until June 1920. The summer of 1920 he was a member of the American Rifle Team at the Olympic Games in Antwerp, Belgium, winning with CDR Carl T. Osburn, USN, nine gold, two silver and two bronze medals. He personally won five gold, one silver and one bronze medal.

From September 1920 until June 1924 he had successive command of the USS *Fairfax* and USS *William B. Preston,* sailing the latter to China Station via the Suez Canal from Newport, RI in 1921. Upon his return to the US he was assigned duty at New York Navy Yard until November 1926. While there he again participated in the National Rifle Matches and in 1925, as captain of the Navy Rifle Team. His next assignment was as executive officer of the USS *Antares* and from October 1927 until June 1928 he was CO of the USS *Lardner.*

After completing the senior course at the Naval War College in Newport, RI, in May of 1929, he served for a year as inspector of ordnance in charge, at the Naval Ordnance Plant, Baldwin, Long Island, NY. During the summer of 1930 he again served as captain of the Navy Rifle Team which participated in the matches at Wakefield, Massachusettes and Camp Perry, OH.

Division of Fleet Training, Office of the Chief of Naval Operations, Navy Department, Washington, DC, was his next assignment and in May 1931 he joined the USS *Pennsylvania,* flagship of the US fleet, for duty first as navigator and later as XO. In June 1933 he returned to the Division of Fleet Training and served as Head of the Gunnery Section for two years as Head of the Tactical Section during 1935-1936. In October 1936 he assumed command of the USS *Concord.* Upon his detachment from that cruiser in July 1938, he reported for duty as operations officer on the staff of RADM Harold R. Stark, USN, who was then commanding cruisers, Battle Force (the *Concord,* flagship). In December 1938 he served as chief of staff for five months while ADM Stark's flag was in the USS *Honolulu.*

In June 1939 he returned to the Navy Department for duty as assistant director of the Division of Fleet Training, and in January 1941 he became director of that division. After the outbreak of World War II in December 1941, he reported as chief of staff to the Commander in Chief, US Fleet on February 1942. After six months in that assignment he was sent to the Pacific Theater where he served consecutively as Commander Battleship Division 6, Commander Battleships, Pacific Fleet (with additional duty in command of Division 6) and as Commander Battleship Squadron 2.

During his service in the Pacific Theater, he commanded a task force which intercepted Japanese forces attempting to recapture positions in the Guadalcanal-Tulagi area. In action on the night of November 14-15, 1942, he won for all forces engaged, the "Well Done", from ADM Ernest J. King, USN, Commander in Chief, US Fleet. He was personally awarded the Navy Cross, with citation.

Following the capture of the Gilbert Islands in November 1943, he commanded a task force which attacked Nauru, and in February 1944, he was in command of the battleships which operated with the Truk Striking Force which took part in the carrier raids against the Saipan-Tinian area and various other engagements. On May 1, 1944, he directed the bombardment of shore installations at Ponape which resulted in great damage to the enemy. Later at Saipan, in the first state of the Battle of the Philippine Sea, he assisted in opening the way for the landing forces. On June 19, 1944, in the Battle of the Philippine Sea, he directed his ships for maximum effectiveness when our Task Force was subjected to full-scale attack by Japanese carrier based planes, and by the expert gunnery of his officers and men succeeded in destroying several hostile bombers. He was awarded the Legion of Merit and the Distinguished Service Medal.

Still in command of Battleship Squadron 2, Vice Admiral Lee died of coronary thrombosis on Aug. 25, 1945, on board a launch bearing him to the USS *Wyoming,* his flagship, in Casco Bay, off Portland, ME. Interment was at Arlington National Cemetery.

He was survived by his wife, Mrs. Willis A. (nee Mabelle Allen) Lee, Illinois, now deceased.

He was posthumously awarded a Gold Star in lieu of the Second Distinguished Service Medal for exceptionally meritorious service.

The USS *Willis A. Lee* (DL-4) has been named to honor Vice Admiral Lee. Mrs. Fitzhugh Lee Palmer (wife of Captain F.L. Palmer, USN and daughter of Admiral Lee's sister, Mrs. Lucy Lee Vallandingham), who then resided at the Naval Air Station, Brunswick, ME, sponsored the vessel at the launching at Bethlehem Steel Company's plant at Quincy, MA on Jan. 26, 1952.

FLOYD GEORGE LEISHING, MM1/C, born Aug. 8, 1923 in Labanon, MO, joined the USN Aug. 8, 1943, and attended boot training at Farragut, ID. Assigned to the *Washington* December 1943.

While at sea he served in battles at Leyte, Mindanao, Okinawa, Iwo Jima, Caledonia, Marshall Islands, Midway and Philippines. He was on board when the *Indiana* rammed the *Washington.* They then went to Pearl Harbor for repairs. He was discharged Dec. 7, 1945.

He married Donna Lee England Nov. 15, 1941. They were married almost 50 years and he passed away Aug. 10, 1991. They had three sons and one daughter: George Lee, Michael Eugene, Sharon Kathleen and Randolph Kurt. *For photo see page 111.*

NICK LEONE JR., S1C, born Sept. 19, 1925 in St. Louis, MO, joined the USN Dec. 15, 1943 and was assigned to the USS *Washington* January 1944 as gunners mate, hot caseman in five inch gun mount.

While at sea he served in all major actions including: operations Flintock and Forager, Leyte, Luzon, Iwo Jima, Okinawa, Kyushu, Saipan and Philippine Sea. His memorable experiences include having his appendix removed during the typhoon of December 1944 and the invasion of Iwo Jima.

He was awarded the Victory Medal, American Area, Philippine Liberation w/2 stars, Asiatic-Pacific w/4 stars.

Leone was discharged April 20, 1946. He married Billie Jean Wessler on Jan. 11, 1947 and they had five children: Nick III, William, Claire, Mary and Angie, 11 grandchildren and six great-grandchildren.

He was the director of the St. Vincent de Paul Society Store and soup kitchen until his death on Sept. 29, 1986.

JOHN WILLIAM LEWIS, S1/C, born Feb. 26, 1920, Laurens County, SC, joined the USN Dec. 11, 1941, and was assigned to USS *Washington* in January of 1942, 8th Div., S1c. He was first loader on a 40mm quad, number 14.

His most memorable experience was the Battle of Savo Island, Nov. 14 and 15, 1942 and the daily attacks by suicide planes at Okinawa. He received an honorable discharge Sept. 19, 1945 and received 13 Battle Stars.

Married to Angie E. Mercer and has one son, four daughters, 15 grandchildren and two great-grandchildren. Lewis and wife, Angie has been traveling over the country for 33 years in evangelistic ministry.

LEN L. LEWIS, CSF, MEC, born April 14, 1918 in Logan, UT, died Sept. 18, 1991 in Snyder, CO. Served in the USN from Dec. 11, 1936 through Feb. 27, 1957.

He became a diver second class March 25, 1940 while on the USS *Enterprise* (CV-6) and remained a diver until retirement. Assigned to the USS *Washington* June 30, 1941 as a SF2/c. Transferred in 1945 as SF1c.

As a civilian he worked in civil engineering at the USAF Academy, retiring to Snyder, CO in 1973. Married Veronica McCartney, Aug. 3, 1946 in Arlington, VA. He is survived by his wife Veronica, Snyder, CO; one daughter, Mary Ellen Johnson and two sons, John and Victory Lewis, all of Colorado Springs, CO; three brothers, Paul and Nick Lewis of Glen Ellen, CA and Victor Lewis of Canon City, CO and eight grandchildren.

BASIL LINVILLE, GM2/C, born March 5, 1924 in Logan County, WV, joined the USN Feb 14, 1941 and was assigned to the USS *Washington* May 15, 1941. He departed Oct. 21, 1944, serving with 2nd Div., #2 turret.

While at sea he participated in action from Nov. 15, 1942 through Oct. 21, 1944. His memorable experiences include his first battle, Nov. 15, 1942.

He was discharged from the USN January 1946 and entered the US Army in 1947. Retired 1964, command sergeant major.

Linville married Irene F. Wojnar April 21, 1945 and they have five childen, (three boys and two girls). All three boys saw service, BJ and Bruce in the Army and Mike in the USN. Presently involved with 40 A Farm in Ashland, OH.

JAMES PATRICK LITTLE, MM1/C, born June 8, 1922 in Hancock, MD, and enlisted in the service November 1940. He came aboard the USS *Washington* prior to the ship's commissioning and served through all ship's campaigns from Murmansk until his discharge October 1946.

He was assigned to main engine room (M Div.) on operational watch where he achieved machinist mate first class rank. He saw action in all *Washington's* battles for which he received six medals and 15 Bronze Stars. (He served on destroyer off Korea October 1950 to December 1951.)

June 1949 he graduated Milwaukee School of Engineering with technician's certificate. He married Ruth Stockhausen September 1950. They were blessed with five daughters: (Anne, Joan, Marge, Mary, Joyce) and has one son (Paul) and 10 grandchildren.

He retired after 25 years as operations engineer at Northwestern National Insurance Company. He died Nov. 8, 1987, shortly after joyfully sharing memorable times with shipmates at Mobile reunion.

JAMES N. LOEWE SR., S1/C, born Dec. 14, 1926 in St. Louis, joined the USN December 1942 and was assigned to the USS *Washington* April 1943, marlin spike and deck seamanship.

Upon being assigned to the "Mighty W" he was told that the 5th Div. would be his home until the war was over. Later he was assigned to mount 3, 5" twin turret, and spent many hours at this battle station.

They were all taught the principle of four different types of 5" shells and when each was to be used.

The majority of his memories of WWII go back to mount 3, and the time spent at his battle station. Comradeship was established there, among ten individuals who were hand picked by their NCO, being so close, they were forced to act in an adult manner, being ready for any situation.

Deck and Marlinspike Seamanship was their other duty, keeping the ship both trim and proper, ready for any eventuality. It seemed there was always a destroyer to be refueled to starboard which they all participated in, as they always had enough fuel oil to go around.

He was always proud to serve on the USS *Washington*.

JACOB ALONZA LONG, SF1/C, born June 22, 1923 in Nixville Section of Estill, SC (Hampton County), joined the USN June 18, 1948 and served boot camp at Norfolk, VA. He was assigned to BB-56 in July 1942. Served with 9th Div. as a gunner on 20mm mounts. Attained rank of SF1. All experiences were memorable, some which he has cherished through the years.

Employed with American Oil Co. for 38 years. Retired in 1983. He married Aug. 18, 1945 to Lily Mae Hix and they had four children: two sons, Jacob Alonza,

Jr. and Harold David and two daughters Glenda Fay and Wanda Jay. He has six grandchildren and three great grandchildren. Lillie Mae died May 28, 1983. Remarried Louise Tison Ferguson Nov. 10, 1988 and has three stepchildren, son Jesse G., Bill and Frampton Ferguson.

WILLIAM R. "BILL" LOZANO, born Oct. 28, 1925 in San Antonio, TX and joined the USN Jan. 4, 1944 and was assigned to the USS *Washington* March/April 1944, serving with I Div., as lookout/radar operator.

Lozano was discharged April 27, 1946. He is married to Lola and they have children: Tony, Laurie and Tracy.

E. "NICK" LUONGO, GMM1/C, born May 1, 1922 in Winchester, MA, joined the USN in September 1942. After boot camp at Newport, RI he was assigned to USS LCT, USS LCG and USS *Miller* (DD-535) serving in the EAME campaigns. He went aboard the USS *Washington* in Bremerton after they replaced the bow from the collision with the *Indiana* and was the ranking petty officer first class bringing approximately 200 replacements from the navy barracks.

He served as first class petty officer in charge of maintenance starboard side 5" and 40mm anti-aircraft guns.

His most memorable experiences include serving as gun captain during Operation Forager; the bombardment of Saipan and Battle of the Philippine Sea; the last cruise with midshipmen from Annapolis on gunnery practice.

He was honorably discharged Oct. 21, 1946 and served in the Navy Reserves for another five years.

He was awarded 11 Battle Stars, EAME Campaigns, Asiatic-Pacific, Armed Forces Expeditionary, Good Conduct and National Defense.

After the war he married Shirley Duffy and they had four children: John, Nancy, Shirley and Janet. Shirley died in 1969. He married Joyce Perkins August 1972. They live in Wolfeboro, NH and have eight grandchildren.

RECHO WARREN MACK, SC/1, born Nov. 5, 1922, in Opp, AL, joined the USN Nov. 19, 1940. After boot camp in Norfolk, VA, he went on the USS *Washington* at commissioning, and served in all major actions through Iwo Jima. Served in the 3rd Div. S/c rating, as helmsman running liberty boat and cradleman on gun station in turret 3.

Most memorable experience was the collision with the *Indiana*. Left ship soon after Iwo Jima, and assigned to Falbrook, CA until discharge on Dec. 15, 1946.

Received Asiatic-Pacific, American Area, African-European, Philippine Liberation, American Defense, and WWII Victory Medal.

He married Mary A. Savage in 1945 and has three children: Carole, Susan, and John. After Mary's death in 1978, he married Hazel Burkett in 1986.

He worked at Naval Coastal Systems Center in

Panama City, FL, as an electrician for 30 years. Retired in 1977 with 37 years federal service. He is presently enjoying retirement fishing and gardening.

SAMUEL EDWARD MAIONE, PHOM2/C, born Sept. 18, 1923 in Madison, NJ, joined the USN at Newark, NJ, Jan. 28, 1941. After boot camp at Newport, RI was assigned to the 6th Div. of the USS *Washington* for ship commissioning. GQ and watch station was in sky control as talker on phones to all the quad mounts. He remained aboard until after the collision with the *Indiana* and was transferred at Pearl Harbor to the Fleet Camera Party in March 1944. After duty at San Diego, CA, Tomkinsville, NY and Philadelphia, PA was discharged as Phom 2/c on Nov. 22, 1946.

He earned the American Defense w/Star, Asiatic-Pacific Theater w/Star, American Campaign, EAME Ribbon. Used the GI Bill to earn a BS in chemical engineering, worked in various companies in cryogenics, pharmaceuticals, plastics, and electrics. Retired from ATT in 1988.

A personal experience while on the USS *Washington:* on liberty the weekend of the Pearl Harbor attack and got back to Norfolk too late to catch the last liberty boat. When he arrived on the pier another shipmate was also there waiting for the mail boat to make the ship. They were cold so, they went to the cafe at the end of the pier for coffee. Later, as they headed back to the landing, they passed a man and woman parked in a car. The passenger door was open obscuring the woman who was sitting sidewise facing out. When they passed behind the car he looked back and saw that the woman had a camera in lap. She was obviously taking pictures of the ships in the harbor and tied up along the wharfs. Since they had just entered a state of war, he knew this was wrong and said to the other sailor that they should confiscate the film. In spite of his repeated objections that "We had no authority" Maione went up to the car and told them that they would have to take the film. As he reached for the camera she broke open the back and he had to pull the film out in two rolls to try to save some of the pictures. Then, to keep it out of the light he held it in his peacoat pocket. They immediately whipped the car around and high tailed it out of there but they managed to get a part of the license number.

Aboard ship he gave the film to the OD and had to make out a written report on the incident. The next day the exec's yeoman looked him up and told him that Cdr. Ayrault was very pleased and might grant the request he had for school, since he first came aboard and found out that he could not strike for the rate he wanted. He never heard another word about it for which he felt very slighted, not to at least been informed of the results. One good thing did come of it though, he was not placed on report for being overleave. *Submitted by Samuel E. Maione*

JAMES H. MALLOY, EMC3/C, born July 5, 1926, Pittsburgh, PA, joined the USN, Aug. 16, 1943. Went to Great Lakes and attended boot camp and 16 weeks electrical school. Assigned to USS *Washington,* March 1944 (E-Div.) First operation, Saipan to Okinawa, back to Bremerton, WA. Down through Panama Canal, two trips to England for troop transfer, to Boston where he was transferred to await discharge.

He was honorably discharged May 3, 1946 and married Theresa Collins in 1950. They have five children and 10 grandchildren. Employed as electrician for Allis-Chalmers, Pittsburgh Div. for 33 years and city of Pittsburgh, seven years. Retired Jan. 1, 1991.

ROBERT H. MANKE, born April 25, 1927 in Portage, WI, joined the USN April 17, 1945. After boot camp at Great Lakes he took a troop train to go aboard the *Washington* at Bremerton, WA, assigned to S. Div.

He spent a short time in the Pacific and went through the Panama Canal to Philadelphia for Navy Day October 1945. They made two trips to England to bring troops back to the US.

One of the more memorable was the second trip in December 1945 when Gen. Patton was to come aboard, but he was killed in France. On the trip a severe storm was encountered and according to reports at the time, swells were recorded 100 feet.

After leaving the USS *Washington* he was transferred to the USS *Wyoming* where it was a privilege to serve with a future President, Jimmy Carter. At the present time he is a hobby farmer in Corning, IA.

JOHN C. "MARCINKOSKA" MARLIN, born June 17, 1924 in Murphysboro, IL, joined the Naval Air Corps in June 1942 and was a member of Carrier Air Group VBF-83. He flew F4U Corsairs from the carrier USS *Essex* and participated in the Okinawa campaign and actions against the home islands.

His Corsair was hit by anti-aircraft fire on March 27, 1945 and he ditched off the Okinawa coast. A Kingfisher from the *Washington* flown by Lt. William E. Lemos and his rear seat man, Henry G. Offney, rescued Marlin. He served on the *Washington* for 24 hours before being returned to the *Essex.*

 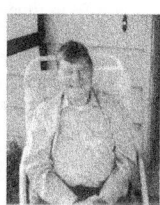

Marlin was discharged in October 1945 as a lieutenant (jg). He was awarded the Air Medal w/5 Gold Stars and the Distinguished Flying Cross w/Star.

He graduated from the University of Illinois in 1949 with a BS in mechanical engineering. His family name was changed to Marlin in 1956. He worked for Caterpillar Tractor and International Harvestor until retirement. He married Odelia M., born Aug. 14, 1948. They have nine children, four son, five daughters and 17 grandchildren. John died Aug. 4, 1996.

ROBERT K. MARSHALL, WT2, born April 20, 1922 in Araphaoe, NE and moved to Clay Center, KS at the age of three months. He joined the USN Sept. 22, 1942 in Kansas City, MO and went to San Diego, CA for boot training. Shipped out of Frisco and sent to Noumea, New Caledonia and boarded the USS *Washington,* assigned to B Div. in fireroom #2. He had a lot of fun crawling into boilers and cleaning the tubes. He was aboard when the collision with the *Indiana* occurred, just off 12 to 4 a.m. watch, in fireroom asleep behind the shaft; went out and helped fire the boilers.

Marshall was discharged Oct. 13, 1945 as a WT2. He received 12 Battle Stars, Good Conduct, Asiatic-Pacific, European and African Campaign Medals.

He married high school sweetheart Irene Spellman. They have one daughter, one son, four granddaughters, one grandson, and one great-grandson.

He went into business as an electrical contractor with his father and brother.

ARNOLD RALPH MARTIN, SF2/C, born Sept. 18, 1918 in Enough, MO and joined the USN Nov. 7, 1939 as shipfitter.

He was stationed NTS Great Lakes, IL; USS *Mississippi;* R/S NYD Philadelphia, PA; USS *Washington;* Rec. Ship, San Francisco, CA; NAV REP Base, San Diego, CA; USNH, San Diego, CA.

He was awarded the EAME Area Ribbon, American Defense Ribbon, Good Conduct Ribbon, American Area Ribbon, Philippine Liberation Ribbon, Asiatic-Pacific Ribbon and Victory Ribbon.

Martin was discharged Nov. 6, 1945. After he was discharged from the USN he went to work as a meat cutter for Krogers. He worked there for 20 years. Due to a bad car accident in 1969, he had to give that job up. He formed his own real estate office and worked at that until he retired. When he found himself with too much time on his hand, he worked part-time as an usher, at these major league activities. In 1991 he developed kidney cancer and fought that battle for three years. He was on dialysis for a year, and died June 19, 1994.

He married Josephine Boscia and had seven children: Ronald, Dennis, Gary, twins David and Donald, Susan and Kathleen and grandchildren: Matthew, Michael, Nicholas, Billy, Brooke, Jennifer and Jill.

WILLIAM HEFLEY MARTIN, son of John Marshall Martin Sr. and Luella Hefley Martin, was born April 16, 1922 in Martin, TN. He was commissioned with the rank of Ensign in the USNR V-12 Program at Fort Schuyler, NY, after attending the US Naval Academy for several months.

Active WWII duty included service aboard the USS *Washington* from July 1945 to May 1946 in various gunnery divisions, and was division officer of a 40 MM battery division. His active World War II duty included service in the American Theater, Asiatic-Pacific Theater and the European Theater. He was awarded the World War II Victory Medal. On April 21, 1959 he was discharged from the Navy as a Lieutenant (jg).

He attended the University of Louisville and graduated from the University of Tennessee, Knoxville, in business administration: including some post graduate courses. On Dec. 4, 1954, he married Mary Margaret Murray, formerly of Pikeville, KY. They had three children: Cheryl Ann, Debra Kay and Barbara Jane and two grandchildren: Laura Porter and Adalan Collins.

After his retirement from federal service in 1990, he and Mary Margaret traveled extensively in Europe, South America, Alaska and other states. They resided in Birmingham, AL and were lifelong members of the Methodist Church. He was a Scottish Rite Shriner and was affiliated with the Zamora Temple in Birmingham. He has been a longtime member of the American Legion and a member of the VFW. He was born on Easter Sunday, and died on Palm Sunday, March 23, 1997.

RAYMOND C. "RAY" MASON,
born June 12, 1918 in Dale, WV, joined the USN in September 1939 and was attached to the USS *Washington* (BB-56) in March of 1941. Commissioned her May 15, 1941. He made convoy runs to Murmansk in 1942. Went to the Pacific, the Third Battle of Savo Island and some of the island bombardments. He was discharged Oct. 19, 1945.

They made a run on Guadalcanal on Nov. 14, 1942. He was sent up to sky control as smoke watch by Lcdr. R.T. Simpson, assistant chief engineering officer. Life photographer and Mason were the only ones not inside the mast. LCDR Simpson wanted a play by play report on the battle. Photographer Shepler clamped four cameras on the rail on the sky lookout, one in each direction in order to get all th action.

When they fired a broadside into the *Kirishima* not only did the camera disappear but the photographer and Mason were left hanging on the rail stark naked. He did have one sock left on, how that happened he really can't explain.

The funniest thing that happened occurred when they were steaming one night, expecting submarine attacks, the galley had sent down night rations for the mid watch 12 midnight to 4 a.m. Lcdr. Simpson was at main control and told the messenger to put a gallon can of baked beans on the top of the engine to heat up. Mason was in #4 engine room on throttle. Suddenly Cdr. Simpson is screaming on the phones. "Submarine attack!" The messenger had forgotten to punch a hole in the bean can and it blew up. Needless to say that was one of the most decorated engine rooms in the Navy. Retired from aircraft factory in Cleveland as a broach grinder.

ALEXANDER WARREN MATOUK, EM2/C,
born Aug. 10, 1923 of American parents in Argentina, joined the USN in August 1941. After boot camp in Norfolk, VA he was assigned to the USS *Washington*, 1st Div. under the watchful eye of Frank Remus, the most feared boatswains mate in the USN. Immediately made "Captain of the Head." Finally transferred to E Div., working in power gang, IC room and galley, where he ate like a king. Remembers shoring up bulkhead after collision with USS *Indiana*. After embarrassing the chief engineer by obtaining electrical supplies from the *South Dakota* which they had refused him, he had him transferred to Landing Ship School. Before leaving the ship he fell on the chow line, hurt his knee and wound up at St. Albans Naval Hospital.

He married Renee in 1948 and they have five children. He owned and operated a hearing aid business for 30 years. Now employed in real estate in Long Island, NY.

LOUIS D. MAURIELLO, QM1/C,
born May 1, 1920 in Boston, MA, joined the USN March 25, 1942, assigned to the USS *Washington* June 1942, N Div. Later assigned to Adm. Lee staff as flag QM aboard USS *Washington*.

His memorable experience includes being stationed to control 2 in conning tower nights of Nov. 14-15 of 1942.

His actions at sea, all BB-56 actions from June 1942 through completion of Okinawa campaign.

He was discharged Nov. 18, 1945. Married to Jo Iosue May 11, 1958 and has three children: Angela Fiorentino, Louis Mauriello and Glen Mauriello and five grandchildren: Brandy Fiorentino, Loren, Amanda, Kyle Mauriello and Paige.

OSCAR H. MAUZY, RM3/C,
born Nov. 9, 1926 in Houston, TX, joined the USN in January 1994 and was assigned to the USS *Washington* at Bremerton, WA in April 1944 assigned to the I (eye) Div., after finishing radar school in Point Loma, CA in March 1944.

He was aboard in all actions from Operation Forager (Saipan) in June, 1944 to Okinawa bombardment in March, April and May, 1945. He stayed aboard for return to Philadelphia Navy Yard (Navy Day, 1945) and two cruises to and from England to return GI's from European Theatre to the states for discharge.

He was discharged at Hitchcock, TX in January 1946. Attended University of Texas, September 1946 until January 1952 on GI Bill, earning BBA (1950) and LLB (1952). Practiced law in Dallas, TX, 1952-1987. Elected state senator of Texas (23rd District) 1966-1986; elected Justice, Supreme Court of Texas 1987-1993.

Father of one daughter, Catherine Anne Mauzy, and two sons, Charles F. Mauzy and James S. Mauzy.

He married the former Anne Rogers Mauzy Feb. 14, 1976. Presently retired and reside at Crestway, Austin, TX.

BERNARD MAYOTTE, HMC,
born March 17, 1915, Webster, MA, attended boot camp, Newport, RI, Feb. 28, 1941. About a week after Pearl Harbor reported aboard the largest and most awesome ship he ever saw, the USS *Washington* (BB-56), H Div.

The most memorable and sad experience was taking care of two young seaman in sick bay and watching them succumb to spinal meningitis. Again surprised when muster was held to find out "man overboard" was the commander of the American Fleet, Adm. Wilcox, and again holding on to his bunk when word was passed "standby for collision", the USS *Washington* rammed the USS *Indiana* midship.

Served 20 years in the USN and when it was time to reenlist he had two loves in his life, adventure

excitement of the sea and his wife, loving, caring, understanding and his best friend. The choice was, what would you have done? Finally retired in 1980 as an optician.

CLEMENT P. MCCORMICK SR., CPM,
born July 6, 1905 in Estherville, IA, joined the USN in 1940 and was assigned to the USS *Washington* in April 1941, in dispensary, Hospital Corps. He achieved the rank of CPM.

He reported aboard in April 1941 and stayed until April 1944. His memorable experiences include being aboard for Murmansk Run and the collision with the *Indiana* and Guadalcanal.

McCormick was discharged in 1955 and retired and moved to Hayward, CA. He died in March 1984 and his wife Olive died in January 1986. They had three children: Clement P. McCormick Jr., Lois Marie Johnson and Michael V. McCormick.

ROY O. "MAC" MCCORMICK, SF1/C,
born June 16, 1915 in Denton, TX, joined the USN Dec. 14, 1934 and was assigned to the USS *Washington* Feb. 6, 1941, SF shop, shipfitter.

His action while at sea was repair 3 anchor detail, diver second class. His memorable experiences include deep sea diving.

He is married to Marie and now retired.

JOHN C. "BLACKIE" MCCOY, CSS,
born Feb. 2, 1920 at Panther Creek, WV, joined the USN Jan. 24, 1938, at Norfolk, VA, serving aboard the USS *Ellis*. He transferred to the USS *Capella*, marine transport, and finally to the USS *Washington* commissioning the ship in 1941. His action at sea includes the Battle at Savo. During his service in the USN he achieved the rank of chief ship serviceman, retiring in 1966.

During the 60s he owned and operated St. Pete Transport, an automobile transport company and during the 70s he owned and operated Mid-Mountain Coal Company. Presently he owns and operates 28th Street Auto Sales in St. Petersburg, FL, with his wife, Mary. John has four sons and one daughter, five grandchildren and two great-grandchildren.

FREDERICK J. MCCRACKEN, GM,
born Aug. 28, 1914 in New Albany, IN, joined the USN in 1939 and was assigned to the USS *Washington* in 1942 as gunners mate.

He served in all major actions and was awarded the Good Conduct Medal w/Bronze Star, American

Campaign Medal, Asiatic-Pacific Medal w/2 Silver Stars and WWII Victory Medal and Philippine Liberation w/Bronze Star.

McCracken was discharged in 1946. He married Eleanor and they had four children and 10 grandchildren. He died May 25, 1986.

VERNON LOUIS MCCREADY, COX, born May 17, 1924 in Lusby, MD, joined the USN July 24, 1943 and was assigned to the USS *Washington* June 1944, deck force. While at sea he participated in the bombardment of Okinawa and air strikes on Kyushu.

He was discharged May 16, 1946 and awarded the Pacific Theater Ribbon, American Theater Ribbon and WWII Victory Medal.

Now retired ordnance technician. He married Virginia Costen, Nov. 24, 1946 and they have a son Robert and a daughter Carol, two granddaughters and one grandson.

JOHN C. MCNEIL, MMC2/C, born in Alderson, WV, Aug. 8, 1915, joined the USN, Dec. 16, 1940 and was assigned to the USS *Washington* May 15, 1951. He left the ship June 27, 1947. He served in the no. 1 engine room as MM2/c and served in the Third Battle of Savo and all major actions while at sea.

His memorable experiences including the sinking of *Kirishima* and *Ayanami*.

He was discharged June 16, 1961 and was awarded 15 Battle Stars, American, Asiatic-Pacific, Philippine Liberation, WWII Defense, American Area Service, EAME, Good Conduct, 5th Award.

He married Helen Perth May 29, 1946 and retired from the shipyard in 1980. He has two sons, William and Robert and one grandson.

PAUL A. MEYERS, FC3/C, born June 22, 1925 in Dubuque, IA, joined the USN June 1943 and assigned to the USS *Washington* late November 1943, as fire control man. While at sea he served in all of the bombardments and air actions from date on board until the war ended. His memorable experiences include standing in chow line and seeing the *Franklin* getting hit; air action during turkey shoot and the big typhoon.

He was discharged Dec. 9, 1945 and received the usual medals and awards: American Theater, Asiatic-Pacific and Philippine Liberation.

Meyers is a retired former science teacher and school administrator. He married Harriet Danner in 1952 and they had three children: Steve, Sandy and Scott and five grandchildren. Harriet died in 1986. He married Ruth Kane in 1989. Ruth has six children and 10 grandchildren.

HARRY LEE MIDKIFF, GM1/C, born April 15, 1923 in Gretna, VA, joined the USN Jan. 23, 1941 and was assigned to the USS *Washington* when it was commissioned, in charge of repair of ships light machine gun batteries, as GM1/c.

He served at sea in action against enemy Japanese forces at Guadalcanal, the Marshall and Gilbert Islands, Iwo Jima, Tokyo and other hostile areas from November 1942 to May 1945.

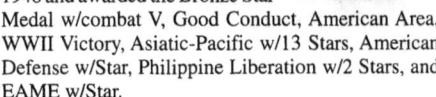

He was discharged April 18, 1946 and awarded the Bronze Star Medal w/combat V, Good Conduct, American Area, WWII Victory, Asiatic-Pacific w/13 Stars, American Defense w/Star, Philippine Liberation w/2 Stars, and EAME w/Star.

He married Helen Ksiezopolski Nov. 10, 1945 and they had a daughter, Linda and sons, Michael and Andrew, a grandson and one granddaughter. Midkiff died Jan. 22, 1973.

PAUL O. MIGNERONE, S3/C, born Sept. 10, 1926 in St. Louis, MO, joined the USN Dec. 15, 1943 and was assigned to the USS *Washington* January 1944 as cook. He was discharged May 15, 1946 as S3/c.

Mignerone is now retired. He married Myrtle May 3, 1947 and they have three sons and seven grandchildren.

VERL ELMER MILLER, CBM, born Aug. 18, 1919 in Gloversville, NY, joined the USN, March 11, 1941. After boot camp at Newport, RI, he joined the USS *Washington* upon completion in Philadelphia. He served as seaman through chief boatswain mate on USS *Washington*.

While at sea he participated in action during the Philippine Liberation, Asiatic-Pacific and EAME.

He was awarded Victory Medal, American Area Medal, American Defense Medal W/A, Good Conduct, Philippine Liberation, Asiatic-Pacific, EAME, Secretary of Navy Commendation.

Miller was honorably discharged Feb. 22, 1947. He married Gwen Laverty Dec. 28, 1946 and they had a son, Stephen, daughters, Rebecca and Pamela and nine grandchildren. He died July 16, 1972.

DAVID A. MING, FC1/C, born in West Orange, NJ, April 11, 1921 and joined the USN, Feb. 20, 1940. He was assigned to the USS *Washington* April 1, 1941, #2 anti-aircraft 5" director.

His memorable experiences include all engagements until July 30, 1949. He was discharged Feb. 20, 1946. His wife of 51 years and his son David Jr. are both deceased.

He is now spending his time playing with his computer and loafing.

HAROLD ANDREW MITCHELL, born Feb. 20, 1921, Coal Valley, PA, enlisted in the USMC Aug. 5, 1941. After boot camp at Camp Lejeune, NC he attended the sea school at Norfolk, VA. He went aboard the USS *Washington* Dec. 14, 1941 with the 7th Marine Detachment.

His military specialties aboard ship were 601 Heavy AA gun crewman, 606 AA machine gun crewman, and 695 Orderly under Adm. Lee's command.

Memorable experiences besides the participation in the war battles and the camaraderie with his fellow shipmates were: the loss of Adm. Wilcox at sea; being aboard ship when King George VI of England greeted

the fleet officers and enlisted men in Scapa Flow, Orkney Islands, in North Scotland; crossing the Equator and becoming a shellback on Sept. 3, 1942.

Mitchell saw action in eight major naval engagements in the Pacific, receiving one Silver Star and three Bronze Stars. Medals awarded were the EAME, Asiatic-Pacific, and the American Defense. He also received the Good Conduct Medal and the WWII Victory Medal.

On Nov. 10, 1945 he was honorably discharged at Bainbridge, MD. He married his high school sweetheart, Cleola Gillingham in Clairton, PA on June 24, 1944. They have a son Harold George, and a daughter Allison Jean and are blessed with one grandchild, Tyler James Mitchell.

He was employed as a machinist for US Steel Corp. in Pennsylvania and Bethlehem Steel Corp. in California until plant closure forced retirement in 1981. On Oct. 2, 1991 Harold passed away and internment is at Forest Lawn, Cypress, CA.

RANDALL C. MOFFITT, born June 10, 1921 in Nashville, TN, joined the USN in February 1941 and was on the *Washington* when it was commissioned in May 1941, in Philadelphia, PA.

He met his wife, Evelyn, June of 1941 and they were married in November of 1941 after the ship returned from the shakedown cruise.

He has many memories of his time on board serving in the 6th Div., memories that are fresh and vivid even 50+ years after they occurred. He remembers the fragrant smell of honeysuckle the night they came up Honeysuckle Lane at Guadalcanal.

To this day, every time he smells honeysuckle he thinks of that night. He remembers the sweet taste of Swanson white meat of chicken on the midnight watch with members of the 6th Div. He obtained the Captain's chicken while they were taking on supplies in the South Pacific. It found it's way into their cleaning locker under a box of salt water soap. He also remembers making cherry wine from the cherry juice taken from the bakery while they were making cherry pies.

Most of all, he remembers their crew members: Jesse James, Sam Maione, Whitaker, the two Jones', and C.B. "Spaghetti" Russ, C.M. Daniel and many more, all good buddies. He has met some again at their reunions and has enjoyed sharing many memories. He remembers Ltjg. Turner, who lost his life in the collision between the *Washington* and the *Indiana*. And he remembers Earl Reed falling overboard while refueling the ship. Earl claimed he floated over the Equator.

Following the war, he settled in southern New Jersey and has been there for over 50 years. He has been married to his wife Evelyn for 55 years. Currently they live in Mt. Laurel, NJ. They have been blessed with a daughter, two sons, seven grandchildren and one great-grandchild.

ROBERT E. MOSIER, GMGC, born March 14, 1928 in Los Angeles, CA, joined the USN Feb. 21,

1946 and was assigned to the USS *Washington* in 1947. He was discharged Feb. 1, 1968 as GMGC and married Phyllis Feb. 20, 1954. They had a daughter Emily, Dec. 22, 1958. Mosier died March 24, 1997.

GILBERT W. NEHER, GM3/C, born April 22, 1922 in Hinkley, NY, enlisted in the USN Jan. 27, 1941. After boot camp in Norfolk, VA he was assigned to USS *Washington* at Philadelphia Navy Yard, 2nd Div., turret crew. Advanced his rating to GM3/c before leaving the ship in 1944.

His most memorable experience was the night battle, Nov. 15, 1942, at Savo Island. His battle station was rammerman center gun turret II. Order came to load, gun captain opened breach; cradleman lowered cradle with shell on it; Gun captain motioned to ram shell in. As he moved lever for ram, could see through the barrel and see balls of fire coming directly at them. The only thing he could think of was to plug that hole up as fast as he could.

He left the ship July or August, 1944 for Gunners Mate Hydraulic School, Treasure Island, CA. Twelve weeks later was assigned to heavy cruiser, *Fall River*.

While aboard, participated in all engagements up to point of leaving for GM School. Since the war was over he took "Convenience of Government" discharge, Dec. 23, 1946. After discharge he was employed with Packard Electric, Warren, OH and Raytheon Co. Missile Systems Div., Lowell, MA, retiring to Florida in 1977.

He married Mary I. Murphy, 1946 and has three children: Richard, Margaret and MaryAnn and three grandchildren. He was remarried to Rosann Brown, 1973-95.

ALBERT E. NELSON, CWO4, born Feb. 21, 1915 in Ironwood, MI, joined the USN January 1934 and was assigned to USS *Washington* February 1941.

His memorable experiences are the battle of Savo Island; sinking of the *Kirishima* and *Ayanami;* Murmansk runs; going after the German battle cruiser along the coast of Norway; losing the Admiral over the side; having King George aboard in Scapa Flow.

Nelson was on board for all major action in the South Pacific until USS *Indiana* collision in 1944.

He was awarded the American, Asiatic w/6 Stars, European w/Star, Philippine Liberation w/2 Stars, American Defense and Good Conduct.

Served on the USS *Tennessee* (BB-43), USS *Monitor* (LSV-5), (APL-53), USS *Keosanqua* (ATA-198), USS *Amphibion* (AR-13), ONC firefighting and damage control school at Treasure Island. Retired CWO4, March 1959 at San Francisco.

He has been married for 51 years to Shirley and has daughter Francine; son Edward, a disabled Vietnam veteran having served on the USS *Oriskany* and grandson John is entering the USN in 1997.

ANDY NERI, S2/C, born March 15, 1926 in Chicago, IL and joined the USN Aug. 14, 1943. He picked up the USS *Washington* in New Caledonia, qualified pointer on 40mm.

His memorable experiences occurred when they rammed another battle station. While at sea he served all over the South Pacific in 10 or 11 battles. He received 10 or 11 Battle Stars.

Neri was discharged March 20, 1946, five days before he was 21 years old.

His wife died March 30, 1994. They had a son and daughter. He spends his time playing bingo and poker. He retired from the city of Chicago, IL.

CAP WILLIAM "BILLY" NEWBERRY, WT2/C, born March 23, 1924 in Sayre, OK, son of Cliff and Cordillia Newberry, enlisted in USN Dec. 16, 1942.

After boot camp in San Diego, CA he was transported to New Caledonia, where he boarded the USS *Washington* (BB-56) March of 1943, assigned to the B Div., fireroom. Also stood smoke watch, became oil king. He was on smoke watch during the bombardment of Okinawa and many others, it was a experience that he will never forget. He was in active duty from first boarding the USS *Washington* until end of the war.

Newberry received an honorable discharge March 3, 1946 as WT2/c. He received the Asiatic-Pacific w/9 Bronze Stars, Philippine Liberation, w/2 Bronze Stars, and WWII Victory Medal.

He received his bachelor of theology from Pacific Bible College in California and is now enjoying retirement. In May, he will be celebrating 51 years of marriage to Gene (Stout) Newberry. He and Gene have three daughters, six grandchildren and 11 great-grandchildren.

JOE E. NEWTON, QM3/C, born May 31, 1925 in Franklin Co., AL, joined the USN July 1943. Completed basic training at Great Lakes, IL boarded the USS *Washington* December 1943 and participated in raids of Kavieng Islands through the occupation of Okinawa and was honorably discharged in February 1946.

He married Jane Taylor in 1950 and they have two sons, Dr. Phil Newton of Germantown, TN and Honorable Joey Newton of Russellville, AL. They also have six grandchildren. Newton is a retired circuit court clerk of Franklin County, AL.

RICHARD E. NEWTON JR., born in Lincoln County, MS, Oct. 12, 1911, enlisted in USN, Sept. 17, 1959 and was on board USS *Washington* as CCSTD when commissioned.

He was awarded the Good Conduct Medal, Yangtze Service Medal, American Defense, Asiatic-Pacific and American Area Medal.

While the *Washington* was in Scapa Flow King George went aboard to inspect the ship. When he came to the galley, Newton showed him a picture of the menu.

He was promoted to pay clerk in October of 1942 and assigned to USS *Concord* after this. Retired in July 1959. He served on seven ships and seven shore stations and held six ranks.

He married Beatrice R. Newton, Sept. 11, 1937 and they have one daughter, four grandchildren and two great-grandchildren. He was employed with the Florida State Board of Health for 15 years. Retired from there in 1974. Maintained his church grounds since and now full retired.

DAVID S. NOE, born Aug. 11, 1924 in Morristown, TN, joined the USN August 1943, took his boot training at Great Lakes, IL, and was assigned to the USS *Washington* December 1943, 6th Div., five-inch gun turret.

He was aboard for most all major actions including the collision with the USS *Indiana*. Many bombardments and air attacks. His most memorable experience occurred when USS *Washington* rammed the USS *Indiana*.

He was discharged December 1945 and received the Asiatic-Pacific Service Ribbon w/8 Bronze Stars, Philippine Liberation Ribbon and American Service Ribbon.

Noe is retired from South Central Telephone and Telegraph Company. He married Grace Bailey, Aug. 7, 1945 and they have two daughters, Nancy and Gail and two grandsons, Justin and Timmy.

ANDREW R. "RAY" NOGAR, born Oct. 5, 1926 in Chicago, IL, joined the USN Oct. 22, 1943 and served in the 8th Div., 40mm trainer.

The encounter with a typhoon on Dec. 18, 1944 with the 3rd Fleet was truly memorable.

His action while at sea includes: Operation Forager, bombardment of Saipan and the Battle of the Philippine Sea, June 12-July 7, 1944; air strikes on Palau Islands, July 25, 1944; Air strikes on Okinawa, Taiwan, Luzon and Visayan Islands, Oct. 10-21, 1944; Battles for Leyte Gulf, Oct. 24-27, 1944; Third Fleet's encounter with typhoon, Dec. 18, 1944; Air strikes on Taiwan and Okinawa, Jan. 3-9, 1945; Air strikes on Indochina, Canton, Hong Kong and Taiwan, Jan. 10-22, 1945; Air strikes on Tokyo, Feb. 16-18, 1945; Bombardment of Iwo Jima, Feb. 19-22, 1945; Air strikes on Kyushu, March 18-22, 1945; Bombardment of Okinawa, March 24, 1945; air strikes on Kyushu, March 29, 1945 and support of Okinawa operations, April 1-May 28, 1945.

Upon discharge on April 16, 1946, he returned to Chicago, learned the trade of mold maker. Married to Lorraine Cremer (Kathy Nogar) and had one son, Dr. Nicholas Nogar, who died in August 1996. Nogar moved to Los Alamos, NM, was employed by the University of California at the Los Alamos National Laboratory and has been retired since 1990.

FRANK G. NOVAK, MM3/C, born May 18, 1925 in Detroit, MI, joined the USN in 1943 and was assigned to the USS *Washington* in 1943, engine room. He served in action 1943-1946 while at sea and achieved the rank of MM3/c.

His memorable experiences include the collision with the USS *Indiana;* sailing through the Panama Canal; sailing under the Golden Gate Bridge; *Indiana* repairs coming apart in the North Atlantic storm after war while bringing troops home from England.

Novak was discharged May 7, 1946 and died May 8, 1996. He is survived by a son, Greg Novak.

MYRON F. "MIKE" NUNN, S2C, born at Independence, MO on Dec. 8, 1925, joined the USN July 9, 1943, and was assigned to the USS *Washington,* March of 1944 at Bremerton Navy Yard while she was drydocked, following the collision with the *Indiana.*

He was aboard from the bombardment of Saipan through the Okinawa campaign and earned eight Battle Stars and wears campaign ribbons for the American Theater, Asiatic-Pacific (6), Philippine Liberation (2) and the Victory Medal. Served on 40mm anti-aircraft quad mounts in capacities from second loader to director operator.

Actions while at sea include: Saipan, Rota, Tinian bombardments; first and second battles of Philippine Sea; Marianas, "Turkey Shoot; Iwo Jima and Okinawa bombardments.

His most memorable experience was observing the Japanese torpedo plane flying "on the deck" coming up the wake trying to drop its "fish" then banking to fly up the starboard side, being shot to pieces by those of them who had reached their battle stations in time. They were in the South China Sea at that time, January 1945. He was honorably discharged from the naval service at Lido Beach Long Island, NY on March 25, 1946.

Nunn retired after 32 years at Cessna Aircraft Co. in Wichita, KS. He is married to Wanda Sue Long, and has daughter to Michaele Van Hook, grandson, Toby E. Leavendusky and great-grandson, Toby J.

BENJAMIN DONALD ODOM, born a twin March 13, 1927 in Shelbyville, TN. He and his brother joined the USN in April 1945. Attended boot camp at Great Lakes and assigned to USS *Washington* June 1945. They served in the 4th Div. and soon learned the art of scrubbing decks, chipping paint and how to holy stone.

He remembers coming through the Panama Canal enroute to Philadelphia for Navy Day October 1945. At that time he left USS *Washington* and finished his duty on USS *Ranger* (CV-4). They were training pilots at NAS Pensacola, FL.

His brother, Marshall Dudley Odom was assigned shore duty at Newport News, VA. After he was discharged he attended college at Tenn Tech on GI Bill and basketball scholarship.

After graduation he worked for Nashville gas company, Robert Shaw Controls Co. and in 1983 became a manufacturers rep. in the appliance industry. He is still active at work and playing golf. His brother died in 1977 of MS.

Left: Marshall Odom. Right: Ben Odom.

DANIEL J. OLSON, born Oct. 7, 1925 in Plainfield, NJ, joined the USN, Aug. 12, 1943. He attended boot camp at Great Lakes, IL and was assigned to USS *Washington* November 1943, where he became a member of the 6th Div. He did daily seamen duties, stood watch at battle stations in mount six. He participated in all the ship's naval actions from the Marshall Islands to Iwo Jima and Okinawa.

His most memorable experience was a kamikaze attack on the USS *Franklin;* Marianas Turkey Shoot; collision with the *Indiana,* Mog Mog and the typhoon.

He was honorably discharged March 21, 1946 and received eight Battle Stars, Asiatic-Pacific, American Defense and Philippine Liberation Medal w/2 Stars.

He was self-employed as a home appliance repairman. Married Anne Kucharski Jan. 22, 1949. They had a son Daniel, and a daughter, Merry Anne, seven grandsons and one granddaughter.

MARTIN L. OLSON, CDR, was born in Minneapolis, MN, May 1, 1918, joined the USN, Aug. 24, 1940, commissioned ensign in March 1941 and was assigned to USS *Washington* April 9, 1941 to participate in the commissioning on May 1941.

He served on the *Washington* in the North Atlantic on the Murmansk Run in 1941. He was also aboard the *Washington* during the battle for Guadalcanal and other Pacific actions.

While on the *Washington* his duties included five inch guns, machine guns, serving as catapult officer. He was assigned to amphibious forces in 1943 in Virginia for LST training. His ship LST 535 was in the Normandy invasion and later action in the Pacific. He was released from active duty in 1947 and remained in the Reserves until retirement at age 60.

He received the following awards: Expert Pistol, American Defense w/Star, Asiatic-Pacific w/3 Stars, Bronze Star w/V, American Area, EAME w/2 Stars, Victory and Philippine Liberation. Olson died April 22, 1991.

EMIL ONKST, MMCS, born April 25, 1923 in Clay County, KY, joined the USN, Feb. 14, 1941. After boot camp at Norfolk, VA, was assigned to the Washington April 28, 1941, No. 1 main engine. He saw all major actions while at sea and received 15 Battle Stars.

His most memorable experience was to see his old hometown buddies on the destroyer that came alongside for refueling. He was honorably discharged Oct. 13, 1945.

Married Jeanette Balling in 1948 and they had one daughter (deceased in 1974). He graduated from Gupton College of Mortuary Science in 1949. Worked in the funeral industry for 10 years and for Oak Ridge National Laboratory for 15 years. He joined the USNR in 1959 and moved to Central Florida in 1969. He then worked for the University of Florida for five years. Retired from the USNR in March 1974 as MMCS.

HERBERT L. OSBORN, born June 25, 1926, Atlantic City, NJ, enlisted in the USN Aug. 21, 1943. Attended boot camp, Newport, RI. Attended Carpenter's Mate Service School, Great Lakes, IL. Assigned USS *Washington* February 1944, Bremerton, WA (BB-56) and got underway for the Pacific Theater, his task at carpenter shop, boat repair, watch, etc. He acquired the job of maintaining all CO2 fire extinguishers charged and ready. GQ station was machine shop, three decks down, that he made secure and watertight. One of the first bombardments was Saipan and the last he remembers was Iwo Jima, the numerous events between are history.

He left the *Washington* in Bremerton September 1945 and was discharged March 31, 1946. Helen became his wife in 1949. The GI Bill provided business administration ICS. Employed as tinsmith for 37 years. Osborn is also a boat builder, fisherman, scuba diver and amateur astronomer. He became a master mason in 1966. Retired in 1983. He's still in good health but has no idea why.

ROY CARL OSBORNE, CMM, born Oct. 12, 1918, Kaufman County, TX and joined the service in 1938. He married Martha and they had a son, Roy C. Osborne Jr. Osborne died Jan. 28, 1989.

WALTER A. PALAC, CEM, born July 31, 1920 in Staten Island, NY, enlisted in the USN Nov. 15, 1939. Attended boot camp at Newport, RI. Served duty on the following: USS *Constellation,* USS *Arkansas,* USS *Washington,* USS *Wisconsin.* Assigned to E Div. in I.C. Attended I.C. School. Received final rank CEM. He was aboard commissioned USS *Washington* and participated in escort convoys to Murmansk and Archangel, Russia. He participated in all major Pacific battles, bombardments and air strikes, including the third battle of Savo Island.

His most memorable was the sinking of the battleship *Kirishima* and *Ayanami.*

He was discharged Nov. 15, 1945 as CEM. He received 15 Battle Stars, American Theater, Asiatic-

Pacific, EAME Campaign, including Good Conduct Medals.

Attended Temple University and employed by Hughes Foulkrod as field engineer; Henkels and McCoy as chief estimator and sales engineer; Williard, Inc. as chief estimator and sales engineer until his retirement.

He married Violet A. Revill Dec. 21, 1943. He has a daughter, Carol A. married to Jerome Shattner; son, Walter A. married to Madeline Braca and son, Robert A. married to Jacqueline Gorski. They have five granddaughters and four grandsons.

RUDOLPH A. PARENT, BM2/C, born June 11, 1921 in Argyle, MN, joined the USN, Feb. 11, 1940 and was assigned to the USS *Washington* in 1941 for commissioning with deck force, 3rd Div.

He was awarded a Good Conduct Medal and discharged in 1946.

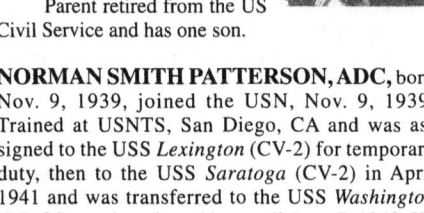

Parent retired from the US Civil Service and has one son.

NORMAN SMITH PATTERSON, ADC, born Nov. 9, 1939, joined the USN, Nov. 9, 1939. Trained at USNTS, San Diego, CA and was assigned to the USS *Lexington* (CV-2) for temporary duty, then to the USS *Saratoga* (CV-2) in April 1941 and was transferred to the USS *Washington* (BB-56), serving aboard her until Aug. 5, 1943. He made aviation machinist mate second class aboard the *Washington* and was plane captain on an OS2U, a sea plane carried aboard.

They flew anti-submarine patrols, then put the USS *Monterey* (CVL-26) in commission. He made chief aviation machinist mate in 1943 aboard the *Monterey*, remained in the USN until retirement on Aug. 18, 1959 as ADC (aviation devices chief), USN, then was transferred to the Fleet Reserve. Patterson is married to Lorene A. and is now retired.

ALVA WALTER PERATROVICH, born April 3, 1926 in Klawock, AK, enlisted in Ketchikan, AK, Dec. 17, 1943 and went to PSC, Bremerton, WA, Dec. 20, 1943. He was sent to Farragut, ID for six weeks training and on February 1943 was assigned to USS *Washington* (BB-56), 8th Div. Participated in bombardment of Nauru; Kavieng raids; bombardment of Kwajalein; Saipan and battle of Philippine Sea; battle for Leyte Gulf; bombardment of Iwo Jima; Okinawa; occupation of Gilbert and Marshall Islands.

His most memorable experiences were Iwo Jima; the collision with *Indiana;* bombardment of Saipan; passing through the Panama Canal enroute to Philadelphia for Navy Day, Oct. 27, 1945; assignment to USS *Nantahala,* USS *Vulcan;* passing through Panama Canal the second and last time.

He was honorably discharged April 23, 1946 with WWII Victory Medal, Philippine Liberation Medal, two Bronze Stars, American Campaign Medal, Asiatic-Pacific Area Campaign Medal and six Bronze Stars.

Peratrovich is a retired lumber mill trimsaw operator. He married Janet Nix of Hydaburg, AK and they had two sons and one daughter. He remarried his high school friend Clara George on Aug. 9, 1975 in Klawock, AK and has five stepchildren.

THEODORE S. "TED" PERLMAN, S1/C, born Sept. 5, 1926 in Chicago, IL, enlisted in the USN, Oct. 6, 1944. After boot camp and radio school he was assigned to the USS *Washington* in June 1945. He performed duties in the radio shack and later transferred to the first lieutenant's office. He participated in the "Magic Carpet" operation when the USS *Washington* was assigned to bring back troops from Europe after war's end.

His most memorable was receiving a message, while on duty in the radio shack, that Gen. George Patton was to board the *Washington* for the trip home from Europe, just before his fatal accident.

He was discharged on July 12, 1946 as seaman first class (RM) and received the American Area and Asiatic-Pacific Area Medals.

He is a retired accountant and is presently performing volunteer duties for the Recording for the Blind organization and as a tax aide for AARP. He has been married to Elaine for 37 years and has a daughter, Susan and a granddaughter.

JOSEPH "JOE PIE" PIECZATKIEWICZ, born Dec. 14, 1924, joined the USN, July 1943. After training at Great Lakes Naval Station he was assigned to the USS *Washington* October 1943, 6th Div. as shellman in a 5" mount. He remained on the ship until February 1946.

 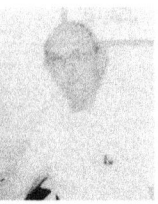

He was awarded the American Theater, Asiatic-Pacific w/9 Stars, Philippine Liberation w/2 Stars, Philippine Independence, Philippine Presidential Unit Citation and WWII Victory Medal.

He married Jean Samczyk in 1949 and they have two daughters, Ellen Koehler and Karen Picchietti and two grandsons, Johnny and Jared Picchietti. Employed in general contracting and a building engineer in a nursing home.

CLIFFORD E. PILCHER JR., born Aug. 11, 1925 in Americus, GA, joined the USMC Oct. 28, 1943 and attended boot camp and sea school, San Diego, CA. Assigned to USS *Washington* March 16, 1944 at Bremerton, WA, statiioned in 20mm guns on boat deck, starboard side forward. Later stationed upper handling room 5" 38 gun mount, near library. He served as Marine detachment company clerk.

He saw action from Saipan to last battle of war. His most memorable experiences were coming up on deck and the first view of Iwo Jima and all the battleships in formation firing one right after the other; going swimming in the Pacific Ocean where the water was over seven miles deep.

Discharged at Camp Lejeune, NC, Sept. 20, 1945. He arrived home on Saturday and began school at Georgia Southwestern College on Monday. Graduated from University of Georgia June 1948. He married Josephine Edwards Feb. 13, 1955 and they have a son, Clifford III, daughter, Ellen A. and three granddaughters. He is self-employed in the accounting business.

JOHN PIZZO, RDM1/C, born Nov. 10, 1919 in Province of Palermo, Sicily, Italy, joined the USN Sept. 6, 1939 and was assigned to USS *Washington* April 1, 1941 as radioman.

While at sea he participated in the Murmansk Run, 1942; Savo Island 1942; Philippine Campaign.

His memorable experience includes the battle of Savo Island.

He was discharged Sept. 17, 1945. He is married to Mary and they have children: Jo Ann Hosier, Terry Lynn Baumbarger and Deborah M. Stein and four grandchildren. He is now enjoying winters in Florida.

JONAS M. PLATT, GEN, born Sept. 21, 1919 in Brooklyn, NY. Commissioned in the USMC June 30, 1940 and joined the Marine Detachment, USS *Washington* in July 1941. He left the ship at Majuro 33 months later. Subsequently, he joined the 1st Marine Div. serving in infantry battalions during the assaults of Peleliu and Okinawa. He commanded an infantry battalion in Korea and was an assistant division commander in Vietnam. He retired as major general in 1970. Until 1977 he worked in the Office of the Assistant Secretary of Defense for Manpower and Reserve Affairs.

His decorations include the Distinguished Service Medal, Silver Star, three Legions of Merit w/Combat V, Bronze Star w/Combat V, Purple Heart, Defense Meritorious Civilian Service Award, Defense Distinguished Civilian Service Award, Vietnamese Medal of Merit and two Vietnamese Gallantry Crosses.

General Platt and his wife, Anne, live in Charlotte, VT and Port Royal, SC.

VALLENTINE GEORGE POPOFF, LCDR, born Oct. 12, 1914, joined the USN in 1940 and was assigned to the USS *Washington* before commissioning as CIC.

While at sea he participated in the Atlantic, Murmansk and most Pacific battles.

His memorable experiences include starting as first class radioman and receiving orders to be commissioned as ensign at sea.

He was discharged October 1945. The Navy sent

him for six months special radar training, then back to the USS *Washington*.

Popoff married Mary Elizabeth Richardson and they had five children. He was employed for the Defense Department in DC for 15 years as aerospace engineer. He is now deceased.

ROBERT D. "BOB" POPPINO, born March 16, 1927 in Martinsville, IN, son of Clarence Edward and Mary Collier Poppino, was assigned to the USS *Washington*, I Div., CIC/bridge, June 1945 at Bremerton, WA after boot camp, Great Lakes, NTC.

His most memorable experience was to see part of a great Navy fleet during the summer of 1945 and later (war over) to travel through the Panama Canal, up the Delaware River to Philadelphia for Navy Day, Oct. 27, 1945. The Welcome Home was unforgettable. Departed the USS *Washington* November 1945.

He also served aboard minesweeper USS *Crag* (AM-214), December 1945-August 1946, Hainan Straits, China and Hong Kong before being honorably discharged as S1/c, Aug. 19, 1946.

He was awarded the Asiatic-Pacific, American Area and Victory Medal.

After college he married Phyllis Thomas, March 11, 1951. They relocated to Miami, FL where he formed a general contracting firm, Bob Poppino, Inc. They have two sons, Thomas and David and three grandchildren: Jay, Matthew and Allyson.

THOMAS L. POTIOWSKY, WT3/C, born April 19, 1926 in Lorain, OH, joined the USN July 20, 1943 and was assigned to the USS *Washington* Nov. 18, 1943, #1 fireroom, #3 fireroom.

While at sea he participated in the Marshall Islands operation; Marianas; Okinawa, Iwo Jima, Philippines; American advances to Japanese main land.

His memorable experiences include the collision with the USS *Indiana;* bomb hitting carrier USS *Franklin;* record steaming - 79 consecutive days and numerous typhoons.

He was awarded the WWII Victory Medal, American Area Medal, Asiatic-Pacific Theater Medal w/8 Stars and Philippine Liberation Medal w/2 Stars.

Potiowsky married Germaine Mudrock, Oct. 1, 1949 and they have children, Louise Leon and Thomas Potiowsky and two grandchildren, Dean and Becky. He retired from U.S. Steel (Lorain Works).

JOHN HENRY POTTER, S2/C, born Sept. 27, 1925 in Chattanooga, TN, joined the USN Aug. 14, 1943, assigned to the USS *Washington,* 40mm in 1943 and departed in 1945.

He was awarded the WWII Victory Medal, American Campaign Ribbon, Asiatic-Pacific w/8 Stars, and Philippine Operations Medal w/2 Stars.

Potter was discharged March 21, 1946. He married Clara and has a son Gary and grandson David.

He is now retired and enjoys hunting, golf and fishing.

JOHN VERNET PREVOST, CDR, born Dec. 10, 1910, West Pittston, PA, entered the USN July 19, 1938 after graduating from the University of Pennsylvania Medical School as LTJG, Philadelphia Naval Hospital. Assigned to USS *Washington* April 17, 1941. Reported to USS *Washington* for duty May 15, 1941. Secured as medical officer aboard ship until November 1941. Departed USS *Washington,* Noumea, New Caledonia.

His memorable experiences include the night on the North Atlantic that Adm. Wilcox was lost over board, he distinctly remembers him sitting in his cabin and obsessively counting peas; the horror of Convoy PQ 17; the night on the Murmansk Run when the KG5 split a destroyer in half and went to the bottom; Scapa Flow when the King of England inspected the ship and came to infirmary, on his inspection.

He was honorably discharged in 1946 after serving as officer in charge of Fleet Hospital of Guantanamo Bay, Cuba. His first wife, Julianne passed away in 1982 and he remarried Kay and they live in Tioga, PA. He has four sons: John, Clancy, James and Louis and a daughter, Sally who have been very supportive and successful over the years. He is now retired and is active with the Senior Citizens Adult Day Program at the Green Home, Wellsboro, PA.

EDWARD A. QUINN, S2/C, born June 21, 1926 in Bronx, NY, enlisted in the USN Aug. 12, 1943. After boot camp at Great Lakes, IL he was assigned to the USS *Washington* which was moored at New Hebrides Island in November 1943. He served in the 6th Div., as S/2 and assigned to 5" gunmount shell loader.

His most memorable experience includes crossing the equator on the BB-56 as a pollywog; being on deck while refueling a destroyer at sea when a Jap kamikaze made a direct hit on the USS *Franklin,* which was off their port stern.

Served on the USS *Washington* until November 1945. Also served at AGC, Brooklyn, NY and the USS *North Carolina* (BB-55).

He received an honorable discharge June 17, 1947 and was awarded American Area, Asiatic-Pacific w/7 Battle Stars, Philippine Liberation w/2 Stars and WWII Victory.

Quinn retired 1970, sergeant MPDC; 1988, retired security manager, Navy Retail System, WDC.

He married Dorothy M. Skinner of Hartford, CT, May 2, 1953 and has three daughters: Kathy, Pattie and Marie and seven grandchildren.

ROBERT W. RANKIN, SF1/C, born Dec. 2, 1918 in New Rochelle, NY, enlisted in the USN Dec. 5, 1939. After boot camp, Newport, RI he was assigned to USS *Wasp* (CV-7) in Norfolk, VA, in 1940. In 1941 he was transferred to Philadelphia, to commission USS *Washington.* He stayed on the *Washington* for over three years.

He participated in all major actions including the battle that saved Guadalcanal, Nov. 15, 1942, when the *Washington* sunk the Japanese battleship, *Kirishima.* He was a shipfitter second class.

In 1943 he was transferred to Braintree, MA to commission the USS *Springfield* (CL-66). He stayed on the *Springfield* until the end of WWII, and was in Tokyo harbor when the Japanese surrendered.

He returned to the US and was honorably discharged at Lido Beach, NY on Dec. 10, 1945 as a shipfitter first class.

His medals and awards include the Asiatic-Pacific, American Defense, European Theater, American Theater, Good Conduct, Victory Medal, Philippine Republic and Presidential Unit Citation Badge.

In 1948 he married Mary Minehan and had two sons, Robert and Daniel. He joined the Port Washington Police District December 1951 and retired as a lieutenant in 1981. His wife died May 12, 1984.

ROBERT M. RAYBURN, LTJG, born Dec. 28, 1916 in NYC, graduate of Columbia University, directly commissioned as ensign USNR March 13, 1944. Served as CO aboard USS *Washington* from October 1944 to December 1945. Participated in Leyte, Luzon, Iwo Jima and Okinawa operations and the first carrier based air strike on Tokyo, February 1945.

Released to inactive duty March 22, 1946 and honorably discharged Feb. 3, 1954.

Rayburn received four Battle Stars, the American Defense and Philippine Liberation Medals.

Before retirement in 1991 he was an optometrist and maintained an active practice in Manchester, CT for 45 years. He married Shirley Mandell in August 1945. They have one daughter, Barbara Ellen.

JAMES ALLEN REISER, PFC, born July 26, 1926 in Carleton, MI, joined the USMC Nov. 8, 1943 and trained at San Diego, CA, boot camp. Assigned to *Washington,* AA machine gun crew 606.

101

He was awarded the American Campaign, Asiatic-Pacific Campaign w/Silver and Bronze Star, EAME Campaign, WWII Victory, Philippine Liberation w/2 Bronze Stars, Philippine Independenc and, Philippine Republic Presidential Unit Citation.

He began working for the Detroit Edison Co. in June of 1948, retiring in 1987. He married Patricia Dugan on April 10, 1948 and they had two daughters and two grandchildren. He died on May 1, 1993.

WALTER N. RESSLER, born April 3, 1926 in Sunbury, PA, enlisted in the USN Aug. 13, 1943 and attended boot camp at the Great Lakes Naval Training Center. After arriving in the Marshall Islands via San Francisco, the USAT *Willard A. Holbrook* and the USS *Rixie,* he boarded the USS *Washington* on Dec. 18, 1943 and was assigned to the 3rd Div.

He participated in 15 operations beginning with the Kavieng raids in late December 1943 and ending with the Okinawan Operation in April and May 1945. Battle station for air defense - a 20mm machine gun, and for surface engagements/bombarments - a cradleman in the #3 turret, center gun.

He was awarded the Asiatic-Pacific Ribbon w/8 Bronze Stars, the Philippine Liberation Ribbon w/2 Bronze Stars and the American Defense Ribbon. He was honorably discharged on Dec. 6, 1945 from Bainbridge, MD.

He began working for the Federal Prison System in 1955 and retired in 1980 with 25 years service as a correctional counselor. He resides in Northumberland, PA and enjoys fishing and hunting in his free time.

WILLIAM "BILL" JOHN REYNAR, PHM1/C, born Dec. 21, 1923 in Los Angeles, CA, joined the USN Jan. 12, 1942. Served aboard the USS *Washington* in 1943 and 1944 in H Div., and was honorably discharged Nov. 15, 1947.

He was awarded the Philippine Independence, American Area, Asiatic-Pacific w/4 Stars, WWII Victory Medal and Philippine Liberation w/Star.

He married Gwen F. Krater April 2, 1944, while on leave after the collision of the USS *Washington* and the USS *Indiana.* After WWII he graduated from the University of Southern California and was employed in the wholesale fine paper business.

Bill passed away Dec. 13, 1996 and Gwen is still living in Beaverton, OR. He is also survived by one daughter, one son and two grandchildren.

VERLYN RICE, S1/C, born April 3, 1927 at Creston, IA, joined the USN in February of 1945, going to Great Lakes Naval Station for boot camp training. After boot camp he was sent to Washington State for S.P. duty and was assigned to the USS *Washington* in 1945 at Bremerton, WA, with 9th Div.

After going through the canal and on to Philly

for Navy Day in October 1945 the *Washington* then transferred troops from England. Rice was then assigned to the Naval District in the Aleutian Island where he served as Adm. Daubin's personal aid until late 1946 when he was discharged as S1/c in Minneapolis, MN.

Today he serves as a county supervisor for Adams County, IA. He has been married to Alice Thompson for 50 years, has one son and four grandchildren.

KING RICHESON, MM2/C, born Sept. 25, 1920 in Hartford, KY, enlisted Aug. 13, 1940. Attended boot camp and metalsmith school at Norfolk. Played on base basketball team that won 21 of 25.

Assigned to *Washington* April 28, 1941 Div. A, evaporators. He was a member of ships basketball team which won all five games before being interrupted by war.

Richeson was aboard during Murmansk Runs and Savo Island. He was machinist mate second class when transferred March 1943 to Midshipman School. Commissioned ensign July 28, 1943. Served on LST 179 during Gilbert Islands action until it was sunk on West Loch and Pearl Harbor May 21, 1944.

Next served on LST 889. Aboard AKA-7 *Alcyone* supplying the fleet at sea when war ended. He was discharged Nov. 25, 1945 as lieutenant (jg).

His memorable experiences include the *Punjabi* incident and seeing *Washington* and *South Dakota* cruising without escorts after Savo Island encounter.

He retired after 35 years teaching. Volunteers for Central Kentucky Blood Center, and is DAV van driver. He married Jean Sudduth June 13, 1949, has two daughters, Margaret Macemon and Sue Finley and three grandchildren.

ALFRED B.K. RODRIGUES, born Feb. 7, 1920 in Kapaa Kauai, HI and was in the USNR when ordered to active duty in November 1940.

Stationed at Bishop's Point, Pearl Harbor on Dec. 7, 1941. He had the 0400-0800 watch. All they had were 30 caliber rifles that they were shooting at the Japanese planes that were strafing the area.

Reported on board the *Washington* in June 1943 and transferred in February 1945. He was in all the action that occurred while in board.

Joined the regular USN after the war and was discharged in June 1964. He received numerous medals.

Started another career with the General Services Administration in Honolulu and retired after 30 years as a manager of a GSA customer supply center.

Rodrigues married Louise E. Schneider from Douglass, WY. They have nine children and spend time babysitting the grandchildren or playing golf.

ALBERT FRED "AL" ROIZ, PNC, born Dec. 29, 1919 in San Benito, TX, son of Ulpiano and Jacinta Roiz. Enlisted USN Aug. 1, 1939 and attended boot camp at San Diego. Reported aboard USS *Washington* March 7, 1941 from USS *California.* Served in various ships and shore commands. Retired as PNC

Oct. 31, 1959. On bridge as JA phone talker during both "man overboard" and "Punjabi Ramming" episodes and in conning tower as JF phone talker during "Savo Island Battle".

He earned nine medals during his career. After retirement earned a BS from U of T and later MS from TAMU. Employed with the Social Security Administration, retiring Jan. 19, 1986. Licensed and worked as realtor until 1994.

He married Anne Estelle Daniel Sept. 1, 1945 and was divorced Jan. 26, 1956. He has a son, Jim, and grandsons, Kevin and Jeffrey.

Roiz married his second wife, Betty Jo Jacobson Aug. 14, 1963, and she died March 13, 1995. He then had a daughter Patricia, and granddaughter Katelin and stepdaughter, Deanne, stepgrandson Joshua and stepson William, and four stepgrandchildren.

Now completely retired. Plays golf and poker for leisure but very poorly. For exercise he jumps to conclusions but he doesn't do that too well either.

SAMUEL A. ROSS, SF3/C, enlisted in the USN Dec. 15, 1942 in Philadelphia, PA and went to boot camp at Sampson, NY 1943. He reported aboard USS *Washington* July 15, 1943 at Pearl Harbor and served on the ship from that date until October 1945 Long Beach, CA, participating in all major actions from 1943 to 1945.

His one clear remembrance aboard ship was their collision the USS *Indiana.* He was on damage control, security watch on the main deck. Their job was to check hatches and lights around the main deck. While walking the main starboard deck, he was knocked down on his side. After getting to his feet, he saw red lights going by him in the opposite direction. He did not know at that time, but he was looking at the red lights on the *Indiana's* mess hall. Their bow had torn a large long hole in her side. They lost men on both ships. It was their worst damage and loss of life.

The only wound he received from the collision was a large bruise on his right hip from the 45 pistol they had to carry. He was awarded the Asiatic-Pacific Campaign, American Campaign, and Philippine Campaign Medals.

Retired in 1980 with his wife Rita who has been with him for 54 years. They have one daughter, Pat Ross, son James Ross and his daughter-in-law Ann.

GILBERT J. ROTH, born Oct. 28, 1921 in Detroit, MI, graduated Hillsdale College and Illinois College of Optometry with bachelor of science and doctor of optometry degrees. Joined the USN V-7 Program on April 25, 1942 and assigned to Midshipman's School at Columbia University, graduating Oct. 20, 1943. Assigned to USS *Washington* and served aboard until December 1945, in F Div. and 5th Div. as plotting room officer. Transferred to Medical Service Corps in 1946. Assigned to Medical Co. 9-5 in Detroit, serving as XO and CO. Assigned to group command in Detroit as medical senior officer and liaison to Wayne State College of Medicine, and CO of Marine Medical Co. 212. Retired on Oct. 28, 1981.

His awards included two Navy Commendations, Naval Reserve Medals (four) and awards for best medical unit for five years in 9th Naval District. Served as consultant to NAS, Grosse Ile for eight years.

Semi-retired from private practice. Fellow, American Academy of Optometry and past president of Michigan Optometric Association. Police commissioner, Grosse Ile Police Department since 1974. He has a son, Edward and daughter, Terry Jo. His wife is deceased.

LORENZO RUSSO, SR., QM1/C, born Nov. 2, 1921 in Utica, NY, joined the USN April 1941 and trained at Norfolk, VA and was assigned to USS *Washington* for duty May 1941.

Aboard ship he joined the boxing squad trained and fought under the watchful eye of their instructor Tom Manuli, a great boxer. While on duty in North Atlantic, he was assigned duty as a lookout up in the crow's nest. After which he joined the QM gang with duties on the bridge at sea and quarterdeck in port. While with *Washington* he earned 13 Battle Stars.

After his discharge he went home and married Adeline Pellegrino and was recalled to duty for the Korean War. Assigned to USS *Stoddard* (DE-566). After discharge went home and started their family, two boys and a girl. Now happily married for 47 years and they have six wonderful grandchildren.

JOHN JOSEPH RUTTER, PHM1/C, born April 24, 1924, joined the service in 1941 and was assigned to the USS *Washington* in 1942, pharmacist mate first class.

Wherever the battleship went, so did he for the next four years. He was discharged in 1945 and is now deceased.

PHILIP JAMES RYAN, born Salem, MA, March 6, 1924, joined the USN March 7, 1941 and was assigned to the USS *Washington* in May 1941 and departed April 18, 1943, stationed with the 5th Div.

His memorable experiences include the third Battle of Savo Islands; recovering from open heart surgeries (one in 1955 and two in 1996). Participated with gun crew, mount 51. He was discharged Jan. 1, 1961.

Married to same girl since March 1951. They have one daughter, an RN and a son, chief engineer on sealands performance largest class container ship under US flag. He is now retired.

VINCENT JOSEPH SABATINI, CMM, born to Italian immigrant parents Dec. 19, 1919 in the small town of Bunkie, LA. He joined the USN in 1937 and three years later was transferred to the battleship USS *Washington* for commissioning of the ship. His tours included the US naval station, Hawaii on board the *Langley* and *Bremerton* in addition to the *Washington*.

In 1941, he was assigned to a small task force which joined the English Fleet in the European Theater of the war. He became machinist first class on the USS *Washington* and subsequently routed to the South Pacific during which time he made chief machinist mate. That tour included invasions and combat missions in Guam, Saipan, and Tinian. During his service in the USN Vincent endured seven years without shore duty. He was honorably discharged on Feb. 4, 1947.

Following his discharge from the USN, he joined the USA for which he served 10 years until his retirement and then entered the civilian world as a professional engineer.

His awards and decorations include the American Campaign Ribbon, European Theater of Operations Ribbon, Asiatic-Pacific Campaign Ribbon w/3 Battle Stars, American Defense and National Defense Service Medals and the WWII Victory Medal.

He married Willa M. Kohler on April 5, 1944 and had two daughters, two sons and eventually two grandsons. He died on Nov. 14, 1983, after a brief struggle with leukemia. Vincent is buried in Houston, TX where many of his surviving family members reside.

ANDREW SABOL JR., S1/C, born Nov. 1, 1925 in Lakewood, OH, joined the USN Feb. 25, 1944 and was assigned to the USS *Washington* October 1944. He served with 8th Div., 40mm gun mount (ammunition loader), deckhand, sea-plane retriever and achieved the rank of S/1c.

While at sea he participated in bombardments of islands of Iwo, Okinawa, Guam, with Adm. Bill Halsey's Task Force.

His memorable experiences include a typhoon; kamikaze attack; seeing the young Japanese pilots in their helmets and white scarves.

He was discharged May 5, 1946 and awarded the WWII Victory Ribbon, American Area Ribbon, Asiatic-Pacific Area Ribbon w/6 Stars, Philippine Liberation Ribbon w/2 Stars.

He married Mary Hadbavny on April 21, 1951 and they have four sons: Andy, Jackie, Tom, Chris, Tim, Richard and two daughters: Kathy Cifani, Rosemary (Steve) Horvath) and nine grandchildren: Robert and David Cifani, Kristine Jennifer, Stephanie and Michelle Horvath, Jessica, Andrew IV and Robert Sabol. His sons have enjoyed coming to reunions, especially Tim.

Sabol has been retired as traffic manager for seven years. Handicapped with Parkinson's, but enjoys traveling to ship reunions, family and friends.

CHARLES M. "CHARLIE" SANDWICK JR., RDM3/C, born Oct. 3, 1926 in Bethlehem, PA, enlisted in the USN, Sept. 28, 1944. Attended boot camp at Great Lakes NTC; radar school at Point Loma, San Diego and assigned to USS *Washington* April 1945, I Div., S1/c, CIC room during GQ.

Participated in Okinawa campaign and *Kyushu* air strikes. After arrival at Puget Sound in June 1945 he was transferred to PT boat base at Melville, RI until September 1945. Rejoined the crew of USS *Washington* after arrival in Philadelphia for Navy Day, Oct. 27, 1945. Enjoyed the opportunity to escort two former female classmates on board the ship on Navy Day.

Transferred to USS *Helena* for Good-will tour of Europe, Middle East and Asia. Last served in Tsingtao, China. Discharged Aug. 6, 1946 with RDM3/c rating.

He received the American Campaign Medal, Asiatic-Pacific Campaign Medal, EAME Campaign Medal, China Service, Occupation Service and WWII Victory Medal.

Sandwick received a BA from Lehigh University and a MS from Temple University. He taught high school science and coached track and cross-country for 30 years. He also sold life insurance. He married "Maisie" Steckel in 1968. They have two daughters and nine grandchildren.

JAMES H. "JIMMY" SATTERFIELD, AM2/C, born April 21, 1924 in Atlanta, GA, enlisted in the USN Aug. 11, 1941. After boot camp in Norfolk, attended aviation metalsmith school in Jacksonville, FL and was assigned to USS *Washington* Feb. 1, 1942, stationed aft on the OS2U aircraft. Attained the rating of AM2/c.

He participated in all campaigns from Russian convoy operations to Philippine Sea battle. Received all WWII campaign medals, Good Conduct and Philippine Liberation Medal. He was discharged April 20, 1947.

Satterfield attended law school earning LLB and LLM. After graduation he was in law enforcement for 37 years with 30 years as special agent with Bureau of ATF. Retired Jan. 12, 1979.

His most memorable experiences were going around the North Cape of Iceland, the Panama Canal, flying over and around an active volcano in the Hebrides Islands; the battle of Savo observed from gun mount of fantail and being catapulted off and recovering of OS2U aircraft.

He married Margaret L. Thomas June 6, 1946 and they had one son and two grandchildren. Margaret died Feb. 24, 1980. He is now presently married to Barbara Peters Satterfield.

KARL D. SAURER, born Oct. 26, 1922, joined the USN January 1941 and went to Norfolk NTS. Assigned to the USS *Washington* March 1, 1941 and was aboard for her commissioning April 1941.

He went to the North Atlantic Theater from July 1941 to November 1941 and was on convoy duty from Iceland to Russia. He went to South Pacific Theater and was in all major battles. Returned to the USA in December 1944.

Sauer was stationed at USN Air Station from January 1945 to March and was sent to US Naval Hospital and discharged April 1945.

He was married and had two children. Employed with trucking company in Ohio for 10 years. He moved to Arizona in 1960 and went to work for a warehouse company. His first wife went back to Ohio in 1970. He met and married his present wife at his place of work and they have been happily married for 26 years. Both retired after 25 years with the company.

He is proud to have been a member of the crew of the USS *Washington,* the best ship of the fleet.

SAM SCALZO, GMC born July 25, 1921 in Danbury, CT, joined the USN March 13, 1941 and went to Rhode Island boot camp, assigned to USS *Washington* on May 1941 and served in 3rd Div., turret 3 as gunners mate striker. September 1941, USS *Washington* participated in test firing 16" guns for the first time to check structural damage. He was part of the gun crew. It was a great thrill.

April 30, 1942 he crossed the Arctic Circle to become a blue nose during Atlantic convoy duty. Iceland to Murmansk to Scapa Flow, rough ocean.

Nov. 15, 1942 participated in the battle of Guadalcanal, sinking Japanese battleship, *Kirishima* and *Ayanami,* eyeball to eyeball, night action, range 85,000 to 11,000 yards.

Served Central Pacific offensive in 1943 as left gun captain during bombardment of Nauru, Kwajalein, Saipan. After 3 1/2 years aboard the USS *Washington* was transferred to advance gunnery school in Washington, DC. After war served on various ships. In January 1961 assigned to NROTC unit University of Illinois as instructor.

Transferred to Hawaii aboard the USS *Radford.* Discharged and retired November 1964 as gunners mate chief.

He was awarded the American Area, WWII Victory Medal, American Defense, EAME w/Star, Philippine Liberation, Asiatic-Pacific w/7 Stars, Good Conduct w/Stars.

He has been a real estate broker since 1965. He married Shirley Hayes Aug. 17, 1962 and has one son, Dr. David Scalzo, neuro-radiologist University of Mississippi Medical Center, Jackson Mississippi and three grandchildren.

E. STANSBURY SCHANZE JR., RADM, born Dec. 30, 1903 in Baltimore, MD, joined the USN, June 30, 1922 as a midshipman at the Naval Academy. During 35 years of active duty, 23 years were spent at sea on 13 ships, commanding three of them. Over four years were spent on the USS *Washington* serving as engineering officer, navigator and executive officer while participating in all of the ship's engagements.

Memorable experiences included sinking the *Kirishima* and weathering the typhoon of 1944.

Awards include the Legion of Merit "V" w/Gold Star, American Defense Medal w/Star, American Area, European-African, Asiatic-Pacific w/9 Stars, WWII Victory, Philippine Liberation w/2 Stars, Korean Area and United Nations.

Following his retirement in 1957, he served as the director of the New York Academy of Sciences for 14 years, died Dec. 25, 1983 and is buried at the US Naval Academy with wife, Marie Louise (nee Moran). He is survived by one son, Edwin Stansbury Schanze Jr. and three grandchildren.

WALTER ALBERT SCHULTE, S1/C, born Nov. 27, 1909 in Detroit, MI, joined the USN Oct. 4, 1943 and served on the USS *Washington* as chaplains assistant. He achieved the rank of seaman first class.

While at sea he participated in all major battles from Jan. 2, 1944 to May 1945.

He was discharged Oct. 13, 1945 and received the Atlantic Pacific Ribbon, American Defense Ribbon and the Philippine Ribbon w/2 Stars.

Schultze married Veronica E. He died June 10, 1991. They had a son Jame L.

NELSON E. SEBRIGHT, CM2/c, born Jan. 20, 1919 in Allegan, MI. He joined the service in November, was assigned to the USS *Washington* June 22, 1942 and stationed in the ship carpenter shop and damage control.

Memorable experiences include crossing the Equator and the night they sank the *Kirishima.* He was discharged at PSC NOB T.I., San Pedro, CA, Dec. 7, 1945.

Married June 1944 to Bernice Powell and family consists of six married children, 23 grandchildren and 15 great-grandchildren. He is retired.

RAYMOND SERENSON, S1/C, born Sept. 11, 1924 in New York City, Manhattan, joined the USN April 23, 1942 and was assigned to the USS *Washington* Aug. 1, 1942, AA Btry., deck. He achieved the rank of S1/c.

While at sea he participated in the Pacific from third battle of Savo Island and most all action to VJ.

His memorable experiences include shooting down a Jap betty with crew of three Jap men, along side the USS *Washington* with 55 rounds of 20mm.

He was discharged Dec. 5, 1945 and was awarded the Good Conduct, 15 Battle Stars and the Asiatic-Pacific Campaign Medals.

Serenson was married Oct. 5, 1947 and has two daughters, and six grandchildren (four boys and two girls). He is now retired as a cargo supervisor for South African Airways, JFK, NY.

DICK ALLEN SHEPHERD, born Dec. 15, 1921 in Triffin, OH. He joined the USN Feb. 10, 1944 and boarded the USS *Washington* May 13, 1944. He was in sick bay when their group had rifle range, he never fired a gun or rifle. Before being assigned to the R-Div. he was a deck hand. While at Anchorage in the atolls, for a number of nights he spent two hours carrying a sub-machine gun. His partner carried the ammunition. He didn't know how to load it and he didn't know how to fire it.

While serving as buglemaster third class, the saddest day was when he played Taps for his first burial at sea.

Shepherd was honorably discharged Jan. 2, 1946. He is vice president of a family owned machine shop making special machines and dies. Retired in 1990 and still plays first trumpet in dance and classical bands.

He married Dorothea Gable and they have one daughter, two sons, five grandsons and two granddaughters.

WILMER SHEPHERD, MM1/C, born Feb. 4, 1923 in Mansfield, LA, enlisted in the USN, Dec. 10, 1940, Shreveport, LA was sworn in to USN Dec. 11, 1940, New Orleans, LA. He went through Navy boot camp at Norfolk, VA. His platoon, #196 was selected to represent the USN and marched in the inaugural parade of Franklin D. Roosevelt for a third term as president of the USA.

He was assigned to the USS *Washington* April 1941, under construction at Philadelphia Navy Yard. Selected by Cdr. Parr, chief engineering officer, and assigned to the #2 engine room. Assisted construction workers and started training in the operation of the steam propulsion system. Advanced to machinist mate first class (MM1/c) and acting chief petty officer.

The USS *Washington* was commissioned May 15, 1941. Secretary of the Navy Frank Knox attended. Shepherd remained aboard the *Washington* until Oct. 20. 1945. Departed to New Orleans, LA and was discharged Oct. 21, 1945.

He was awarded the American Campaign Medal, Good Conduct Medal, EAME Campaign Medal, Asiatic-Pacific Campaign Medal w/15 Battle Stars, Philippine Liberation Medal w/2 Bronze Stars, WWII Victory Medal, Russian Victory MEdal and the Guam Liberation Pen.

His memorable experiences include losing Adm. Wilcox at sea in the North Atlantic. The only Admiral ever lost at sea in the history of the USN; King George VII of England came aboard the *Washington* while anchored at Scapa Flow in the Orkney Islands to inspect the ship and crew.

Shepherd was aboard for all activities in the Pacific in which the USS *Washington* participated. His GQ battle station was "throttleman" in the #2 engine room. Responded to signals from the ships bridge and controlled speed of ships #2 screw accordingly.

May 1946 he went to work for Standard Oil Company (Indiana) at Superior Refinery in North Louisiana.

He married Bonnie S. Cantley Sept. 20, 1947 and they have three daughters, including twins, one son, three granddaughters, one grandson, two great-granddaughters and one great-grandson.

Retired May 1980 after 34 years with Standard Oil Co., now Amoco Chemical Corp. He had great experiences during his work career. He lived and worked in Louisiana, Texas, Illinois, California, Alabama, Japan, Taiwan, Holland and Turkey. Presently enjoying family, life and good health, yard work, travel in travel trailer, lots of golf.

JOHN J. SHIELDS, SF1/C, born Feb. 12, 1923 in Brooklyn, NY, joined the USN Oct. 5, 1942 and was assigned to the USS *Washington* R Div. November 1945.

Prior to being assigned to the USS *Washington* he had 27 months service at submarine bases in Pacific Ocean areas.

His memorable experiences include leaving

Southampton, England on their second run Dec. 14, 1945 for a 5 1/2 day return trip to New York. It turned out to be a rough trip with 40 foot waves engulfing the ship. Finally on Dec. 24, 1945 they arrived in New York. He was lucky he lived. In South Ozone Park which was a subway ride away, (05 cent fare in those days), he was home for Christmas after missing 1942, 1943, and 1944.

His naval time was a wonderful experience which he will always cherish. He also met a great group of men and they still meet every 18 months or so. Shields is widowed and has two sons and has been employed with an engineering company since 1950.

AVIS RICHARD SHIFFLET, CHIEF YEOMAN, born in Washington, DC, Nov. 9, 1922, joined the USN, Nov. 13, 1940 and was assigned to the USS *Washington* in May of 1941. Separated from ship on Nov. 20, 1942.

He was assigned to the dental section shortly, and to the 2nd Div. where he remained until assigned to the staff of Rear Admiral Willis A. Lee. He was officially detached from the *Washington* at various times to serve in other battleships with Adm. Lee, which included the USS *Indiana, Massachusetts and North Carolina*.

His memorable experiences include the third battle of Savo Island where he was in the powder handling room of the No. 2, sixteen inch turret; bombardment of Tawara and Nauru.

While on the *Washington* they had a collision with USS *Indiana* and he returned to the states for reassignment in the *Washington* when she went to Bremerton for repairs.

He was awarded the European Theater, American, Asiatic-Pacific w/8 Battle Stars, WWII Victory, Good Conduct w/5 Stars. Qualified to serve in the Submarine Force. Served in the Commander Submarine Force Atlantic Fleet.

Final discharge June 1, 1965 as chief yeoman. His daughter was born in 1943. He was remarried in 1958 to Gloria Elena Tijerina-Torres. He was blessed with two sons, Richard and Ronald and a daughter Laurie Lynn. They also have nine grandchildren and seven great-grandchildren.

After retiring he worked as a claim adjuster supervisor for Texas Employers Insurance. Retired after 15 years and became a legal consultant for maritime and workmens' compensation claims.

His wife was born in Monterrey, Mexico in 1933 and immigrated to the US in 1953 and became a citizen in 1960. Graduated from the University of Houston, taught in high school for 22 years. He received a masters degree as a professional counselor. Currently occupied with volunteer church work and just plain enjoying life.

JAMES ANDREW SHIRLEY, EM2/C, born March 10, 1923 near Alto, GA and grew up in Lyman, SC. After he graduated from Duncan High School in Duncan, SC, he joined the USN Nov. 18, 1941 in nearby Spartanburg. He was sworn in November 21 in Raleigh, NC, by former heavyweight boxing champion Gene Tunney.

Shirley went through training at the NTS in Norfolk, VA, Platoon 309, and was assigned to the USS *Washington* (BB-56) Dec. 24, 1941. His first onboard assignment was to the 5th Div. His battle station was upper handling room, 5" twin mount #1.

After 18 months, sometime after the ship's first visit to Pearl Harbor, he transferred to E Div. where he continued to serve until he transferred for discharge, Sept. 29, 1945 at Terminal Island, Long Beach, CA. He had advanced to EM2/c.

In July 1949, Shirley took a two-week Naval Reserve Cruise from Charleston to New York aboard the USS PC-1191. While in Brooklyn Navy Yard he saw the *Washington* brought in by tugboats for some mothball work.

His memorable experiences include the early morning they had the collision with the *Indiana*. He was sleeping in one of the mess halls because his bunk, on the third deck over one of the engine rooms, was too hot to sleep in some nights. They didn't have air-conditioned living quarters then. He felt something shake the whole ship. He thought they had taken a torpedo. General alarm sounded and they started passing the word for certain officers to report in. At that time, they didn't know that their staterooms had been demolished.

After hearing a little "scuttlebutt" here and there they finally found out what had happened. Knowing what had taken place didn't ease the shock of going out on deck after daylight, walking forward, and finding the whole bow missing!"

He was awarded the American Theater, EAME, Asiatic-Pacific, Good Conduct, National Defense and WWII Victory w/15 Battle Stars.

He later settled down in Cornelia, GA and married Eloise Cochran, March 3, 1951. He has two sons, Michael and Jeffrey and two granddaughters. He retired March 1, 1989 from a Johnson & Johnson Medical Products plant with 42 years service.

MARTIN SIEGAL, S1/C, born Aug. 23, 1921, joined the USN July 14, 1942 and was assigned to the USS *Washington*. Served in NRS NY, NY, NTS Newport, RI, USS *Alabama*, USS *Washington*, RS T.I. San Pedro, CA, PSC Lido Beach, LI. Honorably discharged Oct. 14, 1945 as seaman first class.

He told his daughter in 1941 that he saw enough action to last him a life time. He earned 15 Battle Stars. Returned home in 1946 after the war and went from job to job until he found a steady one. In 1947 he went out to a dance one Saturday night in Brooklyn and met and fell in love with Lita Citrin. He said, he fell in love with her the first time he saw her.

He married Lita Siegal Jan. 10, 1948. They had four children two sets of fraternal twins, his younger daughter Rochelle Siegal died Feb. 3, 1997. His other children were Ruth Sara, Ira Joel and Charles Barry. He was married to his wife for 25 years before she passed July 7, 1975. When he passed away Dec. 7, 1996, he had two grandchildren he adored, Adam William Liberti and Joel Siegal.

HAROLD I. SLOPER, born in Lynn, MA, received recruit training in Newport, RI after joining the USN on May 27, 1927. He served on the battleship USS *Utah*, the aircraft carrier USS *Saratoga* and the cruisers USS *Trenton, Memphis, Omaha* and *Chicago*.

In September 1939, he first saw service under wartime conditions on the USS *Dallas* (DD-199), a WWI era destroyer assigned to the "neutrality patrol" to protect Allied shipping in the North Atlantic against German submarines.

He was assigned to the USS *Washington* as a boatsman's mate first class on March 31, 1941. Sloper was placed in charge of the 5th Div. and started the task of building up the division's manpower and training to become a battle ready unit. He participated in the *Washington's* commissioning ceremony on May 15, 1941 with his wife Grace, present as a guest.

Sloper remained on the *Washington* throughout it's time in the Atlantic and Arctic Oceans including the tragic sinking of the HMS *Punjabi* and the Murmansk runs, and in the Pacific Ocean through the sinking of the Japanese battleship *Kirishima* in the third battle of Savo Island.

After promotion to chief boatswain's mate, and was reassigned in 1943 to new construction in the US. Sloper returned to the Pacific for the invasion of the Philippines aboard the seaplane tender, USS *San Carlos*, participating in the D Day landings on Leyte. After the capture of Manila and Corregidor, the *San Carlos* was one of the first US ships to enter Manila Bay. With the harbor at Manila locked by sunken Japanese ships, the *San Carlos* was based in the former US naval base at Cavite.

Sloper retired in 1949 after serving as CBM on the USS *Atlanta*. Recalled to service during the Korean War in 1950, he served in San Diego and Long Beach before retiring for a second time in 1952.

He was awarded the Asiatic-Pacific Campaign Medal w/5 Stars, the EAME Campaign Medal w/Star, the American Defense Service Medal w/2 Stars, the American Campaign Medal, the Philippine Liberation Medal w/2 Stars, the WWII Victory Medal, the National Defense Service Medal and the Good Conduct Medal.

Sloper retired from the State of California Military Department in 1975 and lived in Long Beach, CA with his wife, Grace. Harold passed away Oct. 19, 1997. He had one son, three grandchildren and two great-grandchildren.

DONALD A. SMITH, SF2/C, born Aug. 21, 1921 in Freeport, LI, joined the USN, Dec. 6, 1939, serving in R Div., shipfitter shop.

While at sea he participated in all Pacific engagements and the Murmansk Runs.

His favorite stories were the sinking of the *Kirishima;* being on watch at the time of the collision with the *Indiana* (and never feeling good being forward of Frame 21 again); the *South Dakota* (he used a nickname for her) breaking formation and silhouetting herself.

He was awarded the American Theater Ribbon, Asiatic-Pacific w/10 Stars, EAME w/Star, Philippine Liberation Ribbon, Victory Medal, American Defense Ribbon w/Star. Smith was discharged Dec. 17, 1945 and is survived by two sons, Allen and Charlie, as well as one grandson, Christopher. Donald passed away Nov. 6, 1996.

GODFREY A. "SMITTY" SMITH, RT2/C, was born June 27, 1917 in Brooklyn, NY. enlisted in the USN on Dec. 8, 1941, the day after the attack on Pearl Harbor. He was assigned to the Radio Div. aboard the USS *Washington* during January of 1942. While on the USS *Washington,* he participated in all major actions including the bombardment of Nauru and Kwajalein Islands and the occupation and capture of Gilbert and Marshall Islands.

After attending radio school, he was transferred to the USS *Wilkes-Barre*. He was discharged as RT2/c on Oct. 25, 1945.

He was awarded the American Campaign, Asiatic-Pacific w/Bronze Star, Philippine Liberation, Good Conduct, China Service, EAME and Occupaton Service Medals.

He began working for the New York Telephone Co. in Brooklyn during May of 1946 and retired in 1979. He married Peg Gilson on Sept. 13, 1941. They have three daughters and five grandchildren. He died Nov. 1, 1981 and is buried in Hackettstown, NJ.

MELVILLE CLEMENT SMITH, CSM, born Nov. 3, 1919, joined the USN December 1940 and attended Signal School in Chicago. He served one year aboard the USS *Arkansas* and then was assigned to USS *Washington* November 1941. Served as chief signalman in CS Div. for four years.

He participated in 15 battles and received 15 Battle Stars and was honorably discharged in October 1945.

Employed as line supervisor at Timken Co. for 44 years and retired in 1981. He married Charlotte Dlugolecki July 7, 1945 and they have a son who is a captain in the Navy Reserves.

CAREY W. SNELLINGS, SH1, born on Feb. 23, 1922 in Falmouth, VA, joined the USN on Feb. 26, 1940 and served on the USS *Bancraft* and the USS *Texas* before being assigned to the USS *Washington* in 1941.

On April 6, 1944, while the *Washington* was in port for repairs he married Marion E. Limerick.

He served on BB-56 throughout the war and was discharged on March 24, 1946.

After military service he worked as a civil servant at Fort Belvoir and retired in 1972 as a supply officer. On July 15, 1994 he passed away and is survived by his wife Marion, two children and two grandchildren.

ARTHUR H. SNYDER, GM, born Feb. 8, 1922 in Northumberland, PA, joined the USN Jan. 14, 1940 and was assigned to the USS *Washington* in 1941. Served on the *Washington* until 1946, as gunners mate and baker.

His memorable experiences include drydocking beside a ship with a childhood friend on board.

While at sea he participated in every action of the ship and was awarded the Marksman Medal.

Snyder was discharged Jan. 24, 1947. He was married for 38 years and the father of three children. He is now deceased.

RAYMOND A. SPIRES, CWO2, born 1907 in Cape, SC, son of Joseph A. and Ida Scott Spires, joined the USN Nov. 17, 1925. He attended basic training NAVSTA Norva, VA.

While awaiting completion of the USS *Washington,* he was ordered to Brooklyn Shipyard Jan. 16, 1941; Philadelphia, NY; March 31, 1941 USS *Washington* (BB-56).

Spires talked very little about WWII. He never forgot the high seas in the North Atlantic; the loss of Adm. Wilcox; the night battle of Guadalcanal and the ships collision.

His battle station was in damage control. Reluctantly, he left BB-56, March 13, 1944, the proudest ship he ever served on. He was a qualified diver. Transferred to Retired Reserve June 18, 1946 with unblemished record.

His project, Bass fishing. He volunteered for the Korean Conflict. Spires married Irma Rowe May 19, 1928 and they had a son Raymond Jr., and two granddaughters. He answered a call to a higher command March 30, 1981.

ROBERT F. STANZEL, PHM2/C, born Oct. 22, 1915 in Cleveland, OH, joined the USN, Feb. 24, 1942 and was assigned to and boarded the USS *Washington* in drydock Brooklyn Navy Yard, NY. Stationed in sick bay as Phm-striker.

He was aboard for one major surface engagement, third and final Battle of Savo Island.

His most memorable experience was the sinking of the *Kirishima* and *Ayanami* in that night action. Then came duty in Mobile Hospital #5 in New Caledonia and back to the main land and another assignment to the USS *Samaritan,* hospital ship. This ship was active in Peleliu, Saipan, Tinian, Guam and Iwo Jima campaigns while he was aboard.

He was discharged May 10, 1946 as PhM2/c and received the American Theater, Good Conduct and Asiatic-Pacific Campaign Medals w/5 Stars.

Stanzel retired in 1980 from Lewis Research Center, NASA, Cleveland, OH as a mechanic with 30 years service. He has an avid interest in horses and walking.

He is a life member of the DAV. Member of the VFW and 50 year member of the Masonic Lodge. He was married to Patricia Boyd on April 5, 1957. After 21 happy years was divorced in 1978. They had one son, Robert, whom his parents are very proud of. He excelled in knowledge at every level, topped off by MIT. He is his father's greatest accomplishment.

GRANVILLE EDWARD STUART, born April 25, 1925 in Richlands, VA, enlisted at the age of 15. He lied to get into the Navy. His family put his birthdate in the family Bible stating he was 17. The recruiter looked at that page in the Bible and signed him up.

His first assignment after boot camp in Norfolk, VA was the USS *Washington,* May 1944. He was a

plank owner of the ship. He was in the L Div. lookout and messenger watch then transferred to the N Div. as a quartermaster striker.

He loved the USN, it was his family. He had three square meals, new clothes on his back, a pay check in his pocket and his shipmates who were his family.

He worked hard and made second class. In September 1944, he transferred to receiving station in San Francisco for reassignment. In November 1944, he transferred to the YMS 413, the only QM and acted as assistant navigator. After the war was over he was discharged and joined the USNR.

The Korean War started and he was recalled to active service and assigned to the Naval Beach Group One in San Diego and was shipped to Japan.

Their job was to land with the first wave of any landing party and set up control of the beach. Thank God he didn't have to make any of these landings.

He was stationed on an old Japan army base in Yoka Suka. He served his time again and was discharged. He held different jobs, electrician, steam engineer, and county commissioner. He retired in 1989 and lives in Bend, OR with his wife Jill. They have 10 children, 20 grandchildren and two great-grandchildren. His hobbies are fishing, camping and armchair football.

CHARLES E. SUMMERS, GM1/C, born Sept. 30, 1923 in Lafollette, TN, joined the USN Feb. 11, 1941 and was assigned to USS *Washington* April 1941, stationed as 40mm gun battery and achieved the rank of GM1.

While at sea he was aboard for all of USS *Washington* actions during WWII, including convoy duty to Murmansk in early 1942, third Battle of Savo Island, all of the air strikes and bombardment of islands they captured.

His memorable experiences include the loss of Adm. Wilcox at sea in the North Atlantic riding out typhoon in December 1944; the sinking of HMS *Punjabi*.

He was discharged Jan. 16, 1947 as GM1/c and received 15 Battle Stars. He was recalled to active duty from June 1, 1951 to Sept. 15, 1952.

He was awarded the American Defense, EAME, Asiatic-Pacific, Philippine Liberation, Good Conduct and Victory Medal.

Summers is now retired from the trucking industry and Teamster Local 299, Detroit, MI. Retired to Tennessee in 1984 and attends two different Navy reunions and travels.

He married Naomi Hatmaker Phillips on Feb. 11, 1949. They have no children.

ROBERT MERLE "BOB" SUTHERLAND, GM1/C, born March 18, 1920, enlisted in the USN, January of 1940.

After boot camp training in Newport, RI, he was assigned to the USS *Denabola*. On May 15, 1941 he was assigned to the *Washington*. He participated in all major battle engagements from 1941 until 1944. He was a gunners mate second class in number one turret. In 1944 he attended hydraulic school in Washington, DC, and assigned to the USS *Lewis* DE-535 until the end of the war as gunners mate first class.

Sutherland and his wife "Kitty" have been married 49 years. They have two daughters, one granddaughter, three grandsons and one great-granddaughter.

He was employed by the Lansing Board of Water and Light for 27 years. He retired from the active USNR as a CPO after 20 years of service.

FRED SWEARINGEN, CRM, born Oct. 2, 1919, Keyser, WV, joined the USN Sept. 20, 1940 and assigned to the USS *Washington* May 15, 1941, as radio transmitter, achieved the rank of CRM.

While at sea he participated in all wartime actions. Transferred to a new ship in December 1945 by request.

His memorable experiences include being the radioman who set up the emergency transmitter used by Adm. "Ching Chong Cholly" Lee to contact Gen. Vandergriff on Guadalcanal to call off the threatening PT boats who were uninformed of their presence. They had daily drill designed to set up any transmitter on any frequency in one minute or less. They did it too!

During rough seas destroyer refueling operations during January 1945, destroyer USS *Hailey* (DD-556) collided with *Washington's* starboard bow. As a result, *Hailey* left her port anchor on their forecastle before disengaging and departing. In June 1950, at the outbreak of the Korean War, he was detailed to USS *Hailey* recommissioning crew at Naval Station San Diego. He spent the next four years on DD-556. To Swearingen, *Hailey* was a good ship. She now serves the Brazilian navy some 53 years after her birth.

He is now enjoying retirement, has one surviving son with twin seven year old grandsons. He wife died January 1995.

TRUXTON SMELTZER TAYLOR, CPO, born July 7, 1913 in Red Lion, PA to Archiebald and Sarah Taylor, joined the USN Oct. 3, 1934. Found the Navy his way of life for 19 years. Reported for duty April 26, 1941 in connection with outfitting and commissioning the USS *Washington*. While aboard, he attained the rank of chief petty officer.

In 1943, assigned to the Staff Island Commander supplying troops in the forward areas during the Marianas campaign.

During his career, helped commission the USS *Reno*, USS *Cimarron*, USS *Roosevelt*, and the USS *Wasp*.

He received the American Theater, Asiatic-Pacific, EAME, American Defense (Fleet Clasps), WWII Victory, Philippine Defense, European Occupation and Good Conduct Medal, Korean Medal.

He married Louise Smith on Aug. 20, 1939 and they had a son, Truxton, daughter, Lynda, four grandchildren and four great-grandchildren. Taylor worked as an accountant until the age of 72. He died on Oct. 11, 1995.

WILMER ROBERT TAYLOR, EM3/C, born March 14, 1923, Coatesville, PA, joined the USN, July 8, 1943. After boot camp at Sampson, NY, he attended Iowa State College, 16 weeks, electrician school and Gyro Compass School, Treasure Island, San Francisco, assigned to USS *Washington*, Aug. 11, 1943, and served in E Div., EM3/c rating, participating in: Anguar, Pelilieu, Leyte, Luzon, Iwo Jima and Okinawa Operations. Servicing ship's telephones, fire alarm boards and wiring, he stood watch and GQ stations in the secondary battery plotting room.

Most memorable was seeing Iwo Jima; going to Manus Island for dry docking in ABSD-2 and passing through the Panama Canal enroute to Philadelphia for Navy Day, Oct. 27, 1945.

He was honorably discharged Dec. 20, 1945 and received five Battle Stars and Asiatic-Pacific, American Defense and Philippine Liberation Medals.

Employed as an electrician for Lukens Steel Co. for 44 years. Married to Charlotte Simmers, July 23, 1945 and they have a son W. Robert, a daughter, Elizabeth Ann, two granddaughters and one grandson.

FRANCIS E. TELLIER, EM3/C, born Dec. 21, 1923, joined the USN Jan. 28, 1941. After boot camp, Newport RI, assigned to USS *Washington* and commissioned ship May 15, 1941.

Served aboard her in ETO, South West, Pacific, Marianas, Palau and Philippine Campaigns. Left ship at Ulithi in Southern Carolines in latter part of October 1944.

Discharged Oct. 10, 1945, married Lorraine Mellan and they had a son Nov. 19, 1949. They have four children, two boys, two girls and seven grandchildren. Tellier is still healthy after almost 12 years of retirement. He is 73 years old.

STEPHEN TERSTENYAK, SCB1/C, born in Wendall, PA, Nov. 17, 1918, served in the Civilian Conservation Corps July 10, 1939 through March 28, 1940 at Camp F-33A Mayer, AZ.

He enlisted in the USN March 11, 1941 and was stationed aboard USS *Washington* in late 1941. Upon discharge from active Navy duty he was placed in the Navy Reserve from April 22, 1947 until May 27, 1951. He transferred back to regular Navy duty May 28, 1951 to April 25, 1952. While aboard USS *Washington* he participated in the Murmansk Run and was at his battle station being the center 5" mount starboard side when USS *Washington* sank the *Kirishima* and *Ayanami*.

In mid 1942 he transferred to a baby flattop the USS *Sitkoh Bay* where he reached his highest rate of SCB1/c. His decorations include the Asiatic-Pacific w/ 13 Stars, EAME w/Star, American Theater, American Defense, Good Conduct w/Star, Philippine Liberation, WWII Victory and Korean Conflict Medals.

He was the superintendent of a New York State Armory at Jamacia Queens, NY. He served in the Army Reserve until May 1968.

Terstenyak passed away on Nov. 29, 1996. He is survived by two sons, Stephen and Joseph, a daughter Steffina, several grandchildren and one great-grandchild.

RALPH LESLIE "TOMMIE" THOMAS, LCDR, born Dec. 23, 1920 in Jacksonville, FL, enlisted in the USN in 1940 after graduation from Hillsborough High School in Tampa, FL and attended training school in Norfolk. He served on the USS *Washington*, original crew (plank owner) May 1941 to April 1943 (including Battle of Guadalcanal) as RM-2 radio operator (standing radio circuit watches). He served on USS *Reuben James* (DE-153) in similar capacity May 1943-February 1944. The USN put him through school (May 1944-June 1947) as a V-12 student, and he earned a bachelor's degree in electrical engineering at Duke University and the University of Louisville. He was commissioned as a Reserve Naval Officer in June 1947.

From late 1947 to mid 1951, he worked in the U.S. Patent Office in Washington, DC and attended law school at George Washington University at night, graduating in 1951. September 1951 to January 1953 (Korean War) he served as a line officer on the USS *Bearss* (DD-654). Thereafter, he made a career as a lawyer, first as in-house attorney for IBM (during infancy of computer development), and later in private practice in Washington, DC and Northern Virginia. He attained the rank of lieutenant commander in 1958, and retired from the USN in 1965. One of his most lasting memories of his time on the USS *Washington* was hearing the pilots chatter during combat of their hits/victories in the heat of WWII battles. He received numerous merit awards and badges during his service in the USN. He considers his career in the USN, and especially his service on the USS *Washington*, as his greatest accomplishment.

He married Carol Ward April 15, 1961, and has two sons, Ward and Bryant and three grandchildren. He is retired and lives in Nags Head, NC.

He is a tough old salt and never got seasick once.

KENNETH A. TIPPER, born June 27, 1921, in Birmingham, England, joined the Royal Navy on June 5, 1941, and went to HMS *Royal Arthur* for training as a telegraphist. On Jan. 2, 1942, he joined the tribal class destroyer HMS *Punjabi*, then under refit. His job was to intercept German radio signals and use a direction finder to locate ships such as the *Tirpitz*.

On May 1, 1942, while part of a covering force for a convoy to Russia, the *Punjabi* was rammed and sunk by HMS *King George V*, (the story of which appears elsewhere), and he was returned to his home base of Portsmouth for reassignment. He went to the hunt class destroyer HMS *Quorn*, which patrolled the coast of Britain on anti-E-boat missions. On Dec. 24, 1943, after training in interception of Japanese radio signals, he joined HMS *Anderson*, a short station in Ceylon, now Sri Lanka.

He was discharged as a leading telegraphist in February 1946, and on June 1, 1946, married Norah Sollors. They have two children, five grandchildren and one great-granddaughter.

The family emigrated to the US in 1957, and Ken and Norah have made their home in Florida for the past 40 years. He retired as a sales manager in 1985, and is a volunteer bailiff, and writes for several publications, also as a volunteer.

FRED L. TUCKER, P2/C, born Sept. 29, 1921, in Richmond, VA (down where the south begins).

Joined the National Maritime Union 1938, sailed merchant tankers, freighters, colliers until 1941.

Enlisted Dec. 8, 1941, boot training Norfolk NTS. Sent to SOWESPAC March 1942 to Base Beacher, Tongatabu, Friendly Islands in Pacific, after six months of going "rock-happy," managed a "swap" to the newly arrived *Washington*, had previously found a man on USS *Juneau* willing to swap, but they sailed before they could complete the paper work.

Assigned to print shop, condition watch station "JA" phone on bridge. Battle station main battery plot.

Served on all actions until Nov. 20, 1944, when transferred to 11th NAVDISHDQ print shop. Discharged printer second class, March 1946, with usual #1-was-there" ribbons.

Retired after 47 years as printer and supervisor, *Daily Press*. Now handle Honey-Do's, etc., married former Nicholas County, WV, beauty queen Evalyn Huff, son West Point Grad, Class of 1968.

FRANCIS JOSEPH "FRANK" TURZYN, GM3/C, born July 7, 1921, enlisted March 1941. Discharged January 1947.

Upon enlisting in USN, he was told he was too heavy. The doctor gave him a diet and told him to return in a week, he gained two pounds, but was accepted. Trained Newport, RI, grew to 6'2" and gained 20 pounds.

He dove into water on a $5.00 bet, was accused of disturbing the "King's Fishes," like the real Tarzan, when they crossed the Equator. Enroute to Europe, he was on boat deck and saw a man overboard, not knowing it was the Admiral. Passed through the Panama Canal twice, once after North Atlantic. Duty, back and forth from Murmansk to Island waiting for Von Tirpitz to leave Norway to sink convoys. Participating in every USS *Washington* Pacific engagements.

When war ended, transferred to 16th fleet in Philadelphia putting ships into mothballs until discharge. Worked for Republic Aviation making jet airplanes for five years, US Post Office, 25 years. Married while in USN, five children. Divorced after 30 years, married woman with seven children, now grandfather of 24, great-grandfather of one.

HARRY G. VANDERWALKER, BM2/C, born Jan. 13, 1924 in Aurelius, NY. He joined the USN, Feb. 4, 1941 and reported on board the USS *Washington* May 24, 1941. Served at NTS Newport, RI, USNH Newport, RI; USS *Washington*; RS Brooklyn, NY.

He was injured in the leg by shrapnel and was

given morphine twice - once regular time then by a second corpsman who didn't see a tag on him and gave him another shot - for two weeks, he drifted in and out of consciousness.

Vanderwalker was on board for all major actions; the Murmansk runs, collision with USS *Indiana;* was there when *Kirishima* and *Ayanami* were sunk. Many other bombardments too.

He was awarded the EAME w/Star, Asiatic-Pacific w/12 Stars, Philippine Liberation w/2 Stars, Good Conduct Medal, American Area Medal and the American Defense w/Star.

He married Ann Garbarta (US Army), Feb. 18, 1946. They have been married for 35 years. They had one son, Richard, four daughters: Christine, Carol, Linda and Cindy, four granddaughters, and two grandsons. He is a retired farmer, self-employed auto mechanic. Vanderwalker died Aug. 15, 1981.

BEN VIGIL, born Aug. 20, 1924 in Calcite, CO and moved to Salida, CO at the age of six. He graduated high school May of 1943 and joined the USN in June.

He went through boot camp at Camp Pendleton and Signal School at Farragut, ID and was assigned to the USS *Washington* in April 1944 while it was being repaired in Bremerton, WA.

Vigil received eight Battle Stars, six Asiatic-Pacific, two Philippine Liberation. He left the USS *Washington* in Boston in December 1945 and was discharged at Shoemaker, CA March 1946.

He married Clara Lucero May 28, 1947, and they have four children: one son and three daughters and seven grandchildren. In May 1997 it will be their 50th anniversary.

He worked for the US Government for 31 years at Tooele Army Depot in the Security Div. Retired at the present time.

PATRICK T. VINCENT, LCDR, born March 17, 1917 in Chicago, was a 1939 graduate of Dennison University and a past chapter president of Beta Theta Pi.

He served as a naval officer in both the Pacific and European theaters during WWII and also served during the Korean War. He served on the USS *Washington* and USS *Missouri* and retired as a lieutenant commander after 12 years of service.

For 24 years, he and his late wife, Marion, owned and managed the Mountain Home Inn, a German restaurant on Mount Tamalpais in Mill Valley.

He was a member of Friends of La Mirada, the Jesters, the Monterey Peninsula Museum of Art and the Monterey History and Art Association. He also served as a volunteer and "stood watch" at the Monterey Maritime Museum. He was well-known as a storyteller and spent time writing of his war experiences and days as an innkeeper.

He died Feb. 23, 1994 and is survived by a son, Tiff of Fairbanks, AK; two stepsons, Kendall Coburn of Santa Rosa and Curtis Coburn of Petaluma and several grandchildren. He also leaves his companion, Corinne Davis of Carmel.

PETER T. VINETTE JR., MM2/C, born Feb. 24, 1922 in Syracuse, NY, left school after 8th grade and went into the CCC camp at age 15. Joined the National Guard the same year.

He joined the USN Jan. 31, 1941 and was attached to the USS *Washington* immediately after boot camp. Lived in barracks at the Philadelphia Navy Yard until boarding the *Washington*. He was on the *Washington* from time she was commissioned until July 20, 1942.

His most memorable experience was when they lost Adm. Wilcox. His whale boat was called away for rescue. On board they had the coxswain, bow hook, engineer, a pharmacist mate and he believes a lieutenant-commander. Not sure of the officer's rating but his knees were knocking louder than Vinette's. They almost had them in the water (waves 40 feet high). Capt. Benson came out on the bridge and ordered the boat back on board to its cradle. He was also one of the men on watch (smoke watch) that spotted Adm. Wilcox swimming in the water.

Another exciting day occurred while they were taking a load of young officers from the *Washington*, anchored at Scapa Flow to a town called Kirkwall. It was a rough sea and they were taking on a lot of water. Vinette kept using the hard pump but he couldn't keep up. The officer in charge asked if there was anything he could do. He told him to have each one of the young officers to use his hat for a bucket. They did and in no time builges were dry and saved the day.

He was discharged Jan. 31, 1947. He received nine Battle Stars and medals as follows: Good Conduct, American Defense, WWII Victory Medal, EAME Campaign, Navy Occupation Service Medal, American Campaign, Asiatic-Pacific Campaign, China Service Medal, Philippine Liberation Ribbon.

He retired from the US Coast Guard Feb. 24, 1982 and received the US Coast Guard Achievement Medal. Consequently he received the Cross of New York from the state of New York.

ARTHUR H. WAGES, QM2/C, born March 7, 1925 in Queens, NY, enlisted in the USN Feb. 16, 1943. After boot camp at Camp Perry, Great Lakes, NTS, attended Quartermaster School, Newport, RI. Joined the crew of BB-56 in New Hebrides December 1943. Served in N Div. attaining rank of QM2/c.

His most memorable experiences were witnessing kamikaze attacks from the navigation bridge and looking up at 60 foot plus wave crests in the typhoon.

He was honorably discharged Feb. 5, 1946 but remained in USNR through 1951.

Wages was awarded the Asiatic-Pacific Ribbon w/8 Battle Stars, Philippine Liberation w/2 Stars, American Theater and Victory Medals.

After WWII he attended St. John's University and NYU. Enjoyed an exciting banking career with a NYC bank and retired as senior vice president in 1993. Residing now in New Braunfels, TX with wife Michelina, keeps busy volunteering, playing bridge and working out in a gym.

CLARENCE L. WAGNER, S1/C, born July 12, 1908 in Kempton, IL, son of Henry and Dora Wagner, volunteered for service in 1944, receiving basic training at Great Lakes, IL and was assigned berth on USS *Washington* May 12, 1944. Attained the rank of seaman first class and discharged Nov. 5, 1945.

Wagner's awards include the American Campaign, Asiatic-Pacific w/6 Stars, with Philippine Liberation w/2 Stars.

He kept a handwritten personal diary each day of his military service. Following discharge he farmed land 1 1/2 miles west of Kempton until he retired. He also was a school bus driver for the Kempton-Cabery district for 15 years. He married Grace Cooper of Piper City on Aug. 10, 1929. He died Jan. 2, 1989 and Grace died Nov. 25, 1991. They are survived by daughters, Judith Patchett of Marengo, IL and Joyce Tweedt of Kempton, IL, seven grandchildren and eight great-grandchildren. A daughter Doris died at age three.

RALPH WALTON, CPO, born April 4, 1918, Grapeland, TX. Served on the USS *Washington* 1939-45, as chief petty officer in charge of one of the four engine rooms. While on the *Washington* he served in all major campaigns including Atlantic convoys to Iwo Jima.

Most memorable was thanking God he was on a ship during Iwo Jima, almost being washed overboard during a storm when he went on deck during the night to sleep and the kamikaze that was captured.

Ralph married his childhood sweetheart Maurice Long on Feb. 14, 1942. He was the Grapeland postmaster until retirement in 1985. Active in First Baptist Church Choir and served on the Grapeland School Board. Walton spoke regularly to school groups about his experiences in WWII.

He was an adored father and grandfather to four children, 11 grandchildren and one great-grandchild. He died March 2, 1995 and is buried in Grapeland, TX.

HERBERT L. WARNER, CM2, born Dec. 14, 1914 in Brighton, MI. Inducted into the USN Dec. 23, 1943. During boot camp at Great Lakes he made third class carpenters mate and was assigned to R Div. USS *Washington* April 5, 1944 in Bremerton, WA. Participated in all the Pacific Operations from the bombardment of Saipan to the bombardment of Okinawa.

He received the American Area Service Ribbon, Asiatic-Pacific Service Ribbon w/6 Bronze Stars and Philippine Liberation Ribbon w/2 Bronze Stars.

Warner was honorably discharged Nov. 5, 1945 as carpenters mate second class. He worked at Burroughs Corp. for 38 years; 15 years as a carpenter and 23 years as a plant engineer. He married Arlene Richards Aug. 17, 1940. They have one son, two grandchildren and one great-grandchild. Since retiring from Burroughs in 1977, he has been operating an apple orchard.

IVAN WATKINS, S2/C, born Jan. 9, 1927 in South Bend, IN, joined the USN March 21, 1944 and was assigned to the USS *Washington* May 1944, as S2/c, 9th Div. as 20mm gunner.

While at sea he served in the following: neutralization of Japanese bases in the Bonins, Marianas and Western Pacific, June 10-24, 1944; neutralization of Japanese bases in the Bonins, Marianas and Western Pacific, July 3-Aug. 15, 1944; capture and occupation of Saipan, June 11-24, 1944; bombardment of Saipan, June 13, 1944; battle of the Philippine Sea, June 19-20, 1944; capture and occupation of Guam, July 12-Aug. 15, 1944; Palau, Yap, Ulithi raid, July 25-27, 1944; capture and occupation of Peleliu and Anguar, including carrier strikes on the Central Philippines and Luzon, Aug. 30-Oct. 5, 1944; Okinawa Jima, Taiwan (Formosa) raids, Oct. 6-31, 1945; battle of Cape Engano Oct. 24-26, 1944; Luzon raids, Nov. 5-14, 1944; Luzon raids, Nov. 5-14, 1944; Luzon raid Nov. 25, 1944; Luzon Dec. 14-16, 1944; Okinawa Jima, Formosa and Luzon raids, Jan. 3-9, 1945; Cam Rahn Bay-Saigon, French Indo-China raid, Jan. 16, 1945; Formosa raid, Jan. 21, 1945; Hong Kong, Hainan, Canton, China raid, Jan. 16, 1945; Formosa raid, Jan. 21, 1945; Mansei Shoto raid, Jan. 22, 1945; Tokyo raids, Feb. 16-17, 1945; bombardment of Iwo Jima, Feb. 19-22, 1945; Tokyo raid, Feb. 25, 1945.

He was awarded the Asiatic-Pacific Ribbon w/6 Stars, American Service Ribbon, American Campaign Medal, Liberation Guam, Philippine Liberation w/2 Stars, Philippine Unit Citation.

His memorable experiences include kamikaze attacks; total battles of many ships; Pacific; typhoon.

Watkins was honorably discharged May 7, 1946. He married Betty J. Stockton on June 26, 1948. They have been married for 48 years. They have two sons, Daniel and Robert and two grandsons, Jeremy and Dusten.

He is a retired plumber (Local 172) South Bend and member of USS *Washington* reunion group.

EDWARD D. WATTS, GM1, born May 16, 1923 in Mineola, NY, joined the USN Feb. 25, 1941. After boot camp at Newport, RI, he was assigned to BB-56 May 2, 1941. Served in the 4th Div. and attained the rank of GM1. He served aboard USS *Remey* (DD-688) and USS *Champlain*.

He earned nine Battle Stars and serviced 5" and 40mm gunmounts. His most memorable was being on deck watching the battle of Savo.

Watts was honorably discharged May 21, 1946. He received Asiatic-Pacific, EAME, Armed Forces Expeditionary Service, Good Conduct, National Defense, WWII Medals.

Employed as a truck mechanic for Grumman Corp. for 35 years. He married Thelma M. Scudder, June 15, 1947 and they have a son, Edward, a daughter, Linda, three grandchildren and two great-grandchildren. His wife died Nov. 14, 1979. He remarried Edith McKenna Oct. 10, 1981 and has a stepson Alexander, and stepdaughter, Sandra.

JOHN L. WEBB, born March 18, 1918 in Huron, TN, joined the USN Oct. 26, 1936. First cruise, reenlisted Jan. 3, 1941 and assigned to crew of USS *Washington* for fitting out on board when commissioned May 15, 1941.

His first four years were served on board four-piper destroyers, *Sands* 243 and *Reuben James* 245. Discharged from the *Reuben James* October 1940.

Reenlisted on *Washington* until May 1943 at this time he was appointed warrant officer.

While at sea he participated in convoy duty to Russia, Arctic Circle and Guadalcanal Campaign November 1942.

Crossing the equator and the Guadalcanal were the most exciting. When crossing the equator became a shellback. Going through the Panama Canal was interesting.

Webb was awarded the Good Conduct Medal and was discharged February 1946. His married and has four children and six grandchildren. He is now retired.

WILLIAM P. WEIDERT SR., born on Dec. 2, 1921 in New Rochelle, NY was raised in Riga Center, NY where they moved to in 1928.

Enlisted in USN on March 5, 1941 and went through boot camp at Newport, RI for eight weeks of training. Assigned to USS *Washington* (BB-56) May 14, 1941 in the 3rd Div. as a deck hand. His battle station was on the shell flats of turret #3 (16" guns) during the war.

As a crew member of the USS *Washington* for five years, he earned 16 Battle Stars, the Fleet Clasp, Victory and American Defense Medals, as well as campaign ribbons: EAME, Asiatic-Pacific, Philippine Liberation, American Area Service, American Defense, and Good Conduct. He also earned the "Blue Nose" certificate for crossing the Arctic Circle and the "shellback" certificate for crossing the equator. He also is a plank owner.

The only trip he missed was when the USS *Washington* went from Annapolis to New York for mothballing. He was honorably discharged on Jan. 8, 1947.

On May 11, 1946 he married Janet Marie Arlidge. They raised four sons (William, Jr., George, James and John) and one daughter (Judith). They have been married for 51 years and have nine grandsons and four granddaughters. Retired from Gannett Rochester newspaper as single copy district manager.

HARVEY B. WEINER, S1/C, born Oct. 2, 1922 in Brooklyn, joined the USN March 4, 1941 and was

assigned to the USS *Washington* May 15, 1941 and stationed on deck as S1/c.

He participated in all actions while at sea. His memorable experience includes being a bluenose and a shellback.

Weiner was discharged Dec. 9, 1946 and awarded all medals except the Good Conduct. He is now retired and married to Josephine.

CHARLES C. "TODD" WEST, GM1/C, born Aug. 29, 1919 in Kingmont, WV, served aboard USS *Washington* from its commission through spring of 1945 when he was transferred to USS *Dade*. He was a gunners mate first class.

He saw all major actions while aboard and before his discharge on Nov. 20, 1946, and was awarded the following: Asiatic-Pacific w/8 Stars, American Area, EAME w/Star, American Defense, Good Conduct, WWII Victory and Philippine Liberation Medals.

He married Hazel Pauline Drake of Kingmont and had a daughter, Gloria Jean and son, Gary V. Charles passed away on Veterans Day of 1990. His wife and children still live in Fairmont, WV. For the most of his post-war days, he was a short and long haul truck driver for three separate companies. He enjoyed fishing and hunting and was a follower of WVU sports and Pittsburgh sports teams. He was a loved father and husband and a fine gentleman. His descendants can be contacted by e-mail, mellowgrey@hotmail.com. Submitted by Gary West.

JESSE C. WHEELESS, SM3/C, born Dec. 11, 1915 in Texas, joined the USN in Dallas, TX, October 1936. Boot camp San Diego Co. 36-30. Reenlisted 1940 for new construction (*Washington*) Philadelphia, PA and wore crew button #49. He was in first watch (SM3/c) set upon commissioning 1941.

One memorable experience was the ramming of the USS *Indiana*. While he was sleeping on a cot on the signal bridge, found himself on deck and it was very dark. After daylight they found they lost 6 men and 60 feet of bow. Only made approximately 10 knots. After repairs he returned to the war zone.

Wheeless left the *Washington* in 1945. After time and other stations retired in 1957 to New Mexico. He feels rewarded to have been a crew member of a good ship and crew.

HARRY R. WHITNEY, Y1/C, born Aug. 24, 1921 in Buffalo, NY, joined the USN Jan. 16, 1942 and assigned to USS *Washington* in February as Y3c to chaplain and then as yeoman to ship's navigator, N Div.

He was aboard for Murmansk runs in North Atlantic with British fleet and prepared ship's log for signature of King George V in Scapa Flow. Aboard for third battle of Savo Island and other bombardments and air attacks in South Pacific. Left USS *Washington* for Navy V-12 program at Cornell University in January 1944. Returned to fleet in June of 1945 after marriage on June 26 to Ann Tilden, Worcester, MA. Discharged from service as Y1c on Sept. 24, 1945.

Retired from General Motors Corp. in September 1981 and resides in Sarasota, FL with wife, Ann and they have two sons, two daughters, three grandsons and four granddaughters.

HOMER W. WICKHAM, born Sept. 3, 1923 in Greeley, CO, joined the USN with his two brothers March 13, 1942. He was first sent to Navy School of Music in Washington, DC and was part of the replacement band that went aboard the USS *Washington* at Efate Atoll shortly after the battle with the *Kirishima*.

Trained in damage control and assigned to the R Div. battle station was to secure and repair the ship from turret two forward. Liked this because it was quiet and cool up there. All that changed when they ran into the *Indiana*.

Worst duty was standing watch on that smashed and twisted forward bulkhead trying to get the ship back to Kwajalein for emergency repairs.

Left ship shortly after that and was assigned to V-12 program at IIT, graduating as a mechanical engineer.

He has worked as an engineer, farmer, and farm implement dealer. Currently retired, playing with several music groups, and taking college classes.

He married Ruth Molberg Aug. 11, 1946 and they have three daughters, two sons, and nine grandchildren.

FRED WIEGEL, EM1/C, born in Timmer, ND, joined the USN Jan. 3, 1942 and assigned to the USS *Washington* March 25, 1942, forward turbo, engine room, forward control board-powder.

While at sea he participated in all action from North Atlantic and South Pacific including October 1944, Okinawa.

His memorable experiences include the day before crossing the equator, Sept. 2, 1942. This feather merchant and ring leader of the Pollywogs caught Dixon and cut his hair, next was Basetti, cut his hair also, then two more shellbacks, you bet!

The next day, September 3, was their day. The Royal High Court of the Raging Main escorted Wiegel from his duty station to topside and the stocks, torture chamber, water tank, head shave and running of the gauntlet (twice).

He was discharged October 1945 and awarded eight Battle Stars.

He was married for 50 years and has two children. He became a widower on Dec. 21, 1995. Wiegel is living the life of comfortable ease with golf and fishing his top priorities. Carrying a 22 handicap.

PACE WILL WILLIAMS, JR., RM2/C, born Feb. 18, 1923 in Fairfield, AL, joined the USN Dec. 12, 1941 and assigned to the USS *Washington* Jan. 12, 1942, C&R Radio Communications. His GQ station was up at the bow in officers quarters and mess hall.

After collision with the *Indiana*, Sandy and Williams were up in the bow and there was twisted metal and etc. They heard an officer asking for help. They found him and got him out and he was out of his head. They had a time with him.

While at sea he was aboard for all major actions, Murmansk runs, *Indiana* collision and battle of Savo Island.

His memorable experiences: first going through Panama Canal; USS *Washington* not getting hit or damaged.

He was discharged Oct. 13, 1945 and awarded 15 Battle Stars, American Theater, Good Conduct, Asiatic-Pacific and EAME Medal.

Williams is now semi-retired as paint contractor, working five men. Married to Helen and they enjoy Alabama football.

JAMES T. WILLIAMSON, born Jan. 21, 1924 in Tuscaloosa, AL, after enlisting in February 1941 and attending boot camp in Norfolk, VA, went aboard USS *Washington* in May 1941. He served in the 3rd Div., battle station no. 3, as rammer man on the right gun.

He has many memories of his time aboard the USS *Washington,* most of them good and some very exciting. One particular morning stands out in his mind: after weeks aboard ship, patrolling and standing watch, (the usual four on and eight off), the monotony was broken. Usually waking reluctantly to the sound of reveille, an officer on board ship ordered the bugler to play it was a "boogie woogie" swing. At the sound, the sailors awoke laughing and excited. Although the officer was later "chewed out", morale on ship had been restored.

After serving a full six years, Williamson was honorably discharged after the war in 1947. He went home to Tuscaloosa, married Betty O'Quinn and had two daughters, Emily and Iris. He worked as a self-employed building contractor for 35 years. He has one grandson, Bo McBriff.

RUSSELL S. WOEPPEL, F1/C, born in Easton, PA. He was the youngest of nine children and has six brothers and two sisters.

He joined the USN on Jan. 28, 1944 and was inducted from Allentown, PA on Feb. 9, 1944. He was trained at Great Lakes Training Center. He went from Great Lakes to San Diego and then on to Pearl Harbor where he boarded the USS *Washington* on May 12, 1944.

He was at Pearl Harbor and the Philippine Islands and was awarded the Asiatic-Pacific Ribbon w/

6 Bronze Stars, the Philippine Liberation Ribbon w/2 Bronze Stars, the American Area Service Ribbon and WWII Victory Medal.

Woeppel was discharged November 1945. He always looked forward to his ship reunions and seeing his former ship mates, and never lost his faith in his flag and country. He was always proud of his sons serving in the USN, USMC and the USAF.

He married Mary Miller of Phillipsburg, NJ and together they had three sons, Russell W.G., David W and Donald A. He had a total of nine grandchildren and 10 great-grandchildren.

He worked for Kuebler Brewing Company of Easton, PA and the Old Dutch Brewery of Catasauqua, PA. On the closing of these companies he went to work for the City of Easton until his retirement in 1971 at the age of 70. (25 years).

In his retirement he enjoyed biking. At the age of 80 he biked and finished the Lutheran world action bike-a-thon, at which time he felt biking was getting him down, so he took up square dancing (six days a week). He also liked travel, seeing as much of the US and Canada as he could. He was a giving man, always loaning money and a helping hand to whoever needed it. He died Oct. 9, 1996.

JOHN S. WOLONS, EM1/C, born April 21, 1922 in Spencer, MA, joined the USN Feb. 27, 1941 and was assigned to the USS *Washington* May 27, 1941, I.C. and Gyro Compass and fire contact circuits.

He participated in the Altantic convoys, Savo Island and Leyte Gulf while at sea.

His memorable experience includes the collision with the *Indiana*.

Wolons was awarded the American Defense, Asiatic-Pacific, EAME, Philippine Liberation and 11 Battle Stars.

He was discharged March 7, 1947. He married Agnes O'Malley and they have three sons and five grandchildren. Now retired as chief electrician from Bendix.

HOWARD FRANK WRIGHT, JR., PFC, born in Detroit on May 16, 1919, joined the USMC, Jan. 3, 1940, attended basic training at Parris Island, SC and Quantico. Board the USS *Tuscaloosa* and was on board for the famous Roosevelt-Churchill fishing trip.

Boarded the USS *Washington* on May 15, 1941 and served in the 7th Div. His GQ stations, five-inch mount and the 1.1 inch mounts. He was onboard the *Washington* for the Murmansk Runs, through the Third Battle of Savo. After catching pneumonia, he was transferred to a hospital ship on May 16, 1943. He was assigned to the USS *Indiana*. He was on board the USS *Indiana* when the collision occurred with the *Washington*. Special military qualifications: anti-aircraft machine gun crewman, orderly, machine gun crewman, graduated Sea School in 1941.

Wright married Lillian T. Graessle at Camp Lejeune, NC on Dec. 9, 1944 and then shipped out to the Panama Canal, Hawaiian Islands and Japan, and discharged Nov. 19, 1945, PFC. His weapons qualifications: rifle marksman, Browning machine gun first class.

He raised six children including Howard III (associate president). Retired after 30 years as a city bus driver in Detroit, MI. Wright passed away March 30, 1989.

GAY PASCAL YOUNGBLOOD, SK3/C, born Oct. 26, 1917 near the Coldwater community of Calloway Co., KY where he and his nine siblings often boasted that they scalded hogs in Coldwater. Edgar and Alma Youngblood contributed four sons to the war and sacrificed a son-in-law on the European front. He

entered the USN on July 17, 1943, came aboard the USS *Washington* April 1944 and served continuously until Jan. 27, 1946 as a storekeeper third class in the supply office. His vivid recollections include the fires after the tragic skip bombing of the USS *Franklin* seen from the bow of the *Washington*.

He married Edith Smith Oct. 13, 1940. While aboard BB-56, his son Eddie Lee was born and he first saw him one year later. Two more sons and a daughter (Wayne, Diane and Harmon) were born to the 57 year marriage. Youngblood and brothers founded a variety of businesses in Mayfield, KY including hardware, discount center, supermarket and furniture stores, putting his Navy storekeeping skills to good use. Today, his son Wayne manages the True Value Home Center to which you are all invited.

NORMAN D. ZORB, SGT, born Dec. 16, 1924 in St. Johns, WA, joined the service Nov. 13, 1942 and was assigned to the USS *Washington* March, 7, 1943 and departed Sept. 5, 1945, 5" gun merchants.

While at sea he participated in Gilbert Islands, Northern Solomons, Marshall, Marianas, Palau, Philippine, Tokyo Japan, Iwo Jima, Okinawa.

Discharged Sept. 13, 1945 and married June 1, 1946 and has five children, (two boys and three girls): Mike, Sandy, Pat, Vikki, Georgine. Retired and working odd jobs only.

Floyd George Leishing, for biography please see page 93.

USS Washington Associate Members

MARIANNE COMBS ADAMS, born Dec. 14, 1927, Atlanta, GA, married Elton Ray Adams, Dec. 19, 1970. During WWII she went to school and dated service men. She is a writer, artist, illustrator and speaker. Her sponsor is Elton Ray Adams.

MERRIANN E. AUGHTON, born Aug. 6, 1925 in Los Angeles, CA, married Robert T. Aughton, June 21, 1952.

During WWII she was employed at Douglas Aircraft, Long Beach California in August 1943. She is now retired. Her sponsor is Robert T. Aughton.

FREDERICK DAVID BROWN, born Dec. 24, 1961 in Honolulu, HI, married Barbara May 21, 1964 and they have a son Andrew.

He has been employed as commercial and fleet sales manager, Garnsey & Wheeler Ford.

Attended the University of Northern Colorado and received a bachelor of science degree in management. He is a member of the United States Naval Institute.

His sponsor is his stepfather, Alfred B. Rodrigues.

THE BROWN FAMILY, we are the proud family of John A. Brown (Brownie) and Gladys Brown.

Front row: Shane Brown (grandson), John Brown, Gladys Brown, Megan Baisen (great-granddaughter). Back row: Jeremy Brown (grandson), Monica Brown (daughter-in-law), Keith Brown (son), Lori Brown (granddaughter), Sherry Brown (daughter-in-law), Mike Brown (son), Debbie Baisen (granddaughter), and Mark Baisden (granddaughters husband).

We are all associate members of the USS *Washington* (BB-56) reunion group.

John and Gladys celebrated their 50th wedding anniversary last year on April 25, 1996. This is where our family picture was taken. We were all very proud to share this special day with John and Gladys. We love them very much.

MARGARET "TEENIE" BROWN, born April 23, 1933 in El Dorado Springs, MO.

The first time I saw Melvin Brown "Brownie" was in October of 1945 at an old fashioned pie supper at the country school I attended back in Kansas. Gosh, was he handsome in his Navy uniform! We never saw each other again until 1950, when we started dating.

We were married on July 1, 1951 and he was even more handsome then! God blessed us with so much love and happiness, and, of course, as is true to life, some setbacks and disappointments. Our richest blessings are our son, Terry and his son, Toby and our daughter, Tammy, and her son and daughter, William and Megan.

Our multitudes of friends have grown with the reunions of the USS *Washington* group, but one of the heartaches of growing older is the losing of our friends to death. Let us cherish each new day with our family and friends so that we may grow in God's love and live by the Golden Rule, and above all, Let us Love One Another.

ANNA LEE ASH COULAM, born Oct. 16, 1919 in Kansas City, MP, married March 21, 1944. During WWII she taught high school and was a private secretary for Pratt & Whitney Aircraft.

WILLIAM JOEPSH DEAS, born June 15, 1956 in Baltimore, MD, served in the USN, MR-2 E-5 from Feb. 28, 1976-Feb. 28, 1982. He is employed as machinist.

His sponsor is William Joepsh Deas, his father.

PEARLE ELAINE EVANS, born Jan. 7, 1923 at La Grange, IL. Enlisted Jan. 20, 1943 in Chicago. Attended boot camp and yeoman training at Iowa State Teachers College, Cedar Falls, IA. Ordered to DC in May 1943. Injured while on duty and was sent to Bethesda USN Hospital. She had an injured right shoulder. Met her George there and spent six months and then received her honorable discharge, Dec. 18, 1943. She's held her service connected compensation since 1943.

Her husband George died of service connected disabilities 90% on April 9, 1993. He wanted to be buried at sea. He was on the CV-64, USS *Constellation*. He is in 2350 fathoms between lower Baja and Hawaii, 25° and between 125°-130°.

She retired from Western Electric, Chicago, IL and is active in her DAV Chapter. She is a chaplain of South Marin #85 and is a junior vice commander in DAV District #4.

RITA D. GALANTE, born March 21, 1922 in Philadelphia, PA. Married Joseph Galante Nov. 25, 1950. She worked for the Immigration and Naturalization Service during WWII, 1941 to 1946.

Her sponsor is her husband Joseph Galante.

MICHAEL A. GREEN, born and raised in Port Angeles, WA. In 1960, his school wrote local and state officials concerning saving the *Washington*. Unfortunately, at that time, there was no official interest.

He and his wife, Nancy have two daughters and they live in his hometown, Port Angeles. He formerly worked at Grays Harbor Paper Co. in Hoquiam, WA for 22 years and is currently employed at the Daishowa American mill in Port Angeles as a paper machine shift supervisor.

His interest include naval history, ships, railroading, reading, photography, boating, and traveling. From their home they get a good view of the Straits of Juan de Fuca and they enjoy observing the continual maritime activities on the straits.

His is sponsored by John Brown.

MARIAN GILMER HALYBURTON, born in Miami, FL, married Joe in 1949 and has two children, Dan and Donna and one grandchild, Joseph.

Retired from Coral Gables Federal Savings and Loan, (assistant treasurer) in 1986. Resides in Flat Rock, NC.

Her sponsor is Joe Halyburton.

LILLIAN RUTH COLLINS HARDISON, born Jan. 5, 1921 in Corbin, KY. During WWII she went to Army Air Force Technical School in Nashville, TN. Finished and went to Miami, FL, Army Air Field. She worked on all types of aircraft from bombers to fighter planes and was in Miami when the war ended. Then was transferred to Tinker Field (home of the B29s) Midwest City, OK. From there back to Tennessee at Lewisburg. Work for Cincinnati Ordnance as inspector and from there to Redstone Arsenal, AL. Retired from Redstone January 1981 after 30 years of service.

She married James A. Hardison July 1936. They had one daughter, born August 1947, Debbie L. Hardison. She married Charles Casgriff and they had two daughters, Wendy and Penny Casgriff. Daughter and granddaughters live in Huntsville, AL. Also raised a nephew, Charles Edward Collins who was named for her brother Claude Charles Collins, who went aboard the *Washington*. He was on *Washington* when the war was over.

Charle Edward Collins lives in Flat Creek, TN. Her husband James died July 24, 1984.

Her sponsor is her brother, Charles Claude Collins.

KENNETH M. JACKSON, having been raised by a WWII veteran who served aboard the battleship USS *Washington*, he was taught early to have respect for our country, and all those who sacrificed for her. He can still hear the stories his dad still tells about when he was at sea in the Pacific on BB-56 and how she took care of him.

He was born in 1957 and was never called to serve our country. He remained in school and graduated Western Kentucky University on the Dean's List in 1979. He immediately went to work for Whayne Supply, one of the largest Caterpillar dealers in North America. Three months later he married Nova London, his wife of 16 years. They have two children, Allison and Nathan.

In 1996 after the reunion in Wilmington he was asked to be secretary treasurer of the associate group. He respectfully accepted and has began his duties keeping USS *Washington* incomparable history and memory alive.

His sponsor is his father Amon Lee Jackson.

LAVERNE KRUEGER, born June 23, 1924 in Cicero, IL raised in the Berwyn/Cicero area, attended J.S. Morton High School. After graduating from high school she was hired by Western Electric, Hawthorn Works.

She and her husband Raymond, have known each other since they were nine years old. He was discharged from the USN on March 31, 1946, and they were married on April 20, 1946.

Past president of Tractor Post Ladies Auxiliary for three years, also past president of Berwyn Ladies Auxiliary American Legion in the year 1963-64. Served as the Fifth District Children and Youth Chairman Department of Illinois 1965-74. Served as Berwyn Unit Poppy chairman for a period of five years.

In 1959 they attended their first USS *Washington* reunion and only missed one since. Retired from the now Lucent Technologies after 34 years of service and they are now enjoying the golden years.

Her sponsor is her husband Raymond Krueger.

ELNA A. (NYHOLM) KUHN, born June 11, 1920 in Massilon, OH, married Charles H. Kuhn June 22, 1945 and they have two sons and three grandsons.

During WWII she did early GM defense work/Navy Pacific Fleet records, while with WAVES. She achieved the rank of MAM3, serving from May 1944-September 1945.

Her sponsor is her husband Charles H. Kuhn.

NICK LEONE III, born Nov. 12, 1952 in St. Louis, MO, married Mary Neal July 2, 1971 and they have two children, Nick IV, Navy recruiter, Persian Gulf War veteran and Carrie Lynn, RN, and one grandchildren.

His sponsor is his father, Nick Leone Jr.

IRENE F. (WOJNAR) LINVILLE, born in Fall River, MA, married Basil Linville April 21, 1945.

During WWII she worked at Firestone and is now a housewife.

Her sponsor is her husband, Basil Linville.

MARY ANN LOEWE, born Dec. 30, 1933 in St. Louis, MO. Even though only seven years old on Dec. 7, 1941 she remembers the bombing of Pearl Harbor as one of her saddest days of her life.

She recalls her family gathered around the radio sobbing at the news of the day that will live in infamy.

Married James N. Loewe, Sr., Nov. 8, 1975.

Retired from the federal government in 1988 after 36 1/2 years of civilian service with the Department of Defense.

Enjoying retirement and looking forward to the BB-56 reunions.

Her sponsor is husband, James N. Loewe, Sr.

JOHN J. LUONGO, born in Winchester, MA, Jan. 20, 1949 is employed as diesel mechanic. He is a ASE Master Tech member and also a member of the Tail Hook Association, USNI and Mobile Riberine Force Association.

His father Nick Luongo is his sponsor.

MARIE MIOVER MCCORMICK, SPQ3/C, born in Cheyenne, WY, July 22, 1921, joined the USN Feb. 10, 1944. Attended boot camp, USNTC, Bronx, NY; USNCA Nebraska and Massachusetts Ave, Washington, DC.

Assigned as Op20G bomb operator. She almost knocked Adm. Redman down the steps. Speak of a shakey WAVE. But he was very nice about it.

McCormick was awarded the Navy Unit Commendation, American Campaign and WWII Victory.

She was discharged Jan. 8, 1946 and married "Mac" R.O. McCormick. She is now retired.

JON MORAN, born March 15, 1977 in Cleveland, OH is a student. Her sponsor is friend, John Brown.

TIMOTHY MORAN, born Nov. 9, 1947 in Cleveland. Served in the US Coast Guard with the rank of QM2, Sept. 26, 1966-June 25, 1970.

He received the Good Conduct (Coast Guard), National Defense Medal.

Married to Ellen Aug. 31, 1973 and they have children, Christine, John and June. He is employed as a distribution manager and dealer.

His sponsor is friend, John Brown.

MARTHA SHORT OSBORNE, born March 29, 1923 in Dallas County, TX and married Roy Carl Osborne May 30, 1943 and they have a son Roy Carl Osborne, Jr.

During WWII she was employed at a bank.

Her sponsor is Roy Carl Osborne.

WILLIAM PENTASUGLIO, born May 3, 1920 in Scranton, PA, served in the US Army in Europe with the 2195th Trucking Co.

He boarded the USS *Washington* (BB-56) at Southampton, England on Nov. 24, 1945 and was aboard on Thanksgiving and when Luther Oakes was lost over the side and rescued. The ships docked at Pier 56, New York, on Dec. 1, 1945.

He brought aboard a dog in England and an admiral saw the dog as Pentasuglio was shooting clay pigeons on the fantail. The officer asked him how he got the dog aboard and Pentasuglio told him. The officer told him to take the dog off the same way.

He received five Bronze Stars, 50 cal. Marksman Medal Ribbon, Good Conduct Ribbon, ETO Ribbon, American Campaign, EAME Medal, Occupation Medal and the Victory Medal.

When the ship was scrapped in Bayonne, NJ, he was a civilian truck driver assigned to load the *Washington* generator and haul it to Rochester, NY. The name plate was still attached to the generator. He is now retired in Scranton, PA. He has two daughters and five grandchildren.

MATTHEW J. PHILLIPS, born Feb. 7, 1983, now 15 yrs. old. His grandfather is Henry V. Forrest, who served in the Navy and achieved the rank of SFSC, 1941-1953.

He is very proud of his Navy roots. His grandfather has told him many stories of his years spent on the ship. Some sad, some funny, but great memories to have.

His sponsor is grandfather, Henry V. Forrest.

CLARA MAE POTTER, born March 26, 1927. She worked at Patten Food during WWII packing K rations. Retired from the 3M Co.

Married John Henry Potter March 26, 1953 and they have a son Gary Potter and one grandson David Potter.

Her sponsor is husband, John Henry Potter.

DONALD RAMALEY, born July 9, 1948 and married Betty April 17, 1971 and they have twins 17 years old, Amy M. and Kevin M.

Served in the USN as MR2, November 1968 to October 1972. Employed as plant equipment operator.

His father, Russell S. Woeppel is his sponsor.

WILLA M. SABATINI, born March 2, 1925 in Bunkie, LA, married Vincent Joseph Sabatini, April 5, 1944

During WWII while her husband was in the service, she worked in their hometown pharmacy.

She is now retired and does some volunteer work in a local hospital. She spends time enjoying her children: Deborah A. Sabatini Moreland, Barbara F. Sabatini, Robert A. Sabatini and Michael D. Sabatini and grandsons: Stephen T. Moreland II and Jason B. Moreland.

Her sponsor is husband Vincent Joseph Sabatini.

EDWIN STANSBURY SCHANZE JR., born Nov. 16, 1937 in Long Beach CA, married Feb. 15, 1969.

He served in the Army as first lieutenant, USMA 1962. Now employed as training coordinator, Star Enterprise (Texaco).

He has a daughter, Ann Louise and sons Joseph Cummings and Charles Barry.

His sponsor is his father Edwin Stansbury Schanze.

CHARLIE SMITH, born April 21, 1963 in Lackawanna, NY, married Darol Smith, Nov. 11, 1988, Veterans Day.

He has served in the USN as chief petty officer from Sept. 1, 1981 to present. He has been awarded the Aviation Warfare Specialist, Navy Achievement Medal (five awards).

His brother is Allen Smith and mother, Carol Lenahan. His sponsor is his father Donald Smith.

MICHAEL PATRICK SMITH, born Sept. 19, 1947 in Canton, OH, has served in the USNR as commanding officer, Naval Reserve Public Affairs Center Unit, Det. 106, Norfolk, VA. Has been a Naval Reserve officer since May 1976.

Assignments include Public Affairs Officer, Naval Station Keflavik, Iceland; USS *Independence* (CV-62); USS *Nimitz* (CV-68); USS *Forrestal* (CV-59); NATO Brussels; Allied Forces Southern Europe and office of the Secretary of Defense for Public Affairs. He has received the Air Force Commendation Medal, Navy Achievement Medal (three awards). Employed as director, Communications.

His father, Melville C. Smith is his sponsor.

HELEN SNYDER, born March 20, 1925 in Northumberland, GA, married May 31, 1947.

Her sponsor is her husband, Arthur H. Snyder.

IRMA ROWE SPIRES, wife of Raymond A. Spires, born Portsmouth, VA, Dec. 27, 1911. Married 53 years prior to his death in 1981.

Her memories of BB-56 are the highlights of my life as a sailor's wife. Attending the ships memorable commissioning; going aboard her, taking part in memorial service at a Charleston reunion; Johnny Brown taking her top side in the bomb elevator; attending two reunions.

In her book the BB-56 should be titled "The Pride of the Navy."

During WWII she worked for Bn. Ord. made ordnanceman e/c priming 5" 38 and 6" 47 star shells.

She wrote her sailor every day to let him know he was loved and remembered. What a great day when he returned from Japan in 1946.

Her sponsor is husband Raymond A. Spires.

WARD LESLIE THOMAS, born July 23, 1962 in Washington, DC and married Daryl Ann, Jan. 29, 1990. They have a daughter Katelyn and son Taylor. He is employed as an IRS attorney.

His father Ralph Leslie Thomas is his sponsor.

DOROTHY L. TURZYN, born May 30, 1923 in Brooklyn, NY, married MSGT, AF, Francis J. Turzyn, Feb. 18, 1978. They raised seven children.

During WWII she worked as inspector, Sperry Gyroscope, NY. Also worked as executive assistant. Her husband died. She now has 12 children and 24 grandchildren.

Her sponsor is husband Francis J. Turzyn.

LOUIS A. VILLA, SGT, born Feb. 2, 1922 in NYC, served in the US Air Corps as sergeant. He was discharged Nov. 30, 1945.

His memorable experiences include knowing and loving the men.

He has four children and nine grandchildren. Retired and living in Oregon.

DONALD I. WILSON, born Aug. 16, 1922 in Owen County, KY. He married Feb. 17, 1951.

During WWII he served in the USMC as staff sergeant, Oct. 1942 to Feb. 1946 and July 1950-February 1952. Served in Pacific, Marianas Island, Garrison.

His mother Isabell Lee was Adm. Lee's first cousin. His sponsor is John Brown, Vice Adm. WA Lee's second cousin.

GLENN JACOB WINTER, born July 22, 1952 in Arlington, WA, graduated from Arlington High School. Married in 1992 to Mary Krause, have two daughters, owns and operates logging truck company and still living in Arlington.

He has always been interested in naval history, especially battleships. After reading stories of the battles around Guadalcanal, and what the USS *Washington* accomplished, she became his favorite ship.

He obtained this model from a model show he attended. It is radio controlled. He made the cranes, secondary radars, moveable catapults, repainted it, added more guns and lights.

He took the model to the Portland Convention in July of 1995 then had it on display at the Bremerton Naval Museum.

DAVID W. WOEPPEL, F1/C, born to Russell S. Woeppel and mother Mary (Miller) Woeppel, Feb. 19, 1943 in Easton, PA. Served with USAF, A1c, missile maintenance, Atlas, Titan Two, private pilot.

He married Suzanne L. Bryksa, Nov. 16, 1943 and they have a son Matthew David and daughter Monica Denise Fritz and grandson, Nicholas Fritz and granddaughter Courtney Fritz.

He owned and operated Woeppel Refrigeration and is now retired. Employed as operations manager for Museum of Modern Art Film Preservation Center in Hamlin, PA.

HOWARD FRANK WRIGHT, III, is the son of sea going Marine, Howard Jr. first of six children born to Howard Jr. and Lillian on April 16, 1950 in Detroit, MI.

Raised in St. Clair Shores, MI and graduated from high school in 1968. Served in Army as a light helicopter mechanic for three years.

Howard III has worked as an airline station agent and a disc jockey. He has owned two businesses. Now working as a telecommunications specialist.

Howard became involved with the USS *Washington* reunion group in 1989. Elected associate unit president at the 1991 reunion.

Fond memories are of the nights that him and his father watched war movies. His dad would relate some of his war stories to him then. His biggest regret is not being able to attend a reunion with his father.

Howard is responsible for carrying the history of both the ship and the shipmates well into the next century. It is his works that brought about the USS Washington Web Site on the Internet.

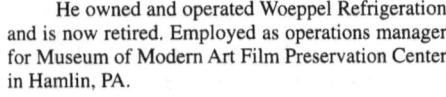

The USS Washington.

BB-56 ACTIVE MEMBERS
FEBRUARY 22, 1998

– A –

Abbey, Ted H.
Absher, Avery W.
Adair, James L.
Adalac, Stephen A.
Adams, William H.
Adams, Elton Ray, Jr.
Allcorn, Melvin G.
Anderson, Albert C.
Anderson, Glenn H.
Anderson, Paul W.
Anderson, William T.
Arts, Laurence J.
Aughton, Robert T.
Avant, Melvin D.

– B –

Barentine, Joel A.
Barfield, Charlton B.
Barnaby, Eugene H.
Barnett, Wayne H.
Barrow, William B.
Baugh, Edmund L.
Baylor, Roger G.
Bays, Vernon J.
Beard, Lloyd P.
Beatty, Paul C.
Beckstrand, Melvin E.
Beene, James V., Sr.
Berc, Harold T.
Bertagna, Dante F.
Bias, James B.
Blanchett, Powertan
Blazes, Leonard J.
Boghosian, John H.
Bogue, George D.
Bohannon, Oliver Lee, Sr.
Boling, Marvin L.
Boss, Richard
Bost, Robert L.
Boyd, Linford, Jr.
Bozeman, Bernard W.
Brantley, Bea
Breske, James F.
Brewster, Charles G., Jr.
Brightwell, Albert W.
Brown, Edward M.
Brown, Jess W.
Brown, John A.
Brown, Melvin F.
Bryant, Billy
Buchholz, Robert O.
Buddenbohn, Kennard L.
Budzinski, Sylvester M.
Bullock, Frank E.
Bundy, Bill L.
Burnaugh, Harold L.
Burns, Roy F.
Burwell, John W.R.
Buse, Roland E.
Butera, Angelo H.
Butler, Jack F.
Byrd, Monroe E.

– C –

Cabeen, Richard H.
Cadwalader, John
Callis, Richard G., Sr.
Calvert, Haydon M.
Campanelli, Hugo A.
Campbell, Luther E.
Campbell, Wallace M.
Canada, James W.
Cannon, Edgar H.
Cargill, Earl E.
Carman, Charles H.
Caruso, Angelo
Cepelka, Emil R.
Chambers, Elmer B.
Cherry, Francis R.
Chesley, Homer C.
Clark, Donald A.
Clark, James K.
Clark, Robert G.
Clark, Willis I.
Cline, Clyde J.
Clinger, William N.
Colasanto, Thomas G.
Colby, Robert A.
Collins, Claude C.
Collins, Raymond W.
Colton, Al
Comstock, Charles O.
Cooley, Leslie V., Jr.
Coolman, Thomas M., Sr.
Copeland, Walter D.
Copenhaver, Jack A.
Cote, John A.
Cox, Elmer R.
Craft, Martin C.
Craft, Robert F.
Cress, W.E.
Cronin, Hunter L.
Cross, Robert L.
Cucinotta, Samuel
Cuff, D. Gale
Curtis, Fletcher
Cusick, Russell P.
Cvinar, Steve

– D –

Daigan, Art A.
Daly, John J.
Davis, Fred L.
Davis, Carl E.
Day, Duane C.
Deas, William W.J., Sr.
DeLoach, Carl J.
DeMann, Raymond J.
Denham, Hubert J., Jr.
Denison, Thayne E.
Dennis, George B.
Derrick, Ralph D.
Dewitt, Russell B.
Douglas, Harry C.
Drewitz, Wilbur B.
Duchin, Alex
Duke, Duane C.
Dunavant, Lonnie
Dupuis, Wilfred E.
Dwyer, Thomas J.

– E –

Elder, Sherwood W.
Elliott, Anthony W.
Elliott, Austin A.J.
Erb, Richard Dean
Eshbaugh, Chester F.
Estevez, Mario V.
Ewing, Dr. Steve

– F –

Fairbanks, Douglas, Jr.
Fargo, Willian B.
Farney, Francis F.
Faulks, Delmar L.
Fehn, William J.
Feist, Bruce D.
Ferrovecchio, Michael J.
Fisher, Theodore F.
Forbush, Alan A.
Ford, Ray E.
Forhan, Thomas F.
Forrest, Henry V.
Fraser, Robert J.
Freeman, Fred A.
Friday, Robert O.
Frix, Lyman C.
Froehlich, Carl G.
Fuller, Russell F.

– G –

Galante, Joseph J.
Galligan, Charles F.
Galvin, William F.
Garcia, Marcel L.
Garrett, Robert L.
Gaskill, John F.
Gath, Leonard T.
Gaudioso, Bart R.
Geisinger, Robert C.
Genovese, Frank E.
Giampopo, Mario, Sr.
Giannini, Joe J.
Gibson, Robert E.
Giele, John H.
Glaviano, James J.
Gore, John M.
Gough, Raymond R.
Greeley, George R.
Greene, Warren P.
Gribler, Robert J.
Groshong, Royal C.
Guidici, Don W.

– H –

Haber, Don P.
Hadsell, John S.
Hail, Elbert M.
Hale, Robert H.
Halik, Lawrence M.
Hall, Troy F.
Hamilton, James A.
Hamlet, John L.
Hammer, Stanley
Hamrick, Jodie, Jr.
Handy, David E.
Hansen, William H.
Harding, Joseph H.
Harrigan, John B.
Harting, Darrel R.
Hartman, William W.
Harvill, Karl V.
Harvilla, Joe
Hatcher, Robert L.
Hatstat, Charles A.
Hayes, Edward P.
Hecht, Paul W.
Herring, Vann
Hesler, Richard W.
Hesselton, Clarence H.
Higgs, Hurley A.
Hill, Frank B., Jr.
Hinzpeter, Richard C.
Hippard, William R., Jr.
Hittle, James Don
Hoffman, William A.
Hoglund, Karl E.
Holbrook, Posey L.
Holland, William C.
Holloway, Martin
Holm, Harold E.
Hoover, Paul J., Sr.
Hopfner, Francis D.
Houseman, Clayton D.
Howell, Thomas
Hudson, Wallace E.
Hughes, Rodney W.
Hughes, William T.
Hummel, Fred H.
Hunt, Nelson Bunker
Huse, Edward W.
Hysinger, Howard D.

– I –

Inch, Thomas P.

– J –

Jackson, Amon Lee
Jacob, Edward K.
Jacobson, Ishier
James, George E.
Jastry, Joseph
Jay, John
Jennings, Howard P.
Jernigan, Emory J.
Jestes, Ned W.
Johnson, Daniel T.
Johnson, John R.
Johnson, John O., Jr.
Jones, Elmo R.
Joyner, Wesley V.
June, Alfred W.
Jungnitsch, Abraham L.

– K –

Kalvaitis, Alexander
Kean, John E.
Keller, Joseph D.
Kenfield, Frank
Kennedy, Robert E.
Kesti, Harold G.
Kinsley, Dave R.
Kinsley, James
Kitchel, William L.
Klaslo, Casimir C.
Kloster, Alexander J.
Knight, George H.
Knight, Paul K.
Knobel, Roland J.
Knowlton, Chad R.
Kobetitsch, William J.
Konecny, Anthony P., Jr.
Korzelik, Roman J.
Kosovan, John, Sr.
Kovachik, Albert J.
Kowcenuk, John F.
Krause, Walter R.
Krechevsky, Herbert Y.
Krohr, Donald S.
Kroschel, Elton C.
Krueger, Donald L.
Krueger, Raymond H.
Kubu, Charles J.
Kuhn, Charles J., Jr.
Kula, Stephen J.

– L –

Lamm, Lewis J.
LaPeer, August C.
LaValle, Angelo
Lawrence, William P.
Lazek, John J.
LeBair, Robert S.
LeRay, Byron C.
Lewis, John W.
Linville, Basil
Lipari, Leonard
Liptak, Edward G.
Lockwood, Harvey C.
Loewe, James N., Sr.
Loken, Marvin
Long, Jacob A., Sr.
Looney, Thomas R.
Lorenz, John G.
Loud, George M., Jr.
Lowe, Robert L.
Lowther, Robert G., Jr.
Lozano, William R.
Luhman, Willard C.
Luongo, Nick J.
Lykins, Lodie R.

– M –

Mack, R.W.
Maione, Sam E.

Major, George L.
Malecki, Robert V.
Malloy, James H.
Manders, Maurice J.
Manke, Robert H.
Manning, James B.
Mariage, Harold H.
Marshall, Robert K.
Marshburn, John M.
Maslanka, Edward J.F.
Mason, John
Mason, Ray C.
Matouk, A. Warren
Mauriello, Louis
Mauzy, Oscar H.
Mayotte, Bernard
McCormick, Roy O.
McCabe, Kenneth A.
McCord, Howard W.
McCoy, John C.
McCready, Vernon L.
McCullough, Wallace A.
McDonald, Ken D.
McKinney, H.B.
McLain, Richard J.
McNeil, John C.
McQueen, James P.
Merritt, Robert G.
Mesimore, John E.
Meyers, Paul A.
Meyers, William M.
Mignerone, Paul O.
Miller, Edward G.
Miller, Jackson A.
Miller, William J.
Miller, John S., Jr.
Mills, James J.
Ming, David A.
Mittleman, William M.
Moffitt, Randall C.
Monahan, Harold W.
Morgan, Frederic H.
Mueller, Robert A.
Musicant, Ivan

– N –

Neher, Gilbert W.
Nelson, Albert E.
Neri, Aldo
Neri, Andy
Nessly, Harry S.
Nestich, Michael T.
Newberry, Cap W.
Newton, Joe E.
Newton, Richard E., Jr.
Nichols, Arthur R.
Nichols, Joe
Noe, David S.
Nogar, A. Ray
Norman, William B., Sr.
Nunn, Mike

– O –

O'Rourke, James N.
O'Steen, Edmund U.
O'Steen, Wallace A.
Oakley, A. Steve
Ocarz, Edward
Odom, Benjamin D.
Olson, Daniel J.
Olson, Fred J.
Onkst, Emil
Orlando, Sam
Osborn, Herbert L.

– P –

Padden, Joseph E.
Palac, Walter A.
Parent, Rudolph A.
Park, Claude J., Jr.
Parrett, Carl P.
Patterson, Norman S.
Pennell, John C.
Pennycuff, Charles B.
Peratrovich, Alva W.
Perlman, Ted S.
Peterson, Carl H.
Phillips, Albert L.
Pieczatkiewicz, Joseph I.
Pilcher, Clifford E., Jr.
Pirfo, Dan Aniello
Pizzo, Johnny
Platt, Jonas M.
Popovich, John, Jr.
Poppino, Robert D.
Potiowsky, Thomas L.
Potter, John H.
Poyet, Edward N.
Prandini, Frank W.
Prevost, John V., M.D.
Price, Dempsey L.
Pyle, John A.

– Q –

Quinn, Carey Kent
Quinn, Edward A.

– R –

Ragusin, Michael G.
Rankin, Robert W.
Rayburn, Robert M.
Reed, Charles D.
Regan, Patrick J.
Reid, Alton E.
Remus, Francis J.
Resnick, Sidney D.
Respess, James W.
Ressler, Walter N.
Rice, Verlyn
Richeson, Edward M.
Richeson, King
Ricks, Benjamin M.
Rink, Robert M.
Rodrigues, Alfred B.
Roiz, Albert F.
Ross, James G.
Ross, Sam A.
Roth, Gilbert J.
Ruff, Gerald P.
Rush, Robert L.
Russo, Lorenzo, Sr.
Ryan, Phillip J.
Ryan, Thomas C.

– S –

Sabol, Andy
Sala, Anthony N.
Sandin, O. James
Sandoval, William, Sr.
Sandwick, Charlie M., Jr.
Satterfield, Jimmy H.
Saurer, Karl D.
Savery, Sylvester J.
Scalzo, Sam
Scandaliato, Anthony J.
Schmit, Wilbur L.
Schweinsberg, George W.
Schwerin, Kenneth D.
Scott, Joe N.
Scruggs, Roderick S.
Searls, Hank H., Jr.
Serenson, Raymond P.
Shepherd, Wilmer N.
Shepherd, Dick A.
Shepherd, Sumner W., III
Sherbert, Charles H.
Shetenhelm, Philip E.
Shields, John J.
Shifflet, Avis R.
Shirley, James A.
Shuey, Richard L.
Sisley, Jim
Sitarski, Jack A.
Sjostrand, Robert W.
Skahan, Robert M.
Slater, Richard R.
Slaughter, J.L.
Smith, Henry J.
Smith, Leo C.
Smith, Melville C.
Smith, Wilbur S.
Soellner, Arthur
Sorensen, Robert A.
Spoffard, Howard A.
Stanzel, Robert F.
Stapleton, George A.
Stenske, Edward J.
Stephens, Julius F.
Stillwell, Paul L.
Stolecki, John
Struck, Robert M.
Stuart, Granville E.
Stumm, Edward R.
Summers, Charles E.
Sutherland, Robert M.
Swearingen, Fred

– T –

Taylor, Wilmer R.
Tellier, Francis E.
Thomas, Ralph L.
Thomason, Harold
Tindall, George Y.
Tipper, Kenneth A.
Tompkins, Edmund M.
Toniatti, Alfred M.
Tucker, Fred L.
Turner, Howard Dean
Turner, Lee A.
Turzyn, Francis J., Jr.
Twombly, Winfield H.

– U –

Uhler, Eugene H.

– V –

Vigil, Ben
Villa, Louis A.
Vinette, Peter T.
Vodola, Vincent J.
Volpe, Herbert M.

– W –

Wages, Arthur H.
Walton, Fernie A.
Ward, Samuel W.
Warner, Herbert L.
Watkins, Ivan
Watson, William A.
Watt, Gordon J.
Watts, Edward D.
Webb, John L.
Webb, John A., Jr.
Weidert, William P., Sr.
Weiner, Harvey B.
Wheeler, Fred A.
Wheeless, Jesse C.
Whitney, Harry R.
Wickham, Homer W.
Wiegel, Fred
Wilkinson, Richard P., Jr.
Williams, Pace W., Jr.
Williams, Donald O'Cain
Williams, Joe G.
Williamson, James T.
Willis, Don C., Jr.
Wilson, Dale E.
Wilson, William R.
Wolons, John S.
Woodard, Glenn E.
Woolery, Bob

– Y –

Yanaway, R.W.
Young, Grover C.
Youngblood, Gay P.

– Z –

Zapotoczny, Stanley
Zinck, Glenn B.
Zorb, Norman D.

USS *WASHINGTON* BB56 ASSOCIATE UNIT, INC. MEMBERSHIP ROSTER

- A -

Abramson, Inah Mae
Adams, Marianne
Albano, Gloria D.
Allcorn, Melvin G., Jr.
Anderson, Edna May
Anderson, Mildred B.
Anderson, Thomas P.
Aughton, Marianne
Austin, Donna V.
Avant, June T.

- B -

Baisden, Debra Michelle
Baisden, Holly Layne
Baisden, Mark Blair
Baisden, Megan Nicole
Barnard, William E.
Baylor, Bettye Sue
Bays, Margaret
Beckstrand, Marie
Beene, Ronald D.
Bertagna, Honora V.
Blanchett, Sara Jane
Boghosian, Ann M.
Bohn, Amy L.
Bohn, Harry
Bohn, Scott R.
Bohn, Terrie A.
Boyd, Doris M.
Braden, David
Braden, Jennifer
Braden, Rita T.
Branciere, Mary A.
Brown, Donald K.
Brown, Fred D.
Brown, Gladys
Brown, Jeremy Keith
Brown, Lori Nicole
Brown, Margaret "Teenie" L.
Brown, Mike
Brown, Monica Lynn
Brown, Shane Michael
Brown, Sherry Olga
Bryant, Leona H.
Budzinski, Brian M.
Budzinski, Mary A.
Bullock, Rosella H.
Burns, Bonnie L.
Byers, Ina M.

- C -

Calvert, Jean C.
Cannon, Evelyn P.
Canty, John I.
Carpenter, Sally M.
Carpenter, Scott B.
Carter, Paula R.
Caudell, Larry A.
Cherry, Stephen J.
Chesley, Naomi P.
Chirico, Judy
Colasanto, Dorothy
Coller, Bernice S.
Collins, Thelma V.
Comstock, Earl D.
Coolman, Beverly
Coolman, Thomas, Jr.
Coulam, Anna Lee Ash
Crider, Anna Marie
Crider, Clifford S.
Croffead, George (Dr.)
Croffead, Georgia
Cronin, Violet
Cuffel, Mary Frances
Cullen, Marie J.
Cusick, Dorothy
Cusick, Mark
Cusick, Shawna
Cusick, Tim

- D -

Davis, Florence E.
Davis, Joan Gaskill
Davis, Michelle
Davis, Glenn B., Jr.
Day, Dora Arlene
Day, Gary W.
Deas, William J., Jr.
DeBree, Judith Marie
DeMann, Angelina C.
Dennis, Carrie E.
Dennis, George B., Jr.
Donohue, Barbara
Donohue, Brian
Donohue, John T.
Donohue, Kevin
Donohue, William F., Jr.
Douglas, Betty R.
Doyle, Margaret C.
Duke, Elizabeth N.
Dunn, Jean
Dutton, Countess B.

- E -

Edwards, Robert Clarke
Evans, Pearle P.

- F -

Farney, Damond
Farren, Marianne T.
Fibbi, Jacqueline
Flood, Bob
Fones, Lisa S.
Forrest, Henry
Forrest, Rose
Frank, Marchon F.
Fraser, Mary Ann
Froehlich, Dolores C.
Froempter, Barbara A.

- G -

Galante, Rita D.
Galligan, Mark
Gamache, Susan
Garcia, Margaret V.
Gaudioso, Gladys
Geisinger, Rolla
Gibson, Jim
Gibson, Judy
Giele, John Carr
Glaviano, Donna M.
Gordon, Barbara J.
Gordon, Marie S.
Green, Florence P.
Green, Michael A.
Greer, Patricia
Gregorio, Ben
Gregory, Robert
Gregory, Mary M. (Wilson)
Grogen, George J.
Gryszowka, Troy
Guzski, Helen

- H -

Hall, Wanda M.
Halyburton, Dan
Halyburton, Marian
Hammer, Fran
Hamrick, Gertrude L.
Hansen, Mary A.
Hardison, Lillian C.
Harrigan, Christopher
Harrison, Betty C.
Harvill, Mary P.
Hathaway, Susan M.
Hayes, Fred E.
Heider, Jean
Hendrickson, Larry D.
Hendrickson, Robert Bruce, Jr.
Hendry, Gladys M.
Herman, Jess F.
Herring, Carleen T.
Herzing, Sherry
Hill, Judith M.
Hinzpeter, Della
Hinzpeter, Elaine
Hinzpeter, Gary
Hinzpeter, Richard
Holbrook, Bess
Holland, Beverly J.
Holm, William O.
Holton, Iris T.
Horak, Mary A.
Howell, Connie
Hughes, Mary L.
Hummel, Gladys D.
Hunt, Caroline L.
Hysinger, Alan Davis
Hysinger, Edith M.

- I -

Imperiale, Linda

- J -

Jackson, Kenneth M.
Jackson, Nathan S.
Johnson, Lois "Sue"
Jones, Daisy Arie
Jones, Helene N.
Jones, Lillian E.

- K -

Kasunick, Rose
Keller, Mark
Kennedy, Betty T.
Kessler, Diane M.
Kinne, Dorothy E.
Kinne, Raymond
Kinsley, Beth
Kinsley, Mary A.
Kinsley, Michael D.
Kinsley, Opal
Klaslo, Frances
Klaslo, Thaddeus
Klopp, James R.
Konecny, Anthony D. (LCDR)
Kosovan, Ruth V.
Kovacs, Henry
Kovacs, Susan
Krawczyk, Adeline F.
Krawiec, Harriet A.
Kroschel, Aaron D.
Kroschel, Ethan D.
Kroschel, Kenan G.
Kroschel, Sonja Ann
Krueger, La Verne
Kuhn, Elna A.

- L -

Lager, Mary E.
Larson, Douglas M.
LaValle, Santa
Leach, Brian H.
Leach, Katherine
Leach, Katherine P.
Leach, Vern P.
Leary, Daniel
Leary, Robert A.
Lee, Iris C.
Leone III, Nick
LeRay, Lucy
Lico, Marie Butera
Linville, Irene F.
Lippman, David H.
Little, Ruth A.
Loewe, Mary Ann
Luongo, John L.

- M -

Mack, Hazel H.
Mack, John W.
Macklin, Elinor K.
Magnasco, Christine A.
Mainous, Carole M.
Major, Elizabeth H.
Marcos, Evelyn
Marcos, George A.
Marcos, Thomas (Dr.)
Marlin, John C.
Marlin, Odelia B.
Marshburn, Wanaga L.
Martin, William C., Sr.
Maslanka, Douglas T.S.
Masserant, Barbara
Matouk, Renee
Matouk, Warren S.
Mauriello, Josephine
McClintock, Jerome L.
McCormick, Clement P.
McCormick, Michael V.
McCormick, Willa Marie Miover
McCoy, Mary E.
McNeil, William R.
Meyers, Ruth K.
Miller, Gwendolyn M.
Miller, Jane A.
Miller, Mabel F.
Miller, Stephen G.
Mitchell, Cleola G.
Mitchell, Lorraine J.
Moffitt, Timothy A.
Moran, John
Moran, Tim
Morris, Caroline C.
Morrison, Patricia D.
Morse, Maureen
Mueller, Harriet E.
Murray, Ann
Murray, Brian W.

- N -

Newberry, Imogeane
Niemara, Alice
Niemara, Claudia A.
Niemara, Mark A.
Nogar, Cathy

- O -

Olliff, Eileen M.
Olson, Helen N.
Onkst, Jeanette B.
Osborne, Martha
Osborne, Roy C., Jr.
O'Steen, Betty B.

- P -

Park, Clermont E.
Parker, Marri
Patchet, Judith Ellen
Patterson, Lorene A.
Pentasuglio, William
Phillips, Matthew
Phillips, Rosemary F.
Phillips, Walter
Popov, Elizabeth R.
Poppino, David Dale
Poppino, Phyllis C.
Poppino, Robert Thomas
Potter, Clara
Powers, Harry W. (MSGT)
Powers, Marie J.
Prandini, Judy J.

Prevost, James W.
Price, Janet
Price, Phillis A.

– R –

Ramaley, Donald A.
Reed, Carroll P.
Reid, Sue H.
Reiser, Denise
Richmond, Ken B.
Rolfs, Joan
Ross, James S.
Roth, Elaine
Roth, Stephen Jay
Roth II, Edward A.
Russo, Adeline P.
Rutter, Frances
Ryan, Dolores R.
Ryan, Jacqueline P.

– S –

Sabatini, Willa M.
Sabol, Andrew J.
Sabol, Jacqueline R.
Sabol, Mary
Sala, Lois M.
Sandwich, Anna Mae
Savery, Helen M.
Scandaliato, Shirley W.
Schanze, Edwin Stansbury, Jr.
Schulte, Veronica E.

Schweinsberg, William B.
Schwerin, Dorothy A.
Sebright, Berneice V.
Selvig, Mark
Shaw, Byron Douglas
Shields, John, Jr.
Shifflet, Gloria E.
Shuey, Roy F.
Sieffert, Debbie
Silvers, Carl E., Jr.
Sloper, Don
Smidt, Jill
Smith, Charles
Smith, Justin
Smith, Michael P. (CAPT, USNR)
Snyder, Helen
Spires, Irma V.
Spofford, Michael
Sprow, Mary Alice
Stankovic, Regina H.
Stere, May L.
Stout, Carol A.
Stout, Jack
Stuart, George W.
Stuart, Gregory E.
Stuart, Michael L.
Summers, Naomi
Sutherland, Catherine R.

– T –

Tarr, Hazel D.
Taylor, Anita W.

Taylor, W. Robert
Terstenyak, Stephen J.
Thies, Marthinia
Thomas, Bryan
Thomas, Carol W.
Thomas, Ward L.
Tindall, Betty
Turner, Ruth
Turzyn, Dorothy
Tweedt, Joyce E.

– V –

Vadino, Grace Susan
Vanderwalker, Ann
Vinette, Peter W.
Volpe, Bettie A.

– W –

Wages, Michelina C.
Walter, Susan
Walton, Dora Maurice
Walton, Maurice G.
Walton, Ralph H., Jr.
Watkins, Betty J.
Watkins, Daniel Lee
Watkins, Robert Gary
Webb, Dorothy C.
Weidert, George Alan
Weidert, James S.
Weidert, John Francis
Weidert, William Paul, Jr.

Wells, Mary Anne W.
Wheeless, Deltha
White, Lynne
Whitney, Peter T.
Williams, Donald T.
Willis, Frances C.
Wilson, Don F.
Wilson, Margaret
Wilson, Theja Jones
Winter, Glenn J.
Winterlin, Victoria Nichols
Winters, Lillian M.
Woeppel, David W.
Womack, Dale J.
Womack, David J.
Womack, Laura J.
Wright III, Howard F.

– Z –

Zapotoczny, Joanna
Zapotoczny, Regina
Zinck, Lois
Zirilli, Joanne A.
Zorb, Shirley

SPONSOR
MISS VIRGINIA MARSHALL
of
SPOKANE, WASH.
direct decendant of
John Marshall, Chief Justice
U. S. Supreme Court 1801-1835

Sponsor, Miss Virginia Marshall of Spokane, Washington a direct decendant of John Marshall, chief Justice of the U.S. Supreme Court 1801-1835.

U.S.S. WASHINGTON

●

The WASHINGTON is named for the State of Washington and is the third Naval vessel to be named for that state, the sixth vessel to bear the name of Washington.

The cruiser WASHINGTON, at present the SEATTLE, was built on the Delaware, during 1903 to 1906, and was the first to be named for the state. She was 502 feet long, 14,500 tons displacement, and carried four 10" guns, sixteen 6" guns, twenty-three 3" guns, and four 21" torpedo tubes.

The WASHINGTON was attached to the Cruiser and Transport force during the World War as flagship. Today, as the SEATTLE, she is the receiving ship at the New York Navy Yard in an unclassified status.

The second WASHINGTON named for the state (Battleship 47) was also built on the Delaware. This vessel was sunk before completion in November 1924, in accordance with the Treaty for Limitation of Armaments. This ship was to have been 32,600 tons displacement and was to have carried a battery of 16" guns.

Battleship 56, to be named the WASHINGTON today, was authorized in March 1934, construction assigned to the Philadelphia Yard in June 1937, and is scheduled for completion in December 1941. Her displacement will be 35,000 tons. This compares with 33,400 tons of the NEW MEXICO class, the largest of our present battleships.

The WASHINGTON is a sister ship of the NORTH CAROLINA (Battleship 55) being built from the same plans at the Navy Yard, New York.

A brief history of the U.S.S. Washington.

BB56 NON-ACTIVE SHIPMATES

— A —
Allen, James S.
Alt, John
Atteridge, Robert H.

— B —
Ball, William J.
Barker, William L.
Bennett, Richard S.
Berentsen, Frank
Beverly, R.J.
Bing, George R.
Blanton, Ray Irvin
Boehme, Lloyd M.
Bohnsack, Homer W.
Breeman, Ken J., Sr.
Brown, Jack G.
Brown, George A.
Brown, Oscar C.
Burden, Ray
Burghardt, Louis
Buser, James D.

— C —
Camp, Vernon C.
Campbell, Herbert G.
Campbell, Robin
Canzoniere, Edmund
Champ, Robert W.
Chard, A. Marion
Chartrand, Donald
Checco, Harrison
Christner, Dick
Ciufo, Charles M.
Clark, Stanley P.
Cormier, Walter G.
Cozzolino, Fred
Cropper, Robert L.
Cunningham, Willard L.
Curren, Calvin
Curtis, Eddie

— D —
Dahman, Les
Dale, John
Daniels, Charles F.
Davis, Dwight C.
Davis, William A.
Davis, Ernest E., Jr.
Dean, James
DeBuher, Claude
DeLena, Alexander Carlo
Dennis, William W.
Depaolo, Anthony
Derr, Eugene A., Jr.
DiRenzi, Mario
DiStefano, John
Divone, Robert L.
Dority, John
Dover, Allen F.
Dowling, Paige
Driscoll, Dan
Durbin, Louis W.
Durgan, Harold J.
Dutton, Granville D.

— E —
Eide, LeGorie S.
Emory, Grady F.

— F —
Fairchild, George
Fargione, Frank
Fassett, Roland D.
Ferguson, Robert
Fisher, Robert C.
Fry, Adam C.
Fulmer, Junior Lee
Fyfe, Earl J.

— G —
Gang, Vernon E.
Garcia, Charles F.
Gheens, Ray
Giannini, Vincent A.
Giorano, Savario Sam
Glass, Orville C.
Glines, Stanley R.
Glynn, Thomas
Goodson, Willard R.
Greenspan, Harry
Griffin, Gordon
Grindle, Frank
Griswold, Vic

— H —
Haber, Don
Halverson, Richard
Hammock, Andrew V.
Hanna, King C.
Harlow, Hugh
Harris, Arthur W.
Harris, Fred
Harrison, W.R.
Harwood, Ray A.
Hebard, Charles R.
Heimark, Jacob V.
Herring, Ernest C.
Herzing, Paul A.
Hilson, Gorman
Hoell, Eugene
Hoppert, Dwight
Houghton, Virgil
Hovland, Arley M.
Hubenthal, Lyman E.
Hueter, Paul V.

— I —
Iademarco, Nicholas

— J —
James, Ed
Jameson, John B.
Jeralds, Bob J.
Johnson, Vernal D.
Jones, Frank M.
Joyce, Robert C.

— K —
Kaemmerer, Kenneth J.
Kaniosky, Carl
Keelin, Thomas J.
Kelly, Charles W.
King, O.N., Jr.
Knox, Kenneth
Kritz, M.E.

— L —
LaRocca, Nat
Ledford, James D.
Lehnert, Wilbur
Lemos, William E.
Lewiton, Jacob
Lindsey, A.J.
Lukemits, Paul J.
Lukinovich, Clement
Lutes, Carl
Lynn, Herman C.

— M —
Mandarich, Vaso
Manders, Dan A., Jr.
Martin, Norman C.
Massey, Sam Clay, Jr.
Matthieu, Charles
McCloskey, James N.
McCombs, William E.
McCrary, William H.
McGuire, Edward J.
McKenna, Joseph A.
McKinley, James W.
Merryman, Dallas H.
Michael, E.
Miller, Charles K.
Mimms, B.M.
Mitchell, Albert
Moehlenkamp, Fred G.
Moore, James C.
Morgan, James C.
Morlan, Melvin
Muehlenthaler, William J.
Muller, David G.
Munzert, Ken
Myers, John E.

— N —
Ness, Dale V.
Newman, Robert W.
Nolan, Marlow H.
Noranbrook, Ernest P.
Novak, Frank G.

— O —
O'Conner, Donald P.
O'Steen, Wallace A.
Oakes, W. Eldon
Oates, Walter M.
Ousley, Whitt

— P —
Pancake, John L.
Pannell, Pete
Patterson, Robert S.
Pawelko, Ed
Peden, James
Pelleritto, Martin P.
Perdue, Harold J.
Peters, William
Pettiford, Sam
Pettingill, J.E.
Pfeifer, Daniel M.
Pietskowski, Edward
Pippin, Billy H.
Pitts, Leonard J.
Plachetzki, Walter A.
Player, Jack
Plummer, John O.
Pomerantz, David
Ponceroff, Raymond
Prendergast, William
Prescott, Charles A.
Pressley, Henry A.
Pressley, Ralph
Price, Floyd E.
Pugh, William Riley

— R —
Rainbolt, W.L.
Ralston, Johnny V.
Rasmussen, George
Remar, George
Retz, Nicholas R.
Reynolds, Jack
Richards, Thomas W.
Richardson, Thomas
Riopelle, Chelsea A., Jr.
Rittal, Ray
Russo, William P.
Rylee, William T.

— S —
Saxon, John
Scherman, Bernard J.
Schesny, John F.
Schwed, William A.
Sebright, Nelson E.
Sedlack, Robert J.
Sheker, Eugene B.
Simmons, Carroll
Simmons, Tom C.
Smith, Alfred E.
Smith, Arthur C.
Spradlin, Wallace
Springmeyer, Glenn
Stanfield, Robert E.
Stanley, Gordon
Stayton, Kenneth
Stechow, Robert H.
Steele, Fred L.
Stiles, William G.
Swenson, Ed

— T —
Takos, James G.
Taylor, Charles B.
Thierwechter, Lester V., Sr.
Thomas, John M.
Thompson, Nicholas S.
Tubb, Ivin L.
Tuminaro, Joseph L.

— V —
Vargo, Charles
Vaughn, Lowell P.
Vontress, Clarence

— W —
Waring, Ernest W.
Warnke, Orville
Whitaker, Phillip F.
White, Ted F.
Wicoff, Gerald D.
Wiggins, Joe M.
Willhite, William C.
Williams, Floyd
Williams, Jesse Gordon
Williams, W.D.
Wills, Victor L.
Wiseman, Glenn
Wolf, John L.

— Y —
Young, Frank A.

— Z —
Zubrod, Gerald F.

USS WASHINGTON, BB56 REUNION GROUP
HONORARY LIFE MEMBERS
MAY 1998

– A –

Absher, Avery W.	March 3, 1998
Adalac, Stephen A.	March 11, 1998

– B –

Bell, James N.*	April 17, 1995
Berc, Harold T.	March 14, 1998
Berman, Naaman P.*	March 29, 1993
Brown, John A.	June 14, 1989
Buzzell, Lehugh C.*	August, 19, 1989

– C –

Cadwalader, John	May 25, 1998
Canty, John T.*	June 25, 1996
Cox, Elmer R.	May 25, 1998

– D –

Derrick, Ralph D.	Oct. 10, 1995

– E –

Ewing, Steve	June 14, 1989

– F –

Fairbanks, Douglas, Jr.	June 14, 1989

– G –

Gale, Grover W.*	Dec. 11, 1993
Gore, John M.	Feb. 12, 1998

– H –

Holton, Albert C.*	April 17, 1995
Hughes, Rodney W.	March 11, 1998
Hunt, Nelson Bunker	June 14, 1989
Hunter, Ray P.*	June 14, 1989

– K –

Kean, John E.	April 11, 1995
Knowlton, Chad R.	Feb.1, 1997
Krueger, Raymond H.	March 3, 1998
Loeffler, George H., Jr.*	Nov. 7, 1994
Loewe, James N.	May 25, 1998

– M –

Major, George L.	Dec. 20, 1997
Morgan, Henry	April 17, 1995
Mosteller, Roscoe*	Oct. 10, 1995
Musicant, Ivan	June 14, 1989

– N –

Neri, Aldo	March 6, 1996
Newton, Richard E. , Jr.	Sept. 15, 1997

– P –

Park, Claude J. , Jr.	April 16, 1997
Pennell, John C.	Dec. 12, 1992
Platt, Jonas M.	June 14, 1989

– R –

Rainbolt, Woodrow D.	July 9, 1993
Reid, Luther G. "Joe"*	Feb. 21, 1993
Remus, Francis	June 14, 1989
Robinson, Roy*	June 14, 1989
Ross, James G.	June 14, 1989
Russo, Lorenzo, Sr.	October 14, 1991

– S –

Sebastionelli, Peter*	June 14, 1989
Shifflet, Avis R.	Oct. 24, 1991
Skarda, E.J.*	Sept. 20, 1993
Slater, Richard	June 14, 1989
Sloper, Harold I.*	April 27, 1997
Stillwell, Paul	June 14, 1989
Sullivan, Richard M.*	April 1, 1996
Sutherland, Robert M.	May 25, 1998

– T –

Talbott, Alton C.*	June 14, 1989
Tidwell, Richard F.*	March 25, 1992
Tipper, Kenneth	June 14, 1989
Turner, Lee A.	April 17, 1995

– V –

Villa, Louis A.	July 3, 1994

– W –

Walsh, Harvey T.*	June 14, 1989
Walton, Fernie A.	July 10, 1997
Wilkinson, Richard P.	Aug. 26, 1996
Willard, Wyeth W. (Rev.)*	April 20, 1992

NOTE: * Deceased

The mighty battleship WASHINGTON arrives at Philadelphia Navy Yard after three years in the Pacific. The WASHINGTON was given full credit for sinking the 30,000 ton Jap Battleship Kirishima during the night in the 3rd battle of Savo Island, Nov. 14, 1942.

BB56 WIDOW - RELATIVE LIST
1998

- A -

Acton, R.T. (Dr.)
Adams, Eleanor M.
Adams, Linda S.
Alben, Carmel T.
Aleo, Pauline M.
Alexander, Wilma H.
Allen, Dorothy E.
Appelt, Dorilyn
Arnold, Bernice N.
Aughton, John A.
Austin, Ruth

- B -

Barfield, E.J.
Bartow, Mrs. Clarence
Baylor, Roger A.
Beckstrand, Bradley
Bell, Debra
Bell, Faye
Bell, Mary R.
Bellison, Ruby
Benedetti, Cynthia B.
Berman, Louise A.
Berman, Michael P.
Bias, James R.
Bias, Robert D.
Bible, Elsie D.
Bigelow, Debbie
Boardman, Elizabeth M.
Boehm, Marcia
Boling, David
Boyd, Bruce E.
Braden, Rita T.
Brandt, Jerry
Brinkley, John L.
Brinkley, Charles B., Jr.
Brown, Jo Ann
Brown, Roger and Connie
Brown, Verline
Bruels, Peggy
Buchanan, Helen F.
Buchholz, Robert D.
Buckner, Kathleen M.
Buda, Florence
Bull, Marian M.
Burchardt, Clara
Burnett, Ken
Buzell, Fred and Mary
Byers, Ina
Byers, John W.

- C -

Calvino, Marie J.
Campanelli, Philip
Campbell, Rose E.
Canty, Edward
Canty, Phyllis L.
Carlson, Margaret
Catlett, Betty P.
Cauthron, Carol
Cervantes, Moses
Chambers, Cheryl
Chasin, Ellen
Clark, Elizabeth H.
Clark, Donald A., Jr.
Clarkson, Richard and Peggy
Cline, Sharon
Cockayne, Jane H.
Codromac, Denise
Cole, Kathryn L.
Collins, John Van
Coner, Mrs. James E.
Crapps, Dorothy M.

- D -

Davin, Judith
Davis, Corinne T.
Deaton, Jacqueline Clemens
DeGrazio, Mrs. Nick
Dehart, Lucille E.
Delong, Maureen
Denham, Gary
Denton, Betty M.
Derrick, John D.
Diamond, Margaret E.
Dickerson, D. Jean
Dio Giovanni, Christine M.
Doke, Levenia
Donahue, Mrs. John W.
Donovan, Elizabeth
Dooley, Janice
Doyle, Margaret C.
Drake, Marie
Duley, Elizabeth A.

- E -

Edwards, Ann
Edwards, Elizabeth
Ennis, Mary
Esris, Betty Lou
Evans, Antoinette
Evans, Mrs. Arlyne

- F -

Fairly, Eleanor
Fallon, Faye D.
Fargo, Helen B.
Farney, Tom
Fialka, Irene L.
Forgach, Catherine J.
Foster, Stacy Solon
Fowler, Betty
Froempter, Barbara A.

- G -

Gale, Helen N.
Gammage, Zinnia M.
Garcia, Mary
Gearhart, Helen P.
Genovese, Robert
Gentile, Albert J.
Gervais, Betty Ann
Giampopo, Mario, Jr.
Giddens, Fay
Giering, Jean M.
Gilchrist, Becky
Giragosian, Kathlyn
Glass, Mr. R.S.
Goodau, Hazel
Grace, Grady F.
Grage, Mary Ann
Graham, Marie
Graham, Mike A.
Griffin, Elizabeth
Groff, Norma B.
Gurney, Amy L.
Gurney, Doris H.

- H -

Hail, Michael
Hancock, Leonard
Hanrahan, Helen M.
Happy, Doris V.
Harrigan, Christofer M.
Harrison, Betty C.
Hauser, Barbara
Hayes, Fred E.
Haynes, Fran
Haynes, Patricia
Highfield, Majorie
Hoffer, Shirley M.
Holmes, Barbara
Holmes, Roy W.
Hook, Mrs. Garold H.
Hooper, Dorothy L.
Hoppe, Merry Anne
Horak, Mary A.
Houseman, Mark
Howlett, Helen
Hudson, Patrick J.
Hughes, Dorothy M.
Hughes, Patricia A.
Hukki, Mary E.

- I -

Ingersoll, Eleanor
Ingram, Maybell M.

- J -

Jacobson, Jonathan B.
Jankowski, Maxine
Jarling, Helene R.
Johnson, David
Johnson, Eric
Johnson, Marguerite C.
Johnson, Nancy and Jim
Johnston, Sandy
Jones, Ann
Jones, Daisy
Jones, Margaret L.
Jordan, Dorothy

- K -

Kangas, Esther
Kaylor, Tim
Keener, Frances
Kelly, Katy D.
Key, Margaret C.
King, Juanita
Kirkman, Forrest J.
Knitter, Sonny
Knoll, Josie Lee
Koch, Connie R.
Korostynski, Florence
Kovach, Mrs. Joseph A.
Kramer, Linda
Krechevsky, Richard
Kretchmer, Margaret E.
Kuhn, Coletta J.
Kyd, Beverly

- L -

Lambert, Ruth
Lange, Emilie W.
Lathrop, Susan
Lea, Patricia
Leak, Stella
Ledbetter, Rose Marie
Lee, Bobby and Bonita
Lee, Mrs. Lucas
Lee, Robert C.
Leishing, Donna L.
Lentz, Elva J.
Lewis, Veronica A.
Liberti, Ruth
Liggett, Phyllis G.
Loeffler, May R.

- M -

Mackel, Marlyn
Madden, Mrs. Henry
Mahoney, Tim and Lorry
Makara, Helen
Manke, Dennis
Manning, Shirley
Maples, Juanita
Marchand, Cecelia J.
Marks, Gertrude
Marshall, Douglas R.
Martin, Josephine
Martin, Mary Margaret

Mathews, Joyce Hughes
Mauriello, Louis, Jr.
Mauzy, Catherine
Mays, Sybil
McCabe, Kenneth A., Jr.
McCartan, John T.
McClung, Kym
McCracken, Eleanor
McDonald, Eileen
McFillen, Maude
McGriff, Emily W.
Midkiff, Helen
Miller, Stephen G.
Miskiel, Norma
Montgomery, Mrs. Ish
Moore, Hazel M.
Morgan, Teresa B.
Morris, Coraline
Morrison, Betty T.
Moses, Elizabeth A.
Moshor, Diane
Mosier, Phyllis
Muir, B.S.
Murtagh, Lorayne A.

– N –

Nacey, Phillip
Neher, Richard R.
Nellis, May
Nelson, Anna
Nichols, Arthur R., Jr.
North, Hazel L.
North, Ivan T.

– O –

Oakley, Nancie
Ohl, Bradford
Oliphant, Bonnie L.
Oliveri, Marie
Olson, Rochelle

– P –

Palac, Walter A., Jr.
Parker, Jerry and Elizabeth
Patton, Kathleen
Peckinpaugh, Genevieve A.
Penberthy, Mary
Pennycuff, Ken
Perlenfein, Phyllis I.
Perry, Betty
Perry, Carolyn
Petretto, Susan
Pientek, Mrs. Ann
Pilcher, Clifford E., III
Pittard, Leita
Pittman, Evelyn
Ponton, Patricia C.
Poplawski, Bernice

Popov, Betsy R.
Potiowsky, Thomas P.
Prescott, John
Preston, Karen
Prevost, Clarence W.
Prevost, Louis E.
Price, Bernice
Pross, Kathline
Pursley, Dan

– Q –

Quillen, Marjorie
Quinn, Susana

– R –

Raby, Victoria E.
Raines, Muriel H.
Reilly, Mrs. Thomas A.
Ressler, Charlie
Reynar, Gwen F.
Rhyne, Ruth
Ritter, Robert Q.
Roberts, Betty Ann
Roberts, Dorothy
Robinson, Joyce
Rockford, Carol
Roensch, Anna M.
Rugo, Teresa A.
Runyan, Mary Ann
Rush, Lee
Russo, Lorenzo, Jr.

– S –

Sacho, Maureen
Sala, Brian A.
Sanders, Cheryl Reed
Sanger, B. June
Sawalich, Eugene W., Jr.
Scalzo, David
Scarffe, Leanne
Schmitt, Linda
Schulte, Veronica E.
Sebastionelli, Flora
Sechrist, Regina M.
Seelenbrandt, Mary
Senkier, Deborah
Shank, Lois
Sharp, Wilma
Shaw, Peggy
Shepherd, Alice Elaine
Shields, John J., Jr.
Simon, Adeline
Siniard, Clifford M.
Sitarski, James P.
Skarda, Fay Dell
Smith, Allen E.
Smith, Margaret C.
Smith, Velma

Smith, M.G., Jr.
Snellings, Marion E.
Solon, Mrs. Harvey
Solon, William V.
Sondergard, Ann Marie
Sowles, Alfreda
Stanzel, Robert P.
Still, La June M.
Stimac, Eileen
Stith, Margaret J.
Stoodley, Helen S.
Sullivan, Leona C.
Swing, Elizabeth Sherman

– T –

Tastad, Nova
Taylor, Helen L.
Taylor, Lillian H.
Thacker, Mary Alice
Thompson, Crystal T.
Thompson, Margaret
Tisdell, Luella
Tolar, Jeraldine
Toniatti, Don
Trahern, Anne
Turner, Maraget Ann
Turzyn, Richard

– V –

Van Baaren, Dorothy
Vincent, Tiff

– W –

Waidley, Sarah
Walkiewicz, Anna K.
Walsh, Dick
Walton, Robert E., Sr.
Ward, William
Watts, Ann L.
Webber, Ed. C. and Catherine
Wells, Robert J. and Cheryl
Whitaker, Arlene
White, E. Deanne
Whiteley, Tia
Whitman, Colene
Wieland, Jill
Wilcox, Arthur
Wiley, Frank
Williams, Jane
Williams, Jo Ann
Wilson, Theja
Winters, Bob and Dottie
Woeppel, Russell W.G.
Wright, Allan
Wright, David
Wright, Mary Lou
Wright, Paul and Theresa
Wynn, Helen E.

– Y –

Young, Natalie
Young, Robert

USS Washington First To Sink a Jap Heavy

By the Associated Press.

BREMERTON, Wash., Aug. 21.—The U. S. S. Washington is the first battleship to sink a Jap battleship in surface action, the Navy disclosed today.

The Jap craft was sunk off Savo Island in a showdown battle the night of Nov. 14-15, 1942, the Navy said, in revealing that the Washington is in drydock at the Puget Sound Navy Yard for overhaul.

Before the Savo Island action, the Washington took part in the attack on Guadalcanal. Later she ranged the Pacific. Participating in most strikes during the Jap war, including Iwo Jima and Okinawa, she was unscathed. Nor did she lose a man.

For five weeks soon after she reached the Pacific early in the war she was "our only threat to Japanese domination of the seas during the darkest hours of the war," the Navy said with elaboration.

The Washington was the newest, fastest and finest battleship in the fleet when she was launched in June, 1940, at the Philadelphia Navy Yard. She was commissioned 11 months later.

New York Times August 1945.

BB-56 DECEASED LIST TO BE HONORED AT BATON ROUGE, LA, MAY 23, 1998

– A –

Abramson, Henry B.
Adams, Charles M.
Albano, Severino S.
Alben, Charles F.
Albertelli, Edward R.
Alexander, Claude T.
Alexander, Donald W.
Appleton, Richard
Arnold, George A.
Auwaerter, Edward A.
Ayrault, Arthur D.

– B –

Baker, Raymond W.
Bartow Jr., Clarence T.
Baun, Matthew L.
Bays, Vernon J.
Becker, Glenn
Bell, Allen H.
Bell, James N.
Bellison, James E.
Berman, Naaman
Berry, Walter H.
Blank, Lambert
Boardman, Ralph F.
Boehmer, Carl G.
Braden, Anthony S.
Branciere, John L.
Brandt, Raymond R.
Brinkley, Charles B.
Broderick, Frederick
Brooks, William R.
Broussard, Gordon R.
Brown, Jesse W.
Brown, John A.
Bruels, Ray
Bube, Virgil
Buchanan, L.B.
Buda Jr., George
Bull Jr., Lester D.
Burchardt, Bill
Burnett, George Donald

Buzzell, LeHugh C.
Byers, John W.
Byers, Robert P.

– C –

Caborne, Roy C.
Caddell, Elbert J.
Calvino, Rocco J.
Cannon Sr., George T.
Canty, Thomas John
Carpenter, Charles L.
Catlett, James G.
Caudill, John T.
Cepelka, Emil R.
Cervantes, Paschal
Chadima, William
Charles, Thomas J.
Chase, Sam C.
Chasin, Nathan
Clark, Harold
Clark, Robert E.
Clemens, Jack R.
Clemens, Marie M. (Jack)
Cockayne, Lee V.B.
Cole, Philip P.
Coller, Edgar J.
Cone, John W.
Coner, James E.
Conroy, John W.
Cook, Jasper A.
Cooke, Thomas D.
Coulam, Noble W.
Cox, Charles W.
Cox, Chester
Crappas, John J.
Crider, Clarence C.
Cross, Frank A.
Cross, Phillip D.
Cuffel, Laurence E.
Cullen, Charles Dudley
Cullen, Michael T.
Cutler, Dave

– D –

Daniel, Calvin

Davis, Glenn B.
Davis, Victor L.
Day, Charles Bryan
Decano, Marino
DeCristofaro, Silvio
DeGrazio, Nick
Dehart, Norman E.
Deppe, Louis F.
Diamond, Earl E.
Dickerson, Wiley P.
DiGovanni, Edmond A.
Doke, Carl A.
Donahue, John W.
Donohue Sr., William F.
Donovan, Michael
Douglas, Frank F.
Douglas, Harry C.
Doyle Sr., Eugene L.
Duncan, Boyd F.
Dutton, Wilbur C.

– E –

Edwards, Clarence W.
Edwards, William W.
Egan, Frank
Estes, Lester L.
Evans, George E.
Evans, Harold W.
Evans Jr., George E.

– F –

Fallon, John
Fargo, William B.
Fialka, Albert C.
Fic, Zigmund
Flaherty, James J.
Forgach, Joseph
Fowler, Beryl M.
Frank, Paul A.
Frankovich, Nicholas T.
Fringer, Volly E.
Froempter, Arthur O.
Froempter, Arthur O.

– G –

Gale, Grover W.
Gammage, James K.
Gearhart, Jack S.
Gentile, Larry Lorenzo
Giampaolo, Hugo T.
Giering, Phillip G.
Glass, Bernard
Goodau, Edward R.
Gordon, Arlie L.
Gormley, Patrick Joseph
Grace, W.R.
Grage, Albert Larry
Graham, Hubert S.
Grissop, Edward A.
Groff, Emerson P.
Grogen, Peter J.
Guilliaem III, Aertsen
Gurney, Harold L.
Gurney Jr., Frank E.
Gurski, Leo
Guzski, William

– H –

Halyburton, Joseph V.
Hanrahan, Edward F.M.
Happy, Walter R.
Harper, Bruce
Harper, Russell W.
Harris, Robert E.
Harrison, Isaac B.
Harsh, Curtis L.
Hartman, Roger M.
Hartzell, Glenn R.
Hatcher, Joseph K.
Haynes, Robert L.
Helmandollar, Hershel
Hendrickson, Bobby
Hensley, Roy H.
Herget, Charles A.
Herman, Royce A.
Highfield, Gerald F.
Hines, Wellington H.
Hocoluk, Edward
Holt, Kenneth C.
Holton, Albert C.
Hook, Garold H.
Hooper, Edwin B.
Hooper, Robert C.
Horak, Marvin W.
Howlett, Willard E.
Huberty, Robert W.
Hughes, Horald M.
Hukki, Olaf R.
Hunter, Raymond P.
Hutto, Woodrow W.

– I –

Ingersoll, Leslie J.
Ingram, Jeff E., Jr.

– J –

Jankowski, Eugene A.
Jarling, Walter
Johnson, Other
Jones, Creighton
Jones Jr., Harry L.
Jordan, Dallas F.

– K –

Karow, Robert P.
Kasunick, Joseph
Katan, Charles
Kaylor, James Brooke
Keener, Charles
Key, Albert E.

The USS Washington fighting off Jap suicide air attacks at Okinawa.

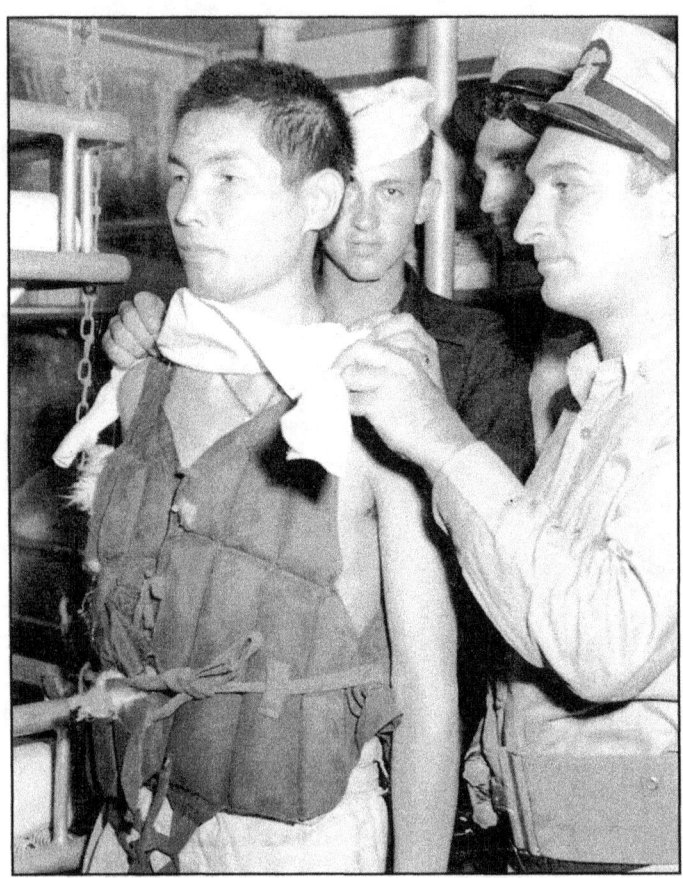
Japanese prisioner aboard the USS Washington.

The USS Washington as seen from enterprise at Panama Canal.

A Japanese prisioner being brought aboard.

King, John W.
Kinne, Walter H.
Kirkpatrick, Robert L.
Knoll, David C.
Koenig, John
Kohlhas Jr., Albert P.
Korostynski, John
Kovach, Joseph A.
Krawcxyk, Stanley J.
Kretchmer, Floyd E.
Kuhn, Ross
Kyd, Charles

– L –

Lambert, Russell
Lamm, Lewis J.
Landherr, William
Larson, Merle A.
Lawless, John J.
Lawrence, Roy W.
Leach, Harold R.
Leak, Patrick T.
Ledbetter, Curtis L.
Lee, Earl M.
Lee, Willis A.
Leishing, Floyd G.
Lentz, Harry L.
Lewis, Len L.
Liggett, Cecil Ray
Little, James P.
Loeffler Jr., George H.
Lowman, Wolliam T.

– M –

Macklin, Robert D.
Madden, Henry C.
Maddock, Joseph
Majors, Roger
Makara, Stepphen
Mandel, Earnest J.
Maples, Leon S.
Marks, Ernest S.
Marlin, John
Martin, Arnold R.
Martin, William Hefley
Martinuzzi, John T.
Matton Sr., George W.
Mays, Rae
McCormick, Clement Patrick
McCormick, James J.
McCracken, Fred J.
McGrath, George
McLaughlin, Merle M.
Miller, Charles J.
Miller, Verle E.
Mitchell, Harold A.
Moll, Fred W.
Montgomery, Howard H.
Montgomery Sr., Howard H.
Moore, Woodrow W.
Morrison, Fred J.
Mosier, Robert E.
Mosteller, Roscoe
Murphy, Ira W.
Murtagh, Francis X.

– N –

Nacey, James E.
Napoli, Dominic
Negroni, Joseph
Nellis, Ivan J.
Nelson, Leonard
Nemara, Stanley J.
Newport, George A.
Niemara, Stanley J.
North, Charles S.
Novak, Frank G.

– O –

Oakley, Steve A.
Odom, Marshall Dudley
Oliphant, Joseph J.
Olliff, Harold S.
Olson, Martin L.
OMalley, Charles F.

– P –

Parsons, William
Paul, Frank A.
Peckinpaugh, Paris E.
Peek, Jerry K.
Pennington, Albert C.
Perlenfein, Russell
Perry, David W.
Perry, Paul O.
Petretto, Allan
Pickett, Eugene
Pittard, Grady C.
Popof, Valentine G.
Powers, Harry R.
Prewitt, Bob C.
Price, O'Neal T.
Pross, Raymond L.
Pursely, Orville D.

– Q –

Quinn, Robert M.
Quinton Sr., Ernest G.

– R –

Rabowski, Gilbert M.
Ramsey, Clyde
Rbowski, Gilbert M.
Reid, Luther G.
Reilly, Thomas A.
Reiser, James A.
Reynar, William J.
Rhyne, Harvey G.
Richjardson, Robert E.
Roberts, James B.
Roberts, Lamar W.
Roberts, William C.
Robison, Roy J.
Roensch, Henry C.
Rugo Jr., Peter John
Rutter, John Joseph
Ryan, William L.

– S –

Sabatine, Vincent J.
Sache, Porter
Sanger, Frank M.
Sargent, Glen
Sawalich, Eugene W.
Scanlan, William E.
Schanze, Edwin S.
Schulte, Walter A.
Sebastionelli, Peter A.
Sechrist, Glen C.
Seelenbrandt, Armand R.
Seely, Hank W.
Senick, Charles E.
Senkler, Robert J.
Senkler, Robert J.
Shada Sr., Victor
Shaffer, Robert T.
Shavely, Boyd A.
Shields, Robert
Shirley, Clark A.
Sidle, Reginald T.
Siegel, Martin
Siegel, Norton
Silvers Sr., Carl E.
Simac, Andy
Simon, Vincent
Siniard, Samuel Gaston
Skarda, E.J.
Sloper, Harold I.
Smith, Donald A.
Smith, M.G.
Smith, Marion D.
Snellings, Carey W.
Snyder, Arthur H.
Solon, Harvey
Stankovic, Roy
Stere, Edward
Stewart, William H.
Still, Edgar A.
Stimac, Andy
Stimson, Robert C.

Stith, Charles E.
Sullivan, Richard M.
Swing, Peter Gram

– T –

Talbott, Alton C.
Tastad, John
Taylor, Frederick B.
Taylor, Truxton S.
Teneyck, Voorhis C.
Terstenyak, Stephen
Thibodeau, Gerard P.
Thomas, J. Charles
Thompson, Frank E.
Tidwell, Richard F.
Tippett, Elbert W.
Tisdell, Edward
Tolar, James S.
Trahern, Charles
Traynor, Peter W.
Turner Robert J.

– V –

Vagianelis, Paul
Vano, Alfred J.
Ver Valin, William
Vincent, Patrick C.
Vincent, Patrick T.
Vov Bible, Amadeous

– W –

Wagner, Clarence
Walker, Aaron R.
Walker, David
Walkiewicz, Walter
Walsh, Harvey T.
Walton, Ralph H.
Watts, Arthur Lee
Wells, Robert B.
West, Charles C.
Whitehouse, Raymond
Whitman, Charles W.
Wilcox Jr., John W.
Wiley, Mayo
Williams, Donald F.
Williams, Joseph H.
Williams, Lesslie H.
Winters, Lonnie E.
Woeppel, Russell S.
Wright Jr., Howard F.
Wynn, Jack C.
Wynn, William

– Y –

Young, Joe L.

– Z –

Zero, Ships Mascot

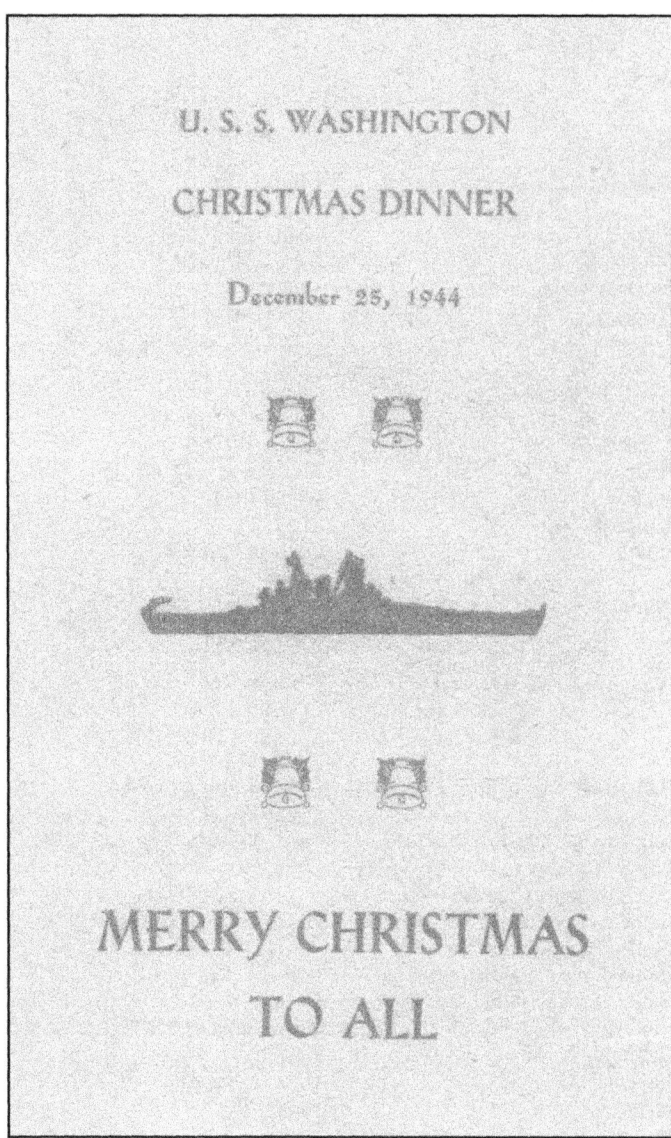

U. S. S. WASHINGTON

CHRISTMAS DINNER

December 25, 1944

MERRY CHRISTMAS
TO ALL

INDEX

– A –

Abbey 45
Adams 32
Aertsen 67
Akagi 47
Alabama 20
Albano 36
Aleutian Islands 15
Allcon 36
Alvarez 57
Anderson 33, 34
Anguar 21
Annapolis 60
Arnold 62
Atago 42, 43, 44, 46, 47
Aukland 49
Australia 15
Ayanami 44, 45, 47, 65, 68
Ayrault 42, 43, 49

– B –

Ballard 49
Baltimore 60
Barnaby 32
Battle of Midway 15
Battle of Santa Cruz 36, 42
Battle of Savo Island 15, 34
Battle of the Atlantic 15
Battle of the Coral Sea 15
Battle of the Eastern Solomons 15
Battleship X 48
Bayonne 23
Beach 64
Belfast 39
Benham 18, 24, 43, 45, 46, 47
Benson 11, 15, 26, 38, 41, 49, 50, 51, 52, 65
Bentinick-Smith 37
Berc 48
Bert 36
Bias 33
Bismarck Archipelago 20
Bismark 38, 39
Black Prince 22
Brancier 36
Brandt 49
Briltz 36
Bronson 38
Brown 19, 32, 34, 51, 62, 63, 65, 66, 68
Bryant 32, 33, 37
Buckner 32
Bullock 32
Bunker Hill 20, 21, 23
Burke 67
Burwell 37
Buse 36, 58, 61

– C –

Callaghan 16
Cam Ranh Bay 22
Camden 58
Camendish 32
Campbell 37, 58
Canada 15
Canton 22
Cape Engano 22
Cape Esperance 18, 24, 68
Cargel 39
Caruso 39
Casco Bay 14, 34
Chasin 49, 50
Chesapeake Bay 60
Chichi Jima 22
Clark 32, 39
Coconut Creek 32
Coffee 36
Cooley 21, 22, 26, 64
Coolman 39
Cox 44
Coxswain 66
Cozzolind 57
Cozzoling 36
Cross 57
Cuff 43
Cybulsky 39

– D –

Davis 15, 16, 19, 26, 42, 43, 44, 45, 49, 52, 61
Dell 49, 51, 66
Devonport 32
Devonshire 39
Dmoch 39
Drewitz 44, 56
Dupuy 61
Dutton 36

– E –

Edmisten 66
Edwards 49
Elgin 65
Ellice Islands 20
Ellyson 65
Espiritu Santo 16
Essex 20
Ewing 36

– F –

Fairbanks 11, 12, 14, 51
Fargo 12, 15, 16, 21, 38, 65
Feist 32
Ferrovecchio 36, 56, 57
Fialka 36, 56, 57
Fiji Island 20
Formosa 22
Fort Lauderdale 32
Foster 38
France 15
Francis 55
Frank 49, 61
Franklin 22
Froempter 36, 57

– G –

Garcia 44
Gatch 47, 48
Giffen 14, 15, 39, 65
Gilbert Islands 19
Gillette 66
Glasglow 39
Good 22, 26
Gordon 44
Gore 61
Gray 61
Great Britain 15
Greeley 37
Griffiths 38
Guadalcanal 15, 16, 36, 42, 44, 54, 56, 67
Guadalcanal Island 24, 49
Guam 21
Gustafson 32
Gwin 18, 24, 43, 45, 46, 47
Gyrtz 58

– H –

Haha Jima 21
Hailey 22
Hall 65
Halsey 19, 42, 49, 57, 67, 70
Handy 36, 57
Harding 43
Harper 61
Harris 66
Hartsell 62
Hashimoto 47
Herget 63
Hiei 44, 47
Hill 56
Hippard 56
Hittle 12
HMS Argonaut 22
HMS Hood 33, 38
HMS Inglefield 30
HMS King George V 14, 22, 30, 32, 39, 41, 51
HMS Marne 30
HMS Martin 30
HMS Punjabi 14, 30, 56
HMS Victorious 30
Holland 15, 36, 50, 57
Honaira 56
Hong Kong 22
Honolulu 64
Hooper 16, 43, 47
Horton 36
Horvath 39
Hughs 44
Hunter 24, 33, 43, 45, 48

– I –

Iceland 51
Indefatigable 22
Independence 20
Indiana 20, 21, 33, 54
Indomitable 22
Iron Bottom Bay 57
Iwo 21, 22
Iwo Jima 22, 34, 65

– J –

Jaluit 20
James 34
Japan 15
Jernigan 11
Johnson 36
Jones 36
Jordan 65
Juan de Fuca 21
Jukes 36
June 36

– K –

Kagero 47
Kavieng 20
Kegaris 44
Kent 39
Kimura 43, 44, 45, 47
Kinkaid 67
Kirishima 19, 36, 42, 43, 44, 47, 56, 64, 65, 68
Kirkam 57
Kirkwall 14
Klieman 57
Knowlton 12, 56
Knox 45
Kohlas 56
Kondo 18, 42, 44, 47, 48
Kovack 57
Krause 14, 44
Krumme 36
Kurita 67
Kwajalein 20
Kyushu 23

– L –

Lambert 57
Land 48
Lang 65
Lappin 36
Leach 39
Ledbetter 32
Lee 16, 18, 19, 20, 21, 24, 42, 43, 44, 52, 56, 57, 61, 67, 68
Lemos 65
Lewis 63
Lexington 67
Leyte 23
Lippman 42, 49
Little 36
Livermore 38, 65, 66
Lockwood 32
Loer 32
Lowman 62
Lundquist 32
Luzon 22

– M –

Mackay 37
Macklin 47
Maclosky 57
Madison 65, 66
Maguire 57
Maher 20, 26, 62
Maione 42
Majuro Atoll 21
Makin Island 20
Malphrus 32
Malvick 57
Marascia 65
Marcinkoska 65
Mariana Islands 21, 67
Maris 57
Marshall 11
Marshall Islands 20
Maslanka 37
Mason 36
Massachusetts 20
Maxwell 44
McCune 36, 57
McGuire 64
McInerney 23, 26
McMasters 66
McNeil 36
McQueen 32
Meade 48
Melnerney 23
Merrimack 64
Merritt 62
Mikawa 18, 42, 48
Mili 20
Minneapolis 21
Mitchell 38
Mitscher 20, 67
Mnehlenthaler 44
Monitor 64
Monterey 20
Moore 57
Morison 61
Morrison 19
Morton 60
Mount Vernon 51
Murmansk 39, 50, 51
Musicant 11, 50

– N –

Nagara 18, 42, 44, 68
Nagasaki 23
Nansei Shoto 22
Nauru Island 20
Nessly 43
Nettle 66
New Caledonia 16, 50, 57
New Guinea 15
New Hebrides 16, 20
New Jersey 67
New Rochelle 51
New Zealand 15
Newton 36, 57
Nimitz 19, 20
Norway 50
Noumea 16, 20, 57

– O –

Ocean Island 20

Offney 65
Okinawa 22, 34
Omiela 57
Onkst 36
Oreck 37
Oyashio 47
Ozawa 21

– P –

Pacific Islands 15
Pack 32
Pagan 21
Page 50
Palac 45
Palau Islands 21
Panama 58, 64
Panama Canal 10, 23
Pardo 36
Parmenter 57
Parrett 61
Parshall 32
Peadrick 64
Pearl Harbor 10, 11, 20, 32, 42
Peleliu 21
Pettingill 36, 57
Philadelphia 64
Philippines 22
Philips 36
Platt 45
Plunkett 65
Poist 57
Porter 63
Portsmouth 32
Pownall 20
Pratt 23
Preston 18, 24, 43, 45, 47
Price 34
Prinz Eugen 39, 41
Puget Sound 21, 23, 58
Punjabi 32, 41, 51
Putton 57

– Q –

Quackenbusk 44
Quinn 41

– R –

Rabaul 19
Raines 36
Raizo 18
Ramey 44
Reid 63
Reigrut 57
Renown 39
Reykjavik 14, 52
Riley 62
Robbins 49
Robertson 38
Rodrigues 56
Roosevelt 67
Roscoe 18
Rota 21
Rowe 61

– S –

Saigon 22
Saipan 21, 62, 67
San Juan 64
San Pedro Bay 23
Saratoga 15, 20
Savo Island 18, 24, 44, 48, 49, 54, 56, 57, 67, 68
Scalzo 55
Scapa Flow 14, 22, 32, 49, 50
Scarborrough 51
Schanze 43
Schauer 62
Schmidt 66
Schmitt 50
Seattle 64
Seeley 16, 52
Seely 44, 57
Sendai 18, 43, 44, 45
Serenson 56
Shaffer 38, 63
Sharpe 62
Sheperd 36
Shepherd 54
Sherbert 39
Sherman 20
Shikanami 44, 45
Shoemaker 54
Shoen 57
Shoun 36
Silver 36, 57
Simmons 66
Simpson 36
Slaughter 67
Smith 64
Soles 40
Solomon Islands 15, 16, 24, 67
South Carolina 34
South Dakota 18, 20, 21, 24, 36, 43, 45, 48, 64, 68
South Hampton 23, 58, 61, 64
Soviet Union 15
Spanish-American War 47
Spitzbergen 14
Stanford 65
Stark 14
Stearts 36
Sterett 65
Stiff 30
Stillwell 67
Stolecki 52
Stoodley 43, 44, 46
Stover 32
Strother 36
Stuart 54
Szalack 36

– T –

Tait 36, 57
Takao 42, 46, 47
Tanaka 43
Tanganyika 39
Taroa 20
Taylor 47, 48
Tenryu 53
Tepper 57
Thompson 46
Thornton 66
Tinian 21
Tipper 30
Tirpitz 38
Tokyo Bay 10, 22, 23
Tomahawk 36

Tonga Tabu 16, 63
Toothill 36
Tovey 30, 39
Trondheim Fiord 39, 41
Tucker 21
Turner 36, 37, 40

– U –

Uehlinger 47
Uranami 44, 45, 47
USS Aldabaran 49, 50
USS Enterprise 15, 16, 18, 20, 42, 43, 48, 56
USS Hornet 16
USS Indianapolis 67
USS North Carolina 10, 11, 20, 34, 36
USS Preston 18
USS South Dakota 42, 56, 57
USS Tuscaloosa 14, 38, 39, 50, 51, 65
USS Wasp 14, 16, 21, 38, 50, 65
USS Wichita 14, 39, 50, 65

– V –

Vandergrift 57
Victorious 22, 39, 41
Von Tirpitz 39, 41, 50

– W –

Wainwright 65
Walke 18, 24, 43, 45, 47
Waller 57
Walsh 14, 44
Walton 36
Washington, DC. 60
Weidert 10, 24
Whitehouse 57
Widder 38
Wilcox 14, 33, 38, 50, 63, 65, 67
Wilkinson 49
Wilson 65
Winchell 64
Winters 36
Wisthoff 37
Woolsey 44
Wyatt 50

– Y –

Yamamoto 48
Yausohn 57
Yorktown 20

– Z –

Zeits 38
Zero 64
Zubrod 39

Maintance work nearly completed on the USS Washington. The ship's scout-observation aircraft are being returned.

Aircraft Carriers Langley and Ticonderoga followed by Battleships Washington, N. Carolina and S. Dakota and Cruisers Santa Fe, Biloxi, Mobile and Oakland - all part of Task Group 38.3. Taken from USS Essex (CV-9) - 1944.

www.ingramcontent.com/pod-product-compliance
Lightning Source LLC
Chambersburg PA
CBHW082142230426
43672CB00016B/2937